BELIEVE IN PEOPLE
The Essential Karel Čapek

Karel Čapek, the youngest son of a doctor, was born in 1890 in Bohemia (now the Czech Republic) in Austria-Hungary, becoming a distinguished novelist, playwright and journalist in pre-war Czechoslovakia. He achieved international recognition for his drama *RUR* (*Rossum's Universal Robots*, 1920), *The Insect Play* (with his brother Josef, 1921) and his satirical novel *War with the Newts* (1936). An unfaltering advocate of humanism and democracy, he campaigned against fascism, which precipitated his death in 1938. He lived in Prague and in 1935 married the actress and writer Olga Scheinpflugová.

Šárka Tobrmanová-Kühnová completed a doctorate in English at Oxford University. She is now a Senior Lecturer in English literature at Charles University's Institute of Translation Studies in Prague.

John Carey is an Emeritus Professor at Oxford University. His books include studies of Donne, Dickens and Thackeray, *The Intellectuals and the Masses*, *What Good Are the Arts?* and a life of William Golding.

'A great writer of the past who speaks to the present in a voice brilliant, clear, honorable, blackly funny, and prophetic.' Kurt Vonnegut

'It is time to read Čapek again for his insouciant laughter, and the anguish of human blindness the lies beneath it … He is a joy to read.' Arthur Miller

BELIEVE IN PEOPLE

The Essential Karel Čapek

Previously Untranslated Journalism and Letters

Selected and translated with an introduction by
Šárka Tobrmanová-Kühnová

Preface by John Carey

faber and faber

First published in 2010
by Faber and Faber Ltd
Bloomsbury House
74–77 Great Russell Street
London WC1B 3DA

Typeset by RefineCatch Ltd
Printed in England by CPI Mackays, Chatham

A CIP record for this book
is available from the British Library

ISBN 978–0–571–23162–1

10 9 8 7 6 5 4 3 2 1

In memory of my grandparents

MIROSLAV BALCAR & VĚRA BALCAROVÁ

and the others of their generation
who remained steadfast
throughout the Nazi occupation

For my late father, DR OLDŘICH TOBRMAN,
'a good doctor who helped'

'The greatest belief would be to believe in people.'

KAREL ČAPEK, *A Factory to Manufacture the Absolute*
(*The Absolute at Large*), 1922

Contents

Preface

In his speech at the time of the 1938 Munich Agreement, which permitted Hitler to annex Czechoslovakia's Sudetenland, British Prime Minister Neville Chamberlain famously referred to Czechoslovakia as a far-away country of which we know nothing.

That, at least, has changed. Thousands of Britons now visit the Czech Republic every year; Prague has become a world tourist capital. Yet most people still know little about Czechoslovakia in the 1920s and 1930s, when the young republic had just gained independence, after three hundred years of Austrian rule, and was enjoying a period of vibrant cultural activity, of which Karel Čapek was one of the leaders. In pieces included in this selection he conveys the excitement of a time when new movements in the arts coincided with the emergence of a new nation that valued democracy, liberty and social justice, and stood out against the absolutism and militarism of the old regimes.

Anyone interested in European culture will want to know about these things. But Čapek is not just a Czech writer, he is a writer of world stature, and he confronts in his journalism subjects that matter to us all. It might seem odd for him to have chosen to raise such issues in short, informal newspaper columns. But he wanted to get his ideas across to as many readers as possible, and he realised that the best way to attract them was by being funny, engaging, irreverent and brief. That is why this selection can, without exaggeration, be called 'The Essential Karel Čapek'. His novels and plays ensure his place among the great writers of the twentieth century. But his journalism conveys his central ideas compactly, directly and appealingly.

Foremost among these is his belief in the inherent goodness of ordinary people. He saw that this laid him open to a charge of sentimentality, and he defiantly retorted that of course he was sentimental, 'just like any decent man' – only 'a rascal and a demagogue' could fail to be sentimental. But in reality he was not sentimental, because he was a thinker. He realised increasingly, as he watched the growth of fascism in the 1920s and 1930s, that evidence against his belief in human goodness was piling up, yet he remained optimistic. He is uplifting to read because he constantly seeks and finds evidence of people's good-heartedness. Sometimes it is a small thing – passengers on a tram smiling benignly as they overhear a young mother telling her little boy a fairy tale. Sometimes it is a global event, as in 'The Rescued and the Rescuers', about the international effort to save the survivors of a polar expedition in 1928. Whatever the scale, Čapek – wise, kind and keenly intelligent – seizes on it as proof that we are not monsters. Despite the evidence of history, we are capable of mutual trust, and that is what prevents the world becoming 'a planet of beasts'. In 1938 he gratefully prints a letter he has received from an English woman expressing her shame at the Munich betrayal. For Čapek it is proof that even at the darkest time the light of common human goodness still shines.

Being a writer, he is naturally a critic of words, and he is on the lookout for the ways in which words diminish and destroy people. He mocks the language of bureaucracy and officialdom because it tries to turn people into machines. He condemns political language because it deletes human beings and replaces them with abstract formulations like the 'class struggle'. Though he was a friend and supporter of Masaryk, the first president of Czechoslovakia, Čapek was not, at heart, a political creature. He seems to have felt that we would be better off without politics, because politics consists largely of clichés, which are 'habitual and mechanised dishonesty', and do terrible things. 'If it were not for clichés, there wouldn't be demagogues'. Politics, he warns, starts with rhetoric and ends with genocide.

Because debased language debases thought, some life-giving linguistic input is constantly needed and this, Čapek argues, is the responsibility of writers and poets. They alone can deliver a language 'unfingered by lies, clichés and averageness'. But he does not see writers and poets as a race apart, elevated above ordinary people. Reality, not art, is the true marvel, he insists. Artists are not 'creators' but simply discoverers of reality. They show us the world we already possess. At best, the artist is just someone who loves reality more than other people do, and who helps them to see it more clearly.

This is a vital Čapek tenet. Reverence for the real and everyday goes deep in his thought. It is what lies behind his idealisation of the tradesmen and artisans whose activities absorbed him as a boy – the cobbler, the organ-grinder, the inn-keeper, the house-painter, the wheelwright, the blacksmith, the grocer, the stonemason. He watched these grown-ups with boyish admiration because they were seriously engaged in what they did, and because what they did was real. Their ordinariness was transformed by their commitment to it. They reverenced the material world as the wood carver reverences wood.

In this spirit Čapek challenges the cultural pre-eminence we normally give to art. He can get as much pleasure, he says, from a fairground or a junk shop, or even from a post pissed on by dogs, as he can from an art gallery. Seen rightly, the world is full of beautiful things. This can sound like a Christian platitude, but it is quite the contrary. Čapek is earthbound. He does not want us to see the ordinary world as the path to some transcendent reality, but to see it as it is. The 'hardest and highest optical task' is just to see. Seeing is the 'great wisdom', and is more beneficial than judging. As Čapek conceives it, seeing is not passive but linked to insatiable curiosity. 'Getting to know' is a 'great and unquenchable passion' for him, and getting to know reveals (as Čapek's God tells Adam in 'Mere') that the world is 'multifarious and promising, full of possibilities and intricacies'.

The 'relativism' for which his adversaries blamed him is, he maintains, merely a recognition of this multifariousness, and of the infinite possibilities it offers. He defines relativism as 'an anxious attentiveness to everything that exists', and it entails an abandonment of all limited viewpoints and dogmas, including the dogmas of religion. His ambivalence about religion does not stem from dislike of its rituals and ceremonies, which he finds quite attractive and nostalgic. He remembers the Bethlehem crib at Christmas, and the Easter processions he watched as a boy with their lights and candles and banners, and memories like these that lovingly embrace old Czech customs and superstitions are among the most winning things in these pages. Rather, he distrusts the tendency of religion to devalue the world ordinary people live in, by directing them towards some superior, heavenly alternative. If heaven is not within reach of our eyes and hands, he insists, it is nowhere, and we shall never get there.

As we should expect from someone with these beliefs, Čapek argues that art and literature should be for everyone, not just for an elite. Literature should be entertaining, and should make people want to read it. Authors grumble about sensation-seeking cinema audiences but, in Čapek's estimation, movie-goers are seeking the same pleasures as the people who, twenty-five centuries ago, sat round a fire listening to the Homeric bard. They wanted thrills, surprises and suspense, and so do people now, and writers should supply them. It is not a matter of descending 'to the level of the people', or fabricating some special sort of 'rougher goods' for popular consumption. There should not be popular literature on the one hand and high literature on the other. High literature should become popular. A writer should be like a baker baking bread for everyone, not a barman mixing cocktails for cafe society.

He did not underestimate the difficulties. Despite his sympathy with cinema audiences, he foresaw, far earlier than most commentators, that visual culture would change people, and not for the better, and might make print culture obsolete. Reading, he points out, makes for contemplation. The reading person is patient and takes time to think, but the 'visual type' wants to take in situations at a single glance, and consequently understands less. Čapek (in 'The Age of the Eyes') predicts that the visual type may become the majority, but because he believes in people he does not despair.

Equally, he sees that most people consume cultural anaesthetics to escape from the emptiness and boredom of their lives. But, again, he refuses to abandon hope. All that is needed is for people to be made aware of what they are doing. We 'need to employ the whole of our brain for once'. When people do that, he is confident, they will be perfectly capable of seeing how worthless and stupid the majority of what they have come to regard as pastimes are.

The columns in which he describes the beauties of the Czech countryside are not diversions from this cultural programme, but parts of it. They are object lessons in how to see, exercises in how to make ordinary things precious. This is true of his comic accounts of gardening or his pet cat, just as much as of his poetic celebrations of trees, or wild flowers, or autumn, or the first snow-drop, or women in Prague cleaning windows at the coming of spring.

A constant refrain in his praise of his native country is that it is beautiful even though it is small. He shows us the bounty and variety to be found within its borders, as when he itemises the many types and colours of its earth in the piece titled 'Topsoil'. Perhaps, he suggests, his country is more beautiful because of its smallness. Because it is small, everything in it cries out to be val-ued, and smallness protects it from the power of big corporations and the grandiose ambitions that seduce big countries into imperi-alism and militarism. Smallness is spiritual health. This was the lesson Britain failed to learn when it cast off empire but retained the illusion that it was still a great power. So for us reading Čapek is especially salutary.

His dream is of a united Europe in which each nation will retain its cultural identity but will renounce any claim to political supremacy, and in which the inhabitants will no longer be forced by politicians to kill one another. In 'Greetings', one of his most inspiring pieces, published on Christmas Day 1938, the day of his death, he imagines the countries of Europe – England, Germany, France, Spain, Italy – as he has known them in happier times – not their politicians or their armies but their ordinary people, friend-ly and peace-loving. It has taken us seventy years, and the most destructive war in history, to realise his vision. In the world beyond Europe that vision is still unrealised, but he has pointed the way. 'We have no right to think', he writes, 'that in a thousand, or ten thousand years humankind will still be so stupid and primitive as to settle their conflicts like dogs in the street.' They are words that deserve to be inscribed on every parliament building on earth.

Čapek's style in his journalism conveys a personality that is friendly, reasonable, whimsical and imaginative. Like George Orwell, he pretends to be an ordinary chap, while leaving us in no doubt that he is brighter and sharper than ordinary chaps generally are. He loves comic fantasy – imagining what an ichneumon fly would say if it could talk, or a bee, or a swallow – but he uses it seriously. He does the same in his love letters to Olga, of which a selection is translated here, and most of all in the wonderfully passionate and funny love-letter in verse, 'God, if I wanted to be anything'. He can write with a pungency that stops us in our tracks ('Imagine the silence if people said only what they know!'), and he is a master of paradox (explaining, for example, that he is not a communist 'because I am on the side of the poor'), which has led to comparisons with G. K. Chesterton. But he is a freer spirit than Chesterton, unshackled by Catholicism, just as his optimism divides him from Orwell. There is no English writer like him. When his playfulness and his thoughtfulness come together they generate little masterpieces – 'Style' and 'Instinct' and 'Nicholas' and 'Cat' and 'A Little Train' and 'Shame before a Beggar' and 'About Birdsong' and 'Owl' and 'Bethlehem' and 'About Dowsing' and dozens more. Journalism may be an ephemeral form, but these pieces are not ephemeral. Like favourite poems, they stay in the mind as unique moments of thought and feeling.

How Czech readers will judge these translations I cannot tell. But having watched them develop over the years, and read many drafts, I do know about the devotion, the depth of knowledge, the acute sensitivity to linguistic nuance, the imaginative ingenuity and the pitiless perfectionism that have gone into their evolution. In these respects, it seems to me, Čapek has found the translator he deserves.

John Carey
Merton College,
Oxford

Introduction

Life

Karel Čapek is among the greatest of Czech writers, and the most loved. To many Czech readers he is not only a master of the word, but a moral example.

The youngest child of a country doctor, he was born in Malé Svatoňovice, a village in northeast Bohemia, on 9 January 1890. Later the same year the family moved to a nearby small town, Úpice. In infancy Karel underwent a severe attack of scarlet fever, which triggered a degenerative disease of the spine. His mother used to offer up a wax replica of the human chest at the shrine of the Virgin Mary in his birthplace, so that his lungs would become strong and healthy. 'But', Čapek joked, 'the wax chest always had a woman's breasts. So I was seized by the peculiar idea that we boys don't have any lungs, and by the futile expectation that, thanks to my Mum's prayers, I'd grow them.'[1] He tried to disentangle himself from his mother's suffocating love, and to be admitted into the company of his elder siblings – his sister Helena (1886–1961) and his brother Josef (1887–1945), who would become a celebrated artist and writer. Čapek acknowledged having 'an eternal boy' in him; he wrote fairy tales for children, and his childhood remained an inexhaustible source of inspiration.

He studied at a grammar school in Hradec Králové, lodging with his grandmother, whose folk language and humour influenced his style. He continued his studies in Brno, the Moravian metropolis, where his sister had recently married, and finished them in Prague, to which his family had just moved. His brother started studying art, and in 1909 Karel began to read French and German, and later English, Czech, philosophy, aesthetics and art history at Charles University. In 1910–11 he continued his studies of German and

English literatures first in Berlin and then at the Sorbonne: 'Paris
was more, indeed incomparably more, important for my development than Berlin, because in Berlin I'd only go to the university,
whereas in Paris I'd go to all sorts of bars.'[2] He recollects how he
and his brother had eyes only for 'pictures of life in the streets and
endless pictures on the walls of galleries'.[3] Back in Prague they
joined the newly founded Group of Visual Artists (chiefly cubists)
and edited its *Artistic Monthly*. Karel's interest in art is also reflected
in his doctoral thesis entitled 'An Objective Method in Aesthetics
with reference to the Visual Arts'.

The brothers also organised a 1914 'Almanac' of modern Czech
poetry. Karel had written verse (often love poems) in his youth,
but he was predominantly a story-writer, novelist and playwright.
During the First World War he attempted to compile an anthology of modern French poetry, with contributions from a variety of
poet-translators. However, the joint project was never realised, and
in the end he translated a selection by himself (published in 1920
as *French Poetry of the New Age*). This acclaimed anthology introduced Guillaume Apollinaire, among others, into Czech poetry,
and inspired the entire post-war Czech avant-garde.

Karel was exempted from the army. He suffered from Bechterew's
disease, which gave him a hunched posture, rendered his neck permanently immovable and caused severe spinal pain and headaches.
He perceived his translations of French poetry as a kind of personal
fight against the Austrian monarchy, and the same applies to his
interest in Anglo-American philosophy, especially William James,
whose influence he acknowledged in a slim book *Pragmatism, or a
Philosophy of Practical Life* (1918). In this way he allied himself and
his culture with the democratic spirit of the West. His philosophy
of pragmatism was no populist opportunism, but a lifelong critical and moral mission. The message that whenever we look for an
improvement we should look to, and start with, ourselves is latent
in his writings.

The optimism he emanates seems to have been the result of a
wilful effort to fight his illness. His physical handicap may have
been the reason why he was not successful with women when he

was young – he was already thirty when he met the love of his life, the actress and writer Olga Scheinpflugová (1902–68), who was then seventeen. During the fifteen years of their troubled relationship, until 1935 when Karel eventually married her, they were in daily contact. His letters to Olga, of which this book contains a selection, are at once informative, dramatic and poetic, revealing sides of his personality not found anywhere else. Besides, they comprise some of the most moving love letters ever written in the language.

Čapek first worked in collaboration with his brother. Between 1908 and 1918 they produced a range of satirical stories and a playful comedy. Their lyrical and ironic *Insect Play* (1921)[4] drew international attention. Karel's fame at home and abroad increased after the success of his *RUR* (*Rossum's Universal Robots*, 1920),[5] a dystopian drama, which gave the world the word 'robot'. But he was also the author of a lyrical comedy, *The Robber* (1920),[6] which exalts love, youth and freedom against social conventions. Between 1921 and 1923, when he became a dramaturge and an occasional director at Prague's Vinohrady Theatre, his dedication to drama continued with *The Makropulos Case* (1922)[7] – a play about the absurdity of immortality that Leoš Janáček (1854–1928) turned into a libretto for his opera (1928). *Adam the Creator* (1927),[8] co-written with his brother, is concerned with the pitfalls of creation and invention, and hence of artifice, warfare and destruction, and also with such topical issues as the individual versus the mass. In the late 1930s Karel returned to drama after a long gap, using the medium to appeal to the conscience of the civilised world. In *The White Plague* (1937),[9] which warns against dictatorship, the ordinary, unromantic hero is trampled to death by the rabble whose lives he had tried to protect. With him dies his medicine – the only cure for a lethal pandemic. Fascists in Czechoslovakia and Germany were enraged by this play, which was rightly seen as a protest against the new dogma and earned Čapek the label of leftist. His last play, *The Mother* (1938),[10] was inspired by a photograph of a Spanish woman crying over a dead man's body in the bombed Catalan town of Lérida.

Though Čapek was an effective dramatist, his chief aspiration was fiction. He confessed he hated having to watch his plays: 'I've always felt like a puppy whose nose is being pushed into his own puddle. All I can see is my mistakes and I'm cross that I can't alter anything.' He objected that drama lies in the hands of directors and actors, so 'If an author wants to express himself fully he must write novels.'[11] The dystopian novels he wrote in the 1920s are still sharply topical, indeed prophetic. His satirical novel *A Factory to Manufacture the Absolute* (1922)[12] is about a mysterious energy that causes wholesale religious conversion. His characters' observations, such as 'The higher the things someone believes in, the more ferocious his contempt for those who don't believe in them', resonate with fresh currency in our time. The theme of scientific invention and its misuse permeates *Krakatit* (1924),[13] but the novel is also the hero's search for one's place in life and love. In the 1930s Čapek began work on his experimental cognitive ('noetic') trilogy[14] – an intricately orchestrated symphony of multiple psychological perspectives. The first part, the threefold story of *Hordubal* (1933), tells of an immigrant's disorientation on his return from America. In the second, the poetic *Meteor* (1934), three different narrators project their own versions of life onto an unknown hospital patient with a bandaged face. The most complex part, *An Ordinary Life* (1934), explores the life of an 'ordinary' dead man, unravelling his motives and experiences, and even his unrealised, potential lives. In 1936 Čapek reacted to the political situation in Europe with a witty, satirical dystopia, *War with the Newts*,[15] that has achieved classic status, comparable to *Brave New World* and *1984*. His 1937 novel *The First Rescue Party*[16] is a celebration of the unromantic heroism of miners, and his unfinished *The Life and Works of the Composer Foltýn* (1939)[17] is an ironic, yet strangely moving, story of an artist who wants to succeed even at the cost of plagiarism. It questions the irony of success while contemplating artistic honesty and responsibility.

Čapek characterised himself as a 'local European patriot'.[18] He admired England and its tradition of liberal democracy. Yet his admiration was not uncritical. For example, in an article about

English theatre, he expressed relief that in his country theatres, and also schools, hospitals and railways, were public, not private and commercial as in England.[19] He confided to Olga that he did not feel at home in England for social reasons, disliking its affluence.[20] He visited England in 1924 as a guest of PEN, where he met George Bernard Shaw, H. G. Wells, G. K. Chesterton and John Galsworthy. His speech, deliberately using a foreigner's common errors, was apparently long remembered for its wit. In 1935 Wells, the then president of PEN, proposed that Čapek should be his successor, but he was not keen and they eventually elected Jules Romains. More resolute was his organisation of an international congress of PEN in Prague in June 1938, which meant to muster cultural support for his threatened nation. When Romains failed to protest against the Munich Agreement, Čapek wrote to the dramatist Hermon Ould, the secretary of London PEN, saying that he could no longer be a member of an international organisation that approved of the crime perpetrated against his country. In a climate unpropitious to anti-fascist advocates it is no surprise that a group of French writers were unsuccessful in urging Čapek's nomination for the Nobel Prize.

Because of his belief in democracy and humanism, and his association with the liberal politics of President Masaryk, because of his unrelenting effort to expose injustice and seek the truth, and surely also because of his international success, Čapek made enemies. He was mostly scorned for his relativism. This was not the simplistic view that everyone is right, but a painstaking open-mindedness, an attempt to make people think and possibly understand each other's opinions. He deeply distrusted fundamentalism of any kind – absolute beliefs, and revolutions that aimed to change the world. He advised people to 'be revolutionary like atoms': if everyone makes 'a leap in himself', 'mankind will change a little too', though very slowly.[21]

The left censured him for his alleged conservative conformism. He was particularly vilified in the communist newspapers after the publication of his essay 'Why Am I Not a Communist?'. The Catholic right disparaged him for his anti-clericalism. As he puts it in 1925, 'it's really curious how similar it feels to speak to the left or the right'.[22] Immediately after Czechoslovak Independence Day in 1918 he cautioned against nationalistic tendencies, and as early as the 1920s he condemned right-wing nationalism and fascism. Before the presidential election in 1927 a couple of nationalistic newspapers that opposed Masaryk attacked Čapek and his 'Friday men' – a loose gathering of writers, artists and scientists (occasionally including the President) – who met in his house to talk about their interests. In 1934 Čapek signed the Writers' Protest against Fascism. Throughout the 1930s he kept alerting intellectuals to the dangers of the new fanatic creed, and was drawn into a number of polemics. The Catholic writer Jaroslav Durych (1886–1962) denigrated his 'civilian' humanistic attitude to the Spanish Civil War, and labelled him as category C, incapable of military service. To Čapek's brave spirit this was the worst insult, especially coming from a writer with whom he had publicly debated matters of Catholicism and loyalty to the new state, and on whose behalf he had interceded with President Masaryk.

Hostility towards him intensified in the lead-up to Munich. He was blamed as a spokesman for the democratic, West-oriented politics that reactionaries held responsible for the impending disaster. He turned down offers from abroad, intent on 'serving' at home. He wrote daily for the paper and radio, and contacted all the influential people in Europe he knew, disclosing the falsity of German propaganda. He co-prepared and signed the Manifesto of Czechoslovak writers and their Appeal to the World's Conscience.

The Munich betrayal broke him, though he still tried to instil some hope into his fellow countrymen, as his last pieces show. After the tragic event the fascist and clerical press launched a slanderous campaign against him. Sadly, a few Catholic writers, whom Čapek respected but who disparaged his alleged 'bovine sentimentality', joined this crusade. Worse still, he was threatened in the street, and his house and office were flooded with abusive anonymous letters, warning him that he would die in a concentration camp.

Yet he also received many letters of sympathy and support from both Czechs and local Germans and foreigners. His widow, however, burnt them on the fateful morning of 15 March 1939 as the German occupying forces were advancing on Prague – otherwise their authors would have been in danger. He was said to be number three on the Gestapo list, and they arrived at his house that same day to find that he had been dead for nearly three months.

His friends had pressed him to go into exile, but even when Thomas Mann sent his daughter for him, Čapek, a believer in personal responsibility, refused. The autumnal events and attacks had left him mentally and physically exhausted. He caught a chill while working in their old country house and garden, and it developed into pneumonia. On 25 December 1938 his doctor concluded that his heart had not been able to endure all the strain. His friend Dr Karel Steinbach, who was also present, writes:

As a doctor I know that he died because in those days there were no antibiotics and sulpha drugs, but those who say that Munich killed him also have a great deal of the truth. It is beyond doubt that the Munich tragedy was a slap in the face of everything he believed in, and that his wounded, disappointed soul hesitated and finally refused to support his sick, fragile body in its struggle.[23]

In Čapek's words, it was 'not just a big part of the country that [was] lost, but a big part of freedom, democracy and many other moral values'.[24] Even though his funeral was a private affair, as none of the official institutions had the courage to organise it, his friends and readers turned up in droves to honour him. They perceived his death as the symbolic end of an era. What followed is best illustrated by the fates of those who, like his brother Josef or his 'Friday' friends, the prominent writers Karel Poláček (1892–1945)[25] and Vladislav Vančura (1891–1942), did not survive the Nazi concentration camps or prisons, or who survived them only to be incarcerated again by the Communist regime, like his brother-in-law, the poet Josef Palivec (1886–1975). Still more were forced into exile or condemned to lives of limited creativity or oblivion.

Despite the unfavourable climate of the subsequent fifty years Čapek's works have never ceased to inspire. There are not many writers who achieve such an intimate relationship with the reader, and who are immediately likable for their understanding of people's

weaknesses and troubles. He knew about suffering and saw literature as a potential therapy of the soul, articulating 'how much it
hurts'.[26] As Olga put it, 'His life was a thank-you for enchantment,
a smile for illness, and a conscious sense of responsibility. Everyday
hours were more generous to him than festive moments are to
others.' In her housekeeper's words, he 'had much more out of his
short life than those who live perhaps twice as long. He saw and
felt a hundred times stronger than us, as if he had a completely
different heart and eyes.'[27]

Journalism

The classic Czech writer, poet and journalist Jan Neruda (1834–91)
perfected the 'feuilleton' – a witty, pointed article on topical issues
appearing at the bottom of the page marked off by a rule. Following
his lead, Čapek became master of the column, and infused the wide
range of his journalistic pieces with an unforgettable style, humour,
irony and with progressive ideas. He virtually created this 'new literary form . . . shorter than a feuilleton and longer than a comment',[28]
which was printed in italics on the right-hand side of the front page.

   He believed in the importance of quality journalism. From his
student years he had published essays and articles in various, at
first regional, journals. Before and during the First World War he
reviewed art exhibitions and wrote on aesthetic or literary issues
for cultural journals. In October 1917 he obtained his first permanent employment on *The National Newspaper* as a writer for
the visual arts and culture section. This newly radicalised paper
was associated with the chief representatives of the anti-Austrian
resistance. For a few months before Czechoslovak Independence
Day (28 October 1918) it was briefly suspended by the authorities.[29] However, its increasingly narrow nationalistic orientation
during the first years of the Czechoslovak Republic did not suit
Čapek's convictions. Between 1918 and 1920 he published a number
of his social and political observations in the new satirical magazine *Nebojsa* (*The Fearless Fellow*), where his brother Josef was the
editor-in-chief. But it was on *The National Newspaper* that he

made his name as a brilliant journalist, unmasking the use and mis-use of language in a series of columns (of which I include a selection), eventually published under the title *Criticism of Words* (1920). However, *The National Newspaper's* mounting opposition to the liberal, democratic politics of President Masaryk precipitated open protest by several members of the team. When Josef Čapek was dismissed at the end of 1920, Karel demonstrated his solidarity by resigning. He had already published articles and short stories in the Brno liberal daily *The People's Paper*,[30] which had recently established a branch in Prague and was keen to take him and his brother on. On *The People's Paper* the Čapeks worked alongside other outstanding writers, such as Poláček and Eduard Bass (1888–1946). They helped to promote the high quality of Czech journalism between the wars, and readers began to associate the newspaper with them. 'The paper for which I write', Karel said in a 1937 opinion poll, 'is so intelligent that it gives me a free hand to write what I want and for whatever section I like, so my "civic" profession is again literature . . . I know that in this respect my position is exceptional in our country – and lucky – such as I wish all writers could have . . .'[31]

Čapek's democratic spirit, seeking to close the gap between high and low culture, made him 'take journalism as seriously as literature'. He believed that 'the writer should live in the world that belongs to everyone'. The advantage of journalism was that it made him take an interest in everything. He thought all writers should be exposed to this 'attempt at universality', and pointed to the example of his favourite contemporary English author-journalists – Chesterton, Wells and Shaw.[32] But his creative mind found any anxiety about influences inane. He observed that 'there are as few good ideas in the world as there are good inventions', and that it would be foolish to sulk or turn one's back on them.

Anyone who reads the Bible and doesn't succumb to its influence has wasted his time. Anyone who has never succumbed to the influence of Shakespeare or Dostoevsky or Balzac should swallow his pride and burst. I have been influenced by everything great I have come across, if only – thanks to my negligibility – negligibly; I would be an enormous chap and a half if I could digest all the influences that have tried to seduce me.[33]

Though it was *The People's Paper*'s editor-in-chief who insti-
gated the new style of column, Čapek was its leading exponent.
He recalled a guide from the monastery of Monreale boasting
about the variety of columns in the cloister, and remarked: 'we
columnists have long known that every column must be unique
from head to toe. With the craft and fondness of master masons
we tap various motives into that delicate thing. Like Romanesque
craftsmen we take care to create each column differently, imbuing
it with that touch of invention that is the joy of ancient crafts.'[34]
These 'compact pictures of life'[35] suited his temperament, as they
were more succinct than feuilletons, and enabled him to start
with a topical, often ordinary, subject, display his observant wit,
and end on a general, ethical note. Apart from the terse linguistic
columns collected in *Criticism of Words*, he got together a volume
called *About the Closest Things* (1925).[36] The rest were published
posthumously. He also introduced a brief form, 'entrefilet', which
was printed among news items and which he used for his reactions to topical events, replies to readers and short profiles. His
longer and chattier pieces – feuilletons and causeries – appeared in
the popular collections *The Gardener's Year* (1929)[37] and *How One
Thing or Another Is Done* (1938),[38] as well as in several posthumous
collections.[39]

Another of his innovations was a Sunday supplement page,
which contained longer pieces or stories with his brother's illus-
trations (from the time of his *Letters from England* he illustrated
his own travel books and writing about pets). He experimented
with the short story, producing a series of delightful parodic tales,
Apocryphas (1932),[40] and a number of dramatic miniatures or 'sub-
stories'. He was also economical with words in creating aphoris-
tic fables and 'little broadcasts' – light verse ranging from political
satires to comic commentaries that drew on the tradition of street
and cabaret songs. These poems reported the news, were usually
stylised as radio broadcasts, and were invented and supplied weekly
by Bass, for whom Čapek often stood in in the mid 1930s.[41] At
that time he used them to criticise Italian, German and Spanish
fascism, and the Moscow show trials.

In 1924 President Masaryk financed the foundation of a weekly, *The Present*, edited by a distinguished essayist, Ferdinand Peroutka (1895–1978), the political editor of *The People's Paper* and Karel's friend. Most of the essays Čapek published in his book *About Common Things, or Zoon Politikon* (1932) first appeared in this journal, which ranked among the most influential intellectual periodicals between the wars. His famous polemical essay 'Why Am I Not a Communist?' was part of an opinion poll run by *The Present*. It was in this journal too that Čapek stirred a controversy about the current state of literary criticism, arguing that criticism should not be arbitrary or subjective, nor prescriptive and full of 'bombast, flowery and imprecise words', but should seek the work's objective cultural value by analysing its form, style, inner logic, psychology, etc. He was censured for being a relativist yet advocating absolute values. But to Čapek, the reviewer's role is to inform readers about the work and offer them a deeper understanding of it, not display his feelings, personality or world-view.

He wrote reviews himself, and introduced English literature to Czech readers, initiating The Anglo-American Library series. As is clear from the present collection, he also contemplated the role of culture. He despised 'the whole of that intolerant, limited, conceited, desiccated and awfully boring intellectual elite'.[42] He brings out the danger of such exclusiveness by alluding to Germany, where so many people 'have stopped being good poets, artists and scholars just because they are Jewish'. For him culture is

a collective, democratic, supremely shared thing, the only thing in this universe that can be shared by everyone. It alone is common and universal, for its mission is to encompass the entire reality; it alone is limitless, for it cannot stop at any final point; it alone does not age, for it will never cease to create. Take one of its relations away, just one, and you will have crippled it.[43]

In 1931 he brought out his collection of essays about popular literature, *Marsyas, or On the Margin of Literature*,[44] which implies that the highbrow should be wise enough to learn from the low-brow. The critic, he said, should be 'as reliable as an ordinary carpenter, at least',[45] and should notice, if not show an interest in, what most people read.

Given journalism's demand on his time (the Čapek bibliography lists 3,149 articles), it is astounding that he never gave it up. From his correspondence we know that he was anxious about his own writing and finding enough time for it. In a 1924 letter to a friend he jokes that he has stopped being a writer and has become a tapeworm because he sheds articles like one of those Articulata. 'Two to three articles come out weekly, but the head won't appear. It's horrible – I'd like to start doing something proper at last.'[46] In the letters from abroad he sent to Olga he complains that he has to turn intense experiences into entertaining reportage for the paper.[47] Yet he was grateful for the long summer leaves that the paper granted him to write novels, in return for the privilege of serialising them. His ability to see the unusual in the ordinary, greatness in smallness, and his belief in the value of useful workaday effort that 'shines and warms',[48] runs like a leitmotif through his works. In a column called 'These Grey Days', which he wrote for *About the Closest Things*, he worries about the passage of time – how 'a day has gone and has left behind nothing but this article on the table'. But he concludes by praising routine work, 'the most awesome pastime of life', and sees it not as a waste but a giving.[49] His aim was not to write for an exclusive audience, but for ordinary people who like to read. This accords with his moral ethos and his wish to be a helpful doctor like his father.

His work also had a practical impact. For example, he used his columns to urge his readers to support *The People's Paper*'s regular Easter collection sponsoring health-holidays for poor urban children. Early in 1934, at the time of the depression, he initiated a project, Democracy for Children, which aimed to engage writers, academic, artistic and scientific societies, and of course readers of his newspaper, in helping to provide food for poor children. One can easily imagine people following his charitable example, and any sensitive person would be moved to action by reading the poetic piece 'Shame before a Beggar', with its insight into human nature. He used journalism as a platform for addressing issues about which he thought it would be immoral to keep silent. He worked for *The People's Paper* for almost eighteen years, from 1 April 1921 right until his death.

Style, Translation and Acknowledgements

This selection is designed to offer the best of Čapek's journalism and some of his best letters. Its contents have, with the exception of a very few pieces, never been translated into English before. The journalism is divided into five thematic sections, each of them organised chronologically. The first relates to culture, the second to language. The third contains impressions of, and ideas about, England. The fourth section is a broad spectrum of observations about people, nature and things, and the last relates to public or political – in his word 'common' – matters. This book also gives a flavour of how diverse his interests were. They encompassed everything from hobbies – gardening, pets, cultivating cacti, collecting Persian carpets, photography and drawing – through literature, culture, philosophy, religion, theatre, film, music, architecture, the visual arts and the natural sciences (entomology in particular), to ethnography and politics. A zestful, ever inquisitive mind, wondering at the richness of the reality around, animates all his work.

Whatever he was writing about, 'from politics to cleaning sewers or a literary article', he cared most about '*how* it was written'.[50] I am aware that I can never do justice to his style. It is frustrating to know what he thought about translation: 'it's a torment for an author having to check how much of the original gets lost even in the most faithful translation.'[51] His style deftly blends colloquial and literary, demotic, fairy-tale and biblical, dialect and formality, terse and metaphorical, plain and poetic. He was among the first to bring idiomatic speech into Czech literature. This is partly the reason why his writing still sounds remarkably fresh. His primary concern is succinctness. He despises clichés and sees their damaging power. The dialogical character of his prose stems from the tradition of oral narrative reflected in nineteenth-century Czech literature. He frequently employs semicolons, often to create the effect of telling a story at one go. And then comes an effective contrast in the form of a short, pungent point. His clustering of images or examples imitates spontaneous narration, but is also an indirect tribute to the inexhaustible wealth of things and experiences the world proffers us. His lists of synonyms are an attempt to grasp reality more fully. He enjoyed exploring the vocabularies of all the branches of human knowledge he was enmeshed in. Czech is special in having developed – thanks to the effort of the national revivalists – a native nomenclature in many disciplines, especially natural science. As an inflected language it has a flexible word order, and tends to employ more adjectives than English. It is not always feasible to retain all of Čapek's nuances in English without running the risk of sounding verbose, which would be just the wrong impression. It is possible to convey his witty energy, verbal richness, and fondness for parallelism and word-play (though not every pun and idiom), but impossible to translate the idiosyncrasy of his diction. Some expressions are folksy or tonal and lend his language a specific, what Czechs recognise as 'Čapekian', tenor. There is no point in resorting to highly unusual English words, which would make him sound obscure.

Given his belief in people, another of his typical usages is 'man' – a genderless human being with whom he sustains a conversation and who merges with his addressee – the reader – or his own self. This has been rendered in translation as 'old chap', 'my friend', 'human creature' and so on, depending on context. The genderless form (e.g. a human or a person) and plural reference have been used wherever possible, but otherwise the masculine pronoun has been retained, as it includes the author's self, and is in tune with the standards of his time.

In a column called 'Do Ghosts Exist?' Čapek jokes about spiritualism and concludes that the best spirits he has come into contact with are alive.[52] Apart from a brilliant Czech mystic poet, interestingly he chooses Shaw and Chesterton as examples. I have been lucky in having had a kindred English spirit presiding over my translations. I first worked with John Carey when I was writing a doctoral thesis on ambiguities in Milton's epic. His sharp insight into my Miltonic 'ghost meanings', as he called them, or those of my prose, was beyond price. When I first read his *Original Copy* I was struck by its keen wit, effortless lucidity and subversive tones that I immediately perceived as Čapekian. His criticism of highbrow intellectuals and his anti-elitist ideas about appreciation of art are also close to Čapek's. I could not have hoped for an abler stylist and a more ideal co-operation, for which I would like to express my infinite gratitude. Čapek has found in this English critic an extremely sensitive, careful – and luckily for me – endlessly patient reader. I am also grateful for the support I have received from Julian Loose and Kate Murray-Browne, my editors at Faber and Faber. The final selection has gained much from Kate's shrewd criticism and enthusiasm, and the typescript from the scrupulousness of its copy-editor, Eleanor Rees. Needless to say, all imperfections remain mine.

Šárka Tobrmanová-Kühnová
Charles University, Prague, 2009

I

CULTURE

Two Kinds of Joy

New Year's Publication 1918, Veraikon library, vol. 11,
Prague, 1918.

I saw him as he was bowing down to the supreme masterpieces
in the temple of the arts, invoking great names: 'By Dante, Homer,
Michelangelo, Phidias and Solomon, by Bach, Rembrandt,
Dostoevsky and the divine Leonardo, behold how I respect Art!
See whether there is, among the gods I worship, a single one who
is small, deficient and dubious! See whether I have not chosen the
best, whether I do not kneel before the highest pedestals! I and
the geniuses! Ich gleiche dem Geist, den ich begreife!¹ Dante, I
understand you! Rodin! Smetana! Sophocles! Jahveh! There is no
beauty but the beauty of masterpieces; there is no art but the art of
geniuses; there is no depth but in the elite of minds. I see only the
Magnificent and appreciate only the Universally Valid. Art is the
innermost expression of a great, renowned genius – my close friend
Lukáš Sobíšek is a profound, creative spirit too, and anyone who
doesn't believe that is an idiot who must be scourged out of the
Temple. Poussin! Sobíšek! Beethoven! My greatest joy and pride
is that there is no iniquity in me: I bow only to the true gods. To
appreciate art is to honour it. The only joy to be derived from art is
the worship of genius.'

Meanwhile, you, the publican, were murmuring your 'Lord, I am
unworthy' at the back of the temple. You often slipped into the
empty temple and stood around in front of the plinths, slightly
weighed down by the odour of incense and drying wreaths, but
now you are walking along the streets of earthly Jerusalem without
aim, and I'm afraid, also without thinking. But your eyes and ears
have a lot to do. You must listen a while to the fiery hurdy-gurdy
near the hot-air balloons, and look at the painted graces, that are
so little redolent of professional models, near the merry-go-round.

You must stop in surprise at a post, watered by all possible descriptions of dog, discovering that it's as beautiful as an obelisk or a primitive god. You must wait till the children at play finish painting their kite. You took to that savage kite very much as its horrid face lifted serenely into the air. Then you stood at the window of an amateur painter, and felt moved as you watched his naïve work, the labour of humility. You found a frameless picture in a junk shop. You didn't know who painted it but were enchanted by a fragment of a painted path, a few trees and a little white cloud. You picked up a trodden label from the dust, studied shop signs and peeped into shop windows full of dolls, postcards and crockery. You saw someone painting a picture that no one understood. You didn't even know if you understood it yourself, but you liked it very much, and they laughed at you when you said so. Now you are going home satisfied and think to yourself: 'Praise be to God, I've seen enough, enough prettiness. What a surprise – how many beautiful things there are in this world! I had a specially happy day today, but I don't even know the names of the streets where I saw it all.'

Instead of Criticism

The National Newspaper, 24 December 1920

Today is unsuitable for the appearance of my usual critical column; Christmas Eve is not the day of judgement. Let there be, exceptionally, 'peace to all people of good will', though good will doesn't mean good literature.

For the whole year I've been reading books and writing about them. Still, I wasn't able to write everything to my heart's content. And now I confess that I often suppressed what seemed to me the most vital thing. I didn't always say what I really liked or what was alien to me in literature; I didn't say what I want from literature and what out of sheer personal dislike I can't bear. Instead of criticism, then, today I'm going to give away my own tastes – I have judged others, you can judge me. I'm not prescribing anything, nor am I prophesying 'a literature of tomorrow'. The literature of tomorrow will be done by the people of tomorrow, and no one needs to think what they should do on their behalf.

First I confess, with appropriate humility, a rather low demand: I'd like literature to be more entertaining, to be, in fact, really entertaining. We all sin against this requirement, more or less. We conceive 'collective literature' as a policy; we speak of the democratisation of literature, about the need to popularise the book. But try to find where the people are. They sit in picture palaces because something's going on there and because it thrills them. It's very easy to break out into harangues against this destruction of taste. But consider whether the people sitting in picture palaces aren't essentially the same as those who twenty-five centuries ago sat by the fire around the Homeric bard and listened to heroic songs, to how the Achaeans and the Trojans chopped one another up, how Achilles dragged Hector three times round the walls, or how Odysseus jabbed Polyphemus's eye out. For film, despite all its flaws, has one primitive advantage: that it is epic, that there is always something going on, that life here reveals itself in its raciest and clearest form – in action. Popular literature will never be anything but epic – I mean, of course, prose epic. Let me just say a word here on the eternal youth of the people. The people remain a boy who lets himself be enchanted by heroism, by great and unshaken characters, by simple passions, by a strong and perhaps even fantastic plot. Their enjoyment of literature is a fierce participation, a co-activity with everything that is going on. They don't want to analyse anything but to live with something, to live through something extraordinary. This is not romanticism – this thirst for a powerful living-through is something more primitive and older than all the divisions of literature into periods and movements. Indeed, if literature does not become epic again, it will be less and less popular.

Now, it doesn't follow that there should be a prescription for writers, that they should in the name of democracy suddenly start dreaming up adventurous and thrilling plots for their future novels. It is not necessary 'to descend to the level of the people' and fabricate some special, rougher goods for them. If we are to talk about popular literature at all, it doesn't mean that there should be 'popular' literature on the one hand and 'high' on the other. I should like high literature to become popular, so that what is written for art's sake, and only for art's sake, could be a pleasure and entertainment for all levels and classes (yes, mainly classes nowadays), just as classical poetry was. Nothing indicates the disintegration of European culture more clearly than popular books, popular theatres and such. It's still common to start from the presumption that the people need something worse and lower than the elite. For once it would be worth trying out in practice the presumption that the people need something healthier and more remarkable than the others, that they need for their excitement great virtues and deeds, whole people, heroic action, miraculous fantasy and, in a nutshell, the great poetic art of a magician, capable of striking the rapturous spark of the unusual out of life.

And now I'm going to confess an even worse lapse. Reading books, I often think that they have yet another task, as it were, apart from forming the characters of the novel – they should form readers' characters too. This brings me, daringly, to the verge of didacticism, which we have, as they say, outlived, but I am prepared to run the risk of this unpopular word. Indeed, literature should form people. It should strive to have an influence on reality itself. And I don't believe so much in a slow educational influence as in the magician's influence, a creative influence that directly begets new realities. I believe that the moment heroic literature emerges, there will be live, genuine heroes running about among us. I believe that morally racy novels will immediately meet with morally racy and magnanimous realities. Look, Robinson Crusoe hasn't slowly brought up thousands of Robinsons, but he has found them – he has found a bit of Robinson in every true boy. Every kind of literature, every construction of a plot evokes the corresponding events out of the fullness of life. It is in this that I see the moral responsibility of writers. Not in that they can corrupt or reform people, but that they directly beget people in the image and likeness of what they write. It is only half true that literature corresponds to life. It is equally true that life corresponds to literature and seeks to accommodate itself to it, however scarce the cases might be. If poets were always aware that they could evoke realities out of the womb of being, they would, I think, stop hesitating about the word didacticism. They would, anxiously inclining their heads towards life, seek to entice magnanimous, genuine and heroic answers out of it. They would appeal to the best, the most lasting, the whole and the self-assured in men and women, and I believe that they wouldn't call in vain. For they create more than images; they create examples. I may be mistaken in my belief that great literature could make life great. However, no sufficiently extensive and persistent attempt has so far been undertaken. We have not yet tried the limits of the magical power present in poetry and art. We write off these possibilities too soon. We are far too fond of decay, dying and the dismal tragicalness of weaklings. Does that mean that we live the life of hopeless weaklings? And even if it is so, have we made enough effort to demand the opposite? It seems to me that the evident lack of novels in our country is caused by uncertainty about what we want from life, an uncertainty which is, ultimately, purely moral. This makes me doubly regret that our young literature is almost entirely unproductive of novels – the only form that could, in effect, become the basis of popular literature.

This is not all I want from literature. But recalling today everything I have read in the whole year, this unfulfilled desire remains the strongest. Entertainment, populism, moralism – these are perhaps the lowest words in the market of literary terms, and yet I think they live; what's more, they live very energetically. They are very primitive, very old, and perhaps that's why they cannot be outlived.

Criticism

The People's Paper, 16 April 1921

Stories about slaps in the face aren't very edifying, not even if they happen in parliament. Recently you may have read about one in a concert hall. There has probably never been a news story in the papers in which a critic has attacked an artist or beaten him up. It's always the artist who beats up the evil critic. Perhaps he regards it as self-defence. This kind of tit-for-tat isn't new; it's been happening for ages. What's new is a different type of defence: if a critic touches a corporate body, such as a theatre or a philharmonic orchestra, a public meeting is convened. And the meeting has a go at the evil, unfair, cliquey and incompetent criticism. Of course, the representatives of political parties must also have their say. A resolution against the evil, etc. criticism is passed, and the papers are urged to sack the evil, etc. reviewers forthwith. The outcome is a summons for libel or for grievous bodily harm, and then we're left waiting . . . for another scandal of the same sort. Something else will come up, you may be sure. For criticism is notoriously evil, unfair, cliquey and incompetent, and a poor artist must defend himself. With slaps. Meetings. Resolutions. Perhaps even by a pogrom.

Look, I've written a few reviews myself. I don't think that I do it out of barbaric instincts, but out of love of literature. Sometimes, even with the best will in the world, I don't like a book, and say so. Now I don't doubt that I have – in the author's eyes – done him a great wrong; I'm reconciled in advance to the fact that he considers me unfair, cliquey and incompetent. It's definitely his right. I, too, use this right when an unfair, cliquey and incompetent critic, who gives my books a bad press, hurts me. To cut a long story short, there's an eternal conflict between artist and critic. 'Praise me, or I'll hate you.' This conflict can never be reconciled. Unless . . .

Unless we artists stop being children and understand how awfully little criticism can do. Keep hammering bad literature for a hundred years, and it will still be read rather than good literature. Inveigh against kitschy pictures in chorus, and they'll carry on selling. Even if a United Criticism of the World were formed, it would not be able to erase a single operetta. If you are a bad artist, don't be afraid of criticism. Be contemptuous of it: it can't get through to you no matter how hard it tries. Your status is unshakeable. Don't give a damn about the scribbling of a few aesthetes. You're invulnerable. If you are a good artist, your case is worse.

Because you'll get hurt, perhaps existentially, but morally for sure. Understandably, you are sensitive, and since you're a good artist, you are able to doubt yourself. But deep down in your heart you need even that doubt. I can't think of a single circumstance in which a good artist, a *true* artist, would assault an evil, etc. critic. And I don't know of a single instance in which incompetent criticism has retained the upper hand over good art. True art wins recognition slowly. Even if a United Criticism of the World were organised with a special view to suppress good art, rest assured that the evolution of art wouldn't fundamentally change. Perhaps it would slow down. But what is truly valuable astonishes as soon as it appears, and then it's useless either to hype it or run it down. Evil criticism is as helpless against good work as good, creative criticism is against pseudo-art.

A Little Reformer

The People's Paper, 23 February 1922

You know how it is. Sometimes you tell a joke on stage, a transparent, surprising, topical, powerful and, why be modest, original joke, and no one laughs. Perhaps they didn't have enough time to realise it was a joke. Perhaps they just didn't expect it at that point. Explain it by any kind of crowd-psychology you like – quite simply, the joke disappears. What a shame: that's a laugh lost.

However, another time the audience suddenly cracks up when nothing you'd expect to raise a laugh happens on stage. There's this devastating moment when the hero stumbles about in pain, and the audience welcomes it with a gale of mirth. Hedda Gabler takes General Gabler's pistols in her hands – it's truly tragic, but the audience howls with laughter. In Synge's *The Well of the Saints* the healed blind man discovers that his beautiful wife is ugly – it's really disturbing, but the audience assumes it's meant to be amusing. If someone punches someone else or utters an obscenity, the audience responds with delighted laughter, though the obscenity isn't necessarily funny and wasn't intended to be. Sometimes it makes your hair stand on end to see what can raise a laugh.

If the audience don't laugh when they have a chance to (and have paid to), and if they laugh, even under threat of purgatorial torture, when they shouldn't laugh at all, the result is disorientation, chaos and uncertainty. There's no knowing how they'll react. What we need is a remedy.

This could be provided in a number of ways. By pressing a button before each joke the prompter could light a little red bulb that would indicate: 'Attention! Joke coming.' The bulb would stay on during jocular scenes, and be switched off during serious ones. Everyone would know right away whether they could laugh. Alternatively a special signal, such as they have on railways, could be set up among the footlights, and manipulated by the curtain-raiser. An arm pointing diagonally upwards would mean: 'The track is clear, no obstacles in sight. Feel free to laugh.' An arm in the horizontal position: 'Watch out! There is a hazard. Don't laugh.' An arm pointing diagonally downwards: 'We're in deep water – something tragic is going on. Pray, if you wish.' And behold, all difficulties would vanish.

Furthermore, bulbs of various colours could light up on the front of the theatre according to what is going to happen inside, whether it's something funny or serious or mixed, and this would, after all, have a decorative effect too.

I offer this idea for free.

Another problem is a bronchial catarrh that only afflicts theatre-goers. An acute fit of it usually erupts when the actors on stage are speaking quietly and perhaps even wittily (I say 'perhaps', because it's impossible to hear). A man (in the third row of the stalls) always gives out a cough, which is picked up by an asthmatic lady (in the pit) and a student with a bad cold (standing in the gods). Hereupon an epidemic breaks out: a choir of about thirty chronic bronchial sufferers (basses and altos) strikes up, supported by laryngo-pharyngeal cases (baritones and mezzo-sopranos). The performance fades out within a few minutes, once the most important part of the dialogue on stage has happily been made inaudible. Some people suspect there's a secret organisation behind the theatrical cough. In my judgement, however, it is a serious epidemic.

Therefore I put forward the proposal that theatres should establish the office of an advance cougher or advance cougheress. This member of the cast would sit on the stage, I mean in the footlights area by the proscenium. At suitable, previously selected moments, he or she would raise a baton (or a truncheon), the actors would immediately stop moving and speaking (just as when a constable stops the traffic at the bottom of Wenceslas Square), and the advance cougher would emit a mighty, lung-clearing, infectious cough, which would stir the audience to a relieving, collective, catarrhal avalanche. Meanwhile, the actors would talk among themselves in muffled voices. After three minutes of coughing the advance cougher would raise his baton (or truncheon), and the audience would finish hawking. A new signal, and in an attentive hush the actors would resume where they had left off. In another few minutes the whole procedure would be repeated. I think that twenty coughs of three-minute duration would suffice for an evening performance.

I trust that the theatre authorities will take this well-meant proposal into consideration.

Where Is Heaven?

The People's Paper, 5 November 1922

Where paradise is, or rather where it was, is a moot point, and where the heavens of the blessed are is all the more uncertain, but good old Charlie Chaplin, well known to you all, tells a story about it that is delightful beyond anything. In his most captivating film, *The Kid*, about which much could be written, the forlorn tramp Charlie Chaplin falls asleep on the threshold of his little flat in the most abject street of a city, and he dreams that he has died and is in heaven. And where is heaven then? Well, it's just in that beastly, sordid street, but now it's clean and radiant, and from each split, rift and crack flower sacred white roses. Heaven is right on the threshold of Chaplin's poor little den, as well as on the threshold of his neighbours and exploiters, as the white roses testify. And behold, the policeman who chases Chaplin so unrelentingly is an angel here; he has a long white shirt and big white wings and a truncheon in his hand; all the neighbours are angels too with bowler hats on their heads, and the women of the neighbourhood with their groovy hairdos, and the scruffy street dog – they all have white shirts and wings and harps in their hands, and all romp around in David's joyous dance, for they are in heaven. And the dreadful boxer, the source of unspeakable terror for Charlie, and the nasty man from the orphanage are likewise winged angels, and even the Jewish junk-shop keeper, from whom the newly ascended Chaplin buys 'virtually new' pinions, is a winged angel, and Karlíček Chaplin begins to float above the flowering street in boundless bliss.

It's tremendous fun, but also tremendous philosophy if you can draw a bit of a general conclusion from Chaplin's dream – yes, it's one of the purest and the most tender moral philosophies I know. To find – if just in a dream – heaven in your street, on the threshold of your home, in the heart of your poverty; to see paradise even in the thing you see every day, within reach, in your most humdrum surroundings, and to see angels in your nearest fellow beings, in your neighbours on the left and right, in a Jewish junk-shop keeper, in a stray dog, but also in a ghastly gorilla-like boxer who beats you, in a constable who runs after you, in the wicked person who has hurt you most, in a paunchy egoist who has robbed you of what's dearest to you, that's the jokey, tender gospel of the sentimental clown Chaplin, a gospel whose comicality conceals the infinite magic of tender and wise goodness.

And I wouldn't be surprised if tonight I saw Eda Bass in the editorial office wearing a white shirt and staggering wings,[1] and Mr Kazetka with wings (which he is careful not to sweep the path with),[2] and Dr Procházka with David's harp, and Messieurs

Rejzek, Keprta and Ondrák with beautiful new wings, and the editorial mice with little white wings, and Dr Šelepa in Brno as, with the help of his wings, he glides smoothly through his editorial office, and the editor-in-chief as he flies in through the window from across the road as if nothing's happened, singing joyfully. And if tomorrow in the theatre I saw Mr Jaroslav Kvapil sporting the enormous wings of a seraph (as befits his rank)[3] and Bohuš Zakopal who has something angelic in him anyway,[4] and the manager Fuksa as he flits about the office amid the white roses, and the eternal villain Vávra and the goody Vojta, and the actors Roman Tuma and Veverka and Strnad and Štěpánek, and come to think of it, everyone, and Mrs Dostálová and Mrs Ptáková and Mrs Iblová and all the ladies down to the youngest, and the porter with wings and a harp, and the tram driver with huge wings on his back, and my dentist with wings (of a lower order, as he's currently doing me much ill). I wouldn't wonder the least bit that they were angels; quite the opposite, I'd wonder that I hadn't noticed it before. And that I hadn't realised they were in fact in heaven. And as for my enemies – though I'm neither afraid of nor angry with anybody – I'd see quite clearly that anyone who was furious with me (an angel with virtually new pinions) might quite easily be an angel of the whitest shirt and most immaculate wings.

Try it yourself. Close your eyes and say to yourself that the setting of your daily caring and toiling is actually heaven, that heaven is your workshop or your office, your four walls, your slightly smelly and, at this time of the year, murky street. And that all the people you know are heavenly angels, though they are formed any old how, and are of various hairs and noses and temperaments and features. Also angels are those who have hurt you in some way, even to the extent that their view on something differs from yours. Perhaps this fantasy isn't all that easy, but if it doesn't seem to you beautiful and like a soothing balm, I don't know what to talk to you about any more.

And I can tell you, if you want to get to heaven by the shortest route, you must follow Chaplin's path. If you find sacredly blooming roses all around you, and a redeemed angel in every human, if everyone is a winged cherub for you, harp-sounding and eternal and worthy of everlasting glory, you'll be in heaven. And then you'll be rewarded like Charlie Chaplin: you'll meet everything you love, and will be happy till the end of time.

For if heaven isn't within reach of life, nay even nearer still, within the reach of your eyes and hands, nay even nearer still, in your very selves, it's nowhere, and you will never get there.

An Emergency Column (Part I)

The People's Paper, 22 January 1923

What is a column? A column is what follows below. It is always printed in italics in *The People's Paper* to bring out the special importance of columns in contrast to the remaining contents devoted to politics, the national economy and culture as well as the courtroom. A column is very important just because it comes out every day as the sun does. If it did not come out, there would be darkness over all the world.

What is an emergency column? An emergency column is a column that needs to be written so that it can come out and darkness does not descend on the world. So there is an urgent need for a quickly written column, made with tremendous wit, say, out of nothing, or out of very thin material that must be deftly expanded so that it will take up a particular portion of type. These emergency materials, then, give rise to the emergency columns in question, which are very popular with readerships as they testify most beautifully to the wit of the writer, and his special acuteness and adroitness, nay, they testify to the writer's soul, which, we might say, they disclose; for, verily, they usually spring from the uncanniest folds of his soul, being fully soul-fed and ultimately having nothing in common with the external world, which is from a columnly perspective insubstantial.

It happens, for example, as it did today, that the Brno editorial office rings up the Prague office to say that they urgently need an emergency column. But there is no column here, in Prague, I swear to God, and it seems that at this moment there is not, has never been and, alas, most probably will never be anything out of which a column could be made. A disastrous situation like this is exactly the kind in which emergency columns have their origin. For they rise out of chaos, just as the universe once did, to which *The People's Paper* and its cherished readers owe their origin.

Since Brno is, in the interest of the readership of that entire universe, very much pressing for the writing up of this piece, two Čapeks have settled down to do the urgent job in order to put together and despatch a column in the quickest possible way, by this means hoping that they might be finished more expeditiously. Note, then, that this has been written by me, *Čapek I*, and that I find I have filled a decent portion of the manuscript without having to resort to digging out shabby and discarded, nay emergency, materials. Quite the contrary, there are so many ideas for columns that this issue alone could publish six of them or even more, and we would not yet have used up all the remarkable things that deserve adept professional reflection, arousing general attention and wonder.

For my part, then, I could pertinently elaborate here on the fact that, say, Shrovetide is at hand opening the door to the first joys of spring. Perhaps I could write about a door, a door that creaks, or does not creak, but I may as well write about the creaking too. Creaking is a thing about which little has been written, a thing that is neglected, indeed, creaky, and that hardly anyone has hitherto noticed, since creaking is, after all, rather unpleasant. I could write a column about unpleasant things of which there are more than enough samples in the world. And I could do a column about what it is like when it is enough. It is almost always good when it is enough. I wish everyone enough, as I realise to my satisfaction that I have enough ideas for columns. I shall be glad to see how many ideas Čapek II has below. Maybe he doesn't really have any or has just about managed one. If he has only one, he could have made it into a column all by himself, and then both of us needn't have been writing. You must judge.

Why Do You Like Your Profession?

The People's Paper, 6 April 1924

Forgive me, but I'll start with something completely different, that is, boyhood. A city boy is a superboy, a born sceptic and lord of the streets, and it's quite natural that he should be contemptuous of clodhoppers, dumblewits, bumpkins, boors and string-beans, or in other words boys from the country. A village boy is boundlessly and rightly contemptuous of urban boys, for he is lord of fields and forests, he understands horses and cattle, can crack a whip, and he has all the treasures of the world in his power, from willow twigs to ripe poppy-heads. However, a small-town boy is by no means the least among the princes of the world, for he beholds more in his sphere than any other earthly creature – he sees into the handling of human crafts.

So when I was a boy in a small town I saw the craft of a doctor at home, and at Grandad's the craft of a miller and a baker, which is awfully entertaining and beautiful, and the craft of a peasant-farmer at my uncle's – goodness, I could talk for ages about that, how I learnt it and all the things I got to know. But our nearest neighbour was a decorator, and that's a wonderfully interesting profession; sometimes he let me mix paint in pots for him, and once, half-insensible with pride, I was even allowed to daub one stencil with a brush – it came out lopsided, but otherwise successfully. I'll never forget how the painter walked with a stepladder as if on stilts and sang, magnificently mottled with all colours, and how he painted such miraculously straight lines, and sometimes freehand, peculiarly roly-poly roses on the ceiling, the colour of old liver – anyway, for me it was the first revelation of the art of painting, and since then I've been addicted to it. And then I would go daily and watch the craft of the publican, how he rolled the hogsheads into his cellar, how he drew the beer and blew the froth off, and how he communed wisely with the gaffers who wiped away the froth from their beards with the backs of their hands. Every day I'd go to keep an eye on the neighbourhood shoemaker, and would silently watch how he sliced the leather and nailed it on the last, and then put on the sole, and I can't remember what else any more because it's a complicated and delicate art, and anyone who hasn't seen leather in a shoemaker's hands knows nothing about it even if he wears shoes made of birds-of-paradise skins or cordovan. Then there was the neighbourhood organ-grinder, Mr Hanousek; I went to see him as well when he was at home, and I marvelled at the fact that he didn't play the barrel-organ there, but sat and looked into the corner so that it made me feel distressed. Further, we had a sad mason there – he hewed crosses and short, plump angels in his front yard; he tapped away all day long without saying a word, and I gazed at him perhaps for an hour as he was tapping in the blind eye of a weeping angel. And then, aha, then there was the wheelwright with his beautiful hearty wood and a yard full of wheels, running wheels, as Homer says; such a wheel, dear folks, is a wonder in itself. And then a smith in a black forge; I was burst-ing with pride when I could occasionally tug at his bellows while he, a black Cyclops, was heating an iron rod and hammered it until sparkles streamed out, and when he was putting a horseshoe on the hoof, it gave off a reek of burnt horn, and the horse turned his wise eyes to the smith as if he wanted to say: 'Don't worry, I'll hold still.'

A bit further off lived Tonča, a prostitute; I didn't understand her craft very well, and I passed her house with a bit of a clutched throat; only once did I peep in through a small window, but it was empty, and there were striped eiderdowns and consecrated catkins above the bed. I watched the craft of factory owners as they ran around the typing room, and I picked up exotic stamps from their wastepaper baskets; and I watched workers, spinning machines full of tow, and weavers at their mysterious jacquard machines; I slipped into the glowing hell of the jute-drying kiln and got burn-ing hot with stokers at the furnace, wondering at their long shovels, which I could barely lift. I used to visit the butcher in his shop, star-ing at him in suspense, waiting to see whether he'd chop his finger off; I was all eyes to find out at the grocers' how they measure and weigh things, I stood at the whitesmith's, and often went to the cabinet-maker's yard, where it all whizzed and pounded with sheer eagerness. I would go to the almshouse to look at the craft of the poor, and I accompanied them on their Friday pilgrimage through the town to witness how begging is done.

Now I, too, have my craft, and do it for the whole of God's day. But even if I sat on my doorstep with it, I don't think that a boy would stop and watch my fingers – standing on one bare foot, stroking his calf with the other – so as to see how scribbling is done. I'm not saying that it's a bad and useless craft, but it's not such a gorgeous spectacle, and the material that I work with is so strange – you can't even see it. But I'd like everything that I've ever seen to be in it: the hammering chime of the blacksmith and the colours of the singing painter, the patience of the tailor and the careful tap of the mason, the nimbleness of the baker, the humbleness of the poor and all that russet strength and skill that grown-ups put into their work before the child's dumbfounded and bewitched eyes.

The Age of the Eyes

The People's Paper, 22 February 1925

You may have noticed that conspicuously few old people go to the cinema. Even if you take into account that older people are as a rule more frugal and more comfortable, and all in all, less profligate than the rest of us, it's not a sufficient explanation for why so few of them indulge in the depraved invention of luminous pictures. The older generation expresses open disgust for this modern spectacle. They mutter something like, 'Don't bother us with such tosh,' and open yesterday's paper or a fifty-year-old novel instead. Meanwhile, the said fifty-year-old novel is being enacted on the screen of a picture palace round the corner, and the rest of us, who are breathlessly watching its flying action, can't understand that an old man has the patience to read such ancient trash. The average film is, in the vast majority of cases, much closer to Walter Scott than to, say, Vít Nezval,[1] and resembles George Sand more closely than George Bernard Shaw. The average film doesn't pick up on modern literature, but on old literature. As a matter of fact, it's the direct successor of old novelistic fiction. The younger generation doesn't realise that in the cinema they give themselves up to the lush imaginative world of their distant fathers. The older generation doesn't have an inkling that the shadowy pictures they are so contemptuous of are bone of their bones, or rather I should say the shadow of their bones. Which is of course a typical, unbridgeable rift between the generations.

It seems to me, then, that the older generation doesn't reject film because it's too modern, or too silly, but for more profound reasons: because it's too fast and isn't rendered in words. I am of the opinion that older people would take pleasure in going to the cinema if texts instead of pictures were projected on the screen. In the beginning of their world is the word, not an optical event. A picture in itself, a picture without language, doesn't mean anything; it must get words to acquire reality. An old man sees just shadows, shadows, shadows on the screen, bolting, and unreal. If they waited for a moment, he could find a term for them and describe them in words. But alas, they've gone, and new shadows are fluttering there in a mute hurry of events. The word lasts, the word can be remembered, the word is solid and firm. But movement doesn't last long enough to be interpolated into what exists and what is valid; it's just a change, a transition, and not a decent, reliable, enduring being. An old man watches the running film as if dreams were being shot before him; if he read in a book about a lissom damsel walking like a doe, he'd believe it, but when he sees a lissom damsel on the screen, walking like a doe, he doesn't recognise this poetic moment because it's not written there with binding words. It doesn't say anything, it's just phoney and monkey business. And the old man leaves the cinema as if he hadn't seen anything. Don't bother me with such tosh, he says.

A kind of re-education of people has really taken place here. A person sitting in the cinema must have found a shorter connection between the eye and the brain without the medium of words; in a technical sense, he may even have found a direct connection between the eye and the brain. The older generation probably lacks this direct connection, this leaping of a spark from the retina straight to the cerebral centres. They are more of a reading, conceptual type, while today's man is becoming a visual type. My late Granny had to read out loud to properly understand what she was reading; for her the word was still an auditory, not a visual, image. In bygone times most readers must have perceived reading through the ear. Later on a more trained reader dropped this aural digression and understood directly by means of verbal signs. In film even the word has turned out to be a digression; we are learning to understand without words. I don't want to decide if it is progress – for the time being it's a fact.

But surely film threatens literature to a considerable extent, not because it wants to replace it, but because it develops another kind of people – a visual instead of a reading type. The reading sort is patient; it takes its time to penetrate the circumstances, to bask in the descriptive passages and follow the conversation from start to finish. The visual type will not be so patient; it wants to seize the situation in a single glance, to comprehend the story without letting it last, and immediately see something new. But perhaps one day people will run from that stampede of pictures back to the book, to take a breather, or rather, they'll have the radio narrate fairy tales and novels nice and slowly for them; they'll listen with closed eyes, letting themselves be lulled by the word, which will re-assume its original destiny – to be spoken language. Maybe – who knows? – maybe the book will die out, maybe it will become a curious cultural heritage like inscribed Babylonian bricks. But art will not die out.

Karel Čapek about Himself

Aventinum Discussions, 15 September 1925

Dear Sir,[1]

You asked me to write something about myself. I have resisted tenaciously and gave in only when it became apparent that you wouldn't let me off. I'm doing it, then, but under protest – for one thing I've written a lot about myself already; you could count everything I've so far published as a kind of pondering about myself, and then I don't have much that concerns just myself to say, except for some insignificant things that I know somewhat better than the people whose job it is to criticise me.

1. I work fairly often and with effort. I may write whatever comes into my head, but I try to say it lucidly. The moment a thing is expressed lucidly, it's immediately evident if it's true or false, sensible or silly, good or bad. I don't write with pleasure, but somewhat irascibly, obdurately, while gnawing my pen. I can't understand how anyone can dictate literature to a typewriter – without savaging the lady-typist or the typewriter.

2. My greatest weakness is an inability to think. I can't think without a pen in my hand any more than a tailor can sew without a needle. I plan very little beforehand – my thinking is expressing. If I can't speak or write, I'm as dull as nature and as scatter-brained as a sparrow. Besides, I'm far too indolent – if I work hard and incessantly it's just because I don't want to be bored.

3. I don't have a special fondness for literature or drama. I read very little fiction but a lot of learned things. If I go to the theatre, it's a rare exception. I think it's because I can't bear sitting without doing anything, and I rather resist the idea of being passively arrested by someone. It's best when I write something myself, otherwise I guess I'd find literature intolerable.

4. As for views on life and metaphysical opinions, I don't know that I have ever done any of that. They've grown on me just like my teeth, and I discover them only when I use them, just as I discover my teeth (if they're all right) only when I eat.

5. Getting to know, that's a great and unquenchable passion; I presume that I write in order to get to know. I could perhaps become a fairly good specialist (what a wasted opportunity!) if I were able to restrict myself to one field. Unfortunately, I

am interested in everything that exists, that's why career-wise, I can't get further than being a writer.

6. Getting to know is one kind of compulsion; expressing quite another. I don't mean expressing oneself, but expressing things. I think I've managed to articulate many things briefly and almost accurately. I've had some success in drama, trying to aim at spoken, not written language. Doing literature is a writer's trade; it's what he's paid for. But doing speech, perfecting language, giving a full value to human talk, that's a special national and social mission – it yields a hidden, mysterious harvest.

7. Influences, influences – that makes me feel awkward, to tell the truth, for it's an *embarras de richesse*. I think that what has had the greatest literary influence on me is children's literature, folk language and Latin prose, and then everything good and bad that I've ever read. I could perhaps name three or four writers who did *not* have an influence on me; otherwise I take care to learn from anything that I stumble on – I don't have a high opinion of my own or anyone else's originality. It's the same in literature as in life: the rich live unashamedly off other people's work. I for my part count myself among those who accumulate future property, and I'll be rather grateful to those who are able to make use of it. I don't really do it for myself.

The rest – apart from literature – is my private life.

Yours Karel Čapek

Culture and Nation

The People's Paper, 27 May 1928

It is not quite so clear to everyone what culture actually is and all that culture includes. It is undoubtedly true that the university department of Indo-Germanic philology is a cultural matter, but a small bunch of flowers on a dinner table is in its way also a cultural matter. The consumption of a good book is a cultural thing, but the consumption of fruit or soap is a cultural thing too. Culture comprises a kitchen as well as a university, football as well as poetry, a home bathroom as well as a comprehensive school. It depends on how every single thing is used. If a distinguished foreigner, say from Syria, visited our country with the special intention of studying our level of culture, presumably he would be interested not only in our libraries, but also in our stoves, he would be interested as much in our parliaments as in our theatres, in our lavatories as in our education. If we decide to consider man as a cultural creature, everything that emanates from his hands and that he uses to live well is a cultural fact.

Take, for example, the fact that man must live in a hole or under a roof. Out of this simple physical need he has gradually made a whole mass of things, like architecture and pictures on the wall, a pattern on a carpet, a vase on a table, nice pieces of furniture, and flowers on a window sill. Nature has given man the need for food, sleep, love, play and knowledge. Out of this handful of needs and hungers he has created community, society, crafts, art, both science and religion, what we call his standard of living as well as what we value as his highest, almost miraculous achievements. Culture is everything that has this mark of perfecting and enriching, of quality and order – a cultural fact is any expression of human activity governed by this interest in a higher level. Culture is at once a luxury and a virtue. It is both a higher enjoyment and a higher discipline of life.

People sometimes cudgel their brains to draw a distinction between civilisation and culture. Of course a motor plough is not in itself a chunk of cultural life, but the freeing of man from harsh, burdensome labour is a cultural fact. Asphalt roads are no more cultural than cobbled ones, but the need for smooth and quiet traffic, speed and cleanness is one of the cultural innovations of our age. A wage struggle is not in itself cultural, but the struggle to raise the standard of living is a big cultural issue concerning us all. All human activity that aims for anything in our world to be perfected, facilitated or organised is cultural. There is no gaping fissure between culture and the rest. I wouldn't contend that the roar of an engine is the music of the present, yet the roar of an engine is one of the voices of the polyphony of cultural life, just as the heavenly sound of the violin or the words of a speaker or the shouts on a sports field are other and other voices. Culture is not a segment or a fraction of contemporary life, but its aggregate and centre.

Culture is not only the creation of cultural possessions but also – indeed particularly – their use. Well, let's not deny that we live in a somewhat abnormal time; our cultural consumption is lower than our cultural production. If, at the Brno Trade Fair,[1] you presented the home of an average intellectual, or middle-class householder, or peasant-farmer, or workman, their books, the pictures on their walls, their commodities and the things that surround and serve them, it would not be a display to which we would summon guests from all over the world, swelling with pride. I know that you might sufficiently explain half of that uninspiring average by reference to the recession, but even if we cut our coat according to our cloth, it doesn't have to be a mucky cloth riddled with holes. We like to go on about our highest cultural values, while forgetting about the everyday and common culture of life. When we utter the word 'culture', we think of statues, university chairs, iconic buildings and state scholarships, we think neither of the man in the street nor of the housewife. Hardly anyone pauses to consider the standard of living in our villages. There is a need for a thorough revision everywhere there, and for something like a programme of domestic cultural propaganda. It matters to us tremendously, for instance, that a Czech book should get to other countries, but a nearer and more difficult aim would be that a good Czech book should get to Kobylisy or Dolní Újezd. National economists call this 'the increase of home trade' and see in it the recovery of economic production. But the success of our cultural production doesn't depend on anything else. The role of the Brno Trade Fair in this domestic propaganda is more important than showing off samples of what we can produce to the world.

However, we don't have to be ashamed of what we can do. So far we have been carving our sculptures with a sixpenny pocket knife, as it were. With modest means, in penny packets we have sought to achieve what has elsewhere been done by ten times more hands, money and interest – and, see, it has worked. We have been able to, and still can, pride ourselves on the fact that our culture hasn't cost us much money; in truth, we have gained it empty-handed. When we, as a nation, didn't have anything else, we had books, the theatre, the university. It was the poet and the teacher who awakened and led the nation. We had nothing, only culture, before we started accumulating materials and power. No wonder that the trump card has changed – by and large, much less interest centres on cultural things today than twenty or fifty years ago. The poet and the teacher, and others too, have realised that they play far too small a part in the public fair. They quietly call it the crisis of culture. But even on this level there is an opportunity for revision. It remains to be seen if we, with our cultural possessions, can switch on the current at home. The point is not so much to show what has been done in the past ten years as to show what we can take with us into the following decades. We wish the Brno Trade Fair to be not just an exposition, but a real cultural fair where everyone finds something to take away with them – and a glorious, popular pilgrimage for all the parishes of the republic at that.

Whitsun

The People's Paper, 19 May 1929

When I was a boy – and, shame on me, as inattentive as ever – and was being initiated into the highest mysteries of faith, such as the Holy Trinity, by the RI teacher Mr Bret, it didn't seem to me at all strange that there were three holy persons. For me there were simply three gods in heaven just as I worshipped three gods on earth: the notary public, my Dad and the Mayor of our district, the three whom I had chosen because of the largeness of their bodies.

I puzzled my head over something else: what does the Holy Ghost actually do, and what office does he hold? The office of God the Father was clear to me – to create the world is, after all, a visible piece of work. God the Son at least became man – even more, he was a child, and I could colour his clothes the most beautiful red and blue in my biblical history textbook. So it was only the Holy Ghost about whom I felt at my wits' end. His face was unknown to me, and his function somewhat indefinable. He seemed to be neglected, somehow, and busy only internally, without any distinct, practical area of competence. I take it that everyone has experienced this trouble with the Holy Spirit.

Since then I haven't progressed much in my knowledge of divine matters. Rather, I have had to deal with human things, and again, it is the question of spirit that I try to get my head around. For we human beings can appreciate work when it is embedded in matter, and admire full mastery of matter, only too well. We can love or hate human leaders, saviours and creators of denominations, but our relation to mere spirit, that doesn't do this or that, is uncertain and hesitant. The human spirit is also what we believe in in man, except that it does not have a demarcated place. We consider intelligence or education as a kind of virtue or ornament, but not as an adequate aim or the purpose of life. Even a recent teachers' poll revealed dissatisfaction with an impractical education that allegedly didn't fit you out for an effective life. Spirit that doesn't directly answer practical needs seems to us indeed to be something useless and undisciplined. We respect it, but we don't know what to do with it. Rather like the Holy Spirit, it does not reign anywhere but sanctifies everything. It cannot be measured by work-performance; its office is ubiquitous.

So let us at Whitsuntide celebrate the human spirit – the tongue of fire, the universal tongue – spirit that neither creates nor leads the world, but sanctifies it, spirit that is wholly impractical and unbound, unserviceable and unconfined within the strict frontiers of efficiency. It is hard to define the function of spirit – or education, or culture. We know that we can't eat it, and that we can't sow a field with it or oil wheels with it. It's perhaps more to a person's advantage to understand the exchange rate mechanism than appreciate music; it's apparently more beneficial to make nails than read poetry; it's of course more useful to produce beetroot than scientific theories. It is impossible to defend culture on any practical grounds, but nor was it possible to defend it on practical grounds ten thousand years ago when people were already perpetrating useless music, poetry and pictures, and counting the stars, and altogether in a hundred different ways wasting their time much as we do today. Education cannot be defended by anything, except perhaps when the one on whom it descends as an ecstasy and a tongue of fire finds that it is, in some mysterious way, worth it – indeed, that it is worth more than any successful, profitable and generally respectable activity. In its highest sense spirit serves nothing but itself: it is here for nothing else but man. It neither feeds him nor leads him anywhere. It gives him one, and only one, thing – it adds value to his life.

The Wireless and the World

The People's Paper, 5 April 1930

A few people have already tried to explain to me how it actually happens that music, speech and other sounds flow out of it, but to no avail. The moment they start throwing around words like condenser, accumulator, variometer, insulation and the like, I'm lost; I'm not even sure if there isn't also a cardan shaft, ruby bearings, a parallelogram of forces and other technical whatsits that have so far remained a secret to me. What I've gathered about the whole thing is mainly this: when you turn that sort of black button, it starts playing or talking, and when you turn the button back, it stops and a pleasant silence diffuses. It's a great progress compared to parliament, committee meetings, theatre and social gatherings where there is no such button.

Besides, the wireless has three big advantages that may even transform our human world.

1. First of all, in effect, the wireless means a return home. When in the past someone wanted to listen to an orator, he had to wend his way to a meeting or at least to a pub; now he wends his way home. When in days of yore a man wanted to give himself over to the passions of music, he had to go to a concert, or somewhere else among people; today he can simply go home. He can go home if he wants to dance, or if he wants to hear the king of England. If he wants to learn the latest news, he can go and listen to it at home. Admittedly, this in a way encourages human laziness; on the other hand, many voices of life come to people's houses, voices that earlier they were too lazy to seek or hear. It's a curious fact that a broader and broader global circumference fits into the four walls of our house. We return to our homes as to a far vaster realm than a street or a concert hall. Like everything else in this world, it has its disadvantages. For example, I know a gentle poet whose friends got him that little black box with a button. Since then he's been lost; he feels a kind of moral obligation to listen to everything that is said or played on the wireless from morning to night. He doesn't have enough brute strength to silence that little box; it seems to him impolite and coarse to do so, as if he was letting someone knock on his door in vain. He assumes that he must give ear to every single voice that demands to be heard. Now he has only one hope left – that one day something will go wrong or wear out inside that box, and he will be rid of the Voices that keep coming to him.

2. This return home, brought about by the wireless, is a fact of more or less personal character, but the wireless has, or at least may have, consequences of a sociological nature. For a few centuries now, flight from the countryside to the cities has been taking place in all civilised states. In most cases, of course, it has been a journey in quest of the sources of employment and earnings, but in very many cases it's been an escape from the boredom and quiet of a small town or a village. The *horror vacui* propels people out of a secluded

place towards what they call a cultural centre, and what might better be called a possibility of seeing and listening. Apart from the social depopulation of rural areas, there is also a psychological depopulation – for many people, life in the countryside has become something like a spell in the desert. But today a country person turns the button and can listen to a Casals concert or the latest foxtrot; a big city gushes into his rural seclusion, among apple orchards and alders. The kind of isolation that an educated person had to endure in the country has now been largely defeated. This means that, to a degree, large cities are becoming a useless hangover from the past; perhaps it will be felt more and more that they are a barbaric hangover. Soon it will be technically impossible for the agglomeration of people in cities to grow at the rate it has done so far. How to carry out a decentralisation of human habitation is a big psychological and sociological problem; the wireless has come just in time to help in its own way with the relative valorisation of rural life.

3. The third aspect of the wireless that is capable of changing our relation to the world is little short of political. By this I mean the international character of the wireless, though it is still in its early stages. If a person hears voices from London, or an opera from Rome, at his fireside, he at first marvels, but then he gradually gets used to the new fact that he is in touch with the whole world, and that in some measure the whole world courts his attention and sympathy. It is, among other things, the wireless that reinforces the awareness of one big, shared world and awakens the belief that there are and can be bonds transcending state boundaries. I'd like to put in a word on behalf of this wireless-opportunity as earnestly as I can. It should be used as liberally as possible, so that each nation, broadcasting its song into our universe, introduces itself to us with the utmost breadth, so that there are days in the universe belonging to this nation, and then days devoted to another, so that everyone announces, as beautifully and resonantly as they can, that they are alive and want to say something of

their own and something pleasing to others. An international congress could take place more often than it has done up to now: it would be a congress of people, each sitting by their own hearth, and yet stretching out their hands to each other in closer and closer understanding.

About the Čapek Generation

From 'About Myself and More Serious Things' (V), *The Present,* 9 March 1932

It's not my fault that it has become common to talk about the Čapek generation: I haven't thought it up, and I wash my hands of it in all innocence. But judging by the opinions of people who presumably see into the problem of generations more than I do, the Wanted Notice of the Čapek generation looks something like this: *Height* – medium. *Nose* – inconspicuous between big eyes, though tends to poke into everything. *Special marks* – relativism, pragmatism, humanism, liberalism. Indulges in the vices of co-operation with the new state and compromise. Is official, and consequently has outlived its usefulness. Fosters earthbound realism, and lives off serving the establishment. And so on. In a word – a terribly irritating generation. Whenever I read about it I have an irrepressible feeling that if such a generation existed I'd rather not apply for membership, and would propose to have my name crossed off the list. But I don't know to whom I should submit an official request.

I'm definitely not competent to speak on behalf of any sort of Čapek generation, but since by a trick of fate I happen to belong to the Čapeks, I shall, if I may be so bold, venture my opinion about certain Čapekian problems relating to the Čapek personal history. If it is in some ways also a bit of the personal history of other contemporaries, if they recognise anything in it they themselves must have gnawed at, let them say it themselves – my attempt will not oblige anyone to a generational or any other solidarity.

We must bring back to life the Czech spiritual climate of the years around 1910, in which willy-nilly swam a young, green, adequately-vigorously-reacting Čapekian individual, who we shall, out of non-partiality and greater objectivity, label Q. If you are familiar with history, you'll know that in those days – until the year 1914 – there was no world war or revolution, that is, there was no turning point that would have split history comfortably and convincingly into what was past, dead and buried, and what victoriously tended towards a better future. In those days, dear folks, everything was wonderfully mixed: ideas and books used to live almost as long as ravens. An inexperienced young man of that time was simultaneously and in a hotchpotch assailed by Dostoevsky and Walt Whitman, Baudelaire and Strindberg, Balzac and Hamsun, Nietzsche and C. L. Philippe.[1] It was awful – all of that lived side by side and didn't in any way appear as something closed and passé; you had to gnaw your way through it off your own bat, and instinctively keep saving your skin from the crushing eclecticism of the *fin de siècle*. It was then that we actually experienced the decades of the so-called coming-to-terms with Europe all at one go. There were too many things at once: spiritually, a young man of that era was (despite the notoriously cramped Czechoslovak conditions) born a cultural citizen of the world, intoxicated and satiated by the evaporations of that witch's cauldron where all the great and peculiar literatures of the world were bubbling up. One might say that, historically, this cosmopolitan orientation was necessary for the cultural evolution of our nation; for those young people it was a great legacy given to them – and at the same time cast confoundedly across their way – by the cultural diapason of the end of the nineteenth century.

I'm talking about literature. At that time, you know, people lived and breathed it much more intensely and deeply than today, perhaps because of the lack of political, revolutionary and other interests. We were politically and socially provincial, and this made us give ourselves passionately over to literariness and other intellectual concerns. Yes, *fueramus Pergama* [we were Pergamum].[2]

We saw the light of the world among spirits who didn't speak to the masses and generations, but who were willing to bite off one another's heads over belonging to this or that literary clan. I still feel ambivalent about taking seriously those who were able to engage so doggedly and so pompously in splitting literary hairs. Apart from those coteries, on our literary leas there flowered realists (who we felt were passé), decadents, sensualists and ironists. Alongside these there took shape a relatively nebulous programme, or rather a postulate, of some sort of cultural synthesis of discipline, style and ultra-personal and spiritual values – all somehow in the abstract. It was a framework in which you could put Catholicism or classicism, the worship of forms or the worship of ideas. All in all, you might say that men of letters were concerned with personal experience and self-reflection – with a dance around their own being. It was, roughly speaking, aestheticism, a state that becomes understandable when literature is isolated from, and feels superior to, the national context – and ultimately to reality itself.

Oh yes, I mustn't forget that those days also saw a peculiar phenomenon, though spirit-and-pen-minded people paid devilishly little attention to it. It rattled into our provincial shelter from all corners: machines, concrete, iron, a spot of sporty spirit, a bit of Americanism, a touch of titillating exoticism, the reckless elbows of technological civilisation, collective power, the advent of speed and dynamism. And the lad Q , enticed out into the world by literary cosmopolitism, could no longer plump himself down in Café Größenwahn or bars on Montmartre. Rather, with a smattering of flabbergastation, he confronted a reality that was far rawer, rougher, more social – and more exciting – than the magical flickers and the personal problems of the books that he had up to then been spoiling himself with so eagerly.

It is true that a new reality was being born in the years before the war, but it is no less true that in them the great, hundred-year-old peacefulness and concentration of knowledge were living their last days. You can observe this in pre-war philosophies. There was the unalloyed, almost chilling need for spiritual discipline in neo-Kantian philosophers, logicists[3] and system-atisers; there was the gentle, aesthetic, cultural eclecticism in Heidelberg's philosophy of values, Simmel's relativism and Rickert's historicism;[4] in the midst of it burst the natural dynamism of vitalists and the magnificent fireworks of Bergson's philosophy of creative life. Among these radiant systems of pure thought, Anglo-Saxon pragmatism – a biblical Martha, not shrinking from intervening in democratic matters – was rolling up the sleeves of its workaday coat. Most of these philosophies breathed out a liberating spirit. Reality no longer appeared in the fixed angle of positivistic causality; it provided a free space for creative development, human initiative and fulfilment, and for a freely chosen order of purposefulness. Reality ceased to be something definite and given, and subjected to eternal laws. A Heraclitean element seeped into it, and with it the possibility of development, history, creativity and the rise of new and unheard-of things. Psychological theories had stopped demonstrating the universal, artificially made model of human consciousness, and touched now on the unconscious, now on the endless individualisation of the human soul, now on the psychology of social groups. Sociology spurted in through all the gaps that were left – in fact, collective interests came to the fore in all philosophical thinking. Things, values and even disciplines acquired a social dimension, a dimension that was evolutionary, historically determined – and indeed relative. You must understand relativism a bit in a philosophical light: it doesn't mean only scepticism. It offers a comforting vista that things of this world are not once and for all finished and eternally valid, but that they can be made better without end. There was an intoxicating breath of optimism in it – if we just make room for life and creativity, we can overcome or realise everything, we can overcome even death, as Bergson rejoiced to think. And just imagine that the historical response to this spiritual optimism was the Great War.

If we put together a living type of man out of all the contemporary philosophies, we would most likely come up with an optimistic and constructive anarchist, believing in human freedom, collective order and radical initiative in a purposeful refashioning of the world. As you can see, I've deftly avoided any mention of revolution. For in that age revolution was neither a programme nor a tactic.

To put it frankly, the political picture of a young man then, say, Q, was a little wishy-washy. Let's give you the low-down on him – he had no time for internal political squabbles, or anti-bourgeois demonstrations, or oratorical feats in parliament. The vortex of literature made the little devil into such a cosmopolitan that the industrialist and politician Mr Maštálka interested him as much as Monsieur Daudet.[5] He sort of lost sight of Masaryk in Vienna;[6] he didn't care about Vienna; he didn't care about the Austrian monarchy either. Quite simply, it was miles away from his concern. The attitude of this naïve world-citizen wasn't some kind of resistance any more, but a silent, logical settling of accounts with a system too narrow, stale and impotent to develop further. He tried to make up for his political sloppiness by directing his attention to social affairs. There something really was happening – it was a time of social revisionisms, Taylorism, trusts and the dynamic accumulation of forces. In short, you could believe in something there: if a revolution professing a new organisation of the world had broken out then, the pre-war Q would have joined it with enthusiasm and conviction. Definitely. All his historical antecedents had equipped him for it.

So this was, in essence, the world of a young man before the war. There was no generation to carry him along; everyone had to gnaw his way through, and alone, in his own manner, grapple with that crush of literatures, ideologies and realities that rushed down on him the more intensely, the more attentive he was. It was a difficult school of versatility – it seems to me that things are easier today, when all's said and done. First, the lad Q had to settle the quarrel with the decadence, the aestheticism and the subjectivism of the *fin de siècle*. That way he got out of the magic circle of elitism and tangled with the anarchic and adventurous world of facts. So

34

he did journalism after his own fashion, he scribbled this or that on the margins of days and compromised himself with interests that were, from a literary perspective, not sufficiently dignified, while tormenting himself from time to time that he didn't write artistically enough, or sublimely enough, or exactly *lege artis*, as a distinguished critic once notified him.[7]

And then there came a coup in the intellectual sphere. It was brought about by the visual arts. Cubism erupted in painting, replacing emotional and sensual Impressionism with a strict, autonomous order, geometry and an independent discipline of the spirit. Concurrently it triggered off a revaluation and a new understanding of all that cultural sediment that had been deposited by art history, ethnography, collecting, engineering, the camera, you name it, even film – it was as if we had suddenly looked afresh, pop-eyed. Architecture rebelled against what had been formal eclecticism, and laid down its own ideal, namely, usefulness, both material and functional – the word constructivism hadn't yet been invented. This pictorial innovativeness and the clear need for formal discipline infected literature. For a time it had tried to muster the help of old formal moulds and rules, but that path didn't lead any further and couldn't catch up with contemporary dynamism. It was necessary to shatter moulds, metre, syntax, literary conventions, the fetishism of style, ornamental language and all that old, richly arrayed stasis.

Fueramus Pergama. It was a devilishly interesting period. But literature-wise it wasn't an exhausted vein, at least not in our country. For all our forlornness, we marched hand in hand with young Europe, with Apollinaire and Paul Zech,[8] with the German expressionists and the Italian futurists, with unanimism and collectivism of all denominations, with the whole of that era that was tendentious and seeking, yet, God knows, somehow more full-blooded and more arousing than the one that calls itself revolutionary (we're talking about literature here). In those days everyone did some kind of little revolution off their own bat. So ... in order that you should know what the war put an end to – all this was a manifestation of a great optimistic belief in evolution.

And I can tell you that I can hardly find in today's literary or artistic manifestos and programmes anything that wouldn't have been more or less expressly said – or done – before the war.

But that's not the last word I'd like to say about the pre-war young man. Literature and art were not the only things at stake then. What was at stake was a new Europeanship, and even more than that – a new relation to the world. To a collective, accelerated and constructible world. Hence the spiritual turn to objectivity. Hence the perhaps almost cumbersome need to get to know. And the perhaps almost unnecessary sense of responsibility.

This was the spiritual state that the Great War brutally interrupted.

About the Čapek Generation during and after the War

From 'About Myself and More Serious Things' (VI), *The Present*, 16 March 1932

Now, God bless, it's understandable that the worst burden of the war fell on the shoulders of the contemporary young generation. Half of them were fighting on various fronts, where they were croaking from dysentery or 'dragging their bowels across the battlefield', the other half didn't find it worthwhile buttoning up their trousers as they were running from muster to muster, from hospital to hospital. It was a repulsive makeshift life; no one would have given sixpence for our skins. It wasn't a generation of the reclaimed and the indispensable; it was simply a crop of the sacrificed, for whom there was no room behind the trenches. No one bothered to employ a young man – it wasn't profitable. I think that it would be hard to find a generation that got to feel in their own flesh as much ruthlessness, selfishness, cowardice, devaluation and humiliation as this one.

But I hasten to note for the record that our instinctive defence and reaction against this disrespect for the human being in us was a peculiar, almost entranced internalisation, warming of the heart, love of man, or how shall I put it – what mattered was no longer the salvation of life but the salvation of soul. Look it up in Czech books from the war period. And anyway, I think that that inner experience hasn't been exhausted even today.

Shipwrecked and scattered to the four winds was the world of the young European from the time before the war; the state of trust, optimism about civilisation, naïve activism, the joyous feeling of collaboration and collectiveness were blown to pieces. The young westerner Q wasn't swept along on the wave of the Slavophile belief in the Russian steamroller. His heart was bleeding from the wounds suffered in Belgium, Flanders and at Verdun. In the first months of the war he tried to get to Italy – he wanted to help the futurists in their anti-Austrian propaganda. This foolish attempt only earned him unpleasant attention from the state police. He was too unimportant to be able to play any decisive part in the national resistance. He would have wanted to serve – he seriously offered to shoot one of the pillars of Austria, but no one would get him a revolver. That oppression of one's own helplessness was worse than the actual pressure of the war. He sought comfort at least in that he tried to organise a collective anthology of modern French poetry, sweating over translations day and night. He had a somewhat mystical feeling that, in doing so, he was somehow helping those out there on the Somme or at Verdun. And when Wilson was giving an ultimatum to Germany, the young intellectual was sending to the press a book on Anglo-American pragmatism. It wasn't, dear friends, 'the philosophy of a generation'. It was politics; it was an intellectual alliance with Wilson's America; it was, in its own way, a tiny crumb of what's called the home resistance. Not that it would have had any weight, but it was felt much more strongly than you might think. It was a creed of democracy and freedom, it was the democratic spirit of the republican and civilian West that stood against – in the words of the simplified war ideology – the absolutism and militarism of the Central European powers. And look – you pre-war chap – where did you find yourself?

Suddenly, you little world-citizen, you were standing with both feet firmly on the national ground, you took its cross upon yourself, lived by its fervid hope, and experienced feverishly things you'd so far looked down your nose at, that is, politics. You were more than a little strongly involved in the new collective interest, and were drawn into the new ideal. You raised your head amidst the wartime misery, and ardently scented the fresh optimism, the fresh faith, and the breezing of the fresh spirit. You found yourself among people who were definitely not artists and poets, but whole, fierce chaps, risk-takers, men of practical life. You felt like a milksop among them. Meanwhile your peers, your generation, were in the legions. God knows it was like an awakening, like a powerful exhalation: for the first time in your life it was possible to believe totally, without objection and collectively.

Every great love is monogamous, every revelation of faith happens only once in a lifetime. Anyone who has experienced this will remain marked by it for life. It is easy to assert today that Homer nodded and that it was a power struggle and a capitalist war, not a conflict of ideals or spiritual worlds. But for our part, we were really concerned about the ideals; to our eye, a world revolution was truly taking place, and soldiers were fighting for a new world order. Our nationhood was at stake, but not just that, the values of democracy and liberty and social justice – all of them beautiful and international things – were thrown into focus. If in doubt, look up the Czech speeches, programmes and manifestos from the end of the war. Never since the year 1848 had Czech political consciousness spoken in such European and progressive dimensions as it did then.

At which point you'll probably say: Aha, there's the rub, sir, you're a fossil from the war years, and can't get over the ideals of that time and move on, whereas for us, the younger and more radical, it's just useless, outdated lumber. Dear friends, I'd politely object to this triumphalist cry that there isn't any question of being a fossil, because the above ideals haven't as yet become reality. Quite the contrary, in many respects we are further from them than in those days. But above all you must forgive me if I am fossilised in the war years, as my memory cannot get over them, over the years of massive slaughter, despotism and injustice, and as long as I breathe I shall protest, foaming at the mouth, so to speak, against anything that brutally puts human lives, rights and freedom at risk. Forgive me, but I'm not so cynical as to be able to pass over that experience as if nothing had happened. The national and social ideals, and the ideals of a world order from the war years, were not born out of comfortable discussions and speculations, but from the personal and collective *de profundis*. It is possible to betray them. It is impossible to outlive them as useless.

The war was over, and the pre-war young were entering practical life. No nice fat-salary jobs were falling into their laps, the revolutionary boom didn't carry them to the top. But even the most trifling function was then, at the beginning of the new state, felt more responsibly and seriously than you can now imagine. It seemed that all things were in a reforming phase. It was necessary to be interested in everything – with a sigh we doffed our old cultural exclusiveness and set out to serve many things. Instead of literary cafes and debates we were faced with an environment of utterly different people, interests and values, and we had to learn – to learn to look in the first place. I think that very few generations have encountered so many various authorities, enterprises, spheres of interest and practical problems as we did. I'd say our artistic priesthood was devilishly secularised. It had its pros, but it was an uncomfortable experience as well.

First and foremost, it was a jolly close-up view – we saw national icons with feet of clay, we saw the flip side of slogans and the underside of great programmes. We saw through narrow-minded partyism, personal interests, intolerant ecclesiasticism and the humbug of big words rather too early in our lives. On the other hand, we got to know people and the situation more intimately, and were forced to put aside intellectual snottiness, comfortable disparagement and what you might call categorical rejection of others' ideas. Believe it or not, the world appeared in a complex light of partial truths and chronic conflict, a conflict that was so historic and collective that no thinking person is now entitled to regard it as resolved by having decided for this or that political belief. 'Up the Guelphs, up the Ghibellines' is a good battle-cry, but a thumpingly oafish motto for the historical process. Especially in the case of intellectuals it amounts to an abdication of the prerogatives and responsibilities of a thinking spirit. One has no other option but to try to make one's way through the jungle of clashing realities with the help of one's reason and conscience. I've always thought that the word for trust in the practical validity of reason and conscience and their role in world happenings is optimism. But I find with embarrassed amazement that it is, in common talk about principles, termed scepticism, relativism, compromise – you name it.

There are, of course, extremely irritating people for whom it's enough to be in the right and to shrug their shoulders at others' mistakes and foolishness – they know better, which fills them with personal satisfaction. I wouldn't wish to give houseroom to this kind of response. I'd swap it even for the smallest possible amount of the moral condition called empathy. The world in which we live hasn't been made for the luxury of being in the right; it is constantly being threatened by something: reaction, bankruptcy, war and injustice. Our country hasn't reached safety, the current national and social achievements are not guaranteed, in human terms we're not home and dry. There is, in the majority of both commonplace and vitally serious things, enough to feel responsible for, and one doesn't really have time for people who care most about their interestingness and opinionatedness. To hell with your so-called positions – that sort of thing is fit for a waxworks, but not for the swarming of life. The world in which you preach, prophesy and babble is no doubt absolute, fundamental and unconditional, but the moment you try to put something into action, you meet a world that is plaguily relative and conditional. But in this, dear friends, lies the great dramaticism of the world: doing something in practice, getting engaged in something actively is much harder and more complicated than just talking. It seems that too many people can transfer themselves to the level of belief only by the method a fakir uses to achieve his mystical trance – I mean, by staring at the tips of their noses. Or, if you like, they cultivate looking at things from the angle of this or that opinion – the sharper the angle, the more cutting their critical judgements. I'm afraid they stop realising that every single angle is only a section of the whole 360-degree reality. The world in which people live truly and fully is three-dimensional. There are nearer and more distant things in it. In a three-dimensional world a bird in the hand is worth two in the bush, and today is closer at hand than the future, and reality is more immediate than programmes. And there is room for both struggle and love, both private life and history, both nations and humankind. It is a pluralistic and an anything-you-like world, but mainly a world that is much more dramatic and human than what reveals itself in the angle and light of a supremely dazzling thesis.

A bird in the hand is worth two in the bush, but a man isn't a bird or a bush. If you don't have any major objections, I take it that concern about contemporary and future man is ultimately the most important thing. Yes, concern to the utmost scruple that people don't suffer any material or moral harm in the first place, and a bid to add value to the lives of all by striving for a better social and world order, and by having a go at practicalities without utopianism or blinkers. But this 'in the first place' doesn't mean that having said all this, we've saved our souls – or have sufficiently taken the souls of our fellow beings into account. Suppose we concede there is a certain drive not to embitter life for others unnecessarily. Or a compulsion to revitalise somehow their trust, their smile, their human relationships. Or not to watch silently when they are inclined to insult themselves as well as others, do themselves harm, torment themselves inside. And so on. Even this is, I presume, a matter of adding value to life. Not to take belief away from people but to relieve them of pain, boredom, despondence and solitude. To try to encourage people to be in a cordial frame of mind, mutual loyalty, obligingness, joy and respect – in a word, morality, in another word, optimism, and in yet another word, un-mucked-up, full-powered life. Admit it – a lie, a cliché, hatred, spinelessness, stupidity, intolerance, hypochondria, demagogy and cynicism humiliate man; they keep him in spiritual serfdom, and shut him out from ascent. Don't you think that our life drags behind it too heavy a load of all that? You can turn away from it indifferently and haughtily, implying, as it were, that you have higher things and ideas in mind, or . . .

Or it is possible to talk with you?

I've described only the antecedents and life experiences determining the conditions of a pre-war young man. How he has come to terms with them, what he has done with them, is up to you to judge. I'd specify just this: if mine is a generation at all, God knows in what many and sundry places it is, but it's certainly not a cafe table. You'd have to dig it out from the mass graves at the front, from ordinary working life, from little offices and schools from Jasina to Cheb,[1] for – incidentally – it is the first crop of active Czechoslovaks. I said it was a generation that was sacrificed. I'd add, in conclusion, it's a generation wrapped up in countless undertakings, and a generation that has so far served as a footstool for both the older and the younger.

Anaesthesia

The Present, 4 January 1933

In his utopia *Brave New World* Aldous Huxley shows us, apart from other fabulous prospects, how easy it will be for future humanity to deal with earthly troubles: you will just swallow a pill, an officially distributed preparation called 'soma', which will immediately provide the desolate soul with forgetfulness. I must confess that when I read this, I was ashamed of the future and transfused by a kind of gratitude that I lived in the prehistoric, primitive and heroic present.

But if a human creature from a primitive, but not all that remote, age came to have a look at us, he might have a similar feeling.

Perhaps he'd find that the primordial human need for disengagement and forgetfulness is not something we satisfy only occasionally: it has become a daily necessity. Radio, film, sport, light literature and theatre – these are just drugs that people take to forget the burden and anxiety of life. Perhaps the visitor from past times wouldn't spot at first that the greatest consumption of these commodities did not reside where there was the heaviest burden to carry. Perhaps he'd conclude that there must be something that gnaws horribly and unrelentingly at today's people, since they are driven to seek an escape from their distress so keenly. Only gradually would he see the light, and realise that the audiences who consume most of these commodities are not escaping from any agony or conflict, but from something else – emptiness and boredom. People are really disengaging themselves from themselves. They are trying to forget the routine of their lives. And the person from olden days would probably be dispirited by what he saw.

If we consider the evidence we have of past eras (such as the nineteenth century), it truly seems that the consumption of cultural anaesthetics has multiplied. Of course there weren't so many opportunities in the first place, but undoubtedly there wasn't this sort of habitual need either. If I recall the people who surrounded me in my childhood, I get the impression that they didn't try to forget their personal lives; quite the contrary, they were remarkably conscious of them and insisted on them with almost comic dignity and importance. They didn't feel the compulsion to transcend the limits of their workaday life; instead, they took care to fill their place thoroughly and solidly. It seems to me that they weren't bored at all, but as far as I could see they were constantly doing something, and when they relaxed, they savoured their own selves, their wisdom, their family, their friends. They didn't look for disengagement, but engagement. One might say that they were downright content with the fact that they lived, with how they lived and with what they did, and they were in no need of escape. Their way of life was difficult, yet somehow more confident; they bore their profession as a perpetual virtue, not a dirty drudgery that it is better to

43

forget. I don't want to glamorise them, but they seem to have been happier, and to have lived their lives more strongly and more alertly. They got more out of their lives because for them life didn't mean forgetfulness and disengagement.

What's gone is gone: it's futile to moan. What's at issue is whether today's production of mass anaesthesia is, in a biological and socio-logical sense, beneficial. I don't want to be a spoilsport, or deny anyone their pleasure. But first, anaesthesia is no true pleasure. We need to be alert even if we just want to truly enjoy ourselves. And second, anaesthesia doesn't cure any disease, or solve any conflict; it doesn't lead anywhere. Biologically, it's better to feel that some-thing is hurting and try to ease it if we can. Socially, it's better not to forget where the shoe is pinching, and think about how to take it off and remake it. Culturally, it's better not to keep escaping from your own emptiness, but make sure that you fill it with something worth having.

If a person gets used to amusing himself with simulacra of life, he loses the ability to amuse himself with life. It's boring to live – let's go to the movies. Observing people and understanding them is baffling – let's go and look at shadows. It's become imperative to have a rest from life, to be in a parallel universe. It boils down to smoking a cosy little pipe of opium. We go to watch sporting con-tests, and it rids us of the inner need to contest anything ourselves. We look for what's new in the papers, so we don't have eyes for noticing what's new in the universe. What a lot of things people have thought up to stop themselves thinking! It's said that religion is the opium of the people, but political utopianism, dictatorship and demagogy are the opium of the people just as much – they deprive them of responsibility, personal initiative and the strain of thinking and judging.

But no, there's no going back. If something isn't right, the only remedy is to rip away its disguise. In other words, we need to employ the whole of our brain for once, and realise how stupid and worthless the majority of what we've come to regard as pastimes are. To raise a protest against the claptrap that we buy as fun and forgetfulness. To find that it's actually degrading and that it humiliates us. You only need common sense to see that. At the end of the day, almost everyone knows that the thing we kill our boredom with is silly and monotonous, but we make allowances for it and explain nonchalantly that we aren't particularly demanding when, basically, it's just leisure. But let's say to ourselves that despite all its drawbacks life is a terrifically valuable thing, and that leisure, too, deserves a bit of our respect. Let's entertain our whole selves, with the full involvement of our intellect. Then we'll find that it's necessary to think, discover, tinker with things, grapple with ideas, create something – well, just be with the thing actively, and stop being a befuddled spectator.

A Personal Letter to President Masaryk

Since the mid 1920s Čapek had been in personal contact with T. G. Masaryk, whom he deeply admired. This letter reveals Čapek's attitude to his international fame and writing.

Prague, 24 March 1933

Mr President,

Head of department Mr Schieszl has passed me your message that I shouldn't insist on my resignation from the chairmanship of PEN. I expect that so far you have been informed about this matter only by the members of PEN who are trying to restrain me from the said move; I beg you then to let me give you my explanation.

1. Nothing about PEN and its activity will change when I am not its chairman. I remain a member, and so will have the same chance and duty to meet foreign guests as I have had until now; besides, a great part of this socialising happens outside PEN. Literary foreigners come to look for me at home or in the editorial office – I shall do this service in the sphere

45

of contacts and propaganda in and outside the organisation to the same extent as I have done it until now. The remaining activity of the chairman is of no special significance, and I am afraid I am rather behind with it, as I don't go to congresses and altogether shun so-called representative duties as a cat shuns water. As far as public service is concerned then, my resignation has, to be honest, a fairly negligible impact, and there is no need to overestimate it. I am sorry that my well-meaning friends from PEN asked you to intervene in a matter that is ultimately only internal and in effect not so important as it first seemed to them to be. After all, the new chairman should be Mrs A. M. Tilschová,[1] so there will be no funda-mental change even in the – let's say, political – balance.

2. The positive reasons for my resignation are not personal, more accurately, not *only* personal. I have observed for years that some kind of alienation has developed between me and our literary milieu, especially between me and the younger generation. They regard me as an *official* representative of Czech literature, and as you know, officialdom is – especially in our country – something like a curse. No matter what I write or do, it is *ipso facto* 'official', and so, as it were, discounted. Common envy has a lot to do with it too – especially because of my so-called successes abroad. It has become habitual to assign them not to my work, but precisely to that official posi-tion of mine. (This is one of the reasons why I try to open the way for other writers abroad; and let me take this occasion to thank you for your kind financial contribution towards the preparation of translations – the whole thing can be very use-ful.) In this respect everyone stands against me, both the older and the younger, both the right and the left; I pay for it by the fact that in our context my work more or less disappears into a vacuum. My resignation from *all* literary offices is part of my effort to shake off that literary representativeness that only ties my hands. I am sure that if I still have something to say, I must say it as a resistance fighter, as a writer who battles for himself and his belief; I think that it is also in the interest of

those truths and that belief – both philosophical and political – that I stand by. Just the fact that I will be able to struggle is worth a lot – I am at the age when it's impossible to sit back and fold my arms.

I do not want to detain you longer, Mr President; I fear that the whole thing is petty-minded for you. You know how highly I shall respect your wishes; I only beg you to pay a bit of attention to my reasons. I shall wait for your reply – a telephone message is enough. Please forgive me for bothering you so exceedingly, but it is the fault of my friends from PEN who first turned to you in this matter.

Mr Ambassador told me that you were working on the *Talks*;[2] I am very pleased because this volume of the *Talks* will contribute in many ways to the sorting out of opinions in our country. That is more than necessary in politics, just as in cultural matters.

With deep respect I remain your devoted

Karel Čapek

Winter '34

The Present, 3 January 1934

Perhaps I'm just imagining it, but I have the strong impression that some sort of silence has fallen. It seems that a few years ago pens were wielded more bouncingly and more mightily, that a greater diversity of cultural possibilities and spiritual paths was propagated, and that there was altogether more willingness to stand spiritually at the front, and lead people out of the chaos of the age, as it's called. Surprisingly this was (as we can see now) in a time of relative affluence and safety in life. Nowadays it's worse in every respect. It's not just material things that are at stake today, but also the responsibility for leading human minds. What's at stake is belief, trust, courage and suchlike essentials, without which it will be hard to carry on. Well then, it seems that in this more difficult, worse time, culture, the intelligentsia and the educated, creative spirit, somehow have miserably little to say.

True, it's said: *inter arma silent Musae*. [Among weapons, the Muses are silent.] But let's hope that the Muses have developed over the past couple of thousand years, and are no longer the ethereal beings who used to fall silent shyly among the tough warriors. A thinking spirit isn't a butterfly that emerges only on sunny morns, and delicately takes shelter on tempestuous days. On the contrary, we might say that the din of Latin arms has long fallen silent, while the classical Muses carry on speaking. Whatever happens, spirit is never silent, except when it renounces its own self. Spirit that keeps silent is like a river hesitating whether to flow – we say about this that it has dried up. We can assume, if only for biological reasons, that intelligence is not a luxury that life has indulged in out of playfulness, or only under particularly favourable conditions. Rather, it is an instrument that has been created for overcoming obstacles and for the better advancement of life.

A thinking and cognitive spirit is never silent, unless it has renounced thinking and cognition. This is not to say that it stands eternally on a platform, ceremonially preaching to the assembled throng. The active intelligentsia isn't a schoolmaster who instructs his pupils about what to think from his dais, but a man bent over a test tube, or life, or a text, searching for discoveries. Let's agree in the first place that the intelligentsia isn't here to lead, but to get to know, and further, to teach the others how to get to know and distinguish, and lastly, not to allow itself or others to sin against the Holy Spirit. Dear me, what a sermon! you'll say. All right, then, so as not to preach eternal truths: we're bystanders at one of the biggest cultural debacles in world history. One whole nation, one whole empire has spiritually acceded to a belief in animality, race and nonsense like that; a whole nation, even with university professors, parsons, men of letters, doctors and lawyers, if you please. Do you think that such an animal doctrine could be propagated if every educated person in that highly educated empire shrugged and said dryly that he wasn't going to join in such primitive imbecilities? Nothing less than colossal treason has been committed here by intellectuals, and it generates a horrible image of what intelligence is capable of. It would be possible to give more examples, and not just from that one country. In every place where violence against cultural humanness is perpetrated we find intellectuals who join in performing it en masse, and what's more, brandishing ideological justifications. This is no longer a crisis or a helplessness of the intelligentsia. It is either a silent or horribly active complicity in the moral and political wilderness of today's Europe.

I know, at this point you'll shake your head and ask what such a more or less isolated and socially dependent intellectual can do; surely it's not enough for him to protest with his weak little voice, even though with deep conviction, against uncontrollable forces. Let's leave it to him what he *can* do apart from that; what's indisputable is what he *should* do. To put it negatively, he shouldn't and mustn't betray his spiritual discipline. All of us have begun to feel that there is something odd and insoluble about the conflicts between world-views, generations, political principles, and whatever else divides us. It is as though we spoke different languages within the same nation, and were no longer able to understand one another. It is as though internationally we were not bound by a common logic, identical terms, and at least a single shared ethical norm. It is precisely in this that the spirit, the intelligentsia and what's called culture seem to me to have failed so terribly. Spirit that is self-defined as universal has failed. Intelligence that in itself means the opposite of every ignorance has failed. Culture that, starting with the school benches, is based on the world treasures of spirit, world history and world knowledge, has failed. To put it more accurately, too many of those who have been entrusted with these values by their education, profession and mission have failed. It's no coincidence that every dictatorial regime turns against the free intelligentsia in the first place; that it furiously suppresses that inner world vision, that divine gift of universality; that it forcibly

49

constrains, or directs, the spirit: thou shall serve one nation, one system, one selfishness, lest we kick you out with an iron-tipped boot. And it's no coincidence, I'm afraid, that it's precisely intellectuals who often assist this yoke or whoredom of spirit with great ideological zestfulness. It seems that in today's state of affairs the intelligentsia has been allocated three paths: shared guilt, or cowardice, or martyrdom.

Perhaps there is still a fourth path left: not to betray one's spiritual discipline; not to deny in oneself, under any circumstances, under any pressure, the untrammelled and knowing spirit. In this, in this solely, lies the special freedom and nobleness of spirit; let's not allow anyone to take it away from us, for it is worth the hardest sacrifices. Can we somehow help the world in this way? If I knew that we couldn't I would be calm and sad, but I feel with awful anxiety that it's still possible to win or lose. It's still possible to face the fanatical dopiness of the world; it's still possible not to preach, but communicate in all the languages of this planet; reason can still be common to all, experience conferrable, knowledge valid and the laws of spirit and conscience obligatory for free men. No International of culture is necessary, but only culture. No spirit above parties, but only a spirit that does not want to swerve from the path of knowledge. We are not judges in the great contention that is going on; however, we mustn't, in the name of honour, remain just onlookers; we should be authentic witnesses. And what the result of that process will be depends on the testimony of those who see more and can shun gross errors. We mustn't be false witnesses; our pledge is stricter and our inner responsibility greater. If the intelligentsia lies or fails, it's a greater transgression than the ignorance or the lie of those others.

And let's not say, 'Not to worry – not in this country!' Come off it. It threatens us from the outside, and something is starting to crack here too, around us and in us; the wound could deepen under the pressure of the current time. Add to it the general state of distrust, dejection and disappointment – any political apeman or juggler could hoodwink people with seeming certainties, or with the mass suggestion of hope, these days. People want to believe and run to little churches; they want to hope and they listen to charlatans; they want to find a certainty that's not in them. It is a chaos that can be stirred by any old slogan, but it is also a chaos in which it's possible to seek firm ground beneath your feet. To find it would mean finding your own self, and meeting others on it.

About a Pussycat, a Puppy and Little Flowers

The People's Paper, 21 January 1934

In the last issue of *Free Directions* Josef Čapek was accused of 'not going to private views,[1] albeit the exhibitions were of the utmost importance', and of 'finding it more important for the nation to look at Dášenka with his brother or write about his cat'.[2] When I discovered this, I sighed with relief – I'm not alone then in being publicly disgraced for looking at God's creatures with interest, and even writing about them. Quite a number of killjoys have already made it clear that they consider writing about a puppy or a few little flowers to be an activity that is somewhat undignified for an author and brings him into public disesteem. That such an undignified activity occasionally becomes world-class literature is of course another story.

Now I could here embark on a speech in defence of flowers, dogs and cats, and profess that they are objects worthy of attention just because they truly exist. But in this context I would rather say a few words about something else – specifically, children. I puzzle my head over the question of whether it is an undignified activity for a man of letters to write about, say, a pup and a pussycat for young readers. I ask if it is 'more important for the nation' if someone runs around smart private views, or if he attempts to write a good read for children. It seems to me that there is something downright muddled about our values. My serious contention here and now is that it is not undignified to write for children but that it is undignified to write for them badly. I think that it's very important for the nation that children's literature shouldn't be written just by Maria Goodbodies or Sophia Hedgeworthies, but that other people should give it a try; and I find thankfully that they are doing it. It can happen that, forgetting his own dignity, an author writes a tale for children. You should read the letters he then receives – letters written by whole classes, and inscribed in a big childish hand: and Mr So-and-so, write something like this for us again, and we like you very much for it, and all that. I can assure you that at that moment the author thinks very frank things (that are, by and large, actionable) about those guardians of culture's cathedral who have expressed their indignation at his profanity.

And I'm taking it further, much further. A man who has, with a certain consciousness, been writing for the papers for years gets used to thinking of the people for whom he writes. He finds that his responsible task is something like baking bread for everyone rather than mixing cultural cocktails for a cafe-table circle. It's not only that he writes for a huge number of people, but something more serious is involved: that in doing so he incorporates himself into a far wider, more complicated world, in which there is room for all experiences, interests and motives. I contend that anyone who encloses himself in whatever narrow spiritual specialisation is a bad journalist and a bad *writer for newspapers*. Being in a newspaper, and writing for a paper, means primarily being in a relationship to everything that exists – finding a lively, direct, democratic interest in the whole of reality without the intellectual snotty-nosedness that fastidiously averts its gaze from the interests and motives of others who kick a ball around, keep canaries, call the government and the weather names, or frown over the columns devoted to the national economy. Any kind of exclusiveness, no matter what it's like, tends to overlook everything else. Even if it is excusable to stay within your own field, it becomes hopeless bungling the moment you impose your value judgements on the life and interests of everyone else. Producing newspapers with any kind of exclusiveness is like ploughing a hundred-acre field with a silver fork. It's more difficult to speak to everyone than to a small select circle – it's all the more difficult when we don't want to become barkers, demagogues and public liars. What I regard as immensely 'important for the nation' is the way newspapers are done – whether well and responsibly, or badly and in a culturally and morally low way. I don't ask if it isn't higher and more elevated, from a literary perspective, to write poems instead of columns or local news stories, but I do ask if these columns and news stories have brought anything decent to the life of a newspaper reader, whether he is a train conductor, a housekeeper or a superintendent. Don't forget that a journalist can do more *harm* than dwellers in ivory towers can possibly realise.

All right then – true, the man who writes for a newspaper, for newsprint, focusing his eyes on the people for whom he writes, doesn't feel that he is fulfilling a super-gentle task, worthy of hand-made paper and a limited edition. Rather, he feels like a worker. But I can assure you that it's by no means a humiliating feeling. And it's absurd when some arty type comes along to lecture him about how he shouldn't do this coarse sort of work but something white-collar, like serving up exquisite values or edifying the people. Such talk is good only in that it makes you look over your shoulder, and eye the person from head to toe. What's to be done, old chap? My world is broader, and there must be room for all and sundry in it. If elevated literature is what excludes all the people I have my eyes fixed on while I'm working, then goodbye, I'm going with them. It is not, you see, only a matter of the profession, but a matter of the heart.

About Global Reading

The People's Paper, 24 February 1934

Just to forestall any objections, I hasten to assure you that I don't intend to meddle in pedagogy. I am not raising the question of how children should be taught reading, but how we actually read. Judging from my own experience, we read globally. We read whole words at once and not letter by letter. We take in the whole word at one glance and immediately know, or think we know, what's written there. The other day I was passing a pub which had a tin plate hung up with a bicycle painted on it, and under it I read: 'HA RECYCLING CLUB'. Only after a few seconds did I start wondering about such a bizarre name. Perhaps I had made a mistake, I thought, and went back again. 'HA RECYCLING CLUB' was what I read for the second time, and my mind boggled at the existence of such a weird fraternity. Only on the seventh reading did I realise that what was really written there was 'HARE CYCLING CLUB'. This instance shows that while skimming cursorily we conjecture words rather than read them. On hasty scanning we see only the beginning and the overall shape of a written word, and immediately conjure up the whole word. We usually read, I'd say, stenographically: to read syllable by syllable is out of key with our reading pace.

I remember how my late Granny used to read her prayer books or the papers. Actually, she didn't call it 'reading' but 'speaking to herself'. By reading she understood something close to suspecting or guessing: 'I read in the sky that it's going to rain.' And she really spoke to herself everything she read with her eyes, silently moving her lips. This old practice of popular Bible-readers and chroniclers was neither global nor fast. During reading, every word was divided into syllables, and then assembled again. Finished words didn't just leap out, but were created in reading; the eye decoded letters and syllables and the ear brought them together. However could we put up with this sort of slow pace today? We no longer chew our spiritual food, we gulp it down in whole chunks, in whole words and almost in whole sentences. My Granny pilgrimaged along the black-letter lines of her pathway to heaven on foot, whereas we whiz through our reading as if we were on a motorbike. Words flash past like bollards. Only when we read something that touches our personal interest strongly and fatally do we stop reading in our perfunctory, global way, and decipher slowly, analytically, syllable by syllable, what's truly written there. It follows, then, that our quick reading fails whenever we are meant to believe, or profoundly come to terms with, what we are reading. Perhaps our grannies believed more because they read more slowly, and so had enough time to sort it all out in their heads.

But there isn't just global reading; there is also global writing, and global style. When we write, we write in a way that stops us having to think too much, or chew our sentences laboriously. It lets us swallow them at one gulp. We find it hard to read older writers, with their unfolding clauses, copious metaphors and adroit, circuitous turns of syntax. We start sprinting through old texts at our usual reading speed, but soon come to a halt in those stylistic mazes, and begin to skip over them impatiently. The ancient style was tailored for slow reading, for readers who analysed the sentence and built word upon word, for people who grasped the point gradually but thoroughly. Our style shows us best how much smarter we are, but also how much more slipshod and superficial than people in earlier days.

Analytical reading seems to us too mechanical. But even that almost intuitive perception of words and sentences we have trained ourselves in is mechanical, just as speed is, and so it is ultimately as thoughtless as pronouncing every syllable. The so-called telegraphic style of newspapers, composed of stock collocations and formulas, political language perpetually reeling off the same clichés and slogans, office-speech and business jargon, these are all global styles that bank on the spiritual automatism of their readers. It's no longer necessary to read and listen carefully, word by word; it's enough to get a fleeting glimpse and we know where we are. But the thought of questioning this global method of generalised reading and speaking doesn't even enter anyone's head.

The Nation Doesn't Need Us

The People's Paper, 9 December 1934

That's how General (and writer) Rudolf Medek has put it.[1] Apparently, if writers are going to be like they are, and won't agree with what is nowadays presented in *The National Newspaper* as the will of the nation, they will have no one but themselves to blame if the nation doesn't need them. It's not clear who has given writer and General Rudolf Medek authorisation to speak on behalf of the nation; it's not clear in which hostelry the spirit of the nation has revealed itself to him and has ordained him to fulfil that mission; but since the statement has been published seriously and even in italics by a number of papers, we must treat it seriously.

The thing is we writers won't let ourselves be thrown out of the nation. Not by anyone. Please note that there are things we won't let anyone take away from us – the first of them is our allegiance to the nation whose language we write in. If anyone wants to deny us this closeness, there's just one answer to it – a punch in the teeth. I'm not going to explain it to you in some subtle way, but no one becomes a writer, no one becomes a linguistic creator and a poet without infinite spiritual love for their nation, for language is the soul of the nation. Without an inspiring love, which not very many are capable of, a writer remains a mere scribe who blots the paper with ink, but doesn't create. And even if a poet has never in his life used the words nation and homeland, he remains the chosen darling of the nation's soul, as long as he is a poet and a creator, of course. Every word of his native speech uttered in his poetic work is as if spoken for the first time, it is bedewed as on the day of creation, unfingered by lies, clichés and averageness. The speech of the nation, threatened by professional gasbags and anonymous scribblers, is always being newly born from two living sources: the people and poets. And then someone comes along, some General-writer or other, some anonymous journalist or whoever, and will say that if things are like this or that, the nation can do without writers. How poor the nation would be if it did without them, if it thought, felt, perceived reality through the language of meetings and editorials! Can't you see, you idiots, what you are depriving the nation of?

Wait, why beat about the bush? I am not going to introduce myself; I hope I haven't discredited the Czech name abroad – for the first time in my life I venture to mention this. I am neither a Bolshevik nor a Marxist; I have no personal motive for feeling tenderness towards the cultural left that some time ago almost excommunicated me from literature[2] – for years I haven't heard much else from that side except that I'm a rightist, a petit bourgeois, a state lackey and heaven knows what. That's evident then. But as long as I breathe, I won't brook anyone throwing, say, S. K. Neumann out of the nation,[3] even though he is a communist and wrote a sentence that I, like others, don't forgive. But besides that sentence, he wrote, if you don't happen to know, *The Book of Forests, Waters and Hillsides*, he wrote *Songs of Silence* and many other things; and no one shall throw those books out of Czech literature, just as no one shall throw the little Svitava River off the Czech map and the sunlit clearings and the paths through hamlets and everything that the poet Neumann articulated in a spirit and language so Czech that its Czechness cannot be matched by . . . well, hardly any Czech politician since Rieger.[4] And no one shall throw out the poet Nezval,[5] who is a communist, but who has turned our language into a sky full of little violins and melody; what lunatic would deprive national speech of Nezval's music? And so on and on and on: so is it true that the Czech nation doesn't need Karel Toman,[6] the most Czech of poets? Don't we need the home-scripture-reading-inspired novelist Vančura who weighs his language on scales as old as the Middle Ages?[7] Don't we need Šrámek and Hora and Seifert,[8] don't we need Šalda[9] – who does the Czech nation need then, if you please? Yes, you've already said that too: dead writers are enough. How convenient for you; the dead can no longer judge the living; Havlíček will not knock big-mouthed patriots any more,[10] Neruda will no longer report on poor people and the battalions of working men,[11] Svatopluk Čech will not defend his big-hearted world liberalism,[12] and so forth – indeed, how convenient for you. It seems to me it will be necessary to protect even dead poets, lest they get dragged into company in which they'll scarcely feel at home.

Enough said. We writers won't let anyone throw us out of the nation; chase after us as you like, we won't give up. We need the nation more than air, and it needs our love more than all the money in the patriotic banks. When the resurrection of the nation was at stake, writers were in the vanguard long before the likes of Hodáč and Stříbrný.[13] And this national tradition is on *our* side.

'Today Needs the Book'

A Contribution to the Opinion Poll, The Annual Miscellany of *The Stem* 1934–5

I can't help it: the combination of those two words seems to me as strange as if we said 'today needs granite stairs' or 'Thursday needs nature'. It may be that a today of some sort is marked by the significant role which granite stairs play in it, and that on a particular Thursday nature is in greater or lesser demand than at other times. Nonetheless, as things pertaining to the order of permanence, the granite stairs and nature are concepts hardly compatible with the temporal value of today or Thursday. I am of the opinion that the book, literature and the art of poetry also belong to the order of permanence. A real book, the book we need, is not a matter of today, and is not defined by the relation today has formed to it. We are not on the right track if we think only about what such and such a book tells our time. Rather, we should have a close look at *just what* the book says. If we want to write good books, if we want to read them or judge them correctly, we will cross in ourselves – even if subconsciously – the boundaries of today and what has been conditioned by it. We will not look for a today man, but simply for a man; we will not look for a today sensation, but for beauty, in which a kind of permanent, universal law finds expression.

A Flu-sufferer

The People's Paper, 22 February 1935

By flu I mean the common or garden species. If you've got yourself some extra variety, crossbred with pneumonia or whatever, these lines will offer you neither advice nor comfort. But the person afflicted by the common flu, with its accompanying phenomena like a headache, backache and ache of some 160 joints present in a sick body (there're less of them in a healthy one), and a cough, phlegm, rage, a total decline in mental power, a sore throat and low spirits of all sorts, is occupied in this manner: if he isn't sweating it out in bed, he swears, blows his nose and groans in pain, and also grumbles, tosses in bed and wants to know 'what's up out there' as if he hadn't gone out all year. He tries to read the paper, but there's nothing in it that would buoy up a distressed creature, and besides he'd have to hold it in both hands, while he just needs one to wipe his nose. That's when he discovers the advantages of literature in book form, because it can be read single-handed while the other hand is squashing the hanky. And further, he finds out with surprise that there're few Czech books that can be read when the flu's reached its flowering phase. They are grim, unaccommodating and without hope. Damn them! Haven't our authors ever had flu and felt the need for something human and cheering? Perhaps just Mr Michelup could manage this lapse into malady[1] – he may have his troubles, but they're his, not mine. So the person with flu is standing in front of his bookcase, looking shivery and despondent, and doesn't know what to choose. A book that conveys reality but isn't nasty to people. Yes, but where to find it?

'What Does Jaroslav Hašek Mean to You?'

A Contribution to the Opinion Poll, *The D-36 [Theatre] Programme*, 31 December 1935

Dear friends,
  They used to tell us at school that humour is the spice of life. Today I rather think that it's not just an ingredient, but a fundamental way of seeing the world. Hašek had humour. He was a person who *saw the world*. A lot of people just write about it.
  Yours Karel Čapek

The Protection of Authors

The People's Paper, 3 April 1938

As is well known, authors, that is writers, are more or less shielded by Authors' Rights, the Geneva Convention, Copyright and other measures of that sort, but this protection is of benefit only to their works, whereas their personalities enjoy no safeguard, not even common consideration. Something should be done, something that would allow authors to be treated like other mortals; that would not require them to do things that no one would ever dream of demanding of other fellow beings, such as doctors, barristers, cabinet-makers, owners of merry-go-rounds and other experts. People seem to regard a writer as a man who loves writing, that's why they bring him books and autograph books to sign. Or they take him for a creature who extravagantly enjoys talking, so they invite him to come and lecture 'about his work or any other subject of his choice. We shall be pleased to pay for all your travel expenses.' No one asks their dentist to pull out their teeth as a keepsake. But an author is supposed to drop some idea or other into their five-year-old daughter's autograph book as a keepsake, just out of the kindness of his heart. No one asks a cabinet-maker to do a bit of sanding on their floor just out of friendship, but an author is expected to move around the world with pen in hand, permanently ready to commit his signature to paper. I've had masses of people wanting me to sign *The Turbine or Antonín Vondrejc.*[1] I was cruel enough to refuse to do it. A lady once came to see Karel Poláček wishing him to sign *A Wonder in the Family.*[2] Karel Poláček is a forbearing man, so he willingly supplied this signature: 'On behalf of colonel Fr. Langer, Karel Poláček, sergeant.'[3]

Honestly, something should be done. For instance, someone should establish a close season during which authors would be kept from harm like wood grouse or roe deer. They should be allocated a month when they could only write, instead of having to sign books and face other predicaments to which their authorial status is subjected. Or there should be an Authors' Protection League, which would promulgate the charitable view that authors are human beings just like everyone else, and so shouldn't be made to suffer unnecessarily – 'spare a thought for our writers' and all that sort of thing. It's a dog's life for authors, and something must be done. Something must really be done, otherwise I'll be forced to warn all parents not to send their kids to school with the aim of having them embark on the authorial profession.

1. The most common and intensive way of persecuting authors is to make them *sign their books* for readers. This awful habit is now so widespread that copies of books that are not signed have almost been rendered obsolete. I can assure you that one day unsigned specimens will be a collectable rarity. You'll see: one day bibliophiles will boast: 'This is one of three hitherto discovered copies that are unsigned by the author – and mind you I got it cheap, just seven hundred.' I've no idea why people care so much to have books signed; maybe they think that the books gain value. That's a mistake, however. In my case, I've signed so many books that I wouldn't give twopence for my signature. You can't imagine how delighted an author is when a grateful reader from Mnichovo Hradiště or Valašské Meziříčí or wherever sends a package of books for signing. The author has to pay the excess postage, sign twenty books, keep an eye on them so that none gets lost, rummage for string and brown paper, wrap them up and take them to the post office – look, this is what teaches an author to swear more colourfully than a chauffeur or a gamekeeper. Or he's doing his thing and suddenly he is informed that a lady has called, who apparently wishes to speak to him with regard to an important matter. Well, it can't be helped, a lady is a lady, so the author goes to have a shave and to change into his best clothes; whereupon the lady bursts into chirrups: 'Maestro, if you could sign this book here for my little Miluška's birthday and include a dedication . . .' I'm telling you one day a murder will be committed on such an occasion,

and I plead in advance for the author's exoneration. It will be a case of justifiable self-defence.

2. Also fearfully sweet are male and female owners of *autograph books*. They send them carefully wrapped up in seventeen silken layers, as if they were the most precious jewels in the world, and with them comes a request for our revered writer, among whose fervent admirers the owner of the wrapped-up thing belongs, to put down some of his sparkling ideas; 'and, if I may be so bold, surely it will be easy as pie for you to secure for my autograph book also the signatures of the President of the Republic, of Vítězslav Novák,[4] Nezval,[5] Maleček,[6] Švabinský,[7] Jarmila Novotná,[8] G. B. Shaw, the pilot Novák, J. A. Baťa,[9] Comenius[10] and other great men and women'. Such a delivery is usually insured for three thousand crowns, return postage not enclosed.

3. Further regular correspondence with authors is kept up by *collectors of photographs*. The author is either to send a few of his photographs with dedications to the undersigned as to his exceptional devotee, or he is to sign the enclosed photograph on which the author as a rule looks like a deaf-and-dumb idiot or a misty mediumistic apparition – God knows where such photographs come from.

4. Again, a frequent request is for *the manuscript* of any of the author's works. 'You can rest assured that I will greatly value your honoured manuscript.'

5. About a hundred times a year the author receives an invitation to sign some manifesto or other, which will stir the conscience of the world. As far as I know, no manifesto has yet achieved this, but that doesn't prevent them from carrying on arriving with unfaltering regularity, vehemently protesting against wars, persecutions, atrocities and injustices in America, Asia, Africa and even Europe.

6. A more troublesome hassle is *opinion polls* asking the author to write, by the 15th of this month, his view on the usefulness of ancient Greek, on women's underwear, on Czech film, on abstinence, on the extirpation of blackbirds, on the decline

of religious sensibility, on boxing, on the reform of special schools, the reform of the calendar, the reform of the examination statutes for female social workers, on women's gainful employment, on modern architecture, on the young generation, on the protection of Prague pigeons, or any other of the 470,000 hot, topical, public issues on which every educated, modern man, hence also the author, is generally presumed to have a firm position, only waiting for the opportunity to express it flauntingly. You have no idea how many things today's educated man is (judging by these polls) supposed to have a distinct opinion on. As things stand, at least twice a week he is expected to come out categorically in support of or against something, without anyone asking him beforehand whether he's an expert on it, or has an inkling of what it's about. That's the reason why you're an author, to be able to write something about anything.

7. Another, not a negligible, hassle is the *questions* the papers sometimes ask authors in order to entertain (in their understanding of the word) their readers, and thus disseminate interest in refined reading and cultural life in general. Such questions are, for instance: what do you like eating best, do you prefer blondes, when did you first fall in love, what would you say about your marriage, what hobbies are you keen on, and so on. If you confronted a publican or a petrol-station attendant with a question like that, you'd probably end up with actual bodily harm, but it's assumed that authors should be glad they've been given the chance to prance around in front of the public. So an author's function is to sound interesting and witty all the time, while the public is encouraged to wallow in his private life to increase sales.

8. Furthermore, everyone who publishes a specialist magazine considers it his duty to wring *a contribution to his journal* from the author. Dear Maestro, please write something about mushroom-picking for our journal. Or an article about hiking. Or a poem for children from six to eight years of age. Or something about glass. Something for women.

Something about interior decoration. Something for our poor, yet beautiful region. Something about the protection of animals. Something for our gamekeepers. Something for the youth in vocational training. Something for the cultivators of dahlias. The deadline for our next issue is the 25th of this month. If you don't mind we shall presume to call on you in order to give you a more comprehensive idea of the mission of our journal, and so on.

9. An author is begged for any contribution, no matter how short, especially for *the first issue of our new magazine*. Let me tell you for the record that at least one first issue of a new magazine comes out every week. Besides, what's also published are:

10. *miscellanies, annuals, almanacs, memorial volumes* and suchlike, to which the author will surely not deny his contribution by 15 October; further

11. various books for the publicity of which it would be extremely helpful if the author could write a few sentences by way of introduction or a no-matter-how-short preface. Quite simply, the general image surrounding authors is that they're something like a magic barrel. You just turn on the tap and any required liquid comes out immediately, in abundance and without effort. Somehow, people can't imagine an author as a man bent over *his own* work or buried deep in his own thoughts. They want him to be a supplier of goods who deals with their orders. You wait. One day authors will set up department stores: children's section – third floor on the left; opinion polls in the secretariat, please, room number 17; hiking and animal protection on the second floor, in the sports and hunting department; obituaries and jubilee speeches – counter number 11.

12. Another inveterate belief about authors is that they *take all journals* and buy all books, not least those privately printed for limited circulation. What a joy for the author to get a few bound sheets with verses by L. V. Seidl Podbořanský, a dedication in the poet's own hand and an enclosed invoice

payable by cheque or postal order. Or how delightful for him to find in his daily mail at least one new journal and the first issue of a new newsletter with a polite reminder that he hasn't yet paid for the subscription to *The Gallant Company of Beer-Drawers* or *The Voice of Young Radio-Amateurs* or *The Avant-garde: The Organ of the Young Literary Generation of the Práchen Region.* It's only thanks to the author's obstinate resistance, which enables him to keep mum in response to these reminders, that after a while he stops receiving these esteemed organs. But meanwhile, of course, a dozen others come to light, by and large banking on the fact that 'we can include you as an unparalleled supporter of all cultural endeavours among our subscribers'. Nothing of the sort. As things stand, count authors among obdurate enemies of all cultural endeavours.

13. Another widespread assumption about authors is that their main profession is to *lecture* on their own work, or anyway on modern literature or some other cultural issue – an occasion 'whereby you will singularly gratify your innumerable admirers who long to meet you in the flesh'.

14. In addition, there's a preconception that authors are expressly designed to make *public speeches* against the violation of Chinese sovereignty or in defence of Brazilian workers victimised by exploitative planters. Such a long-distance campaign requires you to secure the services of at least one outstanding lyric poet, otherwise it just wouldn't seem proper.

15. Likewise *participation in discussions* is regarded as something authors have a special fondness for. Hence they are invited to countless educational organisations, clubs and friendly societies to open debates about their work or some other problem.

16. All in all, *personal participation in national life in general and community life in particular* has been assigned to authors as their public office. In this they're meant to serve as a radiant example for the rest of the progressive public, and take the lead in all revitalising, pan-national and humane activities.

17. Yes, that's one of the most painful things: an author is more
in the public eye than other private people, that's why they
turn to him even with their personal troubles. Not a single
day passes without the author receiving at least one letter
crying for help. Someone is ill: author, help him to get to
a sanatorium! Someone is subjected to injustice, someone
is unemployed, someone is hungry, someone suffers: please
author, help! Find a job for an electrician or a piece of bread
for an emigrant, a loan for a poor man or a housekeeper for a
Ruthenian servant in a synagogue,[11] work for a youngster or
a pension for an invalid. 'You certainly have a heart of gold,'
writes a piteously heavy or a long-experienced, beggarly
hand. Heart or no heart, you feel low and humbled by your
helplessness. If you were to look after a tenth of the cases you
consider honest, you wouldn't have enough days to manage
them all. Not a day dawns without this sort of meeting with
human misery – and yet one is supposed to be writing about
unusual and comforting things! It is difficult, dear folks, it is
the deepest shadow on the author's everyday life!

So we should wish, for the sake of authors, an alleviation of misery among people in the first place, and next to that a little more
respect for the fact that writers work and need all their time and
concentration for it, and also a somewhat greater consideration for
their privacy. Stand up for the human rights of authors!

II
WORDS

From Criticism of Words (1920)

There is criticism of books, and God knows if that's good or evil. The only certainty is that it hurts all too often and that it's necessary to have a truly patient spirit so that if someone smites you on the one book, you can offer him the other. It's difficult to write a book, but it's easy to let a word out of your mouth. The book is yours but the word belongs to everyone – hence a *criticism of words* won't hurt anyone, even if it doesn't prove to do any major good.[1]

Supposing you wanted to attempt a critical portrayal of today's prevalent attitudes, you would very likely write a criticism of great philosophical systems, life currents, political ideologies, artistic schools and so on. My plan is humbler: I'm going to write just a criticism of words. These words are more or less public property. So I don't criticise their spiritual fathers, predominantly unaccounted for, but their general use.

A word is more likely to catch on than an idea, and it also wields more public influence. Therefore it's not quite pointless to write a criticism of words. Mistakes, ignorance or lies don't start with an idea but with a word. And since we use words more often and more effectively than ideas, criticism of words should have two goals: (1) to criticise the content of words, (2) to criticise the use of words. The two are not quite the same.

Logic would look for the content, or *the meaning of the word*, in its inner self. In reality, the word doesn't conceal its meaning inside it, but is overgrown with meanings like a stone with moss or a tree with mistletoe, or it's covered with meanings as a rock is with a deposit of silt. Every period lets words be grown all over with different meanings. That's why it is unrewarding to question which of the hitherto possible meanings, or perhaps of all the possible meanings, has more right to overgrow or cover a particular word than any other. Wherever a meaning finds some soil, it grows. It's hard to impede it.

This criticism of words, then, engages in the second rather than the first enterprise, that is, *the use of words*. But any use points to the problem of practical life, hence it has not been in my power to prevent my criticism of words from degenerating into excursions on questions of, oh well, definitely not only verbal ones, but those of life. That's how my critiques have turned into sermons, and that's the reason why there are fifty-two of them as there are fifty-two weeks in a year.

Novelty (IV)

For most readers this word evokes the idea of something unnatural, artificial and forced, whereas everything old and primordial is *ipso facto* natural. For example, there's no doubt that the telephone is unnatural. Today we no longer feel this, but let's recall our first encounter and initial struggle with it: it was dreadful. It croaked and didn't hear you; you shouted and pounded the box to no avail; the more you shouted the worse the thing shaped up. Finally you left it, your body and spirit broken. That was a long time ago. Since then you've invented a way of dealing with it. It was a chain of small inventions of which you were as proud as Bell and Edison were of theirs. You, too, have invented the telephone.

Things may seem unnatural, but invention is not unnatural. On the contrary, invention is the very nature of man, the very spontaneity and energy of life. A novelty, a new *thing*, is of course something unnatural, but to invent, co-create, co-discover a novelty, this *activity* is endlessly natural. And I didn't, dear reader, have the telephone in mind. I was thinking about new ideas, new currents and new art. Even here, dear reader, it's pointless to shout, and pound these seemingly strange, unnatural, unbending things with your fist. The more you shout, the worse the thing shapes up. There is no other way that novelties can happen but by invention. Novelty answers the active and spontaneous side in you. It's not a mere thing but an activity. It's up to you to take it up, and when you've done it, you'll feel that it's as natural as a heartbeat, the growth of a flower, work in the field or a child playing.

Dog's weather [2] (XI)

Underlying this expression is the nonsensical idea that weather which is too bad for man – that is, hurricanes, sleet, forty-day-long precipitations and hail – is just the thing for a dog and closely related to his nature. There couldn't be a more monstrous lie. A dog's actual weather would be more beautiful than you could possibly imagine: June for the whole year, a warm sunlit yard with cool shade, short dewy rain, a multitude of interesting scents, moist tall grass, no full moon, no pianos, no beggars, no inequality, many children and enough meat for everyone.

Similarly false is the saying that when things are exceedingly nasty they are 'fit for a cat'.* In reality, and from a rightful cat-perspective, what is 'fit for a cat' is a cushion, sweet milk, a careless sparrow, mysterious attics and haylofts, a woman's lap, a soft hand, a ball of wool, moonlit nights, a quiet house and a garden – things that are altogether lovely, natural and intimate.

These idioms show, with pitiable clarity, a human prejudice whereby the animals' scale of values is monstrous and dismal. But there is reason to believe that if animals were endowed with the power to adjust, or even create, the world to their own taste, it would be – despite many a cruelty and inconsistency – not the least happy of worlds. *Man* in particular would, in this world, be an endlessly mild and good animal, as holy as a lama and as affable as Dionysus.

Superstition (XIII)

I was going to write about a different word, but when I put down 'thirteen' in the heading, I thought of the unfortunate, derogatory word 'superstition'. Yes, we have outlived the age of superstitions. If I go to the office by tram number thirteen, I don't think about the dire and fateful consequences it may bring me, and none of the pedestrians regards my resolution to go just by number

---

* This idiom is not only a lie, but also a Germanism. Pardon me, but I'm more interested in the lie.

thirteen and no other as a sign of special intrepidity. There's no doubt we live more comfortably if there are no unlucky thirteens, inauspicious Fridays, places marked out by fate, and thousands of other omens. But it's doubtful if life is richer and more interesting. To tell you the truth, I don't really know if it's better for a little spider to be an indication of the future, or just an indication that the corners haven't been dusted. I don't know if on hearing that the clock has suddenly stopped it's more important to call distant relatives to mind with loving concern, or call the nearest clockmaker. The profit from comfort and certainty is only relative. Something always gets lost, something that can't be easily replaced. Superstitions used to lend things a deeper meaning and greater diversity. By outliving superstitions we've attained a greater indifference towards things. It seems that things have been getting their revenge by showing indifference to us. A little spider runs across a wall thinking not about good luck but about the nutritious goo in some corner or other. A flea leaps onto your hand and doesn't magic the postman to bring that expected letter. The sky doesn't send you auguries of comets, nor the rainbow of peace, nor bloody swords, as it used to do during wars in the past. The clock stops obstinately and foolishly, and if your ears ring, no one is thinking of you just as you are not thinking of them. The relation of things to man is precisely the same as the relation of man to things.

Style (XIV)

This word expresses something distinctive and individual. So composers say they cultivate a particular style, and every painter uses colour in his own special style. And if you haven't developed an idiosyncratic style, you are left wondering at the playfulness of nature and at the fact that while one musical master is endowed with the style of Smetana, another genius sprouts a style like Slavíček's.[3] Nature is powerful and eccentric.

But if I were able to communicate with the little bird that occasionally sings in front of my window, I think that he would tell me this: 'I'm singing, true, but not because I'm possessed of a singular style, but because I'm terribly overflowing with love. You know, sir, art is not a matter of a special style. It's a matter of the heart, and God's gift. God is teek teek tiuitee, tio tio trrr to to to netia teek. This is a great mystery, dependent not on style, but on soul.' However, I can't understand this tiny bird so well, so I just listen to him singing. It seems to me that he doesn't really mean anything overly special and original by his singing. That he, indeed, very much enjoys his little song, but not the greatness and individual remarkableness of his style. His artistic mission is to sing, not to have a style. A singular style is the privilege of human artists.

Aim (XV)

Once or twice a day in our 'serious and critical' times, as they say, some 'aim' or other materialises before our conscientious eyes. All kinds of dark nooks in newspapers and magazines suddenly light up with a new aim that shows us the way to a better future. I don't know any more what our national aim is and what not: to have healthy children, to be a member of the Museum, to buy the Golden Book by V. B. Třebízský,[4] to join a party, to be a eugenicist, to remember the hungry, to support an infinite number of worthy causes, to build a new theatre, to establish new schools . . . you name it. For God's sake, I don't argue against the good, useful things that descend on us as aims, but only – and diffidently – against our turning them into aims. For they could be all sorts of other things: a liking, a pleasure, an entertainment, a matter of pride, relief, love or craziness. I wonder if the Czech lands wouldn't be a merrier place if people found it a delight, and not an aim to be a member of the Museum; if it were a national entertainment, not a national aim to build nice new schools; if we gave food to the poor because we desperately enjoyed doing it, and not because we saw it as an aim; if we opened our bags of gold out of our untamable charitable temperament; if we did 'everything for the child' because we love children, and everything for adults or science or art or the future out of blithe and sympathetic motives. Aims guide and rectify life, whereas personal impulses live it. We get humanity from an aim, but we live it from the heart. The word 'aim' is the antithesis of 'nature'. I don't exactly know what a national nature is, but I'd like ours to include at least the majority of what we nowadays term 'national aims'.

Outlive (XVIII)

I can't even enumerate all the things that we have, as they say, 'out-lived'. We've outlived Impressionism and realism, the Middle Ages and superstition, speculative philosophy and Darwin, Tolstoy and art nouveau, scepticism and Ibsen, Wagner and romantic sensibility – in short, it seems that having outlived such an enormous amount, we can't rest on anything except our laurels. To outlive something always means to outlive something bad. Each of us has outlived a cold in the head, but no one with a cold in the head will say that he has out-lived a period of health. We outlive winter, but not spring. If we have outlived Impressionism, we imply it was like a cold or an unpleasant winter. But in fact, it used to be so marvellously healthy and charm-ing that we ought to say it has left us in the lurch. We have outlived romantic sensibility, but will anyone say that he has outlived youth? We have outlived Darwinism because . . . we are just being outlived by vitalism, and we shall outlive vitalism when we have again been outlived by something else. Yes, we can outlive yesterday, but tomor-row, when we have outlived today, yesterday will be immortal history. Today, yesterday seems like a mistake, in a year it will be a historical era. In a hundred years our 'outlived positions' will become sacred sacrificial sites of the human spirit. In a hundred years our alleged victories will be just moments of transition. And when we ourselves have been definitively outlived, we, too, no doubt, shall enter history, dignified and immortal as the past itself.

Principle (XIX)

– a mysterious and powerful word. You take a walk before dinner on principle; your aunt isn't a theatre-goer on principle; your wise cousin avoids crowds on principle, while your late grandad on principle drank mulled beer. If you took a walk out of habit or dyspepsia, if your aunt spent evenings at home out of indolence and parsimony, if your cousin were simply afraid of crowds and your late grandad mulled his beer out of tender consideration for his catarrh, the world would undoubtedly be more colourful and language richer, but life would presumably lose out on moral commitment. If you take a walk on principle, you fulfil your moral duty importantly and faithfully. It matters more to aerate yourself on principle than to call on a sick friend without principle. If your aunt plays patience alone at home in the evening, as she, being a principled woman, doesn't hold with the secular vanity of music and the stage, it is a dignified act of moral will. You can turn any habit, any laziness, weakness and inertia, into a matter of principle. The world may not gain anything by it, but you will – you'll please yourself and, as a bonus, feel like a person of character.

Ism (XXI)

A critic usually treats an artist like an animal. He captures him, and first of all he identifies him and gives him a name. So damp forests are the habitat of the naturalist, in cool highlands flits the intellectualist, the futurist lives wildly in cities, the realist resides in poor, working-class regions, the sensualist occupies fecund nature, the Impressionist occurs only in certain areas, but in abundance, and so on. It's not a disaster if it's just the critic who harbours the scientific superstition that there are species and families, not individuals. But it's worse when the reader or the spectator is led to believe that instead of poems and pictures he is presented with nothing but isms. 'How come!' the disappointed art-lover cries. 'I wanted to see a feeling, not a theory; I wanted to experience an image of reality, but you fakers offer me some kind of abstract, made-up ism! But that's enough, I don't want to know about your isms! I'll go out by myself to be surrounded by nature, and I'll find true, unfeigned beauty there with my own senses and my own heart.' So this beauty-lover walks out and lies down on his own back on the grass; he loves the scent of hay and the tinkling of herds, listens to forests, floats with clouds and recollects his childhood. And suddenly a Tempting Spirit comes unto him, whispering: 'Lying and sniffing is sensualism, perceiving the variegation and fluidity of phenomena, that's Impressionism, and loving the bleating of the herds, that's barefaced, cynical naturalism. A recollection of childhood is primitivism. Fusing with nature is monism and pantheism. O man, in every proper ism there is as much theory as in your lying down, as much of a system as in your pleased nose, and as much abstraction as in your flowering joy. Wherefore go and enjoy art with the same vigour and skill as you use when you are lying here and loving.' I believe that the Tempting Spirit is right.

Creative (XXII)

This word is a standard burnt offering of critical praise. To call a work or a person creative is strong acclaim. But if the acclaim is strong, the idea is weak. 'Creative' means a great deal for God, but very little for man. The only thing we know about creation is that it means 'making something out of nothing'. According to all available legends and reports God created the world, but none of them says that he learnt to do it. It's nowhere written that he couldn't do it at first, but had to perfect his technique bit by bit, and that he gradually became bolder, more experienced and adroit until he achieved proper mastery, beginning with the heavenly bodies and finishing up with fleas and people. Indeed, since he created everything out of nothing, he obviously didn't need any preparation. But a man – an artist – doesn't have such an easy time, because he doesn't create 'out of nothing'. The reality from which he takes his material is such a huge 'something' that the artist feels, with sorrow, if I lived for a million years, I wouldn't be finished with all this. I'll never watch away, hear away and feel away everything that exists, right to the depth. And this something, this reality is so special that he jumps for joy when he manages to get a bit of it into his work. A painter doesn't throw his cap in the air out of delight that his picture is a creative feat, but out of the greater delight that he has managed to paint space into his canvas. Homer didn't feel joy at his own creative divinity so much as at the heroic divinity of Achilles. An artist is a bit like a cabin boy on Columbus's ship who sees a distant shore and cries: 'Land! Land!' That boy did not imagine that he had created America, but he was the first to behold a new reality. Cabin boys, Columbuses, artists are not creators of Americas, but discoverers and admirers of reality. There's a bit of truth in the idea that an artist loves dreams above all, but there's more truth in the idea that he loves reality more than other people. Or you could say that an artist is like a good cabinet-maker. A good cabinet-maker makes a beautiful table out of a beautiful piece of wood, and he loves that beautiful wood more than the nothing-ness out of which he could perhaps, by Pure Potency, magic a table and chairs. A good artist creates a beautiful work out of a beautiful reality; and even if he were to discover that reality in his own inner self, it is far more than the creative 'nothing'. His craft is not God's.

Instinct (XXVI)

This word is commonly used by artists when they want to lay claim to, or want to show that they feel, a distinctively mysteri-ous kind of power or gift. They are almost ashamed to say that they have composed this through careful deliberation or painted that following a rational plan. On the contrary: 'This', they say, 'has sprung up instinctively, and that is an intuitive expression. An artist creates instinctively, driven by something that is stronger than him.' Indeed, there are even theories of art like this, there are critics who resolutely believe that an artist creates by instinct just as an ich-neumon fly lays an egg into a mindless caterpillar by instinct, or a swallow finds the way to Italy by instinct, or bees, by instinct, collect honey for winter. I have no problem with believing that the ichneumon fly, the swallow and the bee do by instinct every-thing that natural science orders them to do. But the moment they had enough human understanding to be able to communicate with us, they would most likely speak differently. 'We Ichneumonidae', the ichneumon fly would probably say, 'are terribly clever insects. Mind you, we have such big brains that we, for example, lay our eggs straight into caterpillars.' – 'And we', the swallow would make its voice heard, 'have such wonderful perception and consistency, yes, consistency is the right word – if we want southwards, we fly southwards!' – 'And in our case, you know,' the bee would conclude with a few buzzwords, 'we observe an old law whereby honey must be collected, and whoever does not obey this law is a drone or a stupid crone, and no honourable bee.' – 'But my dear animals,' man would object, 'you do all these feats without even knowing why, by pure, unadulterated instinct . . .' – Whereupon the animals would look offended and say: 'Are we cattle or what? You, you just don't know what you're talking about!'

This fable shows that nature boasts not about its method, but its success and thirst for life. Do you have lunch out of nutritive instinct, or because it's sensible to eat well? Both of these are true, but it's even truer that you simply like the food. In the same vein, an artist should say: 'I've done this because I had to, somehow; also, I considered it rationally, but mainly I jolly well liked it, and deep down in my heart I hoped that you'd like it too.'

Cold (XXVII)

Common usage has it that reason is cold, and the favourite philosophy of our time holds that it's not only cold, but also mechanical. That's why, as I was saying last time, people prefer instinct. However, I talked about it, as I often do, downright badly. I presupposed that if a sand wasp could speak, she'd show off her intelligence, and not her instinct. Well then, if she really did that, I'd throw into her face a terrible example of her unintelligence, an example related by the reliable, wise Fabre.[5] A digger wasp called Bembex excavates a horizontal burrow in sandy soil. At the end of it there is a little chamber where the larva is placed, as well as the flies that the Bembex has brought in and stored there for it. And even if the digger wasp flew miles and miles away, she always comes back, with ungraspable certainty, exactly to the opening of the burrow. And if you buried the tunnel or blocked it with little stones, the wasp would push her way through with passionate, fervent diligence, so as to feed her larva. Oh, what an example of maternal love, you'd say. But the wise Fabre cut the upper part of the nest off with a knife, so that only a little channel and the little chamber without a ceiling, with the poor hapless larva, were left. And the mother with a new prey rushes straight to the opening – but, alas, the opening is no longer there. The digger wasp is looking around, clawing, feeling the ground, rummaging for the opening with untiring pig-headedness. She is searching even in the former burrow, she even gets into the uncovered chamber where, on the white bottom, the little larva is writhing on the heap of prepared flies. But the mother pushes it aside as if it were a parcel or a dead obstruction, mulishly looking for one thing: *the opening!* The opening leading to her child! The digger wasp doesn't know her child, she only knows that she must get to it through the opening, and if there is no opening, there is no child. 'What a gaping gulf between intelligence and instinct,' cries Fabre, who, despite everything, liked insects. 'Among the debris of a collapsed home a mother, led by intelligence, hurls herself straight to her child; led by instinct, she obstinately stops where the door once was.' Again and again Fabre shows that the instinct of insects is truly astonishing, but mechanical. Particular procedures must succeed one another. If you disturb the routine it's all up with instinct. Instinct is sophisticatedly perfect as long as it works within the conditions it's been fashioned for. Change a single one, and instinct will become the most sophisticated idiocy. Instinct is perfectly adjusted to the conditions; reason, however, adjusts and sets up the conditions by itself, even if imperfectly. Instinct is the wit of nature, but the idiocy of an individual. Reason, though poor in comparison with nature, gives the individual wit and inventiveness. Instinct is conservative, whereas reason is the organ of invention. Where instinct marvellously manages thousand-year-old acts, reason, if it succeeds at all, leads to new achievements. And that's why I'm begging you, for God's sake, to respect reason and not say that it's cold. It's quite the opposite – good, spirited reason is hot all over from strong friction against the conditions and situations it is trying to overcome. Now it is inventive like a child, now simple like a craftsman; it invests honest labour, but then with a light jump it skips over the chained links that instinct must follow. It offers you an endless possibility of mistakes and adventures, but also the possibility of choice.

World- (XXIX)

Beside the World War, there are also world exhibitions and world-views. A world exhibition is a big, neatly organised heap of all kinds of exquisitenesses – you find industry and ethnography, science and art, technology and nature, all the world's continents, all possible products there. You can't see how any of those things is produced and what it really does in its place, but that's irrelevant. The crucial thing is that everything fits in there and can be lined up. A world-view is very similar to a world exhibition. It has everything in it: biology and history, hygiene, politics, sociology, literature and even a God in a separate pavilion. You can't see how this or that thing works and what uncertainties it is tormented with, or how a particular idea runs untamed in the virgin forest of reality, but all that is irrelevant. The main thing is that all the sciences and ideas fit into a limited space, and are accessible all at once, for a low entrance fee.

And now, dear friend, after you've worked yourself to death by looking at the world exhibition, after you've run through the pavilion of minerals and fossils, a zoological garden and a botanical orchard, an industrial palace and one of the world's most beautiful collections of kitsch, tell me, do you really know anything about the world? Drink this glass of water (don't worry, the water is genuine, and doesn't belong to the world exhibition), and confess if you didn't have more to do with the world, with the *whole* world, when, for instance, you told your first love that you'd go 'to the end of the world' for her, when you set off for the first time 'to see the world', when you were gradually getting to know what 'the dearest things in the world' were to you? Tell me if these world feelings didn't resemble the world more than world-views. For the world, the real, intriguing, unknown world, lies on the path of interest, not opinion; it lies in the direction of intensity, not comprehensiveness. If you observed one ant strongly, with love and understanding, you'd form a world-view, for you'd have looked into the depth of the world's interestingness. What is a world-view good for, if it isn't an aggregate of the passionate interests and experiences that the world can offer?

Angle (XXXIII)

An angle of vision is an optical invention just like glasses or the telescope, only more magical. For example, from the angle of eternity you see the world as if you stood high enough to view everything from above: Lo, how tiny it is; lo, what swarming multitudes creep down there on earth, how great we are and above everything! Or you can see the present from the angle of history if you position yourself adroitly, as if you didn't give a damn about anything: Oh, all the rest of you, if you only knew what a heavenly prospect of your ephemeral deeds I have from here! The special deliciousness of an angle of vision is that it's much easier to decry things from it. From the angle of humanity you can denounce nationalism, from the angle of nationalism you can denounce socialism, from the angle of socialism you can condemn property; from the angle of property you can condemn an ideal, from the angle of an ideal you can write off reality, and so on until once again you've come back full circle. It's enough to adopt a suitable angle and a judgement is made. You shake it out of the angle abundantly, with ease and without question, and what's more, this angle is a pure horn of wisdom; multitudes draw their pearls of wisdom from nowhere else but its depths. For the wisdom of many people hinges on being judgemental. But there is also another type of wisdom that doesn't judge but looks. Even the God they scared us with when we were little just looked and 'saw everything', but left judging for the Last Judgement. And I believe that seeing is great wisdom, and that it's more beneficial to see a lot than to judge. I even believe that the more a person sees, the less he can judge and the less he desires to be a judge. But where are you running to, my friend, with your angle of vision, if all you want is to see? The angle of vision isn't a means of seeing, but of judging. Open wide all 360 degrees of your soul and pack up all your angles; they're good for nothing, they're really utterly useless whenever you want to assign yourself the hardest and highest optical task – to see.

Mere (XXXIV)

This adjective is often used critically to mean a palpable and mysterious lack. You are, for instance, a 'mere' intellectual; if you were not that, you would be a 'mere' realist or a 'mere' romantic. In any case you are lacking in something, presumably always in the opposite faculty. Your non-belief is 'mere' materialism, your belief is 'mere' dogmatism – you can't be delivered from this dilemma, not even by 'mere' scepticism. You can be either a 'mere' expert or a 'mere' dilettante: which one will you choose?

Suppose Adam in paradise had turned to the Lord God with discontent, saying: 'Look what you have created. In your poor paradise a stone is a mere stone, a tiger a mere tiger and a lily of the field a mere field lily. And Eve? A mere woman. And yourself? God is a mere spirit, isn't he?' Whereupon the Lord God would have been bemused and abashed. Only after a while (in a few thousand years) would he have realised that he could have answered the moaner something like this (unfortunately, we always think of the best replies too late): 'O Adam! A stone is not a mere stone; it is a weapon, a demarcation post, a wall of a house, a stepping-stone, a future sculpture – everything you turn it into. A tiger is not a mere tiger; he is a cub, a father, a fur, a sylvan god or an adventure in the jungle. Nowhere, not in a single instance, did I create any mere entities, Adam. Everything is multifarious and promising, full of possibilities and intricacies. Your eyes are to blame, Adam. You have turned my tiger into a mere animal, my substance into mere materialism, my reality into mere realism – poor Adam!'

Superlatives (XXXVI)

One of the most popular form of words in both criticism and life is the superlative. You're forever coming across 'the greatest Czech poet', 'the most outstanding work of our time', 'the best humorist' and suchlike, almost as you do in advertisements – 'the best alcohol-free drink', 'the best factory of its kind', 'the most this', 'the best that' again and again without end. We live in a world of superlatives. However, Alpha fizz or Omega pop may be the best alcohol-free drink, and still not be good. The greatest poet of the Trebizond tsardom doesn't in effect have to be great, and the greatest humorist of our time doesn't have to be good at all – quite simply, good is better than best, great is greater than greatest, and the positive is more serious, more absolute and weightier than the superlative.

If a woman wants to be the most beautiful in society, she's a vain coquette; if she wants to be simply beautiful, she accomplishes a classic, God-pleasing work. If someone wants to write the greatest Czech novel, he commits a grubby piece of competitiveness against no fewer than 150 best Czech novels. If, however, he wants to write a good novel, his ambition is great and honest. When Leibniz tried to prove that our world is the best of all possible worlds, he justified God very unreliably; he'd have done better if he had provided (of course an impossible) proof that our world is good. Nothing more than good. Yes, of course, we have invented superlatives mainly in order to wriggle out of the difficult examination of whether things are good, great and beautiful. We speak in superlatives not because we like to exaggerate, but because we don't have the courage to speak in positives.

Fight, struggle (XXXIX)

These are perhaps the most frequent words in our public vocabulary. We fight for bread, recognition, women's rights, the suppression of prostitution, the establishment of specialised schools and what not, and if a peaceful inhabitant of Saturn got hold of our declarations and took them literally, he'd be horrified, imagining our world devastated by everlasting civil war where pedestrian attacks pedestrian and fights to the death to gain bread or recognition, and where murderous campaigns are regularly waged between workers and employers, between the sociologists and the clientele of the Red Lion, between everyone and everyone else. In reality a man 'fighting for bread' sits in an office quite unheroically, or sews shoes; an artist 'struggling for recognition' waits at home or in a cafe until fame shines on him, without spilling the dull critic's blood or engaging in a scuffle with the first citizen who doesn't respect him. If the bloodthirsty word 'fight' or 'struggle' meant nothing but an illusion of heroism in our non-epic life, it wouldn't be worth taking it away from people. But as an idea is often the father of an action, so a word is often the father of an idea. If we didn't say 'the fight for bread' but the earning of bread, people wouldn't sit in their offices or workshops with such enraged, antagonistic feelings. If we didn't say that an artist 'struggles for recognition', but that he looks forward eagerly to fame, there would be less bitterness in the unlucky fate of being an artist. And if 'class struggle' weren't used at all, but replaced by getting enough to eat or the longing for justice, don't you think that life would be at once infinitely kinder – and perhaps even more generous? And if you flatteringly called my writing 'a fight for better understanding', you'd infuse me with the idea that I'm fighting against someone, that there's an enemy somewhere, whom I must hurt or at least hate. Meanwhile, I'm writing without a shadow of hatred in my heart. Sometimes I get absorbed in thought, sometimes I smile, and if I occasionally think I am at least a bit right, I feel as if I were offering my hand, and not struggling for anything, not even for the truth.

Material fixation (XLIII)

– or materialism, is said to be the disease of our time, and is defined as worship of matter. However, the most conspicuous feature of the present time is that it doesn't worship matter at all; it devalues it rather than worshipping it. An old wood carver reverenced wood, but a wholesaler in wood hasn't a speck of respect for the wood he sells: make it into sawdust or rotary paper, it works out at so much a metre. An old mason revered good stone, but today's mason reveres his political party or health insurance or nothing whatsoever, perhaps because no good stone gets into his hands, but just a substitute. Yes, our time honours matter so little that it surrounds itself with nothing but substitutes. It's so little matter-oriented that it has absolutely no serious and solid friendship with matter. It consumes materials but doesn't honour them. Honouring wine doesn't mean swilling bottles at fifty or a hundred crowns each, but pouring drops of wine to the gods, composing anacreontic poetry, or sipping and seeing the heavens open. Honouring a woman doesn't mean buying her, but loving her. Worshipping matter means carving and hewing, painting, building cathedrals and doing beautiful weaving, cherishing the soil as Boaz did and tending sheep as Paris did, uttering flights of poetry, loving nature, singing while you work, bowing to the Maker and having tons of rich experiences that cost nothing, through your eyes, ears, tongue, nose and fingers. Honouring matter means getting yourself furniture as eternal as idols and as beautiful as churches. Matter is honoured by a master craftsman and an artist, not by factory owners or workers. A factory owner and a worker do not appreciate matter, but the profit it yields. But money is not honest matter; it's the basest and most nonsensical substitute. Now and then it's perhaps possible to find some kind of idealism of spirit in our time; more importantly, however, we lack the idealism of matter. If this very minute I received divine power, I'd take all the genuine, venerable matter away from people and would leave them just with two things: words and money. And maybe most of them wouldn't even notice that something in the world had changed.

To play (XLIV)

There's nothing wrong with this word, except that it's misused in the idiom 'to play a role'. So Napoleon 'played a leading role' in world history, or sugar 'plays a considerable role' in the exports of our republic. It's doubtful that Napoleon 'played'; I suspect that he took his mission in history quite seriously, and without pretence. But if he 'played', more should be said about it. It's not enough to say that Vojan[6] 'played the leading role' in *The Merchant of Venice*; even the worst reviewer tells us more – *how* he played it. Imagine a historian writing: Mr Napoleon played a leading role in world history, graphically and inimitably; he rendered the battle scenes with rapturous verve, his emperor's mask was exquisite, but on St Helena he played insipidly and without tempo. Or imagine this being written about sugar: This time sugar has not fulfilled expectations; it played its hitherto considerable role in export feebly, it didn't even know its part and would have flopped if foreign audiences didn't cherish the memory of its sweet performance.

In saying this, I don't want to blame people for not taking Napoleon or sugar seriously, but for not taking play seriously. In this paragraph I'm concerned with the merits of play. You tell a lazy worker: 'Stop playing with your work.' Well, if he really played with it, he'd do it with the ardour of a child who forgets about time and focuses all his strength on the perfection of his play. For perfection is at stake even more in the case of play than of work. Play is a purely qualitative employment. It matters supremely that playing is done well; that's why play is the mother of ambition, the first and eternal field of competition and self-improvement. We don't take play seriously enough – that's evident also in the failures of our civilisation. If we *only* played with work, our work would acquire fabulous perfection. If we 'played our role' in life, we wouldn't be such cabbages, and so morally shapeless as we often are. Come to that, playing would teach us to honour fair play and the real skill that you need to win.

Tomorrow (XLVI)

This word is often used in the combination 'tomorrow's art' or 'tomorrow's world-view' or something like that; as often as not a more definite instruction follows stating what the imminent art or wisdom must, should or will surely look like. Tomorrow's novel will be collective, for instance; tomorrow's historiography will be socialist; tomorrow's philosophy will be either mystical or realistic – tomorrow has nothing else to do but fulfil our predetermined programmes. And it's clear that the fondness for prophesying hasn't petered out, though its technique has deteriorated. An old prophet foretold the future conditionally: 'And when there appears a sword like unto a flame of fire in heaven, destruction shall come upon the earth'; or 'when a beast with four horns reigns, there shall be a great famine upon the whole land'. But no contemporary prophet says: 'When there appears a green star with a red tail, a collective novelist shall be born.' He no longer has the patience of a mystic to wait for the fulfilment of the conditions; he wants to see the result immediately, today or tomorrow, and that's why he prophesies 'tomorrow's art'. Fools! It's easier and safer to predict what the world will look like in a thousand years than in one year. I can safely say that in a thousand years everyone will fly, but I can't say if I'll fly in five years. I can have the revelation that in a thousand years a beast with four horns will wield power, but no revelation will tell me if Mr Tusar will be in power next year.* Tomorrow's prophecy is the riskiest of all possible soothsaying. And yet one prediction about tomorrow is possible and safe – I mean the one that no one cares to make. What will remain of today will be there tomorrow. If we have any good art today, it will be at least a bit of tomorrow's art as well. If we have any good idea now, it will become a part of tomorrow's world-view, at least in some minds. If there is a spark of eternity on earth today, it will be as bright a spark tomorrow and the day after tomorrow. So we don't have to make prophecies about tomorrow; we can make tomorrow straight off, without any uncertainties or queries. Tomorrow will be, at least in some part, just what we make it today. And some of the future can always be read in the palms of the present.

* Stop Press: Upon my soul, not any longer!⁷

Form (XLVII)

This word very often occurs as part of the phrase 'mere form', which implies something empty, useless and dead. Church rituals, for example, are dismissed as 'mere form', and the rigmaroles that go on in the law courts are just legal form, and thousands of social conventions are mere form as well, which is to say that they can happily be held in contempt from a higher, liberal perspective.

Now I am not setting up as a Catholic apologist, nor am I keen to make a career as a form-specialist, either in heaven or on earth. But I value form – the more so, the longer democracy continues. Just think about the 'mere forms' of the church: the birth of a child becomes a festival, a celebration, by the sanctity of christening. Confirmation ostentatiously and ceremonially sanctifies puberty. Marriage is not just a contract, but a rite. Dying is again a solemn, sacred moment, and a man's funeral is sheer festival, I'd say, really the most beautiful day of his life. So the whole of man's life is framed by a glorifying and comforting order. Both entrance and exit are solemn, so are the great turning points, and even if all the celebration is mere form, you must admit that it is more glorious than, say, roast goose. All the pagan religions, all irrational but elevating superstitions, all the churches, have imbued and sanctified human life with a whole system of celebratory forms, whereas politics has brought only electoral junketings and vacuous speeches.

Or take legal form. England is the classic country for a feeling of citizenship, so they say. I have no doubt that this has to do with English formalism and judges' wigs. Medieval law was an enormous structure of forms, for only form, not an idea, could tame those half-barbarians. Magic was nothing but sheer formalism; you didn't have to be possessed by demons – it was enough to pronounce a certain formula correctly and the spirits of all the elements were at once under your sway. And I affirm without embarrassment that a bit of magic art lingers in any form even today. You poets, you are aware that rhyme and rhythm are pure magic; and you, priests, know the same is true of your rituals, and you, judges, of your formalities. Every revolution is more of a revolution of forms than of ideas. If you entirely destroy ingrained forms, you end up with collapse. It is particularly states that are just in their infancy, and authorities that want to sanctify human life, and rulers who want to rule truly that should grasp the sorcery of forms. Only the driest rationalists, who don't believe in magic art at all, dismiss forms. But if magic is needed – and our souls thirst for it – forms are what we need.

A question, or a problem (XLVIII)

These amply and successfully circulated words can give your speech a profound and scholarly tinge. Don't say 'a table', but 'the problem of a table', don't speak about drama, but 'the question of drama'. Don't say 'women', but 'the woman question', and if you want to pray before going to bed, don't pray to God, but to 'the problem of religion'. The advantages are readily grasped: (1) If you speak about realities, you must speak clearly; if you speak about problems, you can – indeed, you should – speak in a complicated way. (2) You have to have knowledge, or at least experience, to talk about realities, whereas you must have uncertainty or inexperience to talk about problems. (3) A question, or a problem, is a very rewarding topic because it allows you to speak as much about what there is not as about what there is. We won't quarrel about the actual transmigration of souls, for God's sake, but we can discuss the problem of the transmigration of souls endlessly. Naïve certainty only knows that something exists or doesn't exist, but a problem poses something between being and non-being, some kind of shadowy half-existence, a noetic purgatory where the quadrature of a circle and God, gender and infinitude, co-education and the Jews dwell side by side, along with other problems and questions that we have littered about in such profusion that they are gradually consuming the whole of our mental universe. And this advance of problematisation isn't finished by any means. It seems that we have more taste for questions than answers, or at least that our problems are

more interesting than our solutions. Perhaps we shall finally be able
to put problems in place of all realities, but until that happens, we
can cry out with the last remaining bit of naïve (too naïve) certainty: a problem is the work of passion, not the work of reason; the
work of reason is reality-based and assuring, whereas questions and
uncertainties arise from the lustful passion of intellect. And having
pronounced that, we can expire in the problem of our own being.

Relative (LI)

'Relative' is a wise and modern word. Values and truths are relative.
Both space and time are relative. Notions and knowledge, science
as well as human experience – simply everything is relative, even
absolute alcohol – if you want to be wise, son, believe absolutely
that everything is relative.

Ah, for how long absolute truths have been pulling the wool over
our eyes! Every, even slightly, self-respecting idea has told you: I am
the only truth, the crystalline hundred-per-cent philosophical truth;
only my registered trade-mark guarantees the true methylated-
spirit embrocation of knowledge; only mathematics, Catholic faith,
empirical science, positivism, theosophy, or heaven knows what, is
the absolutely true opinion, and everything else is *ipso facto* an absolute error, a load of old cobblers and an *ignis fatuus*. Those absolute
truths, how many of them there have been! What a ferocious ceme-
tery of absolutes history is! *'Everything is relative!'* These consolatory
words sound across the burial ground of ideas like some 'Remember,
man, that dust thou art, and unto dust shalt thou return.' All truths
are relative, but then all errors are relative too. You can't, relatively
human creature, throw a stone at any error. If there isn't even a tiny
shred of truth in it, well then, at least it must have had good reasons
for coming about and existing. Success, happiness, good are relative,
but then failures, pains and sins are also relative, and leave us some
hope that it's possible to rectify them – at least relatively; and verily,
a twenty-per-cent rectification is better than a hundred-per-cent
condemnation. And if this relativism drifted out from philosophy,
or 'the empire of spirit', to the life of us people who quarrel and

torment ourselves with our hundred-per-cent notions, opinions and despairs, it would be a great gain – a relative one, of course, for 'Everything is Relative!'

Forgive me, I don't want to play with words, but when I said that everything is relative, something quite unrelativistic slipped out. For the sinful word 'everything' stinks of covert and obdurate absolutism, as if I were to say with Pythagoras' followers that 'everything rests on the number three', or with Hegel that 'everything that is, is rational'. Get thee behind me, Satan! Genuine, hundred-per-cent relativism must come to a better insight: almost everything is relative. Everything is relative except for certain exceptions. And now, relativist, you have just done a good piece of work; not only have you thought your relativism through to its consequences, but you have opened for yourself a delightful vista of something that is an exception in this relative world, of things that are not relative, of truths that are not delusive, of beings that are perfect and infinite. Definitive relativism tells you (and be sure to appreciate the weightiness and gratification of this truth): there are things that are not relative. Something absolute is present in the world, we don't know how many per cent of it there is, but it is present – to be believed in and enjoyed.

Life (LII)

Reading through the preceding pages, I found the word 'life' so many times that in the end I was overtaken by doubt: what does the word 'life' actually mean? And then an amiable, chirpy voice from some up-to-date book replies: What? You're asking what life is? Life is creative, warm and pulsating; everything alive is good; life is always right, and always in the right.

Ah, my friend, I too love to live, I too like that word – it has answered umpteen kinds of uncertainties for me, and I don't find anything wiser and better in me than life. And yet I was exasperated the other day when I read that 'it's sweet to live', and I'm driven to protest when someone tells me that life is warm and pulsating. For just here, a couple of inches away from this paper, everything is not warm and pulsating, and yet, it lives, wants to live, would terribly like to live. For even the feeble, the unhappy and the abortive are life that wants to be right and in the right!

And suddenly a Tempting Spirit comes unto me, asking: 'Do you regard life as something perfect or imperfect?' – Very imperfect. – 'Do you admit, then, and believe that there is something more perfect and higher than life, something above life, or not?' – Yes, I do. – 'Why don't you want to serve the perfect and the higher by your pearls of wisdom, then?' – Because I sort of want to be of service to life. – 'And why do you sort of want to be of service to life?' – Because it's very imperfect. – Whereupon the Tempting Spirit laughs and says: 'From this it follows that you are lost in a vicious circle.' – *Yes*, Mischievous Spirit, but *noli tangere circulos meos*. Don't disturb my vicious circles.

Poor Language

The People's Paper, 18 April 1923

No wonder it is poor when it is, poor thing, getting weaker. Some of its words have been weakening so oddly that they've become – well – good for nothing. They no longer say anything and must be supported by others. Take the word 'only', for instance. In days of yore, in the age of Duke Přemysl, it was still possible to see a shop window with an inscription: 'A metre for only thirty-five crowns'. Today this must be written: 'A metre for a bargain of only thirty-five crowns', or 'A metre for a bargain of only as little as thirty-five crowns', or 'A metre for a bargain of the amazingly low price of only as little as thirty-five crowns'. In Charles IV's times you were able to find a notice 'Special lacquer shop' above the door. Today it is written: 'Exclusively special lacquer shop', or 'The world's greatest exclusively special lacquer shop', or 'The world's greatest exclusively special lacquer shop – the ultimate in paint 'n' lacquer choice', or 'The best for less – superb money-saving special offers for astonishingly low prices: buy one get three free for only . . . !' It's not enough to say 'pure honey', but at least 'one hundred per cent pure and exclusively genuine, smooth, luxurious, exquisitely delicate and rich in taste, the finest premium quality, reliable, solely original bee-collected & wholly meadow organic produce obtained from carefully selected organic plants, the best ever extracted, simply irresistible, natural granulating process legally guaranteed, first-class health-certified & patented, registered trademark, absolutely natural and intrinsically pure special honey'. Otherwise we don't believe it.

From National Customs

The People's Paper, 3 August 1923; Nos 4 and 6: 8 August; Nos 13 and 14: 14 October

To start with a definition: national customs have, to all intents and purposes, only one function – that they should be performed. At times they are combined with a modicum of entertainment. Typical national customs are constructing a may-pole, throwing a corn-dolly into the river, overeating on feast days, and the like. These are collective national traditions. Besides, there are national family customs, such as lighting consecrated candles, collecting horse-shoes for good luck, or making the home spick-and-span before Christmas and Easter. Ethnography has so far paid scant attention to the national customs that people perform in their closest circle, that is, just for themselves. I should like to devote some space and study to these neglected yet widespread practices.

(4) Worshipping one man

This custom is rather enigmatic. We must presuppose that once upon a time there existed an impeccable male personage who turned up punctually and reliably whenever required. He rose to his feet in an especially prompt and ceremonial manner, that hasn't even now evaporated from people's memories, and in every other respect behaved in a downright exemplary way. Nothing else is known about this man, neither his name, nor even the era in which he lived – he is simply referred to as 'one man'. His bright example has been remembered to this very day, whenever it's said: 'everyone came together as one man', for instance, or 'the assembly rose to their feet as one man', or 'the crowd began to march as one man'. Actually, it's good that we don't know his name. It sounds more urgent and cryptic than if we said: 'everyone came together as Václav Říha', or 'the assembly rose to its feet as František Šedivý'. I suggest that a monument be erected to One Man. I hope you'll agree as one man.

(6) What is blessed

Two things have remained blessed even in our secular century: 'marrow and fatness' and old age. Marriage, for example, is no longer blessed, even though it's just as unpleasant. At best it's blessed with children. The fact that you can be blessed with marrow and fatness is perhaps an atavism from cannibalistic times. The blessed old age is the one when people die. 'He shuffled off this mortal coil, having been blessed with eighty years.' So the four years of age when he got his first trousers wasn't in any way blessed, nor was the fourteen years of age when he fell in love for the first time, nor was a much later age when he was, at least partly, brought to his senses. It's tragic that you can reach a blessed age only by dying. That's a bit late for a blessing.

(13) Put a question

This is a practical trick for conquering a question, because the moment you put a question, it can't defend itself. It's as if you put a boxer on the ropes or on the canvas, or even tied him up and started beating him. In reality no real topical question can be pinned down or expected to keep still or stand in a particular way. It runs around the world, twists and turns, and has hundreds of shapes and uses. Instead, we drag a stuffed dummy into the ring, which resembles a question a bit, though it's filled with sawdust, and then we put this lump in place of the question and that's it.

Think I'm playing with words? If the majority of questions weren't just stuffed dummies, the majority of our answers and solutions wouldn't be so futile.

(14) Take the floor

I'm probably just being deluded by usage here, but when I read that someone 'has taken the floor', I like to imagine that he has taken it as if he were taking pity on an orphan, so generously and selflessly. I like to imagine that the floor was ill-treated or oppressed or forgotten, and so this particular person got up and said: 'For goodness sake, my good souls, please be kind, I don't know how to put it, but here is a floor that lies between us like a little beggar, and none of the speakers has bent down to help it, so I wanted, you see, to ask you to take pity on it.' Hereupon he would take that orphanly, down-trodden, universally forgotten floor and pity it with the word 'love', for example, or 'let's forgive one another everything', or 'after all we're fellow beings' – words that are truly under-represented at political meetings and general assemblies where people 'take the floor'. But this is definitely not a national custom.

A Handful of Sayings

The People's Paper, 30 May 1929

A little bird told me is often said about news and rumours. A little bird apparently tells someone that a certain lady is two-timing, or a government minister is in a jam about something unmentionable, or that something has gone altogether wrong with someone else. It's usually public secrets, official indiscretions and social scandals that a little bird tells us about.

Now, I pay considerable attention to what birds chatter about. For the most part, they tell you things quite publicly, they shout them from the rooftops as loudly as builders on building sites, yet, I swear to God, they chatter about bird matters and never, never, I can assure you, do they meddle in human affairs. I've never caught them telling other birds in a self-important way about things that are absolutely none of their business, for example, the private lives of neighbourhood ladies. Their tweets never relate to politics; they don't swap stories about what's rumoured to have happened, or may happen, in the next few days. It's true, though, that they swap chirrups, they even whoop, shriek, quarrel and fight, but I'm damned if they gossip. Gossip is for the press and pressure groups, but not for birds. A little bird is better than its alleged reputation: chirping away, it tells us none of the things that hearsay ascribes to it. Only humans tell others about things that don't concern them or they know nothing about.

Every schoolchild knows that. I heard this from a motorist when I confessed that I wasn't exactly sure what a cardan shaft was. Since then I have looked upon every schoolchild with a sense of awe as upon a creature who knows what a cardan shaft is. When many years back I didn't know what a cosine was or when Charles VI reigned, my headmasters told me reproachfully that surely every schoolchild knew that. The other day I even read in a national-economy feature that today every schoolchild knows whatever there is to know about the gold standard and preferential customs duty. These children, dear friends, are wondrous prodigies: they are omniscient. What every child knows, according to the assertions of us adults, would, if it were collected, make for a pretty decent fourteen-volume encyclopaedia. If a single adult knew everything that every schoolchild knows, he'd be unbearable. He'd be just bursting with information and erudition. It's easier with children. Every child may know what a cardan shaft is and that bimetallism is an outdated system. But it doesn't flaunt this fact so that the rest of us have to notice it.

Like a dog with two tails. If someone feels very proud about something in private, or among a small circle of his friends and opponents, that's his business. But if he does it publicly at a representative meeting of the Dog Association or at a national congress of the Political Party of Dogs, that's quite another matter – his two tails acquire a broader significance, and he speaks roughly along these lines: 'Ladies and gentlemen, as you know, a dog's tail – our tail – surpasses all the other tails. Only our tail is capable of splitting in two, in a flash of ebonite lightning, thus producing electricity, radio, and global progress. And what do we get for this magnificent tail? Sheer ingratitude, and no recognition. (*A storm of approval.*) No other animal in the world is treated as brutally as dogs are. (*Hear! Hear!*) We are told that the lion, who always gets the lion's share of everything, is king of beasts, though his tail has no electric qualities. Even the fox is better off than we are, though he wags his tail uselessly and inefficiently. (*Voices: Away with foxes!*) Sleeping in a comfortable manger is denied to us on the pretext that horses need to eat. (*Shame!*) We want our tails to be granted the status they deserve. (*Applause.*) So far we dogs have faced many injustices and insults, but all dogs will now realise their leading mission and will move forward with their tails in front.' (*Frenetic approval and cheers.*)

Against Little Goose Legs

The People's Paper, 1 November 1930

Just to forestall any misunderstanding – I don't mean to raise serious objections to little goose legs, sometimes sold as giblets or part of a gosling, but to the little goose legs called inverted commas, or quotation marks. As is well known from grammar, inverted commas should serve to 'indicate direct speech'. Unlike grammar, however, inverted commas have adopted the habit of indicating speech that is very indirect, not to say sneaky. There are papers that can't write about socialists, but only about 'socialists'; some others don't know of humanity, just 'humanity'; there are journalists who would never in a million years be able to put down the word pacifism, but only 'pacifism'. It's such an enigmatic knack. Once you've put inverted commas around pacifism, it becomes suspect, as if it were fake or a cock-up. You don't need proof for any of this, little goose legs are enough, so there! The moment you enclose humanity within inverted commas, it dawns on the reader that it's some kind of falsity or perversion, even a conspiracy. In this way 'humanity' is undermined, and exempted from all possible justification.

So this is what's unpleasant about these popular little goose legs. We can devalue everything with them, without having to exert ourselves or concoct something approaching plausible criticism. It is as if we had spat on someone's coat and took a perverse pleasure in the fact that the person was running around with spit on his clothes. If I write that Mr Novotný or Mr Kratochvíl is a 'butcher', presumably it means something indefinite yet incriminating: that he may not really be a butcher, or that he's a bad butcher, or that his butchery is suffused with a shameful overtone – simply it calls for physical violence. Suppose a compositor, used to setting up newsprint, had turned his hand to the Bible and printed:

In the beginning God 'created' the heaven and the earth.

Thou shalt 'love' thy 'neighbour' . . .

'Honour' thy father and thy mother . . .

And so on. I think your stomach would churn at the destructive power of the little goose legs. They are just tiny little lines, but they can turn all the values of life upside down. They can make Žižka into a 'hero',[1] and every virtue into hypocrisy; they can deny and devalue anything without the writer's having to pause even for a second and ask himself what he in fact wants to say. Keep a sharp lookout for little goose legs: if they don't introduce direct speech, they usually introduce some foulness. Sometimes I have fits of cruelty. For example, I wish that every journalist who has committed little goose legs 144 times should be tattooed with indelible inverted commas on his forehead. With others, I'd have a question mark in brackets burnt into their foreheads, as that is also considered to be an innocuous (?) means of public polemic. But I'm afraid that government minister Meissner will not incorporate these punishments into his new press law. Consequently these dirty little goose legs will carry on treading the Czech leas and groves and, believe me, will do more harm yet than those historical hooves beneath which no grass grew.[2]

About the Verb to Want

The People's Paper, 12 April 1931

I was peeping over the masons' shoulders as they were building a wall from solid stone. Naturally I was also interfering, asking them how many kids they had, what their world-views were and suchlike, but I was really all eyes to find out how stone walls are built and what needs to be done while making them.

'Damn it,' said the younger and more skilful one when, with the help of a bricklayer's mate, he put a new stone on the top, 'it don't want to sit here.'

'Some 'tother will,' said the gaffer with a pipe, and paused to think over the heap of coarse stones. 'Maybe this one'll sit there.' And so he picked it up to comply with its will and put it in an appropriate place.

'This one wants to sit here,' volunteered the first chap, 'but it has a bum on 'tother side. Turn it over, it wants to sit on its bum.'

So it came to pass and the stone was seated on its bum as was its hidden will.

'Okey-doke,' said the mason, 'but this paunch wants out.' So he took a chisel and chipped off the paunch that wanted out. And then the stone fell in its place, for which it felt destined, it fell there firmly, comfortably and with a look of evident gratification. And so it went on, stone after stone, and every block fitted in the right place where it wanted to be and to persist with so to speak stony immovability. And so I found that for a stone wall to come into being, it is necessary to fulfil the thousandfold will of the stones that want to become a firm, unbreakable wall.

That verb 'to want' is not, however, a masons' monopoly. To people working with wood, this plank wants to be a bit shorter and this batten wants a bit of filing here; with woodcutters, the tree wants to fall to this side, not to the other where it would destroy the undergrowth; with tailors, this coat wants taking in, and so on. Every kind of work with matter reveals that things have not only their own independent existence, but their own will, which it is desirable to satisfy, for I can assure you that only then good, durable work, properly serving its purpose, can be accomplished.

Well, you can explain this mode of expression variously, as philosophical voluntarism, or primordial animism, but I think that it testifies to something else, I mean to a certain optimism flourishing among us despite all difficulties and miseries. It is trust that a stone is willing to lie in such a way so as to become a good serving part of the wall, and isn't possessed by a mean will to wobble or stick out of line or in some other way rebel against the human attempt to turn it into a chunk of masonry. If a coat, as tailors say, wants to be taken in a bit, it implies that the coat itself doesn't mean to chafe the person's armpits or make life difficult for him in any way, but to fit like a glove and add comeliness to his figure. The coat has a good, complaisant will towards man. The tree that is being felled doesn't want to crush the undergrowth, but wants to fall down dextrously and harmlessly. It would be horribly pessimistic if woodcutters expected that it wanted to fall right on the other young trees and nowhere else. A tacit premise of all human work is that matter really wants to be what is made of it, and that it wants it fully and, if possible, purposefully.

Only in human affairs do we not have the optimistic trust in the objective good will of things. We don't say, for example, that customs duties want to be reduced or that sugar wants to be cheaper. About these things we only quarrel. They alone don't speak to us.

In the Grip of Words

The People's Paper, 6 December 1933

Cliché. A cliché is defined as a stereotyped saying, but when someone greets us with a stereotyped saying like 'Good evening', we don't denounce him as a cliché-monger. Many of our utterances in everyday life are complete commonplaces. The sentences 'I have a headache' or 'The days are drawing in' have been said zillions of times, and yet they are not clichés. The people's speech mostly consists of sayings that are perfectly stereotyped; even so the people don't speak clichés, at least not among themselves and not about things they know very well. There must be something false, something untrue and spurious about a stereotyped saying for it to become a cliché. A cliché is always a bit of a lie. It is not a stereotyped saying but stereotyped lying. A cliché is habitual and mechanised dishonesty.

Hyperbole. It is characteristic of clichés and hackneyed expressions that they nearly always contain hyperbole. A simple, matter-of-fact, sincerely meant utterance can't become a cliché even if it were reeled off by millions of mouths a day. Even the greatest gasbag can't turn the sentence that someone's aunt has died into a cliché. But a gasbag doesn't say this; rather, he announces that the Grim Reaper has snatched his much-loved relative away. A gasbag doesn't say that people are fed up with taxes, but that our people groan under the burden of unbearable taxation. A cliché's hallmark is to exaggerate and embellish everything that enters its mouth. For that reason the structure of a cliché is chiefly attributive: it is mostly made from adjectives. The word 'peasant' is a bare, I'd say, honest, fact. Just add 'our', 'Czech', 'our sturdy', 'our class-conscious' peasant, and you have a cliché sound as a bell. 'Enemy' means something so definite, soldierly and no-nonsense that the word is scarcely used in civilian life. It's necessary to say a 'cowardly', 'despicable' or 'sworn' enemy, it must be larded with adjectival emphasis so that the word can lose its clear blade and be thrown around like a verbal dummy.

The philosophy of the cliché. The cliché has a special logical place among assertions and utterances. Above all, it doesn't count on being taken literally. If our people groan under the burden of taxes, it's not meant to suggest that we can hear tax-payers wailing and whining and sobbing in the streets. Since a cliché is presented as a more or less figurative expression, it possesses a priori a kind of mental alibi: it escapes the control of having to correspond to facts. But a real cliché is time-worn, pedestrian and unambiguous. It has no claim to aesthetic quality, and cannot be mistaken for a creative fiction or a product of fantasy. It is neither an expression of reality nor a display of imagination, then. It is unreal and yet without invention; it springs neither from reality nor from spirit, but counterfeits both with mere words.

So you see that as a verbal mechanism, a stock phrase, a more or less affected exaggeration and a lexical decoration, a cliché has nothing to do with the seeking, critical formulating and conveying of experiences and knowledge. But the worst thing is that it is not a conscious, deliberate lie. It's impossible to refute a cliché as you can a wrong idea or untruth. It's beyond truth and falsehood. No logical deceit, no absurdity, corrupts human thinking so much as a cliché. It is impossible to convince a cliché-monger because he lies unwittingly, he is himself deceived by the words that he takes for things. If a man hears or reads thousands of times that we have a sworn enemy and today's world is useless, he no longer needs any proof of that, just as there is no need to prove that Palacký's Bridge is Palacký's Bridge. A certain collocation of words becomes a habit, and so a conviction too.

In the spiritual economy, a cliché really has the function of a substitute. It is a cover-up for education, thinking, opinion, interest, feeling, knowledge, conviction, faith: it is a fundamental faking of all spiritual values. But unlike the faking of food, it is a legal activity – indeed a respected one. Not infrequently it is taught at schools, and hallowed at political meetings, and, since the invention of printing and the rotary press, it has become the object of industrial mass production.

The morality of the cliché. The cliché is blamed for spoiling language and style. While this may be true, its destructive power is much more profound. The cliché blurs the difference between truth and untruth. If it were not for clichés, there wouldn't be demagogues and public lies, and it wouldn't be so easy to play politics, starting with rhetoric and ending with genocide.

About the Word Robot

The People's Paper, 24 December 1933

Prof. Chudoba's[1] mention of how, according to the *OED*, the word 'robot' and its derivatives caught on in English reminds me of an old debt. For the author of the play *RUR* didn't think it up; he only brought it to life. This is what happened. At an unguarded moment the author came up with a subject for a play. So while it was hot, he ran to his brother Josef, an artist, who was just standing by a ladder, painting away, his hand whizzing over the canvas.

'Hey, Josef,' the author started, 'I've had an idea for a play.'

'What sort?' muttered the painter (he really muttered because he was holding a brush in his mouth).

The author told him, being as concise as possible.

'Write it then,' advised the painter without taking the brush out of his mouth or pausing in splashing the canvas with paint. It was almost insultingly indifferent.

'But I don't know what to call those artificial workers,' the author said. 'I'd call them laborators, but it seems to me somewhat stilted.'

'Call them robots then,'[2] murmured the painter with a brush in his mouth, and proceeded with his painting. And that was it. This was the way the word 'robot' was born. So let it be attributed to its true originator.

About But-people

The People's Paper, 30 December 1934

But-people are a separate species who greet whatever they encounter with 'but'. They always have some reservations at hand. Their speech is neither 'aye, aye' nor 'nay, nay', but 'yes, but' or 'no, but'. If you tell them that two twos are four, they will promptly reply with a certain superiority: 'Yes, *but*, my friend, two threes are six.' Whereupon they leave you, feeling satisfied that they didn't yield any point, and that they put your statement, and you, right, so to speak. If you sigh that the days are, thank God, drawing out, they'll object: 'Yes, but this will not make our economic misery any better.' If, for some pressing reasons, you expressed your indignation at the fact that Tom was a thief and a rotter, they would reply: 'Yes, but Dick and Harry are no better.' And so on.

As is well known from grammar, 'but' is an adversative conjunction. But-people neither refute nor deny anything, they only take up the position of an adversary. They show a kind of adverse resistance to every idea. They are by nature poor conductors, so the passing spark of communication disappears in them. They don't deny that two twos are four, they only make you feel that it doesn't much matter, that you can stuff your four, and that there are more important facts in the world – that two threes are six, for example. If you dragged a drowning child out of water before their eyes, they wouldn't tell you that you shouldn't have done it. Rather, they'd say that you acted correctly, but that three hundred – or whatever – passengers drowned on board the *Principessa Mafalda*, and no one had rescued them – or something along those lines. You can help a poor person, but mind you, they'd say, that still doesn't solve the social issue. In short, you can't do anything, or even utter anything, without having a potential 'but' hovering over you. That's what we have but-people for – they always know better, they always think of something that the situation in hand excludes or fails to take account of, and so can be reproachfully pointed out as a defect, an incompleteness and an erroneous solution.

To be a but-person has its advantages:

1. A sense of intellectual superiority with which we correct the action and knowledge of our fellow beings and put them in their place.
2. A favourable opportunity to do nothing, to be preoccupied only with taking up our own position and raising our objections, and in doing so, boosting our ego, as it were.
3. And finally, a deep satisfaction that this way we can most successfully annoy other people.

This crucial 'but' is for the most part an intellectual disease. A simple person is concerned with things rather than taking up positions on them; he doesn't try to distinguish himself from others by making objections or emphasising his specific viewpoint.

That's why intellectuals lose out when it comes to common matters – for all their cavils they become incapable of a simple, decisive 'yes' or 'no'. For them, all necessary truths always have 'buts' hanging over them, and that ties their hands. This is the reason why truths often get lost in public life and something infinitely more primitive takes their place, I mean slogans.

But-people diminish everything they touch; they are left with just their 'but'. God save us from but-people!

If I Were a Linguist

The Word and The World of Letters, February 1935

If I were a linguist, I'd probably do the same thing as linguists have been doing from time immemorial: I would listen carefully to how people speak, and wouldn't stop pondering about it until I managed to detect some general rules, laws, classes and systems in words and collocations, sentences and cadences. I don't think, however, that I'd be able to abstract language from people and imagine speech as a pure linguistic phenomenon. Rather, I'd see it as a manifestation of particular people, human professions, types, groups, cultures, and come to that, particular world-views. I know that this approach is in no way new, but I maintain that linguistically we haven't as yet got so far as to be able to use the analyses and critiques of speech for an analysis and critique of people and their imaginings, ideas, opinions, social attitudes, cultural and political schemes, and the like.

Supposing that it was possible to investigate how education, social status and group allegiance affect the number of generalising words that crop up in speech, and further, what kind of social and political outlook corresponds to the ability or inclination to use broad, vague words. The political behaviour of a person who thinks and expresses himself in down-to-earth images will surely be different from that of a person who thinks in loose terms – no doubt there will be more generalisations, more radicalism, more intolerance on this side. It would be important to study what sort of people have a fondness for using words of foreign provenance that they don't understand well, or big words that lack precise contours; what disorder of the human spirit, what social derangement, what inner uncertainty this linguistic incidence reflects. Gorky's barefooted peasant who has become intoxicated with the word 'organism' is now a collective phenomenon; in politics, too, a man like that will undoubtedly follow big, vague words, enchanted by their resonance.

It would be conceivable to arrive at a diagnostics of demagogy through linguistic analysis. It would doubtless be found that speech-wise, demagogy must be at once demonstrative and, if possible, imprecise; it must enter people's heads easily, but mustn't cling to facts, so that it is easy to subsume many diverse perspectives, interests and imaginings under its formulations. Its distinctive means are equivocation, emotionalism, the changing of ideas into hackneyed slogans, and rapid dynamics that carry listeners or readers over blatant obscurities or inconsistencies.

Linguistic analysis would further be able to bring out the profound difference between the imperative and the persuasive linguistic systems: in other words, between the language of dictators and the language of democracy. It's enough to turn the button on the radio and listen to the voices of states and their representatives. It's possible to judge, purely linguistically, how the diction, syntactical constructions and presentation give rise to the manifestation of authority, power, mass pathos, will and decisiveness, or, by contrast, to the manifestation of public musing, argumentation and persuasion, which more or less chimes with the parliamentarian system. Analysing authoritative and parliamentarian styles, we would see, with considerable precision, what kind of intellectual qualities and human and social aspects a particular regime turns to, hinges on and assumes.

This linguistics of public utterances would inevitably become social criticism: not in the sense of evaluation but spiritual diagnostics. Disclosing the disorders, abuses, incoherencies and imprecisions of expression, it would lead to the recognition of similar flaws in social thinking. I have no doubt that sooner or later linguistics will evolve into this kind of diagnostics. For human speech is just such an immediate and unmistakable intimation of our spiritual life as heartbeat and metabolism are the signs of our body's viability.

About Two Types of Agent

The People's Paper, 9 May 1937

There is one sub-species of human being (and almost all of us belong to it) that possesses a special and inexhaustible aptitude – namely, a talent for saying what should be done. The state should do this or that, and we'd be out of the wood. Financial means should be found. Such-and-such a thing should be introduced into our schools. The town council should . . . Writers should . . . Parliament should . . . The public should be influenced in a particular respect. All people who want rectification should unite. This should be strictly prosecuted. There should be a law against it. The papers should pay more attention to . . . The theatre should . . . This should be built. There should be enough money for that, et cetera, et cetera.

Characteristic of this 'it-should-be-done' entrepreneurship is that:

1. it's used for proposing things that are by and large good, beneficial, urgent and in the public interest, and could be carried out in the twinkling of an eye and at the drop of a hat, if the executive had enough enterprise, energy and good will;
2. it concerns things that can and ought to be effected by someone else than the proposer, and that lie beyond his personal

effort and control. No one comes up with a suggestion as to what he himself should do to put things right; no one says that his profession or department or kind of chap should do this or that in the public interest. What should be done is always someone else's responsibility. Our reforming fantasy works most exuberantly when it can assign reforms to someone else. The thing would lose its lustre the moment it dawned on us that we alone should turn our hand to it.

The other sub-species of human being (that almost all of us belong to) is exactly the opposite. They like to raise difficulties. The long and the short of it is, such-and-such a thing is not so easy. You have no inkling what technical hurdles it would meet with. It's just not possible. It would have its darker side. Impossible in today's state of affairs. It would be great, but in practice it's unfeasible. There wouldn't be the resources to cover the costs. You can't change the whole set-up just like that. Administrative or other problems. As it stands, we can't even meet our own targets, et cetera, et cetera. Characteristic of this kind of protest is that:

1. the objections are practical and matter-of-fact, falling back on long-term experience and taking into account so-called realism;
2. they are used only when something is delegated to us, or to our department or profession. No one insists that the thing isn't so easy if it concerns other sectors, but in our own domain we are adamant that nothing can be done to remedy the situation. Here it's simply impossible, but of course in someone else's bailiwick it could be done . . .

So the two kinds of people complement one another perfectly and harmoniously. For each 'it-should-be-done', an 'it's-not-so-easy' objection lurks in the womb of possibilities. The interplay and balance between the two ensure the permanence of phenomena: all sorts of new stuff should come about, but because it's not so easy we'll carry on making a botch of things. It's pleasant to suggest what the public interest demands, but equally pleasant to put it securely out of reach.

Nevertheless, if something new is to get done now and again, or something amiss remedied . . .

In short, we need more people who say 'I should or we should . . .', as well as more who prefer to say: 'Dash it all, it's not easy, but we can try; it's in our own backyard and we won't be afraid of it.'

So this should be done . . . But I know it's not so easy.

From A Few Idioms

The People's Paper, Nos 1 and 5: 16 January 1938, Nos 7, 9 , 10 and 12: 23 January 1938

1. *The time is serious.* Or the situation is extremely serious. This idiom is generally used when things have already gone to the dogs. A tacit and curious assumption behind this is that times that don't overflow with misery can't somehow achieve a correct level of seriousness. For example, the time is serious when millions of people are unemployed; on the other hand, a state of affairs when everyone does something useful by the sweat of their brows is presumably deemed to be insufficiently serious – as if human creatures worked and earned their living out of sheer exuberance and light-heartedness. Or a serious time is when there's a general expectation that the first aerial bombardment is about to hit some city or other; on the other hand, it's not considered to be quite serious when houses are being built for people, when they are being born or living out their old age, when they are producing or creating something, when they are getting to know about things, and so on. I'd say that all these activities are very serious, even more serious than smashing something up or sending someone to kingdom come, whereas the times that are termed serious disrupt and devastate the great and constant seriousness of human life. What's characteristic of serious times is that they usually

terribly degrade life. Serious times are the ones that turn the world into a desert. Are you saying that the time is serious? Well, something insane must be happening to the world.

5. *To ensure peace*, it's often necessary to increase armaments on land, at sea and in the air. What can be done? That's how things are. But imagine it being equally common and matter-of-course to say: in order to ensure harmonious co-existence in our office, I'll take a loaded revolver with me. To secure quiet in our street, I'll stuff my pockets with grenades. It would be a bizarre world. It is a bizarre world.

7. *To deliver a speech* pertains only to statesmen. It's not written in the Bible, for instance, that Jesus delivered a speech on a desert place near the city Bethsaida, but that he spoke, answered and taught. It's not written that he delivered something, but said something. Likewise God, as far as I know, doesn't deliver speeches; at best, he delivers us from evil. It's necessary to become a government minister at least to be able to deliver speeches.

9. *Tense relations* – one of those turns of phrase that cannot be replaced with the active voice of a verb. You can say that the relations between two states are extremely tense, but you can never say that someone has taken extreme pains to tense relations. The best you can say, without resorting to a personal agent, is that international relations have darkened, just as we say that the sky has dimmed or the illness has deteriorated. From this it's clear that we still regard politics, especially high politics, as something independent of human agency, just like natural phenomena and disasters.

10. *To recognise*, or not to recognise, is a magic word that can turn non-being into being and being into non-being. For example, some state or other can declare that it doesn't recognise the Chinese government, at which point there is no Chinese government, China doesn't belong to anyone, and it's permissible to kill the Chinese without scruple.

However, let me draw attention to the fact that only governments and states are allowed to use this power-word.

If any of you took it into your head that you didn't recognise the board of directors of the Živnobank, and so could enter its nearest branch, shoot the cashiers dead and empty the tills, you'd most probably be condemned as a bandit. In the international field it's not really seen like that.

12. *Power interests* are among the most successful terms of international politics. They have only one flaw. That they can be neither defined nor restrained.

III
ENGLAND

I Want to Sit Down

The People's Paper, 23 September 1924

A woman has written to me that she would like me to say something more about England. Just imagine! OK then, if need be, but let me sit down first. If you're supposed to write or talk, you must sit. Right, now in England . . .

Forgive me, but this chair is too high and uncomfortable. If you're supposed to talk well and think well, you must sit well. I'll start in a sec, just as soon as I've changed my seat. Well, note, then, that the English . . .

Damn it, how am I supposed to sit on this? This back chafes my spine, it's hard, and it has an edge here, and this whatsit seems to be here just to make your shoulder blades calloused, doesn't it? I'd rather stand if I may. What was it I wanted to say? Oh yes, note, then, that the English are the nation that can sit best and most comfortably. A fundamental portion of their culture resides in that. Perhaps that's why they write so well, because they sit well while they're doing it. Their prudence, probity and hospitality and other exquisite qualities have decidedly been sat through. It's only after they've eaten that they go and sit really properly; for that they have *sitting rooms*, or rooms for sitting down in, and *lounges*, or rooms for lolling around in and snatching forty winks. They are of a settled disposition, because they settle back well in their seats. They have such low, wide, well-worn easy chairs, quite shabby, but immensely willing. Each part of your body settles into them as if into the palm of a hand, you sprawl your legs out in front of you, lean your head against the back, and put your hands here on the arm-rests, and now, bliss, you sit and you're conscious that you're safe and that nothing will poke you between the ribs with its treacherous edge, and so you indulge yourself in mild and magnanimous thoughts, and sometimes you even say something, something that is quiet, and stuffed with scandal-free humour like a good old armchair, something that won't stab anyone in the back, or cause them to feel that they're sitting on pins. Oh no, these aren't leather club-armchairs, nor are they architectural thrones, or monumental sarcophagi, or carved settles – nor a sofa, nor a prie-dieu, nor a plush divan, but a kind of little den for just one person, who stretches out a bit in all directions. It is styled for sitting and has the shape of a man's shoulders, short legs and a high back over which the good spirits of comfort, fantasy and inspiration hover. And there is one even in the poorest household. It seems to be at once the badge and the emblem of England.

By contrast anyone who's forced to lower himself onto a high, spiky, edgy, unfriendly and, simply, Central European chair becomes an irascible, discontented, peevish, grumbling, cross and impatient Central European. He can't write good, wise novels, for novels must be sat on till they hatch. He doesn't arrive at tidy opinions or trustfulness, but on the contrary at sour, resentful thinking.

In Italy, on the other hand, the very climate prompts you either to lie on your back or drift around and aerate yourself standing on your legs. That's why poetry has flourished there, and especially painting, which is produced while standing. The English have never been great artists, because it's impossible to paint well or chisel sculptures sitting by the fire, whereas novels, parliamentarianism, philosophy and history are done by and large sitting down, but it must be really good sitting.

Besides, in Italy and France it's possible to sit on cathedral steps, on thresholds and on the plinths of statues, or you can sit there in pavement cafes. But you don't sit just to sit, but to look around and have a good time, and eye up the girls and altogether enjoy life. The real, fundamental, deep, thorough and perfect sitting has evolved only in England.

So I want to sit down, but here God knows we somehow aren't equipped to do it like that. We aren't respectful and attentive enough to sitting, because we aren't respectful and attentive enough to things you do while sitting. While sitting, you keep silent, or think, or talk just a bit and without agitation. If you want to curse and lament, you stand or run all over the place. But while sitting, you cultivate conservative and social virtues in yourself. Traditions, too, live sitting comfortably at home. Family life is simply a sitting-together.

Now and then you still find an old easy chair in which it's sweet to sit. But what our designers and cabinet-makers fabricate is likely to be inspired by covert hatred of the peaceful, settled values of life. It's simply impossible to sit in it. If we want to have a rest, we just have to go and sleep. But we aren't allowed to rest with a book in our hands or talking to our fellow creatures. Indeed, life is hard on us, even when it comes to sitting down.

About England

A talk for British radio, *The Present*, 15 December 1927; broadcast by the BBC 12 December 1927

There are people who'd be prepared to travel to Tibet to lecture the Tibetans about their country, its natural conditions, Tibetan mores and religion, woman's status in Tibet, and what have you. There are people, like Mr G. B. Shaw, who are willing to deliver a talk to doctors about what medicine is. For my part, I confess that I don't feel competent to tell the English what England is. I take it they might know themselves, not so much because they live in England as because they often travel outside England. An Englishman living in England, like Mr Pickwick, may imagine that he lives in Europe, or more generally, in the world. An Englishman who takes a trip across the Channel, however, may come to the reliable conclusion that England is an island, more still, that England is a different continent, even more, that England is another planet. If the travelling Englishman doesn't recognise this secret, it's presumably because he stays in England all the time even when he happens to be somewhere else, say Naples or Tibet. I myself first entered England not at Folkestone, but in Perugia. One of my friends has been to England only once, in Spanish Granada. England is not just a certain territory;

England is a particular environment habitually surrounding Englishmen.

So even if it seems obvious to the voyager that on stepping onto English ground he has alighted on another planet, where there are different creatures, different customs, different meals, and even different chimneys, still, he may notice that in historical times this strange planet probably had fairly close relations with our continent. He finds almost everything there that he meets with on the continent, yet everything slightly differs. For example, he observes that trains run on the track as they do in Europe, but – if he watches carefully – he finds to his astonishment that there is no guard with a little flag standing by the rails at every kilometre. So the traveller makes the discovery that English rails are on the whole unprotected, and that there must be a national mystical belief that it isn't necessary to safeguard the tracks. It seems that the European view that man is by nature inclined to tear up railway tracks or blow up trains hasn't caught on in England. So as early as between Folkestone and London, the newcomer makes the first fantastic English discovery that England has a kind of audacious local tradition – that is, trust in man.

The second discovery that the traveller makes is trees. Nowhere else are so many big old trees as in England. At first the foreigner isn't sure whether the English live in trees, or whether they worship them in a pagan way on moonlit nights, performing ritual druid dances around them. But because they do neither of the two, the traveller comes to understand that England has so many old trees because the English like old things. They like old trees, old walls, old customs, old ways, even old people. They like aristocracy because it's old; they like democracy because it's even older; they like the family because it's the oldest of all. So the voyager realises that in England there's something immeasurably alive – I mean, tradition.

Another discovery is, of course, English lawns, not only because they are thicker and more beautiful than in our world, but mainly because one is allowed to walk on them without getting a scolding from an owner or a watchman. When I first set foot on English grass – it was in Hampton Court – initially I had the feeling that I was doing something forbidden. Only later was I overcome with a sense of unrestrained freedom, that I could just follow my nose. Earlier on I imagined freedom somewhat vaguely as a woman with a Phrygian cap, waving a flag of sorts. Since my visit to England, I've known that freedom is a green lawn *without* a notice saying 'Keep off the grass'. If England isn't, despite all this, a country of paradisal liberty, it's without doubt only because there are other things besides green lawns there. I take it that when God expelled the English Adam from the garden of Eden, he didn't have a tablet hung on the gate of paradise, saying 'No entry', but simply one announcing 'Private property', which didn't prevent the English Adam from going and spending a weekend there with his family, and the Lord didn't mind, silently letting them do it. 'He's an Englishman,' he probably said to himself, 'and so is used to this kind of freedom; not to worry – he won't do any damage to the place.'

Another of the foreigner's findings is Hyde Park, more precisely its speakers. Anyone on whom the Holy Ghost descends can stand there and preach, sing, flourish their arms and enunciate a faith without the passers-by bursting out laughing, or the nearest constable trying to calm them down and pack them off home. To an outsider, it's not only an unusual spectacle, but also an unusual experience, as he sees a constable listening peacefully to a communist agitator, or a gentleman in a top hat engaged in a serious discussion with a ragged enthusiast, or a Catholic disseminating the truth of his faith alongside a Calvinist, or a supporter of a free market alongside an advocate of customs duties. Beholding all these wondrous phenomena in Hyde Park, the foreigner shakes his head in amazement, asking what to call it: freedom, or equality, or tolerance?

A further result of exploration is – wait a minute – is marbles. Not marbles as such, but the great unwritten law that only graduates can play it on the steps of the degree-ceremony hall in Cambridge, but not undergraduates. I believe firmly that there hasn't so far been a single criminal undergraduate who has tried to play on those steps. I strongly suspect that the English play their games of marbles everywhere: at home as well as in clubs, in sport as well as in parliament; that they have lots of unwritten laws and rules, carefully observed, in life and conduct. I'm convinced that all these games of marbles had and have two decisive influences on English life: first and foremost, they promote geniality, or if you like, a sense of playfulness, and second, a sense of loyalty.

I could enumerate many other things that a stranger finds in England, but to finish with something that is at this moment probably closest to the listeners of this broadcast, I'll say that apart from all these other peculiarities, the newcomer discovers English easy chairs. I'm telling you that nowhere else in the world are they so comfortable, broad and low as in England. It doesn't follow, though, that the English supremely value easy chairs. Rather, they supremely value people, so the comfort of a human being isn't the last and the lowest ideal for them. A person in an easy chair is, to a degree, a person on a throne; he is a king who no longer fights, but just enjoys his dignity. When a foreigner sees English easy chairs he doesn't think that Great Britain is a big empire, but that England is a comfortable home. But perhaps this is exactly the great political secret: perhaps we must first create comfortable homes before we can found and maintain empires. But since I haven't been in *all* English households, I conclude with undiscovered things – consider those yourself.

England from the Outside

Written for the *Spectator*, *The Present*, 5 December 1934

Two or three times already I've been honoured by the invitation to tell the English about how a foreigner views them. So I'm tempted to repeat what I've already written about the matter two or three times. But as far as I know only scholars are allowed to repeat what they've already said for the rest of their lives. I could, for example, describe again the discoveries I made in England as a wayfarer:

English insularity, which reveals itself not only geographically, but also in the manners and customs of people who were born on that island, and wherever they come, they bring their island withdrawnness and difference with them;

English traditionalism, more precisely, the worship of ancient things, like cathedrals, university towns, monarchy, aristocracy, clubs, old trees and many old and picturesque customs;

English sobriety, which, however, has its counterbalance in English fantasticality; the evidence of both these is in English literature, English humour and other institutions.

And so on; I could enumerate (for the umpteenth time) everything that to my knowledge makes the English differ from other nations, tribes and clans. But England isn't only a geographic and ethnographic reality; seen from the outside, England is in many respects something like an ideal. Or let's say more accurately, there are certain ideals that the world has more or less universally accepted and behind which it sees, more or less rightly, England as the country that has generated and multiplied these valid ideals of the educated universe. You might say that it's a mistake and that the ideals have been attributed to England by historical accident. Or you could affirm your allegiance to them as to something originally and deeply British – but then it must matter to you that, seen from the outside, England really shows herself as the hub of those ideals.

The first of the ideals that the educated world accepts as English is the ideal of a gentleman. I could cite wittier definitions about what a gentleman really is, but for practical reasons suffice it to say that a gentleman is a man we can trust. We can rely on his word, and that he will live up to his duties and commitments. If nothing else, he'll do it because he enormously respects himself. But it's not just the willingness to live up to commitments that constitutes a gentleman's character, but also the willingness to take on commitments, to stand actively and any time by the side of those who are threatened, who defend themselves against iniquity or represent the more legitimate interests in a conflict. I'd put it this way: gentlemanliness is a guarantee that things within our reach will happen as is proper. This concerns relationships between individuals as well as social relations, and ultimately, it also concerns relations between classes, nations and states. A world in which nations and countries deeply distrust one another is fearfully ungentlemanly. If one needs to be afraid of violence and iniquity, human society becomes something that does not in the least resemble a society of gentlemen. I'd say that there exists something like the mission of a gentleman in international politics: ensuring – no matter where it is – that fears of violence and iniquity subside and room is made for trust between nations and states. Given the way things look these days, the ideal of a gentleman is one of the most urgent aims of the world. Would it be possible to achieve this British ideal without the closest and most active participation of Britons?

The second of these ideals, in which we outsiders see a special expression of English temperament, is something puritanical, or it may be called probity if you like. Of all nations in the world the English judge things and deeds most according to what's fair, decent, true to God's will and, in a word, moral. More than other people, you Englishmen have a fixed idea that there is one morality and one differentiation between good and evil valid for all people. The French believe in the universality of reason and ideas; you British believe in the universality of moral principles. In today's somewhat desolate state of the world we feel the need for both beliefs. We find that it's impossible to unite nations pacifically if they aren't equipped with some common reason and common perspectives on what is decent, right, just, human and moral – if they are unable to agree on what violence is, what an attack on human freedom and dignity is, what coarse and unjustified egoism is, and so forth. Here is the second British ideal that is further from its realisation in today's climate than it has ever been, and it's an ideal that is more than any other worth enforcing perseveringly and scrupulously by all those who assume their share of responsibility for the present and future shape of the human world.

The third British ideal, to a greater or lesser extent adopted by the entire world, is democracy: not only institutional democracy, to which France made an equal contribution, but also moral democracy, which consists in respect for the individual liberty of every person. As you know, this old and famous ideal of individual liberty, freedom of faith and conviction, is today being denied or suppressed in a considerable part of Europe; and that means that a piece of Britishness, which passed into the evolution of humanity by the will of history, is also being denied and suppressed. So you can perceive the current course of things as the course of certain ideal English values; and you can't be indifferent to how they are faring. The ideal of individual liberty hampers, so it seems, another modern ideal, which is called Power. It's precisely in the name of Power that the moral freedom of man is being thrown onto the dump. Yet what power the solidarity of all free people in the world could have!

Behold, this, too, is 'England from the outside'. For England from the outside is not only foreign wayfarers' memories of the thousands of sweet and strange things they have seen in your country, but also the questioning and expectant look that the countries on the other side of the Channel fix on England. The strongest impression that a foreign wayfarer gets in England is the awareness that England is really infinitely English. Today a lot depends on the fact that in the area of universal ideals and their realisation, England herself remains infinitely and obstinately English.

About Discovering England

The People's Paper, 18 December 1937

For a long time people from the British Isles have been discovering different continents and islands, and have even made them into a kind of collection of their own. Now, in the most recent time, this state of things is, so it seems, changing: people from different continents and islands are beginning to discover England. According to my observations, books and articles whose authors describe the customs of British islanders and the idiosyncrasies of their life have patently proliferated. Little by little it's becoming generally known that no other country – perhaps with the exception of Tibet and the inner Chinese provinces – has preserved so many curious customs, national peculiarities and picturesque institutions as the *terra nebularum* on both banks of the Thames. It's certainly true that this exploration of England has enriched our image of the world with clubs and colleges, Hyde Park and the East End, the idea of a gentleman, the English-woman type, and so on. Gradually we are beginning to realise that British politics, which the indigenous people of other countries sometimes find hard to understand, belongs with the other historical oddities and traditions of the British species: that it's as consistent and irrational as the wigs of English judges and the bearskins of the royal guards.

So continental observers revel in what's special, fantastical, ancient and, to be honest, a bit funny about England. If I'm not mistaken, there are signs that a good number of English people, too, have been swept along by the general interest in the British Isles, and are beginning to discover them as well, though from quite a different side. They don't so much see what's old in England as notice what's new. Now and then in English novels the reader comes across a dark and disturbing recognition that even in England quite a few things are changing. For example, sex life has been discovered in some post-war books. Elsewhere indications of social uncertainty, or fears for the future of man, have cropped up. A different type of person is somewhat hazily, yet implacably gaining prominence, a human being resembling far less the old rosy-cheeked gentleman who plays golf and maintains a dignified silence in his club, and considers looking at everything from a purely British perspective as the highest wisdom of life. Something is changing in England; it seems that she's becoming less British. Maybe some of these discoveries will go further, insensitively, and be destructive. But maybe one day someone will discover that England has stopped being an island – and it will have to be a Briton who'll find this out.

To be being discovered only now: that's not a bad start for such an old country.

One of Many Letters

The People's Paper, 15 October 1938

This is how an unknown English woman (who at the end of her letter makes it clear that she supports the Conservative Party) writes: 'I shall not waste time on describing the shame and worthlessness that I, as an English woman, have felt for weeks. I am only asking you to put down my address and let me know one of these days what I can do, and if I can do anything at all, to help your country. The only thing I have come up with for the time being is to spend the little money I have in Czechoslovakia, or on things produced in your country, if you could tell me where I can buy them. Believe me please that I mean it sincerely, and that many of us feel as I do.'

Umpteen similar letters expressing sincere sympathy with us keep arriving especially from England, but this one differs from the others by a nice practical idea, which it would be good to notice. We would, no doubt, be happier if help weren't given to Czechoslovakia as a gift, but if it were earned by the honest work of our able, diligent hands. The wave of sympathy, which we mustn't, for all our disappointment, underestimate, could at least launch a demand for what we can produce better than any other nation, whether it's glass or embroidery, gloves or a range of other small products. And not to waste time. We must feed our people and employ their hands in the first place. Here is a possibility that would help our home industry, that means our poorest working men and women.

A Letter from Czechoslovakia

Written probably sometime in late October 1938 – unfinished and
unpublished; the original in the Prague Literary Archives

I am writing this letter to unknown readers, and I am writing it
with not a little unease. For I do not really know in which things
we still stand on common ground and in which we can still understand one another without difficulty. If, for instance, I put down
what my heart is overflowing with, I think that the British reader
would shake his head and say that some people just give free rein
to pathos. I probably wouldn't persuade him that we – I mean I and
he – have shared reasons for pity, shame, protest and disappointment, or that what has happened on Czechoslovak ground is in
large measure a part of British, as much as French and European,
fate. Recent weeks have shown that only the stronger can persuade
successfully. We were not allowed to persuade anyone even about
what the life interest of our people and state is; how can we persuade anyone, then, about what would have been or what will be
in the life interest of the British people or of European civilisation
or of true peace?

All right then, I will not try to persuade you, unknown British
reader, that what has happened is good or bad. I'd rather, with your
help, reach some certainty about what has in actual fact happened.
Indeed, it's not entirely clear. We do see the sharp, distinct lines on
the map that are called the new delimitation of the Czechoslovak
state, but that's just the outer contour of something that has so far
remained totally unexplained. To put it quite simply – and it's not
meant to be criticism or accusation, but a plain and sober pointing
out of the historical facts – the Berlin conference, with the participation of Great Britain and France, dealt with Czechoslovakia
as if it were a defeated enemy state. No one has yet explained to
us why – what the reasons were why this radical change of the
British and French stance on Czechoslovakia occurred, and why
it has been concealed from the world. Some such U-turn must
have happened because otherwise it is beyond comprehension

how the representatives of Great Britain and France could have taken over the responsibility for the particular resolutions made in Berlin. What's at issue is not that the resolutions are unfavourable to Czechoslovakia, but that these are resolutions contradicting the principles that Great Britain and France accepted as part of the solution of the so-called German Sudetenland question, the acceptance of which they also assigned to our state under the title of a sacrifice for the sake of European peace. I raise the question, which the whole Czechoslovak people are asking with horror, of why these principles have suddenly been discarded, and have been replaced by something that can hardly be called anything but *Vae victis* [Woe to the defeated].

I beg the British reader to believe me that this is no exaggeration of the actual state of affairs. The principle whereby the minority problem in Czechoslovakia should have been settled laid down that the regions with a prevailing majority of German population should be ceded to the German Reich. Now, with the consent of the British and French representatives, regions, towns and villages in which the absolute majority of population is Czech are ceded to Germany. The boundary demarcation should have been carried out according to the actual ratio of the nationalities, but with the consent of the British and French representatives the demarcation was done according to statistics that are thirty years old, were compiled during the Austrian regime, and reflect neither the former nor the current situation. Counter to the very principle of ethnographic delimitation, about a million Czech nationals are now to fall under German rule. According to the British and French governments' proposals, the new Czechoslovakia should have remained a country capable of an independent political and economic life. Now, with the consent of the British and French representatives, the great majority of all its coal and virtually all its water resources have been taken away from it; its main transport connections have been severed, and transport-wise the country is torn in two parts. No defeated enemy state seems ever to have been treated so ruthlessly, with such lack of consideration for its continued existence, as Czechoslovakia. After all, we can't hold it against Germany that it doesn't care about the fate and life of Czechoslovakia, but we can't understand what interest the representatives of Great Britain and France had in such a crippling of our country, and why they joined in with everything that was to paralyse its future existence. I beg you, help us to unravel this question: did your country, did France, really have any interest in ensuring that it should all turn out in the worst possible way for Czechoslovakia; and when, why, and in what British or French interest, was the conclusion reached that the healthy life of this small and relatively happy country must be vitally broken?

IV
NOTICING PEOPLE AND THINGS

Decadence

The Moravian Region, 2 December 1905

What I want to write about today does not relate exclusively to students, but to youth in general. I think exclusively of the young while I am writing this, and dedicate it to them only, because it is about their sorest side. I think that the thing itself is very important, because it is so terrible. And it is I, a student, writing about it, because our elders cannot write about it sincerely; they cannot write about it because their time of youth has long been over. Today I want to write about the sex life of students.

By no means do I intend to deal with the question of how a young man should act, I do not wish to give medical advice, I do not want to strike the pose of a holy preacher who issues warnings and reprimands – that is not my aim. My essay is meant to be a bare stating of necessary facts; it is to show the inner decay of youth – and that is not, I presume, pointless.

So at fourteen, at the time of puberty, after the previous phase of sentimentality and indefinite longing, a young boy enters a stage marked by a despairing battle with his own body, burning youth and desire. The fight is not long: the body must win. Youth no longer has firmness. We no longer have any Saint Aloysiuses.

After gruelling sessions at school, bending over his work, a young man is physically so tired that his body is unable to enforce its claims. So the searing drought of a day passes. But then nights arrive, those horrible nights on a hot bed, under the black ceiling, where the staring eyes seek a beautiful woman, beautiful and terrible in her nakedness, nights when the inflamed body cries out for its right, irreversible and not nice, nights which make the head smart and the dry lips crack, nights when the body squirms and the fists are clenched in cramp, when the overheated nerves faint in sweetish stupefaction – during those nights the desperate battle between body and soul is being decided. One feels the unconquerable power, raw and repulsive, above him – arising from the dark, it lies on his chest stiflingly, fuelling the atoms of his blood. This enormous force, having the privilege of youth, surpasses human powers. And then – *iacta est alea* [the die has been cast]. A young man with a feverish head and raging blood and parched brain falls – it is a kind of drama too.

Or to put it shortly and realistically: at that particular time sexual tension overcomes will, and so the man succumbs. He must succumb because he is young, and so flaming and so weak. It is natural, and necessary. Sexual desire is hunger. What to do about hunger? It must be satisfied. Even if it were satisfied with mud. It is so ordinary, so natural. What an unhandsome image of man!

So the young man yields all right. On a hot bed, exhausted by the struggle with that terrible force, he yields to masturbation. Oh, how disgusting, you will say! But a young man never succumbs without struggle. First he looks yearningly for salvation, he runs away from the circle of male thoughts, he flees from himself. And then he sees that it is futile. The blood in his veins is mad and the head has turned stupid. See how sad it is! Is man an animal, not in control of himself?

Or a young man disappears among narrow alleys and into a certain house, sick with desire and passion. At that moment, when he goes there for the first time, he is *unzurechnungsfähig* [insane]. He does not understand what he is doing. He only feels that he must go there, a poor lunatic without will and strength. And then he goes there for a second time, already knowing what he is looking for. And then he drowns in that 'cloaca of humankind', he plunges into the life where it is so easy to forget the other life, unsympathetic and cold.

I do not want to find excuses for anyone in any way. I know that young people are often sybarites who savour and encourage their bodily desires. I know that these people feel no shame before themselves, that they do not even want to suppress anything, though they could often do so. But this human animality has a great deal of tragicalness mixed in it. For even this animality grows from the circumstances of life, even these sick wretches are tinged with the guilt of life.

It is a terrible thing. And the proportional numbers sound horrendous, I do not exaggerate: three quarters are masturbators, the rest are given over to prostitution, or are weirdos. I do not believe in the existence of the innocent. This is youth as I know them.

Oh, how hot are the nights when the body has for once lived a life of its own! Those nights, white-hot with passion, charged with wild pleasure and love – they are like deep pools in which one sinks forgetting the world above . . .

And then comes awakening. With a muddy soul, an aching, mournful head and an exhausted, as if emptied body, with incomprehensible disgust and sadness clutching his heart, a man returns to the other world, cold and arid. Everything has become repulsive, everything tastes of mud that weighs down the head and gradually settles in the bottom of the soul. One is weak to work, impotent to think, ill with surfeit and exhaustion. Here, in this life, there is neither beauty, nor joy, nor warmth – now then, what shall one do with that irritable soul and sorrowful head? Behold, the man steps down again to that nether life that is deep, deep down below us. It is too late to break away from it.

And then he drags himself along through life, sated, fed up, listless to the point of stupidity, sick to death and burnt out like old age, resembling a hedonist of the nastiest type, a male animal with moist piggy eyes and Bacchic lips. Youth has been wasted, feeling wasted, reason wasted – behold the man!

My God, my God, how terrible it is! Having this grim, ugly image before my eyes, I curse my youth and am afraid of my future days. Deep below me is that nether life, and from its darkness a red glow beckons. The sky above me is starless and has no gods. I am a human and am afraid of myself and for myself.

Why is it like this? It is impossible to speak about the causes that imprint the stigma of passion on the soul. It is life – life as it shapes a young soul. From early youth spiritual circumstances form human nature. Hence passion too is the resultant of the living conditions of early youth. Why curse those weirdos, those sick wretches? They are miserable creatures who are not to blame for their lowness and badness. They are born with it. This of course leads to the complete negation of crime – but that negation is perhaps the truest thing.

There are many theories about how we should arrange our life in order to be better. But they are just theories. Payot seeks the reason for this terrible evil in the weakness of the will.[1] And he is right. But we cannot win this fight. It is said that the will should be trained. The strength of the will grants salvation. Oh, what a utopia, utopia! The human will has been going to the dogs since the dawn of history – the decadence of the will is long-standing. And then they say – train it! What an idealist that Payot is!

The First Step on the Path of Vices

The People's Paper, 12 February 1922

has been taken by the scribe of these dolorous lines. It wasn't just a step, it was a whole leap, straight off, at my first attempt – I mean a leap from a pulling-out tram, which was, however, only a teeny bit in the process of pulling out, such a teeny bit that there were six of us who jumped right into the arms of Constable No. 2031. 'So, gentlemen, that'll be a couple of smackers,' the constable said, looking pleased, and gave us each a 'receipt for a fine of 2 CZC for disturbing the night's peace' (though it happened in grey daytime). So a man who had been a spotless citizen since birth, a man who hadn't committed any offence whatsoever (except, on one occasion, high treason),[1] a man who had never come into conflict with the law, be it cosmic, civilian, natural or moral, received his first punishment. The first stain was left on a hitherto blank slate. And if this person, who had been innocent until yesterday, died (God forbid) today or tomorrow, and were summoned before the divine court of justice, the Almighty would ask him: 'What trespasses have you done in your life?' And the sinner would stand abashed in silence, and would want to sink back to the earth for shame. 'What are you guilty of?' the Almighty would thunder again; whereat guardian angel No. 2031, with a starry truncheon in his hand, would open the book of life and read: 'Fined two crowns for disturbing the night's peace on 8 February 1922'. 'That's serious,' the Almighty would say. 'To disturb the night's peace, that's a sin, a filthy business and a rebellion. For that, wicked soul, you'll get twenty-four thousand years of hard purgatory without suspension, with a dark spell in the lock-up every thousand years, and after that you'll be put under angelic watch.' And the guilty soul would look for the way to purgatory, but would never find it, because he'd be afraid to jump from the pulling-out planet onto another one, 'being in motion', and so would keep standing there till the end of time, amen.

Unanimity

The People's Paper, 11 October 1922

Occasionally you get tired of your inner loneliness and exclusiveness, of what is called originality or an independent view; occasionally you are sick of being yourself at all costs, and being other than all the others. Occasionally you no longer want to think, feel and act in a mode of proud and enclosed individualism. You'd rather think and speak, feel and act, as everyone else does, just like the simplest and the humblest. All of a sudden you are gripped by a feeling that despite the differences between classes and opinions, beliefs and political parties, religions and languages, interests and dispositions, there is something common to all people – a kind of pan-human intercourse, an ineffable mutuality. I, you, whoever is out there, the man in a village, the man in a town, all carry in them an indefinable something they share, something about which they can be in total accord. Now then, give utterance to what is the same and internally social for all people, what emanates simply and unanimously from all hearts. Do you want to, oh, do you really want to utter it?

Go and stand by the window, then, and say: 'Damned weather!'

About Different Judges

The People's Paper, 22 November 1922

It happens to everyone some time or other, that, not to put too fine a point on it, he treads in something nasty and it sticks to his shoe. It's not in itself a huge misfortune, nor does it cast a shadow over the fate or the character of the afflicted person, but it throws a light on his fellow beings, since at times like this they reveal themselves in a number of ways.

For example, one type of person notices the accident, and, to add insult to injury, looks at it with the most demonstratively merciless and triumphant stare. What's more, they come up to the victim and tell him loudly (with what they would call wonderful directness) something like this: 'You've mucked up your shoes, mate; dear me, you've really made an exhibition of yourself! Yes, of course it shows, no help for it – the more you hide it, the worse it looks. Ugh! I'm not going to hang around here with everyone looking at you.' With that, satisfied and proud of themselves, they leave you crushed and ashamed to the roots of your hair.

The second type of person doesn't even acknowledge that they know you. They give you a wide berth, and run away in conspicuous haste saying to themselves: 'Why should I let him embarrass me? Enough is enough. It serves him right, anyway. What a scream! Let him run around with it; I'd be a fool even to tell him! Paddle your own canoe. Adios.'

The third sort (whom I want specially to talk about) notices your injury and turns scarlet with embarrassment. 'Oh my goodness,' a person of this ilk says to himself, 'I can't leave him in the lurch! But I can't tell him either, because – well – first, it's bad form, and second, he'd be embarrassed, and hurt and anxious. And, poor chap, he doesn't know about it. Better he never finds out, poor chap!' And then this person takes you under his arm and draws you aside somewhere, and says: 'Listen, it's awfully pleasant to shuffle around here; please try it, you'll see you'll really like it. Or how about a bit of paddling through the grass? For dear life, try it!' And when at last he manages to rid your shoes of the disgraceful appendage in one way or another, he's relieved, and overflowing with happiness bids you farewell, leaving you with the impression of a slightly weird and childish person, for it's the fate of good intentions that they usually remain unappreciated.

Everyone willy-nilly treads in something nasty in their life; everyone sometimes makes a mistake, a foolishness, a clumsy step; in some ways everyone occasionally gets stained or spattered or sunk. And then everyone gets to know these three kinds of people: those who, with 'wonderful directness' and personal gratification, rub your nose in that embarrassing and deplorable mess that's happened to you, and, as they say, 'hold up a mirror to you'; next, those who, with a touch of irony and covert satisfaction, leave you in the lurch, above all feeling pleased that it didn't happen to *them*; and finally, those hesitant good souls who pass over your injury, your humiliation, your wrong step as if nothing's happened, and try to conceal it not for their sake, but for yours.

Whenever the first type meets you, they tell you, with all the agility of their love of truth, that you are a bad, incompetent fellow and that you've done this or that idiocy, though you more or less know it yourself or absolutely don't want to know. The second lot just make you feel uneasy with a suspicious smile, an evasiveness or a general hint, and then silently gloat over how sharp their blade is; they want neither to put you right nor offend you, but only to revel in their own superiority – these reticent judges are the cruellest. The third type takes your guilt or weakness on themselves, as it were; they are ashamed of it, torment themselves with it, and desperately strain to sweep it away or atone for it, as if they were accomplices in your blemish, as if it were up to them to apologise or be punished for it. There are such people, albeit you may think they are but few.

And one day, at the Last Judgement, everything we have trodden in bunglingly in our lifetime will come to light. Then we shall stand either before the infinite Justice of the Peace, about whose jurisdiction we know none too much, or perhaps before a three-member senate, as the ancient Greeks assumed. But then it might be possible that those three, I mean Minos, Aeacus and Rhadamanthus, divide their roles in exactly the same way as our judges here on earth. Minos, a fanatic for the truth, will thunder out all our sins, guilts, mistakes, follies, vices, daftnesses and the highly undignified stains that we're covered in from head to toe; he won't hide anything, and we'll stand as if drenched in his immortal, ruthless harshness. Aeacus will just be sniggering, and will drop a remark about 'certain people' and 'certain behaviour that it is unnecessary to elaborate upon', and will pierce us with his cold, undying, heavenly contempt. But Rhadamanthus will blush and torment himself and sweat on our behalf, and then, instead of blaming or judging us, will say in his celestial embarrassment: 'Look, how beautifully that little star over there shines, hang on, what's its name – Procyon,' or something equally pointless and well-meant, and we'll feel he is the only one in whom we have an advocate.

Well then, whatever I might have committed at any time, or whatever I might have trodden in, I appeal to the judge Rhadamanthus.

Nicholas

The People's Paper, 6 December 1923

Poor old thing, now he's walking along the Prague streets, jumping clear of the traffic, trotting through the beastly muddy slush, and squeezing his way through passers-by with his crozier. He has a holy white beard made of cotton-wool, a mitre, beautifully mellow blue eyes, a basket with a gramophone on his back, and he is, quite simply, serving as an advertisement for some business enterprise or other. How low St Nicholas has sunk!

His devils are employed by the Baťa shoe company, and a rival St Nicholas is parading himself in the shop window of what I presume is the Moravia engineering plant. Where the angels are, I don't know. Let's hope they're in heaven, where they wring their hands and flutter their wings woefully, and little feathers fall to earth, and that's why it snows all the time – but even those feathers are somewhat tricky and fake, because they immediately start thawing, and that's how we get the mud through which the hired, numb Nicholas with his blue eyes and a spattered holy vestment is pattering along.

When I was little, the real Nicholas was still going round the houses. Even the devil was real. Not the angel, though, that was only Julie, and since then I've realised countless times that no angel is at all real, and that ultimately he's only a woman. But Nicholas was a genuine, miraculous saint, for he brought gifts.

Gifts are the most miraculous thing in the world. In fact, they are the only unarguably miraculous thing in this materialistic world. God knows, I can buy a hot dog myself if I really fancy it that much. But if someone in the street suddenly gave me a hot dog, I wouldn't believe my eyes, and would have to pinch myself, thinking it was an angel or something. A given thing has about it a special awesomeness – it is as though it had come from heaven. There isn't a shred of fairy tale in the fact that someone has been scrimping and saving until he has scrimped and saved a fortune. But it's fairy-tale if he gets a bag of ducats as a gift, or if he finds a cave inlaid with rubies and gold like Rechner's shop. Getting something as a gift, or finding it, that's the magic kernel of a good half of all the fairy tales of all the nations in the world. So, a gift is fairy-tale, magical, miraculous. Don't look a gift horse in the mouth, not because it's probably wooden, but because it's a divine horse, fallen from heaven, and a mysterious one. Don't look a gift horse in the mouth, but put your arms round its neck, hide your face in its mane and, with your eyes half-closed, dream of the wondrous wonder that has been given to you. If you buy a pair of slippers, you know what to expect from them. But if someone makes you a gift of a pair of slippers, that's different. Mind you, they might be seven-league slippers, or they might bring you good luck, or whatever – in any event, they are somehow different from all the other slippers on earth, more enigmatic and simply out-of-this-world.

And now I know why gifts are brought by the baby Jesus and St Nicholas. It's because no true present is of this world, but comes from heaven. It's magical and supernatural in itself, and so can't be given by a human hand. And that's why the baby Jesus really exists, and St Nicholas too, cross my heart, they do. They dwell supernaturally in those little somethings, and that's why when you open them, you get a whiff of such a heavenly, bewitching scent that your heart leaps with joy. Gifts come from heaven, albeit by the earthly means of human choosing, haggling and paying. Of course here on earth you only pay the shopkeeper for wrapping up that godlike thing and having it delivered. But the thing itself, the thing intended as a gift, can't be paid for with money, for it comes from paradise.

May you get lots of gifts.

A Little Candle

The People's Paper, 25 December 1923

Let's stop being negligent and at least once a year light a little column in the paper for the dear Lord God.

So, Glory be to God on high. Although he's everywhere, he's more alone and more at home on high. See for yourself: ascend on high sometime and you'll meet him. On the high of beauty, on the high of love, on the high of knowledge and I don't know on what other highs. And when you get there, you'll feel pleasure and horror, an inexpressible joy and a terrible chill, and that's him in person. But anyone who has never ascended on high hasn't met him, and doesn't know anything about him or his glory. For there is no true glory but God's. He alone smells of wild thyme, and has the stars in his hair and birds on his shoulders and a cricket in his lap, and beneath his feet flow rivers and small brooks. Glory be to God on high.

And on earth peace, good will towards men. For nothing is sweeter than peace, so leave us in peace all you who think that you've been called to administer and rectify the world. Peace to men on earth. Glory belongs to the Lord God, and peace to man;

wonder and awe are on high, but may there be peace on earth. Heart of man, be peaceful when you turn your face towards the earth; and if there is anything that we should dread, may it be the terrible high with its glory. May the scourge of eternity and the fear of God smite us, may we shudder with mortal apprehension and bliss meeting the Lord on high, but may there be peace to the earth and men. Peace, that's the greatness of small things and the depth of everyday ones. A peaceful thing is consecrated, and a peaceful man is good, and a peaceful heart is happy and a peaceful day is blessed, amen. Glory be to God on high.

And peace to men of good will. Perhaps there are greater and finer virtues than good will, choose heroism, magnanimity, self-sacrifice or whatever you like, but nothing is so good as good will. Good will is like a good path or a good roof or other quiet, good and reliable things we don't even notice. Only when they aren't good, do we start to kick up, and when we encounter ill will, we feel as if all certainty in the world is collapsing. And that's the reason why good will is the best thing – all reliability and trust depend on it. Good will is the horizontal basis of all the world's good. Glory be to God on high.

And on earth peace. All over the earth. I feel it, you feel it. When it's crumbling somewhere in our neighbourhood, we no longer have firm ground beneath our feet. There is just one earth. Even so, humans had made mincemeat of half their race before that began to dawn on them. All is not well on earth, that's why we don't feel well or safe. So we strain our ears to detect what is happening in the far distance in case we hear the dreadful cracking of the earth. No, nothing yet, thank heavens: glory be to God on high.

And on earth peace, good will towards men. It's the shortest, smallest prayer. If you repeated it a thousand times, as if you had a Tibetan prayer-wheel inside you, you'd always find a new, pleasurable taste in it. Because there are glory and height, earth and peace, as well as good will in it – only good, great, holy and tender things. I, a miserable sinner, keep repeating it, not counting lines, and I don't even know if I'm now thinking more about the one for whom

I wanted to light a little candle, or about the men of good will, or about the earth thirsting for peace, or about the peace of my soul; I just hear a harmony, a voice at once angelic and familiar.

An Invention

The People's Paper, 13 February 1924

I like all kinds of technical inventions, not because I take them for granted, but because I marvel at them beyond measure. I don't like them as real practitioners – an American, or the engineer Mr Vesely[1] – do; I like them as a primitive does. I like them as wondrous, mystical and incomprehensible things. I like the telephone because it offers you plenty of incidents, such as when the switchboard puts you through to someone else and you greet him chummily: 'Listen, you old bastard' or what have you. I like the tram because it's temperamental, whereas walking is thoroughly even-tempered and unadventurous. I've got myself an American stove because it requires so much attention and constant personal contact, as if I had an Indian elephant or an Australian kangaroo at home. So now I've got myself a Swedish vacuum cleaner. I don't know if I shouldn't say that the Swedish vacuum cleaner has got me.

The man who brought it told me that there was an engine inside the cylinder; he seems to be right, because when it starts off it makes noise like a biggish factory. Other bits that belong to it are a wire and all sorts of small tubes and extension what-sits – about ten pieces – you can play with them like a Meccano set. You stick the wire into the socket and run the other end over the floor, or whatever you like, while the cylinder is yowling like a steam-lathe and heats up with all its bellowing. As you can see, it's quite simple. And then, aha, I almost forgot the main thing: there's a little bag in the cylinder, and you pull it out and turn it upside down on a piece of newspaper, and after that you only keep saying, 'Gadzooks', and 'You'd never believe it' and 'Blow me!', and call up the whole house to come and have a look at how much dust there is in the little bag. I can assure you that the amazement of the assembled throng is the chief delight in cultivating a vacuum cleaner, and that it provides you with priceless satisfaction every day.

I've so far believed in a whole range of things: the Ancient of Days, the moral laws of the universe, atomic theory, and other things more or less inaccessible to human reason. Now I am obliged to believe in the Swedish vacuum cleaner. I'm even obliged to believe in the metaphysical ubiquity and the supernatural existence of dust. I now believe that dust I am and unto dust shall I return, yea, that I constantly keep turning into dust. I think that I drop dust wherever I tread or sit. I think that while I'm writing this, a little heap of dust is forming under me on the easy chair. My thoughts are floating down on the floor in the form of thick grey dust. When I talk, I surely spray a cloud of dust through my teeth, though I speak the holy truth, the whole truth, and nothing but the truth. Everything turns into dust. Otherwise it would be thoroughly impossible to explain the presence, the volume and the exquisite consistency of dust in my electric cleaner. In that little magic bag, I mean.

Every faith and every idol requires certain rituals. Every morning, since the time I started waiting upon the Cleaner, my house has seen the ceremony of the ritual Shaking Out of the Bag. It looks very much like when a conjuror shakes a dozen glasses out of his sleeve, or a rabbit, a stack of paper and a live girl out of his top hat; in short, it's miraculous. You shake the bag in a special formal manner, lift it up in suspense, and a heap of dust emerges – I'm telling you, it's pure magic. The Dust from the Cleaner is not ordinary dirty dust; it's dense, even, heavy and mysterious; it's somehow conjured-up, for you can't for the life of you understand how so much dust has materialised there.

If it happens that the size of the dust heap is somewhat modest, you're immediately alarmed – just as pagans must be alarmed when they feed their idol and it doesn't tuck in. It is a matter of faith and a sort of ambition for you that the heap of dust should be staggeringly big. You look for a forgotten corner where there is still an unused-up and cryptic stratum of dust. If you didn't feel ashamed, you'd go out and suck dust from the street just to pay homage to your idol. When you go to visit people, you envy how much beautiful, unsucked dust they have in their place. I think I'll start secretly taking dust home once I've swallowed up the last pinch of mine.

As I say, I have awesome respect for technical inventions. If I had enough money, I'd also buy a three-phase motor or a steam threshing machine, and maybe even a cylinder for rolling out glass. Or that machine that makes boxes for matches. For the time being I only have an American stove and a Swedish vacuum cleaner, but I serve these two idols with steadfast wonder. The other day my American stove was burning for a whole fortnight, and yesterday you should have seen how much dust there was in the bag. It was dazzling.

Cat

The People's Paper, 18 January 1925

Can anyone explain to me why a cat gets so strangely agitated when you whistle to yourself very softly and tenderly? I've tried it on Czech and even English, Italian and German cats – there is no geographical difference. When a cat hears you whistling (especially if you whistle, 'It's a beautiful night, a time of love, Everything makes me want you, my dove', as soulfully as you can), she's fascinated and starts rubbing herself against you, jumps on your lap, sniffs your lips in astonishment, and finally, in a sort of amorous ecstasy, begins to bite your mouth and nose with a pleasurably perverse expression. At this point, of course, you stop, and she starts purring diligently like a little engine. I've thought about it many times, and still don't know what primordial instinct makes a cat delight in whistling. I can't think there was ever a time in the primeval past when tom cats whistled instead of summoning their females in a harsh, metallic alto as they do nowadays. Perhaps in wild, bygone days there were cat gods who spoke to their worshippers in magic whistling, but it's just a hypothesis, and the musical enchantment I've been talking about remains one of the enigmas of a cat's soul.

We think we know cats just as we think we know people. A cat is a thing that sleeps curled up on a sofa; sometimes she wanders away to pursue her feline interests; sometimes she knocks down an ash tray, and she spends most of her time fervently relishing warmth. But it was only in Rome that I got to know the mysterious essence of felineness. It was because there I didn't look just at one cat but fifty, a whole herd of cats, a large feline pool round Trajan's Column. There is an old forum, excavated like a basin in the middle of the square, and on its dry bottom, among the lopped-off columns and statues, lives an independent cat nation. It subsists on fish heads that the benevolent Italians throw down for them from on high, and observes some sort of moon-cult. Other than that it doesn't seem to do anything. Well then, it was there that I had a revelation. A cat isn't simply a cat, but something enigmatic and impenetrable – it is a wild animal. If you see two dozen cats walking you are surprised by the sudden recognition that a cat doesn't walk, it creeps. A cat among people is only a cat; a cat among cats is a creeping shadow in the jungle. A cat seems to trust a human, but a cat doesn't trust a cat because she knows her better than we do. 'Like cat and dog' is used about social distrust. However, I've often observed a very intimate friendship between a cat and a dog, but have never seen an intimate friendship between two cats, unless we speak about cats' love affairs, of course. The cats on Trajan's forum ignore one another as ostentatiously as possible. If they sit on the same column, they sit with their backs to one another, jerking their tails nervously, to make it apparent how displeased they are about having to put up with the presence of that slut behind them. If a cat looks at a cat, she hisses. If they pass in the street, they don't cast a backward glance at each other; they never have a shared interest; they never have anything to say to one another. At best they tolerate one another with contemptuous and repudiating silence.

But with you, my dear chap, the cat is on speaking terms. She coos at you, looks you in the eye, and says: Open this door for me, human creature; give me, mighty devourer, some of what you are consuming; stroke me; tell me something; let me on my sofa. To you she isn't a feral, solitary shadow; she is simply a domestic puss, because she trusts you. A wild animal is an animal that doesn't trust. Domestication means trusting.

And come to that, we people are not wild either so long as we trust one another. Suppose, for example, that on setting out from my house I didn't trust the first old buffer I came across, but roared sinisterly as I approached him, and secretly tensed my thighs as I walked along so as to leap at his throat if he so much as blinked an eyelid. If I didn't trust the people who travel with me on the tram, I'd have to ram my back against the wall and spit so as to frighten them off. Instead, I hang on the strap peacefully and read the paper, exposing my unprotected back. When I stroll along the street I think about my work, or nothing in particular, without considering what passers-by can do to me. It would be terrible if I had to eye them askance in case they should devour me. A state of distrust is savage and primitive. Distrust is the law of the jungle.

The politics that thrives on cultivating distrust is the politics of the wilderness. A cat that doesn't trust a man doesn't see a man but a wild animal. A man who doesn't trust another man sees a wild animal too. The bond of mutual trust is older than civilisation. Mankind has always had its ups and downs, but if you abolish trust, the human world will become a planet of beasts.

And let me tell you, I'm now going to give my little puss a stroke. That's what I'm going to do. She's a great comfort to me because she trusts me, even though she is just a little grey creature from God knows where, who has strayed to my place from the unknown wildernesses of Prague's backyards. She's purring and looking at me. 'Human creature,' she says, 'rub me between my ears.'

A Little Train

The People's Paper, 9 June 1925

As it happens, I wanted to write about something else. But just as I was taking my pen in hand and, turning, glanced towards the window, chasing a flitting fly and a fleeting thought, my eye caught a little train, a far-off, gurgling, long-distance train in full motion – a regular international express 'stopping at Benešov, Tábor, Veselí, Vienna'. It bustled away over there beneath Bohdalec towards Hostivař, and before I could say Jack Robinson, it burrowed into the fields somewhere and was gone. I was left pen in hand, and with the typical, quiet, dumbfounded envy of a stay-at-home for the people who are bowling away into the distance.

   If the Creator himself had come up to me an hour ago and said, 'Karel, come on, get ready, in an hour an express will be going to Benešov and Veselí; look, you'll be able to travel beneath Bohdalec towards Hostivař, and the whole world – all of them that can see the track – will be silently jealous that you're tearing along on the little train into the vast, free world, while they're bewitched behind their everyday windows. Off you go, then, and God bless.' If God had said that, I think I'd have wriggled, and stammered that, as luck would have it, just today wasn't really convenient, that I wasn't kind of feeling quite the thing, and that I was really supposed to be writing an article. I'd think up fifty excuses to talk him out of it, and I'd be relieved when the great tempter shut the door behind him and left me at home. And you would, I think, do exactly the same – but that doesn't prevent us from following the next little scudding train with sorrowful eyes, thirsty for new horizons and unknown goals. How about that, we think to ourselves, those people on the train travelling along, while poor me . . .

   A gentleman is standing at the carriage window, watching how the vast, unknown world whizzes by. How about that – there he is travelling. But the man is standing, watching the little far-off windows and thinking to himself: They must live a nice life over there behind that window; the net curtains are flying, and it's so quiet and fresh – I feel like going there right now and knocking: You don't know me. I am so-and-so. I was going by train through these parts and a kind of longing for your little window came over me, how it's possible to live behind it quietly and deeply. And that path down there – I'll never walk along it; I wonder what there is further on in that valley? It's something beautiful and surprising,

some trees or a little well, I'll be bound. To be able to walk to the
end of that path, to see what the world looks like beyond that hill,
to walk round the corner of those houses to find out who or what
there is behind them, to linger around there and get to know everything – what enormous, adventurous and mysterious possibilities
I'm being rushed past like an animal in a cage! Hello there, hello
folks who have stopped to wave at the train; what a nice life you
have here, I'd like to be in your place, but see, I have to travel, I
must, and can't do what I'd like to.

And do you really think that the gentleman at the window
of that carriage will arrive in a far-off country? Even if I rule
out the possibility that he's headed only for Benešov, he'll
never be in a far-off country; even if he went to Italy or Java,
he'd never be in a far-off country because a far-off country isn't
the one that is far away, but the one where we are not. A far-off
country is the one we'll never reach or the one we always leave
behind. I've never been in a far-off country, and sometimes I've
travelled by train or boat for many days, only to find that a far-off
country is somewhere else, or back home. So, regardless of where
the gentleman at that carriage window travels, he won't meet with
an adventure, for the moment something truly happens and must
be truly lived through it stops being an adventure – it becomes
nothing but a confounded reality. To be in Java or on the moon
isn't the least bit adventurous for the person who is there, but it's
incredibly adventurous for the person who isn't. For a person who
is waving his hat to the train, romantic distances are where the
train is heading; for a man in the carriage, romantic distances are
all the places where the train doesn't stop. I don't know, perhaps
it seems special and romantic to someone to be sitting behind a
window, writing an article, while I find I'm tempted by the mysterious
possibility of travelling to Benešov ...

Yes, come to that, what did I really want to say? Aha, just that
this is precisely the reason why everyone's eyes look lingeringly
after a little dashing train, and that this is precisely the reason why
the most beautiful and enticing landscapes are those that randomly
unfold behind a train's rattling windows.

From Philemon, or About Gardening

The People's Paper, 6 September 1925

Savoy cabbage

I was pleased with it: it was full, a bit hoary and as curly as František Langer when he was younger.[1] But all of a sudden, God knows where from, caterpillars of the cabbage white variety appeared that, as their name indicates, should have been stuffing themselves with white cabbage near Strašnice and should have left my Savoy in peace. However, they devoured everything apart from the beautifully branched ribs.

Prior to this disaster I was inclined to modify the floral hierarchy and regard the Savoy cabbage as the queen of flowers. Well, it's not true. The rose is still the queen of flowers, seemingly because it's no good as fodder.

Presumably man, too, must have been very inedible to become Lord of the Creation.

Earth

I was talking about earth to a gardener, and he took offence. Garden soil, he said, is not earth; it is topsoil, humus and refined, living matter, while earth, you see, sir, is clay and dead or stony ground. I felt a bit ashamed. The gardener is right. But why did the Lord create man from the dust of the earth and not from topsoil then? It is not written that Adam was created from humus. Nor is it recorded that the Creator made him from delicate leaf mould. No doubt he was saving humus and leaf mould for the Garden of Eden. We gardeners don't waste the best topsoil on shaky experiments.

How clouds are cultivated

It takes quite a lot of effort. You have to weed very thoroughly, extract all the rubbish and stones from the topsoil and discard them, stoop, kneel, dig, water, pick off caterpillars, exterminate greenflies, make the tilth crumbly and minister to the earth. And when your back finally hurts from all this, and you straighten up and look at the sky, you have the most beautiful clouds. QED.

In Praise of Butterfingers

The People's Paper, 20 December 1925

Some people are the victims of a malicious quirk of fate: they are called butterfingers, as if it were their fault that things come alive in their hands and reveal demonic tendencies. Really and truly they should be called magicians, because their touch breathes unpredictable luxuriance into things. When I try to knock a nail into the wall, the hammer springs from my grasp with such wild animation that it breaks the plaster, or my finger, or one of the windows on the far side of the room. When I try to wrap a parcel, the string is possessed by serpent-like subtlety, gathers into a coil, breaks free, and ends up tying my finger to the parcel – its favourite trick. A friend of mine, who meddles in politics at such a high level that everyone marvels at his audacity, doesn't dare to screw the cork out of a bottle. He knows that the moment he tries, the cork and corkscrew will stay in his hand, while the bottle will jump to the floor with startling nimbleness. People are foolish to laugh at those who have this kind of enlivening relation to the physical world, and to characterise them as bunglers or butterfingers or bulls in china shops, instead of appreciating their special magic.

In reality, the whole difference lies in the fact that these bunglers treat inanimate things as if they were animate, that is, refractory, untamed and endowed with a will of their own, whereas dextrous people treat inanimate things as just inanimate, and subject to their domination. A shop boy doesn't treat string as a savage and subtle snake, but as an obedient, spiritless ball. He's finished in no time, and Bob's your uncle. In a bricklayer's hand a hammer isn't a barmy, obstreperous ram that butts its head against whatever it fancies;

it's a docile instrument, as dead as mutton. From a blunderer's viewpoint taming things like this is sheer wizardry. But handy folk should concede that clumsiness has its own mysterious powers too.

I for one am of the opinion that fairy tales about things that have the power of speech weren't thought up by deft people, but by magical butterfingers. I think that Hans Christian Andersen must sometimes have fallen off his chair, or his chair must have fallen on him, and that this must have given him the idea that chairs sometimes come alive and can speak. When Simple Simon greeted a footbridge and wished it 'God bless', he was no doubt afraid that if he didn't it would catapult him into the brook. If he had been a member of the Tourist Club, he wouldn't have talked to it because he would have felt sure that walking across it would be as easy as falling off a log. Skilful people enrich our world with heroic ideas of boundless possibilities. But butterfingers contribute the fairy-tale idea of boundless difficulties, accidents, obstacles and resistances. The image of a glass mountain peering over chasms, dark lakes and impenetrable wilds reflects the bungler's vivid experience that it's terribly hard to get anywhere or do anything, and that you will get drenched and bruised on the way.

But I don't praise butterfingers just for this imaginativeness – their significance is more substantial. I'd like to emphasise what they've done for the world's evolution and progress. It's the bunglers who are the authors of mankind's greatest invention. It was exactly the butterfingers you look down on who brought about division of labour. The first pathetic blunderer must have been born so that his more skilled fellow Neanderthal could push him away from chipping a flint tool or tanning a bit of animal hide and say, 'Chuck it, mate, I'll do that.' It was the botcher who created the specialist. If all people were equally neat-handed, there'd be no division of labour, and in consequence, no progress. While some prehistoric men could knap flint and others could kill mammoths or reindeer, there were rare, radical individuals who could do nothing. Or perhaps they could just do what was good for nothing – one of them killed time by counting the stars, another twisted his jaws to make all sorts of noises that others laughed at and started to imitate, and a third idler played with coloured clay and soot, and daubed the first frescos on a rock in Altamira. They were probably quite helpless, weird butterfingers who weren't able to so much as split a marrowbone. Proficient people discovered you could make a knife from stone; clumsy ones made the further discovery that you could leave that to others, and so they created society with its supportive structure. Strong, adept men found that it was necessary to be hunters and warriors for humankind to survive; butterfingers showed that a few hunters and warriors were enough for other kinds of people to survive too. Man stopped being a mere hunter when the individuals who were bad hunters first saw the light. If all people could sew shoes there wouldn't be any shoemakers. If it hadn't been for us butterfingers, there would have been no Prometheus and no Edison.

Good Resolutions

The People's Paper, 25 December 1925

With some it regularly happens on Christmas Eve, with others it doesn't occur until New Year's Eve, with yet others it makes itself felt on their birthdays or at some other regular time – in short, everyone has their own day when they are inspired with a good resolution. It comes over them out of the blue like a mystical experience or a cold in the head. At first they're just troubled by a bit of discomfort, then they suddenly start feeling morally queasy, and finally they tell themselves that they alone are to blame and that everything could be different and better if they reformed their lives. That's the moment when a good resolution takes possession of a person's mind. He makes a firm resolve, there and then, that starting with tomorrow or the New Year he will get up earlier, or do horrible hygienic things to improve his metabolism – exercise for five minutes first thing every morning, or have a cold bath, or read a few pages of Marcus Aurelius on an empty stomach, or smoke less, or stop smoking altogether, or give up drinking or politics, or devote three hours a day to self-education and contemplation, or start saving and pay off all his debts, or perform some truly great deed. I take it that at least once a year each of us suffers an attack of good resolutions. I even think that seriously famous people, like ministers or saints, feel the same terrible temptation at least once a year too. I honestly believe there isn't a single person who doesn't intend, at least once a year, to turn over a new leaf and start a new life.

Now, heaven knows, it's perfectly true that once a person has made his resolution, he won't get up earlier tomorrow, not even five minutes earlier, he won't knuckle down to physical jerks, nor will he start performing a truly great deed. Not that it couldn't work – quite the opposite, but just this particular day doesn't seem right, sort of, and one must get used to it gradually, and anyway, I could start tomorrow, yes, definitely tomorrow. That normally is the end of the resolution. It may be the end of it, but it's by no means wasted, for the very essence and point of a resolution is not that one should carry it out, but simply make it.

If in the hour of good resolutions I'm seized with a virtuous and heroic resolve that from tomorrow I will get up earlier, I'm demonstrating a great liberating fact: that I could get up earlier, for it depends only on me and is in my power. It would be terrible if I believed that I couldn't get up earlier, and that doing so was absolutely beyond me. It would be dreadful if I thought that I got up a bit late out of some health-related inadequacy or under the remorseless pressure of circumstances. Good resolutions confirm that we can still change our lives and ourselves. It would be shattering if we came to the conclusion that there was nothing about us or our everyday existence we could redo and alter. If a person cultivates the heroic idea that he will start getting up early, he simultaneously sustains in himself the miraculous possibility that he will start living newly: that he will see the sun rising or even a splendid sunrise in himself. If a person takes it into his head that he will start physical jerking, he leaves open the possibility of becoming as beautiful as an Olympic athlete. In cultivating good resolutions, we deny fatalism. A good resolution is an unconquerable assertion of free will.

As long as a man is capable of good resolutions, life stretches ahead of him like a great, untried promise. Good Lord, what wonderful things I'd write if I began getting up at six in the morning! And exercised for a quarter of an hour, and had a cold bath while reading Marcus Aurelius, and educated myself two hours a day, and did a bit of cabinet-making or hoed the garden instead of reading the papers, and learnt to play the accordion, and ran across the fields every day for a couple of hours, and immersed myself a little in Eastern philosophy, and regularly mingled with the populace, and grasped the basics of the national economy, and read Plato in the original, and created a radio station by myself, and learnt to be an expert skier, and boned up on astronomy, and practised rhetorical skills, and went in for hiking, and experimented with the crossbreeding of the dianthus, and kept pigeons, and replied to all letters immediately, and contemplated great thoughts on a daily basis, and initiated some far-reaching measure for the benefit of all fellow beings, and got to know everything that a human should know and at the same time didn't waste a single minute. For all that, and many other things, are embraced by my good resolutions. Thanks to good resolutions our lives are immensely and inexhaustibly rich.

I wish you many good resolutions for the season of good will.

Shame Before a Beggar

The People's Paper, 21 February 1926

Now it's a grandpa with white curls, or a mum with a muffled-up baby, or a granny bent over at right angles as if she were constantly looking for something on the ground and couldn't find it; now it's a blind man tapping in front of him with a stick, or a woman with two numb tots, or a scary oldie, or people without arms or legs, variously gnarled and misshapen, people with stumps, stricken with the shakes, dwarfish beings, or with gobbled-up noses, mumbling, coughing, selling matches or a small bundle of birdseed, standing by a wall, crouching in a corner like something thrown away, pilgrimaging along the pavement praying, wrapped up in rags, or strangely scrubbed, or just pairs of pleading eyes – in truth, it's a tumultuous collection of the human breed, a very specific but diversified assortment. Curiously, no extravagant millionaire has yet materialised to found a collection of beggars, to walk around towns and cities and collect these specimens, both run-of-the-mill and unique, just as someone else might collect ancient clocks or rare old snuff-boxes. It would be a hugely huge collection. It could be the biggest gallery in the world.

I can't help it: I can't regard begging as undignified. I don't think it undignified for a person to receive something as a gift from a fellow human being. I don't consider it humiliating for a person to ask for something. Quite the contrary. It is entirely dignified for us humans to ask and give. Generally speaking, a man is good not only as a source of profit, but also as a recipient of gifts. A true beggar is a man who is of no use; he is only fit for living on people's mercy. But his special, hidden usefulness is that he lives on mercy. Nature lets its beggars die: a tree that cannot sustain itself withers away; an animal that cannot feed itself dies; a man who cannot support himself – may he live! Where I grew up, beggars used to go begging collectively every Friday. For me, a wildly marvelling boy, it was a festive and exciting day. While they were still a great distance off, I'd watch out for that lame, limping, grunting, stumbling procession, and then I'd run back home with a triumphant shout, 'They're coming,' as if the Three Kings were approaching in all their glory; and then I couldn't take my eyes off my Mum as she walked to the threshold and sliced bread for Them while They were shuffling their feet and mumbling. If I ever had a sense of a feast day at that time, it was on Friday morning, not on Sunday.

There are professional beggars who have their stations as a shopkeeper has his shop; there are shy beggars who ring your doorbell and reel off their 'for-God's-mercy'; there are beggars who patrol only the more expensive shops, where the boss quickly packs them off with a sixpence, impatient to see the back of them; there are others who latch on to you in the street and rasp into your ears that they've just lost their job, and have nothing to eat.

Of course, every police inspector and every constable and every man who prides himself on knowing what's what will tell you about all these various cases, that they're for the most part twisters and lazy-bones, that they could work but don't, that those mums have borrowed the kids from someone else, that the hunched granny over there has a daughter who married a caretaker, that the white-haired grandad blows it all on booze, that all begging is phoney and loafing and a craft, battening on silly, trusting people, and – in a nutshell – you shouldn't give them anything, and that's that. All this has been said many times before, and even in public. If it has had any practical effect at all, it's not that the class of beggars has disappeared, but that it has given rise to a new class of people – shameful and hesitant givers.

Admit it, if a begging hand reaches out to you from a dark corner, you're quite likely not to give anything. Perhaps you say to yourself that you don't have time to fumble about for small change in your pocket, and besides, begging is phoney, and something or other should be done so that this kind of thing doesn't happen on the streets. But no sooner have you finished thinking that than you feel a bitter aftertaste mixed with shame. You're ashamed that you didn't put anything in that held-out hand; you feel embarrassed to go back to it; you're angry with yourself that you didn't decide to return straight away, because now it's definitely too late. That six-pence wouldn't have saved the man's life; all the same, he stretched out his hand to you and was waiting. Oh well, it happened; and burdened by a dissatisfaction that will not easily dissipate, you go about your business.

And another time you put your alms into the first palm held out before you. With the next step you feel a surge of awkward displeasure: How stupidly sentimental of me! The old thing is a drunkard anyway, and the woman has a fake baby stuffed with rags in her arms; professional begging shouldn't be encouraged, and blah, blah, blah. Oh well, it happened, but you're somehow miffed. Not to give alms is harshness, but to give alms is false sentimental-ity. Not to give is a sin, but to give is silliness. Only very simple, and usually poor, people can give alms as a matter of course and without hesitation. But as for the rest of us, the mite we give in alms cannot save us. Rather, it embarrasses us, and if we give, our giving is hasty, perfunctory and almost cowardly.

But an authentic, honest-to-God beggar doesn't have an enemy in the miser who keeps his purse tight, nor in the constable he runs away from when he spots him far off. His enemy is the twister who spoils his craft; his enemy is the false beggar, the pretender to poverty, the impostor who only plays the beggar, and so takes away from him not only his alms, but also the special and great dignity of beggarliness.

At the Bonfire

The People's Paper, 24 October 1926

We were being driven between the two walls of a valley – two wings painted in some creative frenzy. It was as though someone were playing the piano, burying all his ten fingers into the keys. So the deep tones of purple and brown and black-green boomed; the voice of copper, ochre and scarlet rang with the blare of a French horn; and the sharp sound of diaphanous yellow cried out with the highest string. Where have you gone, simple little summer song, green reed song, clear pliant female voice? See how the divine grapevine of colours has ripened. Let's press it into a goblet and drink the rough must of autumn. Isn't your head swimming, wandering through this vintage of groves!

Yes, it is, so that's why let's take a deep breath on this high meadow, this green meadow, a green raft on the brown waves of the mountains. Wave after wave, mountain after mountain; from the deep valleys trumpets the dark, ferocious roar of harts. It's like heavy drops – thump! thump! – the falling acorns, beech mast and hard wild pears, pouring down and drumming. Why should you go anywhere else, since you're standing on top of the world? There are, in every direction, beautiful and distant things that you won't see; be happy that you're in their midst. All this is in front of you:

ginger groves with blue shades, golden beeches, paths drifted over with leaves, meadows with meadow saffrons, a red roof of solitude. But all this is just a beginning, for beyond it are the earth and the heavens, and if you walked without end, you'd get through only in one direction and get to know just the margins of your path. Look, the sun is already setting.

The sun is already setting; you must follow it with your eyes as it touches that mountain over there, no, as it is cut in half, no, as only a golden shaving of it pokes out over the blue edge of the world. Now the sun isn't there at all, it's only amber light suffusing, only the mountains blueing, only a chill from the long valleys blowing in. Can't you hear the mild bell on the cow's neck, can't you hear the curfew of the flocks? God bless the hour of twilight!

You little flame, fire, glowing pile of embers, blazing bonfire! You burning bush, pillar of fire, tongue of fire, you fire of the first people, you first brand! What fire-worshippers we people are, what a primeval god that high flame is, dancing, snapping his fiery fingers, shaking his thatch of hair, jumping in frenzied ecstasy! We no longer understand it, we people of today; if we understood it, we, too, would start dancing and jumping round the fire; instead, we stand as if under a spell and stare into the fire in astonishment and dazzlement. Look at those sparks, hark how a new tuft of flames is shooting up, buzzing, how the logs are caving in, red-hot and crumbly, how it lives, how madly it lives! Yes, we, too, could . . . we, too, could flare up with a terrible flame, but we humans are made of different wood; our lot is to burn slowly like an erect candle; for a long, a very long time we must carry our flame, but we, too, could . . . What an adventure fire is! We, too, could set it ablaze, but never mind; quiet and slow is the fire of life that gives light.

You, too, are here, heifer with big eyes and a bell on your neck; you, too, have recalled some bygone times with shepherds' fires aglow all night long; you, too, once took your journey, following the pillar of fire. She is looking into the fire, forgetting to chew; then she wriggles her tail, dings her deep bell and carries on grazing. But it was a moment when she felt one of us.

So you see: you'll never fathom where darkness comes from,

nor the moment when it began, but it is here, all-encompassing and voluminous, so huge that people are suddenly smaller, they are quite tiny on the background of darkness; and as it is dark, they sit closer to the white-haired husbandman and talk quieter; as it is dark, even the fire has reddened and has sunk and is breathing with familiar warmth. It's not a dancing, savage god any more; it's a family fire; it's a little red fire that has cut us, who are sitting by it, out of the infinite world of darkness, and has made us into people belonging to one another. As if we were holding hands. As if we didn't run around the world after things, everyone along a different path. How many more people should be here for our circle to be complete! If only there were enough room for millions of us under this wild pear tree, around this heap of lambent embers! We would all be touching shoulders, and we would be looking very seriously, very pensively into the one and only, common little fire . . .

Children, it's already night. Peace be with you. Thank you for that bonfire, husbandman.

Home Life

Weekly Variety, 31 December 1927

Laundry

'Hey, Mary,' a man says to one of the women in the household, 'could you sew this button on for me tomorrow?'

'No chance,' the woman says firmly.

'But why not?'

'BECAUSE WE'RE DOING THE LAUNDRY.'

These words are spoken by women with such a special, almost ritual dignity, as if they had announced, 'We're giving birth,' or 'Tomorrow we're celebrating the Great Mystery,' or some such thing that precludes any objection. Tomorrow we're doing the laundry, that means: tomorrow is a day when no one has the right to boss us women around, a day when you'll be a useless creature, just about put up with, and that's all, you'll get your beef in tomato sauce, and from morning to evening you'll be heedful of the fact that you're an ineffectual man, a mere sponger and a good-for-nothing.

Don't tell me anything about the equality of the sexes: on laundry day there's no such thing as equality; on a day like that we men are terribly inferior. That day we almost avoid the women, oppressed by that . . . what's it called? . . . that inferiority complex. A slave-like desire to revenge ourselves on them for their showy superiority awakens in us – to go to the pub, to shout the odds and perform swashbuckling escapades. But we don't matter – when the laundry is being done, no one is interested in our spiritual moods. Just as men seek refuge in clouds of smoke so that, concealed behind them, they can deal with big male affairs, such as politics, the confounded current situation and all the rest of that jiggery-pokery, so women enter clouds of steam so that, concealed behind them, they can confer about the great womanly matter, that is laundry. If you peeped into the laundry room, you'd see nothing but women's backs rising from white clouds – what a curious ascension! Walk away on tiptoe. It's not just work; it's a rite.

Water pipe

But you take your revenge on women as soon as something stops working in the house: usually – I don't know why – it's a water pipe. Once in a while a woman comes up to you, looking conspicuously humble, and reports that over there, in the toilet or somewhere else, water doesn't run or, just the opposite, won't stop running, and that the man should, like, go and fix it. At that point the man realises with pleasurable smugness that now he's the master of the situation, and starts thundering, 'You women break everything,' and 'I'm always having to fix something or other,' and with the important countenance of an expert he goes to inspect the site of the catastrophe. The moments when a chap is needed for something in the household are rare, that's why he must make the most of them.

'You'll never learn to use it in a million years,' the man declaims, addressing this insult to the entire regiment of women worldwide, as it were. 'Bring the small ladder over here!' As you can see, this time he can command, and so makes sure not to miss the opportunity. 'And a chisel!' He says this, already sticking his head into the hapless mechanism. 'Aha,' he grunts as if he knew where the problem was; whereupon he fiddles with some mechanical gizmo or other, thrusts his fingers into it, wondering silently which whatsit does what, gets terribly dirty, and after a few minutes climbs down.

'That's it,' he says complacently, crushing the women of the household under his contemptuous look. 'Now it's a bit sorted, and you, Mary, go and fetch a plumber.'

Ironing

I don't know why the iron isn't counted among musical instruments, just as the piano, the violin or the aeolian harp. For it is a fact that the iron emits all kinds of songs: 'When I weeded flax', 'In Bohemia, where I was born', 'I loved, oh but just once in my life', and countless other lays, mostly in the loving vein. Likewise the brush is an instrument, a singing instrument beyond measure, especially when the stairs are being scrubbed. There's something like a law of rhythm, when you think about it. On the day of ironing the house is sunk in dry, somewhat singed warmth, and in such a peculiar white smell. The man is treated fairly amiably, or at least patronisingly, but he mustn't put anything down anywhere. He's handled with a certain magnanimity like a big child or some other half-tamed animal, unless he takes it into his head to throw his hat on the freshly ironed shirts or a book on the neatly folded linen. The very minute he does, he's made to feel in one way or another that he's a creature dirty by nature, whose touch, or even whose very closeness, threatens the immaculate whiteness of the great womanly work.

The man then avenges himself for this contempt by looking with glee for a burnt spot on his shirt.

'What's this?' he asks reproachfully.

'That?' the woman announces with a perfectly innocent face, 'that came during ironing.'

About Toothache

The People's Paper, 17 February 1929

So when it was at its worst, when I jumped out of bed at three o'clock in the morning and started running round the room in circles, holding my head and squealing like a scarified mouse, I said to myself: No, I can't leave it like this; it's impossible for mankind to keep quiet under such suffering; something must be done against it.

Well then, I'm fulfilling the promise of that more-than-hard moment by writing an article against it: I mean against periostitis.

The normal progress of the illness is this: first the sufferer, suppressing how he feels and trying to say it as lightly as he can, announces to his fellow beings that he has a bit of a toothache. Whereupon the fellow creatures say comfortingly that it's nothing, that it's just a little chill from a draught, and the best thing is to put plum brandy on it, or vinegar, or tincture of iodine, a cold poultice, a warm woollen scarf, peroxide, acetate of aluminium and whatever else anyone thinks of. The gain of using all these devices is that the pain, till then indeterminate, becomes keener and begins to prod, drill, dig, twitch, pierce, glow, prick, gnaw, blow up and rise like dough. This precipitates the arrival of the second stage of the illness, when the patient decides that he won't tolerate this, and embarks on swallowing various pills, such as aspirin, amidopyrin, novamidon, rhodin, trigemin, veramon and loads of others. It really helps a bit, the drilling pain gets blunted, but the invalid starts to bulge and feels the swelling with trembling fingers. It seems to him bigger than anything he's ever touched in all his puff. Meantime, his fellow beings divide into two camps: one claims that he should put cold compresses on it to stop it from dilating, and shrink it, while the other propagates the idea that it should get fomented under a cloth so as to quicken its development. The sufferer does both this and that by turns to the effect that the swelling fattens and hardens – you can almost see its exuberance making it gleam –

and pain surfaces from it, refreshed, agile and aggressive, launching bayonet attacks to the right and left, while the tooth in question grows, as it were, and juts out from the others, so that it keeps bumping against the teeth opposite, which gives it, every time this happens, the welcome opportunity to have a dazzling lightning-flash of pain strike through it. At this stage the sufferer growls something horrendous, sticks a hat on his head and steams out to see his dentist. There are moments when a human being is capable of such a heroic resolution.

Against all expectations your dentist doesn't display any excessive sympathy; he only mumbles brusquely: 'OK, we'll have a look at it.' He's tapping on your teeth with an instrument of some sort, ignoring your protests, and then he falls to musing: 'You know,' he says frowningly, 'this tooth really wants to be out.'

That very moment you are overwhelmed with a burst of peculiar generosity towards the wretched tooth; you're like a father who exerts himself to angelic patience over a reprobate offspring before he disowns him. 'Perhaps we'll give it another chance,' you suggest eagerly; 'look, perhaps it'll come to its senses and we'll be able to save it, don't you think?' At that moment that beastly creature is honestly hurting a teeny bit less, perhaps its character is already taking a turn for the better –

'All right,' the dentist grunts, 'we'll wait another day.' And he dismisses you, having prescribed some painting and anointing and poultices. Already on the way home the tooth changes its mind and flares up like mad. Running home, your pockets stuffed with small flasks and gallipots that you've bought in the apothecary, you can't wait to commence rescue works. So then you try to rescue the hapless tooth with super-human self-sacrifice (for you do it because it's in *its* interest, not yours). You gargle, rinse, rub yourself with pungent tinctures, paint yourself with evil-smelling iodine ointment, compress yourself with white-water pads, and do another rinsing round, and put another soothing little poultice on it, and in between you bang your head against the wall and try to count to a hundred and run in a circle and altogether make an effort to kill time, for there is no intellectual distraction that can quell an inflamed tooth for five minutes. One day, once in my lifetime, I'd like to write a book that would be so good and strong as to grip a person suffering from an inflamed tooth, but no one has as yet managed to do it. For my part, I've tried books tested during other ailments, for example, the Bible, *The Three Musketeers*, Dickens, detective stories and gardening price lists – in none have I found relief and forgetfulness. The sufferer concentrates on one thing: the rescue bid. Just as a sailor on a sinking ship ceaselessly pumps out water, so the person afflicted with an aching tooth ceaselessly administers poultices, swabs his jaws and drenches them with tinctures, and if his dentist recommended him to say 'Our Father' backwards, or spit three times northwards every seven minutes, or keep winding a red thread round his left leg, or rub green vitriol on the tip of his nose and swallow a spoonful of horse-dung infusion every quarter of an hour, he'd do it with passionate precision, and get really engrossed in it – and, moreover, it would make another of his days tick by.

Indeed, a day did pass and night fell. This night can't be described just as it's impossible to describe any endless thing; suffice it to say that with the first peep of dawn everything's been weighed up and sealed. The tooth must be taken out. I'll go to see the dentist first thing in the morning and will say firmly: Doctor, the tooth must be taken out, do with me whatever you like, I'm prepared for anything. Surprisingly, this heroic resolution lasts through until the morning. In the morning it turns out that it's Sunday and there are no dentists. There's a curious law whereby tooth inflammation usually culminates on Sunday. As a rule, it's Saturday night when it becomes apparent that the tooth is ripe for plucking. This phenomenon is surely related to the fact that on Sundays dentists don't run their surgeries.

The sufferer greets this fact with a double-edged feeling: on the one hand, he's furious and utters profanities against dental surgeons, the nonsensical custom that there are Sundays and public holidays at all, the whole world, and particularly that he can't have his tooth pulled out. On the other, he denies and suppresses a kind of profound relief that it's impossible to go to see the dentist, and so the tooth doesn't need to be taken out. At least not today, not yet. One has to wait.

The last day is an enormous wait, then. The patient no longer applies compresses, nor does he rinse his mouth, nor dab it with a wad of cotton wool, but waits curled up, writhes in agony, and runs in a circle staring at the clock in goggle-eyed consternation – when the devil will all this stop? Or he sits and rocks his body from side to side to stupefy himself. Every half an hour he gulps down some painkiller or other, the result of which is that he begins to feel really sick. In a state of paralysis he at last sees night and crawls into bed. It's the last night before his execution.

The pain that has so far gripped one tooth is now sprawling around; it's already up as well as down, in the ear, on the temple and in the throat, hot, glowing, pulsating; the sufferer is shaking with ague and raging impatience that makes him gnash his teeth – heavens alive, what a rough deal! He has no sooner gnashed his teeth than he hurtles out of bed, squealing and whining and running all round the room with shivering knees; when he can't go on any longer, he sits on the bed swaying his trunk; when he can't go on, he collapses among the eiderdowns and gnashes his teeth in raging impatience, whereupon the whole thing repeats itself. At three in the morning he decides that it can't be left like this, and that mankind can't carry on suffering in this way. Then he lies down and suddenly falls into a half swoon. In my case, I began to dream that the sore tooth and its counterpart weren't teeth but two divines; one of them, the sick one, visited the pope, and consequently the other one was forbidden to touch him. Any time he touched him I woke up with a painful wrench. Why is it, I wondered, that this divine can't be touched? That's a stupid custom, isn't it? Yes, came a clear and uncompromising answer, it's just an old regulation from Robert Guiscard's time. I've put up with it, as I reverence traditions. Whereupon I began to dream that I didn't really have teeth in my mouth, but cacti; the sore tooth is a spiny opuntia, while his counterpart is a cereus with long prickles; the moment they get close, they thrust those spikes into each other, and I have to wake up. I said to myself with tears in my eyes: I cultivated them from seedlings with so much care, and this is what I get for it. Hag-ridden by such dreams, the patient finally sees dawn.

The end is short and abrupt. With trembling knees the sufferer creeps to his dentist's.

'Doctor . . .' he tries to stammer.

'Sit down,' commands the dentist.

'And it won't hurt, will it?'

'No,' the dentist says, rattling some instruments.

'And does it . . . really have to go?'

'Absolutely,' the dentist replies frostily and draws nearer to the patient.

The martyr grabs the forearms of the armchair. 'But . . . will it hurt?'

'Open your mouth!'

The sufferer deals the dentist's stomach and chest several blows with his legs and fists. He's pressed down to the back of the chair, and is about to shout out, at which point he receives an injection.

'Did it hurt?' the dentist asks.

'N-n-no,' opines the martyr uncertainly. 'Could we wait till tomorrow?'

'No,' the dentist grunts, looking dreamily out of the window. Outside, people walk by as if one of the greatest tragedies on earth were not taking place here, by this window.

'Well, it'll be done soon,' the dentist says with satisfaction. 'Open your mouth!'

The patient closes his eyes so as not to see that God-awful instrument. 'But . . .'

'Open wider!'

Something crunched inside his mouth; most likely the doctor's pincers have slipped.

'Will it hurt?'

'Rinse your mouth,' the doctor rumbles, as if from a great distance, and shows something whitish in the pincers. For God's sake, wasn't that tooth any bigger?

For three days after this the former sufferer goes from one human being to another and relates what he's been through with his periostitis. But people are so ungenerous. When your story is at its height, they say: 'That's nothing. But when I had periostitis . . .' And then they launch into some highly coloured saga about how the doctor had to cut through their jaw with a chisel, or something like that.

Others say indifferently: 'Periostitis? I've never had that.' And take no further interest in your case.

Forerunners of Spring

The People's Paper, 9 March 1929

They have a different one in each paper: some write about seagulls, others about starlings, some about snowdrops, others about daphnes. We have run throughout the whole of Prague these past few days, from the Strašnice quarter to the National Theatre, yet we haven't met any starlings, nor have we seen a single snowdrop, nor a shoot of daphne coming up through the snow and mud. And still, we have seen

the true forerunner of spring,

which always arrives out of natural necessity once the overly long, mean, murdering and merciless winter is doomed to disintegrate. It is an unmistakable, poetic foreshadowing, and yet no paper has so far mentioned it. For note that the moment spring is drawing near WOMEN START CLEANING WINDOWS!

They haven't been able to wash them since December because the water would freeze on them. Hence we have looked at the world through murk and gloom, succumbing to cheerless, melancholy rumination. And behold – now when we look through a window, we see conspicuously brighter horizons, and the whole world is somehow lighter and cleaner even though it's sinking in mud. Consequently, we look future things in the face and with greater confidence. So when we extol harbingers of spring, let's not forget women cleaning windows.

Spring Overture

The People's Paper, 31 March 1929

You are the first thing we have after such a long wait through this ghastly winter – you snowdrop, or crocus, or little flower of a winter aconite, or catkin on a pussy willow. As soon as the first bud swells and the first leaf unfurls, there is an open flower; as soon as nature begins to breathe, it blossoms. Love comes first. Everything else arrives only later: the eagerness of growth, the work of roots, the quiet, tenacious struggle for life. But to sustain you, the first floweret, the plant takes energy from nowhere but itself. The ashen earth is still closed, no roots have yet sucked the still-slumbering soil. The plant gives out the first flower from its own essence. Because there is nowhere else to turn to, it puts its whole heart into this spring enterprise. That's why it's good.

As for us people, don't, little spring flower, believe every bit of gossip – it's not so bad. We, too, would like to have a paradise on earth and God's peace and resurrection and eternal spring and other such things, but for the time being we quarrel over how to arrange it, and where to find the money and who should do it, and this, that or the other. It seems that the earth on which we live has not yet opened so that the Garden of Eden can begin to 'vegetate', as gardeners say. In short, it's still impossible. But if we are properly attentive, now and then we find people who put their whole heart into this Edenic enterprise and draw the means to make our world better from their inner selves. Love comes first.

But I'll testify for that first snowdrop (it doesn't have any Christian name, and has performed its clever little feat anonymously, in honour and praise of its family) that it was extremely courageous of it to embark on the said spring enterprise. It must have crunched its way through the snow and ice – a positive tiny icebreaker. It knuckled down to its own personal spring off its own bat, taking the risk of night frosts and morning rime. Make no mistake! A dinky flower like this is not a sunshine idyll. It is toughness, guts and adventure. The first envoy far ahead of the lines, bravely waving its white flag of truce. A pioneer and a conqueror. The first settler in an inhospitable region. The first white sailboat on the ocean.

It is guts, and it is quiet naturalness as well. That's why it's good.

Well then, as for sprouting, it's really beginning. Now a chubby bud is protruding from the ground, a nub, thick and closed, now a tender young leaf is unfolding its frills so beautifully green that no other time is there anything as green as this. But that's not all. When you look more closely, you can see that the infant life is forcing its way out of the mouldering and putrefaction of last autumn, that it's stuck fast up to its neck in the common burial ground of last year's vegetation. Only in the spring is last year's leaf buried, only in the season of sprouting is it turned to dust and ashes. If we observe the springtime earth carefully, we find that it's not so much spangled with flowers as strewn with dead foliage and decay and the disintegration of what happened last year. It's only now that the previous year is being buried; it's only now that dead life is going back to the earth from which it came. There is no resurrection of the dead; there is a resurrection among the dead.

Wait a minute, fresh little leaf amid the rotting sparrowgrass, that's what you wanted to say all the time, wasn't it? – life and death eternally coexist.

About Birdsong

The People's Paper, 9 June 1929

Various commonplace ideas about birdsong are pervasive: that birdsong is delectable, for instance. Conversely I heard the other day a lady, who lives near Rieger's Orchards, lament that she must move out. Apparently the birds in the park keep shouting so loudly from four o'clock in the morning that they don't let her sleep. I consoled her by saying that all birds didn't do this, only blackbirds.

Where blackbirds are concerned, it's of course necessary to admit that they are black, rumbustious scoundrels who don't have a tang of feeling for poetry. Besides, blackbirds have almost entirely alienated themselves from nature; they have become townies and, consequently, turned into boors. They've got used to the city as sparrows have; more precisely, they've seized control of the city and don't suffer any decent species of bird into it. A thrush wanted to settle down in my garden. He sat on the fence, tilted his head to one side and whistled that, basically, he'd like it there. That very moment a pair of blackbirds pounced on him ruthlessly with a hell of a racket and drove him away, somewhere beyond Červený Dvůr. With that this black, yellow-beaked louse hopped about victoriously on the palings of his garden, bawling out: 'See him? See him? See him? He's gone!' Then he wagged his little tail and spat energetically.

That was last year's blackbird, a big shouter and a lout in the sight of the Lord. He had his favourite hackneyed utterances, which only uninformed people took for singing – they were actually insults. For example, he enjoyed shouting around at full blast:

'Leave her alone! Leave her alone! Leave her alone! I c'n seee!! I c'n seee!!'

When he'd had enough of that, he asked just as little urchins do when they lose track of time for all their playing:

'What's the time? What's the time?'

This year's blackbird (one of the offspring of the previous one) is less personal. He can say only a few words – God knows where he got them from. At four o'clock in the morning he starts shouting persistently:

'Veeaal! Veeaal! Veeaal! Veal!'

Then he makes a little jump and eagerly bursts into:

'Crap! Crap! Crap! Ha-ha-ha!'

At which point he gulps down a worm, as if it were a piece of macaroni, and carries on repeating his repertoire, to which his consort, a diligent little brown individual, patiently keeps replying:

'I know. I know.'

And the husband snaps back rudely:

'See her! See her! Yyyuck!'

It's a well-known fact that blackbirds are not great singers, but I must confess that when I heard nightingales for the first time in my life, it was a sheer shock for me. It happened in Fara Sabina, a couple of miles from Rome. I was having a nap on a cosy little train when suddenly I jumped out of my dream with a terrible feeling that somewhere near me six xylophonists had gone mad, pounding the wooden bars with their sticks with all their might. It was the nightingales' jugging.

Maybe – who knows? – there live among us larger beings than we are, cherubs or seraphim, for instance, who speak a different language and have other things to do than us. Maybe they sometimes put down their pens or instruments, and for a while listen absentmindedly to the voices of *our* life. Maybe at that very instant a child is screaming somewhere, a drunk man is swearing at his wife, chaps in a pub are brawling about politics, thumping their fists on the table, news vendors are calling out the evening editions of the papers, a driver is shouting at a pedestrian: 'You fucking idiot, get out of the road!' Perhaps at that moment a cherub smiles at a seraph and says, just as we do about birds: 'Can you hear how the people are *singing*?'

Sisters

The People's Paper, 14 July 1929

Like it or not, it's part of a sort of male prestige to talk about females a little disparagingly. It's not so much ill will as an awareness of physical superiority. It often looks as if women needed our protection, but there are moments, and indeed difficult ones, when we find that we need theirs. The great superiority of woman is that she is a mother, and second, that she is a sister – I mean, a sister of mercy. A man can be a brother to a man in a religious community or in battle, but rarely can he be a brother to a sick person. He can treat him, or at least regale him with something, but he can't accompany the sufferer on his path of pain silently and softly so that he isn't alone. A man is crudely active; he is incapable of dividing his activity into tiny, patient deeds so well. I've seen surgeons at work, quick and determined as if in an attack; I've seen sisters in their silent vigil, and I can't tell which of them was more beautiful.

I've seen two types: one, still rather a novice to that Samaritan order, slight and shy, was sitting at the head of a bed for hours on end, and nights on end, and didn't avert her eyes from the patient's face. I don't know what she was thinking about, but surely nothing heavy or sad, because her face was unclouded and calm, and was a pleasurable sight for the patient's eyes when they woke up from the sleep which had virtually become never-ending. Nothing was going on in that stuffy chamber; only the regular breath of the invalid and the regular footfalls of passing seconds were heard, but the quiet sounds floated upon something even more quiet, upon the peaceful vigil of a small, rosy deaconess, who was neither reading, nor praying, nor sewing, but only looking radiantly at the face of the sleeping man. She resembled a glowing lamp that doesn't blink, but stilly and silently pushes back the dark that hurls itself down upon us. And the patient opened his eyes and calmed down, for he saw that little bright human light shining above him.

The other was an old veteran of the Samaritan service, fat and heavy, half-blinded by thirty years of vigil. She sat bending over the sick man, with her hand on his pulse, and listened, watching out for every murmur with the experienced, unfailing attentiveness of an old bloodhound. Nothing escaped her, no quiver of breath, no attempt of an exhausted arm to stir. Before the patient lifted his arm, she had been there with her strong, sure, yet light hands, and helped him to make the movement or rest his arm more comfortably. And she accompanied that last struggle with those experienced palms; she helped the arm to defend itself still, the chest to breathe, the head to repose, and she served the burning-out body to the last holding of its breath. Then she wiped her eyes, and promptly went to wash and straighten out the body of the dead.

I believe, then, that this is roughly how it was: the good Samaritan, having found a half-killed man, cleaned his wounds with wine, and ripping his robe, bound them up, and set him on his beast, and supporting the insensible body, brought him to his tent. And then – and that's what the New Testament failed to mention – then a woman Samaritan came quietly, and sat by the patient's bed; she kept vigil all night long like the tranquil, lambent flame of an oil lamp, she kept lifting the invalid's head and moistening his lips. This is not recorded in Scripture, but it must have been like this. And unimaginably long hours passed – the wounded man groaned, and the woman Samaritan kept vigil at his bedside without Scripture having written about it and without either the Levites or the good Samaritans caring about her quiet work.

Return to Nature

The People's Paper, 1 January 1931

Just to make sure you don't get me wrong and don't think me ungenerous, I wish all of you who're gadding about on the mountains during these winter days twenty inches of good powdery snow, terrific downhill schusses and all the rest of it. Let it be.

However, when I see the mass migrations on public holidays or Sundays, those myriads of lads and lasses with skis on their shoulders, that crazed, collective exodus to the white majesty of the mountains, the first thing I say to myself is that not all of those pilgrims and pilgrimesses are processing towards the sporting delights of telemark turns or Christies or whatever those knacks are called, but that they will come a cropper and roll downhill like snowballs and get dreadfully winded and feel their legs are dropping off, because not everyone is endowed with the kind of grace you need for every mode of self-propulsion. Further, I'm sure that not all these wanderers are led into the misty distances by the ardent urge to surrender themselves to the white sublimity of the mountains, and worship their divine purity. For if there were such a powerful mass movement towards beauty, sublimity and purity, it would have to be a shade more visible in our cities, and even in our habits and civic arrangements. Grumblers and inveterate cynics would say that this winter crusade to the mountains is nothing but a fashion. For my part, I think that it's something even blinder than fashion. It's something like an instinct. An atavism. A return to nature.

Naturam expellas furca, tamen usque recurret. Throw nature out of the door and you'll climb after her through the window. Expel her from the city and you'll go after her to the mountains. It was bound to happen. Because the snow on our roads has become a traffic hindrance, we must look for somewhere where snow is simply snow still, yea the snowiest snow. Since we live less and less commonly in wild wooded dells, we go on camping pilgrimages to the forests. We chase after sun and water because we're no longer farmers and fishermen. We've discovered sun and water with inordinate and unprecedented zeal. Through long-term sitting, we've discovered our own legs and have started using them fanatically, calling it sport. Such a discovery is, first of all, an evaluation. We've come to value snow and water, sun and air, we've made the world more beautiful and more precious. Achieving control over the forces of nature is a great gain, but equally gainful is valuing them. A boy who sledges and builds a snowman and sucks icicles has a much deeper relation to the cosmic phenomenon of winter than the town council responsible for clearing snow from the roads. I'm not saying that the council isn't useful and necessary, but I'm glad that on the whole the boy with a sledge wins.

Discoveries aren't over and done with yet. Perhaps one day we shall discover and value the moon and the stars, perhaps we'll get to like rain, building runnels and things, and find something good in the wind like children with a kite. And there are still flowers and animals left. And perhaps a time will come when we discover our streets and cities as pieces of the universe, and people as bits of good old nature, and start to cultivate them with collective relish and passionate enthusiasm. Let it be.

How I Have Come to Be What I Am

A talk for radio, *Lumír: A Review of Literature, Art and Society*, 16 June 1932; broadcast on 8 May 1932

When I was assigned the task of saying something about my writing, what first crossed my mind was this question: how did it in actual fact happen that I had come to be a writer? Since I was very little, my Dad, himself a doctor, had got me used to the idea that I would be a doctor. After a few other plans (like becoming a tram conductor) I also reckoned that I'd do doctoring. I don't want to shift onto others the responsibility that my life has eventually taken a different direction; but to be frank, the greatest blame lies with my home and my family.

First and foremost, there was my Dad, a country doctor and, moreover, a good example of the – today already very out-of-date – generation of cultural revivalists. He was a voracious reader; since our childhood he had kept us supplied with books, which didn't stop us from reading through, more or less secretly, the whole of his library, from Havlíček and Neruda to forensic medicine.[1] Apart from that, our old man took a hand in politics, was an orator at open-air rallies, lectured to workers, chaired the local amateur actors, and was a regional poet; even today I can still see him spending evenings composing festive speeches in the silence of his surgery, which smelt of phenol, and then reading them out to us in a moved voice. Because he was big and strong, we boys imitated him wholeheartedly; ever since we were about eight we composed congratulatory rhymes and other occasional verses of that kind. He liked to see it and encouraged us. Then – it was about the time of the Ethnographical Exhibition – our Mum recorded national songs, fairy tales and legends. That's when grandpas and grandmas from the corner of the world around Granny's Valley came round,[2] and sang and narrated tales over a pot of ersatz coffee, while Dad collected folk embroidery, chests, ceramics and antiques. He accepted them from people instead of fees – quite a few things are in the Ethnographical Museum; and Mum's bundle of national songs and fairy tales is somewhere there too, I think.

And then we had Granny, a miller's wife from Hronov, godly, wise and at the same time as perky as a sprite, full of songs, sayings, proverbs and folk humour. She was the living embodiment of the folk spirit and language of our region. The longer I write and work in our language, the more I realise how much I owe to her and what I learnt from her and am still learning even today.

Mum was the romantic element in the family; she was ardent, vehemently emotional, gifted and utterly non-practical. In her youth she sang romantic songs, and wrote well. It's from her I have that bit of romantic sensibility and that fantasticality without which my writing would look different in many ways.

Dad was – besides that revivalist humanism – a typical spirit of the so-called scientific century: he was a natural-science materialist, factually engrossed in the enigmas of nature; he was interested in prehistory and history, philosophy and natural science, the order of evolution and the secrets of unknown regions. His library was a layman's compendium of all possible branches of learning, and in one way or another he dabbled in each of them. Apart from that he gardened and did carpentry, kept bees and grafted roses, drew pictures and looked after communal affairs. He was versatile and simple, entirely objective and fully turned towards all the things of this world. He never made a big deal out of his inner self, he lived in what he was doing, and was a good physician. I am aware of how much of what I do and how I do it is his inheritance.

In addition this was, while I was still a child, joined by my sister's passionate musical world and my brother's objectivity as a painter. And then the environment determined by my Dad's profession: the world of pain, journeying around the cottages of paupers and the dim rooms of millionaires; the small-town environment of crafts-men and shopkeepers, of the almshouse and factories, of work-ers and spiritualists and old-world cottagers; the environment of German peasant-farmers from the linguistic borderland and of a radical little Czech factory town – the extreme social and national contrasts were there as if in the palm of your hand. It seems to me that I have taken something from all that.

I know that it's only a part of what I have picked up and endeav-our to gather in life, but I think that it's the basis, and I have noth-ing better than this basis by which to explain to myself what I have written. And come to think of it, I haven't, it seems to me, really betrayed all that much the profession that my family background destined me for. In my own way I also try to do doctoring, if I can, to heal people, to help them in their pain. I'm not a surgeon, but a physician, as country practitioners often are; now I give drops, now a compress, whatever the daily practice brings along – and I, too, would like to be a good doctor who helps.

A Fairy Tale on a Tram

The People's Paper, 26 November 1932

Just to avoid any misunderstanding: this is not an imaginary fairy tale but a real one. A pretty young mum is sitting on a tram, a little boy like a bear cub by her side.

'Mum,' the tot suddenly sings out in a clear childish voice. 'Tell me a fairy tale!'

The mum bends towards him and whispers: 'Which one?'

'Well, the one about the frog princess,' chirps the boy.

Softly, very softly the mother starts narrating the story.

'And how big was the princess?' asks the little one loudly. The whole tram begins to smile.

'And what did the prince do to her?' the young gentleman enquires again. And the mother on a rattling tram carries on whispering the fairy tale about the frog princess. The entire tramload has fallen silent so as not to disturb, and looks as if it does not concern them . . .

At that moment the story-telling mum and her little boy were completely self-sufficient. They filled in their own world, just as a mother who is breastfeeding doesn't care about those around, and the others look somewhere else because they feel that they don't belong in the magic circle drawn round the mother and the child.

Topsoil

The People's Paper, 24 September 1933

It would be a lovely map that would faithfully capture the colours of our country, copying nature. There would have to be, it goes without saying, the black green of pine woods, the saturated green of spruce thickets, and the pale green curliness of broadleaved forests. But the greatest number of colours would be supplied by the soil as we see it now towards autumn, freshly ploughed, not yet crumbling or faded by frost and drought. This map would of course tally to some extent with the geological one, but it wouldn't be so scholarly, and it would serve the joy of the eyes more, because it would be beautifully colourful with a rich spectrum of shades, like the work of an artist who fondly mixes various pigments, reliable and unfading, on his palette.

It's a whole gamut of colours, from white sand to the greasy black of the fattest soil. In some places the kinds of topsoil are creamy or light grey, as if trodden into dust or bleached by drought; some kinds are dyed like very light cocoa, almost bluish, or like milk with a drop of coffee in it. Then you find clayey yellows in various tints of ochre and rust, and flaxen and golden and gingery soils, and some in the shades of Naples yellow, Indian yellow or baked ochre. The broadest, however, is the range of browns, from straw-like paleness to the deep, strong tones of sepia, from an opalescent gleam to rich ruddy hues like chocolate. There are coffee, chestnut, the brown of baked crocks and the warm charred crust of bread loaves, the dry, blanched brown of shallow, stony topsoil and the powdery hints of deep loess and silt. And finally there are red or russet soils, from bashful rust to maroon, playing with a tinge of purple, in all the intensities of sienna, reddle and terracotta scorched by fire; there are stretches of pink and tracts painted over with blackening blood, or blushing as if they were ablaze in an infinite sunset. Region from region, virtually village from village, there is a differently tinted dominant, and a different paleness; now when the harvest is over, the colourful map of tilled earth speaks to us loud and clear.

All the things that are dug into it! Lumps of lime and heaps of black manure, nutritious sediments, slag and meal. How strange that hundreds of years of work couldn't lacquer over or dissolve the native colour of earth. For so many hundreds of years man has manured and turned over that thin peel of topsoil, year after year he has covered it with the cultural deposit of work, but the russet region still is and will remain equally russet and the yellow region equally yellow. Earth can't be re-dyed; not even the ages can take its speech and its colour away. It can be transformed neither by tractor nor hoe – after the strawberry-blonde grain and the dark potato rows, the brown or flaxen earth resounds with its original tone again. Soil will never be uniformed; nations and cultures may succeed one another or merge, but what they trample on can be neither crushed and dispersed nor mixed. Perhaps this is the reason why we so much like to talk about native soil; we want to hold on to its steadfastness. Just look at how solid and colourfast our earth is, my friend – it will outlast us.

So, talking of autumn colours, let's not forget these beautiful, warm colours of topsoil uncovered by the plough. Even in this respect we are, thank God, a blessedly dappled country, clothed in an iridescent robe. We are, so to speak, kneaded out of all possible samples of soil, and all the geological eras have contributed layers, so that this rather small bit of the world could be formed. It's only people that are not so easily tolerant of their various shades and colours – perhaps it's because they have been here, geologically speaking, only since yesterday. It will be a very long time before people look at the colourful map of nations and states as fondly as at the colourful map of soil.

Autumn

The People's Paper, 25 November 1934

Where nature's concerned, nothing's ever over and done with. You think, leaves will fall and all the finery will be gone, only the bare boughs will remain. But if you look at them more carefully over time (a couple of decades should be enough for you to notice properly) you realise how much has been left on those bare boughs – how much of character and personality. If we start with the bark – a bark that's russet as in dogwood, green as in laburnum, yellow as in weeping willows, white as in birches, silvery grey as in beeches, and also brown, cinnamon, ochre or black, and smooth, so taut that it shines, or wrinkled, furrowed, scaly, cracked or peeling – we can see straight off where each twig has grown from, each has the characteristic of a whole tree or bush. And when it comes to ramification and the structure of the crown, there we really run out of words, unable to find an expression for every single variant of growth and arboreal composition. There are branches that are splayed out, lateral, curvy or rigidly spiny, or set on the mother bough stiffly or sinuously, or running up smoothly and delicately as if they had been combed; others stream upright, or square their shoulders; still others are trailing, protruding, twiggy or fanning out, or muscular or skinny like a skeleton, or dense like a thick shock of hair, or velvety and pulpy, or firm and dry like brushwood. Each bush and each tree does it differently according to their family and variety.

Only when the leaves drop off can we look at this infinite diversity thoroughly – and best when hoarfrost descends.

And I haven't yet talked about roots. How many extraordinary and individual differences in colour and growth there are, in the hairiness of soft fibrous ends, in woodiness, and rhizomes and expanse! That's something a man can't really appreciate, perhaps just some Creator or other watches it all with delight, admiring what a beautiful crown of roots this tree or that bush has. What a lovely underground landscape, he thinks.

We look at it only from a human, or in other words wrong, perspective when we say that in autumn nature resigns herself to dying, or bunkum like that. First, nature is lucky because nine times out of ten she doesn't die, and second, she doesn't indulge in such a sentimental weakness as resignation. Quite the opposite, she goes at it, incredibly active and determined, as if she meant to say: What kind of talk's this! We must get ready; we must gather and mobilise all our strength to be able to defend ourselves. It's impossible without sacrifices, we'll give up all our foliage, we'll tighten our metabolic belts, we'll draw our glucose, starch and all those chemical compounds into our roots. To work, to work! Grieving and lamenting won't help. It may hit us any minute now, but when it does, it will find us with ripened wood and capable of endurance, but capable of sprouting, too, and fit to flower the moment we get out of the blasted winter. To persevere and have the groundwork done for next spring, that's our watchword.

As you can see, when autumnal nature says something, what she says doesn't sound like resignation but robust encouragement.

And one night grey frost strikes brutally and without notice. Suddenly the bare boughs reveal their contours with a beautiful, new distinctness that has previously escaped our attention. All at once everything is so petrified, austere and stern that it comes near to jangling like steel rods or wires. Everything is ready – each hard leafless twig is an armed front behind which life is being defended. We call it bare boughs, but it is vegetation clothed in armour-plate.

A Legend about the Horticultural Species

The People's Paper, 3 March 1935

He's sitting over gardening catalogues and ticking items with his pencil. I must have this new medium-height *Aster amellus*, he's saying to himself, and this salmon-pink astilbe, that's for sure, and what about *Bergenia delavayi*? Well, let's go for a *Bergenia delavayi*. But I haven't got a buphthalmum in my garden yet. I must definitely try buphthalmum. And so he goes on until he has ninety-eight new perennials ticked and ready to order, that he finds he can't carry on living without.

Whereupon he buries himself in shrubs (well, only in the catalogue). One day I should really try an abelia, and here they have a new *Acer japonicum* – look, they say it goes a magnificent colour in autumn – it would be a sin not to have it. And this dwarf amelanchier, surely I can fit that in somewhere. And so on. With a heavy heart he restricts himself to choosing twenty-three new arboreal species that he yearns to have, ought to have and must have if he's ever to have a happy life. Oh, and five dwarf conifers, which, they say, are unusual, delectable and an enhancement for any garden. But wait a minute. Where can I plant all those little fir things?

And so the gardener puts on a winter coat and makes off eagerly into the garden. Here, in this bed, there's some free space; wouldn't it be possible to put the salmon-pink astilbe there? No, it wouldn't, there's already a monarda there, but you can't see it just now. OK, what about here? No, there's an *Anemone hupehensis* there already. He walks around the whole garden, seeking a spot that isn't already occupied. He's standing and looking pensively at a bit of land where anyone else would see just a smattering of manure and dry leaves, but for him the snow-white stars of moon daisies are swaying in a June air. God, if only the plot were half a yard broader so that a few more things could be fitted in. There's so much space in the world, take that manchuria or whatever it's called. Please, God, it wouldn't do you any harm if I had an extra half a yard.

Then a Tempting Spirit comes nigh unto man in the office of gardener, who is sniffling with cold and goggling at his desolate plot: 'Look,' he whispers, 'I'll give you as much land as you like if you bow down and worship me.'

The gardener raises his head. 'You know what, this plot needs to be a yard broader.'

'A yard?' the Tempting Spirit queries contemptuously. 'Don't be silly, man. I don't work in yards, believe me. If you like, I'll give you everything as far as you can see for planting.'

'As far as Bohdalec?' the gardener asks distrustfully.

'That's nothing. As far as Krč Forest, and over there beyond Spořilov and Záběhlice,[1] and OK, why not – I'll round it up from sea to sea for you. So, it's a deal?'

'Hang on a sec,' the gardener hesitates. 'No, I couldn't manage all that.'

'So I'd add in a magic power. For example, you could just look at a place and a big tree would immediately spring up there.'

'Which tree?' the gardener asks, livening up.

'A maple, if you like.'

'Well, it's easy to say a maple,' the gardener grunts. 'There are many kinds of maple, old chap. I'd put an *Acer ginnala* there, it's smashing in autumn, you know, like fire. But there would have to be free space around it. It's not just a simple matter to plant a maple. I'd prefer to put a few birches around, the birch is our sort of tree.'

'Put your birches there, then,' the Tempting Spirit rejoins a little impatiently.

'Yes,' the gardener meditates, 'but what shall I put in front of them as foreground? A cornus with coral branches, perhaps. That would be beautiful in winter: the red stems of dogwoods and the white trunks of birches, but a berberis with red berries wouldn't be bad either. Hang on, it would take a lot of thinking to get the best possible effect.'

'You think it out later,' the Tempting Spirit insists. 'Now say – do you want it or not?'

'Well, it's not just that,' the gardener ponders. 'I'd like to, but for a chap to plant it all thoroughly, so that it's perfect, you see, is not as simple as ABC. To put the best thing on each spot so that it thrives there, and also goes with the other stuff – that would take a devil of a lot of work. I don't know, a chap mightn't be up to it.'

'But surely you won't go on fiddling with every bit of land like this,' the Tempting Spirit rumbles. 'Come on, you'll have such a whacking great tract of land in your power, from sea to sea! Why should some paltry inch matter?'

'I beg your pardon,' the gardener stammers in a peeved voice. 'It's clear you don't understand gardening! I'll show you how it should be done. For example – well, look, do you think you could extend this plot by a yard for me?'

'Certainly not,' the Tempting Spirit retorts with absolute finality. 'Dear me! I haven't come to please people but to seduce them. I'll either give you power over the world from sea to sea, or . . .'

'If you don't want to do a yard,' the gardener concedes, 'even half a yard would do. Or just a tiny patch so that I can fit in a salmon-pink astilbe!'

'Go to hell!' the Tempting Spirit spits furiously and leaves the gardener standing over his narrow plot covered in dry leaves.

What to Give to Each and Every One of Them

The People's Paper, 25 December 1935

When Christmas is coming near, the normal course of family life is approximately as follows: at the beginning of December the sensible members of the family (except for children) agree with immense relief that *this year* they won't give one another any presents – besides, they're all useless things, and you don't have time to shop for all that, and after all you need nothing *at all*, you're up to your ears in other expenses, and anyhow, no bones about it. So that's it – just a matter of agreeing on things and they can be made wonderfully easier.

After about ten days each of the above-mentioned adult members of the family begins to feel a sense of unease, something like this: *I know* that we're not going to give anything to one another, and I'm *terribly glad* I won't get anything from anyone, but I could still give something small to the others – they'll not expect it and will be all the more pleased. We did promise one another that there wouldn't be any Christmas presents this year, but never mind that, I'll get just a little trifle.

The method of choosing presents varies. Some people simply walk along the streets and look into shop windows until they spot an article, and feel something like an inspiration or afflatus: yes, this is the one thing I'd like to give to Uncle Hugo, and this manicure set has appeared in the universe only so that I can give it to my sister Agnes. People of this sort choose from what they see – they're a rather carefree but generous kind. A more cautious person tries to discreetly investigate beforehand which gift would be welcomed and would fill a particular gap in the life of the one to be endowed with it. So he stops by at his sister Agnes's, announcing in a loud, cheery voice that he's 'just popped in'because he's passing on his way somewhere, while scanning everything in the room to find out if there's anything missing. (A barometer? A nice little vase? A bedside lamp?) Sister Agnes begins to feel somewhat uneasy and embarks on a barrage of explanations that she hasn't 'tidied up today' because she's got 'so much work to do, what with this season'. Alternatively, the careful giver starts up a conversation with Uncle Hugo so as to get out of him imperceptibly what he'd like to have. He eventually finds out that what Uncle Hugo would like to have most is thunder with which he could strike the Inland Revenue or something. Lastly, the most methodical of all (among whom I count also myself) takes a sheet of paper and jots down a list of all the family members, and what to give to each and every one of them. Such a list looks roughly like this:

Marjie
Agnes
Tony
Uncle Hugo ... wine

George
Betsy
Grandad ... tobacco
Francie
Mrs Hedvik
Brother-in-law Joseph
Annie

And now the methodical giver starts pondering over what to give to each of them. He recalls all possible objects that exist in the world, lock, stock and barrel; wherever he goes, he keeps muttering: 'Wait, so here we have a tie, stockings, a picture, a thermometer, a pocket knife, a sewing kit, a tie, a pocket knife, a thermometer, a tie – and, damn it, what else? And a handbag. Then a pocket knife and a thermometer – a tie – and a handbag ...' A feeling of mounting intensity that there aren't enough present-able things on earth grips him. He reads, advertised in the papers, that 'the most suitable Christmas present is net curtains', but he can't really buy that, or 'get your dear ones sophisticated books', but how can he know which sophisticated books wretched old Tony already has? He strains every nerve, turning it over in his mind, and in the end he gives something that the other person thinks a nuisance, and gets purely useless things himself and pretends that he's awfully pleased ...

Next year we must *really and truly* agree that we shall give nothing to one another. (A note for the composing room: Keep the copy and print it again next year!)

Haymaking

The People's Paper, 7 June 1936

Let me pillory the poets for the wrong they do by keeping quiet about nature's beautiful and magnificent feats. Oh yes, at times they weave garlands of forget-me-nots, sing of the rose and interlace their verses with the lily or the convolvulus. But they do not, to my knowledge, pluck the mouse-ear chickweed or the speedwell, do not exalt the ragged robin and do not spare a tender word for the woodsorrel; the globe-flower does not open its buds for them, nor does the buttercup, nor even the pretty little saxifrage; they do not stoop towards the blue ground ivy, do not marvel at the meadow vetchling and are not dazzled by the awesome gleam of marigolds. Just this once I shall do it for you, poets, albeit in the rough language of unmetrical speech, but make sure that in future you voice a sincere testimony, concealing nothing in your verses of what demands to be seen and appreciated.

So, then, this is the lustrous and lionhearted marigold whose yellow is mighty and rich, quite unlike any other of the world's yellows: a yellow so thick, pitchy and deep, so strong and ripe that it is as though the flower of the marigold has been working on it for centuries. And when the plant casts off its legendary crown, what remains is a bristly, firm ovary – a small, erect mace. I'm telling you, the marigold is strength, a square-built, substantial and patulous strength, a sturdy, broad-shouldered chap, the really strapping lad among all flowers. Small and stout let it be – the marigold is a jolly good fellow.

And this is the saxifrage: an overflow of flowers, a cream-white bouquet, a glistering profusion on a stalk as firm as a rock; the meadow is smothered with them as if it were covered with snow; every single one soars and climbs from the huddled rosette of leaves like a tiny poplar. How come you don't bloom yourself away, you rigid, plentiful flower? I know, we all do our best, but anyone who has broken rocks comes to understand what achievement is.

And what about the speedwell? A little blue cloud in the grass, out of the blue; a bit of hazily blue sky, powdered, as it were, with a dusting of peace, a mild and poignant colour of countless blue eyes that peer among the stalks of grass as children look through the pales of a fence to see what goes on in the street. No, nothing's up, only a stranger is walking by. And who are you, little boy with flabbergasted eyes? I'm Speedwell. I see, so you're the Speedwell boy. That's good, you have nothing to feel ashamed of.

The buttercup, that's slimness, slender suppleness and a brilliant, sulphurous, soprano yellow: high above the grass glitter glossy, cool cups on such tenuous stalks that they seem to be floating in the air. You don't flower on earth, golden buttercup, but in unconfined space as the heavenly stars do. You aim too high, you little poisonous flower. Can't you see how the honest, amiable cinquefoil crouches near the ground?

And here is the noble, tall globe-flower: a pale, slightly exhausted yellow of round blossoms, too dignified ever to open them up entirely. Half-unfolds them like this – look – just to allow them to give out a delicate scent. And if the meadow were saturated with globe-flowers, each would still remain an individual – there is something like aristocracy in it.

Chickweed, chickweed: those are the bounteous little white flowers whose every petal is heart-carved. The chickweed: when it comes to blooming, it displays no less than whole carpets and cushions. Why do these flowers on short stalks flourish so densely, so luxuriously and en masse? Perhaps because they are very close to the earth and its strength. Or perhaps because an area ought to be covered and filled up, whereas in space it is possible to float. We shall never fill up space, but we can cover our land with a carpet of our work.

And here comes the ragged robin fluttering its fringy petals, the pink flags, the wind rippling the meadow, the white foam of chickweed and the airy corals of ragged robins above it, the gingery panicles of the woodsorrel and the little blue cloud of the speedwell; the straddling marigold is firmly waving its minute maces while the large flakes of the saxifrage are snowing: children, flowers, stars, it's time for haymaking.

Icicles

The People's Paper, 31 January 1937

So one morning I looked into the paper to find out what was new (and bad) in the world, and then out of the window, up to the heavens, to see what was new under the sun, and at that second glance I noticed to my astonishment that above the window of my attic hung twelve icicles lined up in a row. The biggest and most beautiful was over two feet long and as thick as an arm, the others were a little bit shorter and weaker, perhaps to make it plain that there is no equality even among icicles. I don't mean to claim that my twelve icicles were an especially unusual sight; the only strange thing about them was that out of a clear blue sky they made me walk on air. And while I was wondering why I was beaming with so much pleasure and rubbing my hands in glee, I got it: like so many other things (for example, snow, caterpillars, shells, rabbits and marbles) icicles are inseparably tied up with childhood memories.

Take my word for it, only a little boy can properly appreciate an object as interesting as a stick of ice hanging from the roof. The moment he comes across his very first icicle he discovers in joyous surprise

1. that it can be broken, giving out a pleasant clinking sound;
2. that it can be sucked – well, it's terribly cold and makes the little wet childish paws numb, but it's a tasty seasonal hit;
3. that it's possible to fling lumps of snow exquisitely at icicles on the eaves, especially if there aren't any windows nearby. To knock down a good solid icicle, which smashes into crystal splinters with a dry crash, that's indisputably one of life's greatest enjoyments and most fabulous successes; and anyone who has never hit his icicle doesn't know what youth, winter and the beauty of the world are, and above all doesn't know the true nature of an icicle.

Yes, that's what it is: an icicle has an awful lot to do with child-hood. That's why you're now looking at it in enchantment, old fellow, and smiling enthusiastically, and feeling that the day is a bit nicer and more cheerful because it's framed by these twelve icy stalactites. Look, you could reach out your hand and see how it breaks with a pleasurable clinking sound, but you won't – you think it would be a shame to spoil it. You could break off a bit and have a suck, but somehow, that doesn't interest you at all. Has all your childish curiosity about what an icicle is good for, and all the things that can be done with the world's odds and ends, dwindled away? No, not really, it probably hasn't quite gone, but now I'm looking at something I didn't notice then – at how icicles grow, for instance. Ring after ring is pieced together, layer upon layer accumulates until it builds into a kind of stalactite. It only looks as if the icicle is dripping down from the roof; in reality it's a work of patient adding-up. When you look closely, you can see little horizontal lines. And, what's more, you can see where the wind blew from while the icicle was growing. What happens is that a little swelling forms on the reverse side of the icicle, as a droplet of freezing water is wafted there. The whole icicle is made of those little ledges like the articulated stalk of a horsetail. And before I've managed to study it thoroughly, my biggest ice-stick has grown longer by another whole joint. So I can now say that I've seen icicles grow.

And perhaps it's like that with all human cognition. Perhaps what first interested man about things was if they could be broken or sucked or used for something else. Only hundreds or thousands of years later did he begin to be interested in how things originate and what laws they obey. Perhaps humankind is very young so long as it keeps trying out what things and materials can be used for – for eating or fighting, say. When it becomes more mature, it will observe more slowly and carefully what things actually look like, how they evolve, and what morphological or genetic laws govern them. It seems that with far too many things we are still at the stage of sucking or damaging them out of curiosity.

March Parade

The People's Paper, 21 March 1937

As yet it's more a matter of a tickling in your nostrils or a rustling in your ears rather than your seeing it. The air is pregnant with it, it blows from the soft soil, it bubbles in drains, it gurgles through a brook, it whistles flutingly in a blackbird's song. What if the grass in the meadow is still flaxen and rusty like a hare's fur! Look more carefully, and you find all sorts of things already. Something green-ish is squeezing its way through last year's straws, under the dry leaves – it may become a creeping cinquefoil or a starkly green celandine – God knows what, screaming with sheer green. But now you have to search for it among the shaggy strawberry-blonde bristles of last year, like lice.

But why bother? Just now we're not concerned with this little God-sent weed, let it grow in its own way, when its time comes; we have a more serious candidate for spring here. You'd call them twigs or little witches' brooms but we know they will be lilacs and an elderflower, dogwoods and barberries, currants, hawthorns, guelder roses, a honeysuckle and a privet. For the time when spring asks you what you planted in the autumn is now approaching. Just for the record, I planted all this, and in addition weeping willows and cotoneasters, a philadelphus, a deutzia, a spiraea, a maple and a laburnum, a sumac and a rowan, an oleaster, a bird-cherry as well as a flowering cherry. I should really wear a white coat like a hospital doctor, who walks from bed to bed to find, by sight and touch, how his cases are doing. God bless you, it's not too bad. The patient is still asleep but the inner bark is green and full of sap. True, this branchlet is poor, I'm afraid it will mean yet another operation, dear little shrub, but after that you'll come round and start sprout-ing for all you're worth. And as for you, I don't know, I don't know. We replanted you without any hairy roots; you were more dead than alive. We can't do magic, I'm afraid, but we can still hope that 'Nature will help itself', as we doctors say. Sometimes you can only bend over the patient and carefully poke the bark with your nail – well, I don't know. And here – this was done by hares. They have gnawed the bark of the bladder-senna down to the living wood. God knows how we'll manage to recover from that. Well, we can only shrug and forward the whole issue to the aforesaid Nature.

Those were the patients then, but the others, thank God for them! They're already bustling with life, I can tell you, it's all go here already, just look at those buds. Yes, just look at them – some look like tiny bundles, others jut out at the end of branchlets like bludgeons or the hard points of spears. But most often they resemble some insect with folded wings stuck on a twig. It sits there with its head downward, crouching and immovable, and sucks and sucks so that it chokes with it. Here on the guelder rose it looks like a downy grey fly with a little thin bum; here on the barberry, it's like a sated red tick; here on the dogwood, there's just a teeny flat bedbug that you can almost not see as it presses itself onto the twig. Look, everything puffs up, sucking greedily and relentlessly. A bit more time, and the squatting fly will jerk its little folded pinions, the motionless aphis will carefully spread its wings, and, still shrunk and crumpled, they will unfurl and straighten out in the sun, and hover on the twig from spring to autumn. We humans call these leaves, but they're something like the extended wing-cases of the buds when they take to the air.

Little wings of leaves, floating pollen and humming insects. I can tell you, flying is one of life's strongest dreams; and spring truly begins only with the fluttering of all the wings of the world.

Owl

The People's Paper, 30 May 1937

Perhaps it wasn't a barn owl but just a Central European little owl (*Athene noctua noctua* Scop.), nonetheless everyone started calling her our owl. It is common knowledge that owls live, stuffed and somewhat eaten-up by moths, in school natural-science rooms, where they sit on a branch quietly and persistently, smelling of naphthalene, and serving for the edification of young folk. They further appear in *ex libris*, where they sit on two or three thick books, which is meant to signify their special, indeed professorial, wisdom and profound bookishness. Screech owls, on the other hand, most often crop up in the papers, where they screech about the decline in youth's morals, about the heavy gloom on the European horizon, or about some impending economic disaster or other. So it's an even greater surprise for a modern person and a graduate of several schools when he finds that an owl (or a little owl) also exists in a live form and in a so-called state of nature. It happened on a sunny day, to make it even better: the owl was sitting neither on thick books nor on the ruins of a castle, as you might expect, but on the ground in the grass, and was quietly asleep. At a distance she looked a bit like a small shabby grey tree stump. Only when we got closer did she begin to show some signs of life in that she turned her head in our direction. But did she open her eyes? Presumably, we weren't worth the bother. She seemed to have been implying that she was very pleased to meet us, but that we could go away again. That's why I couldn't subject her to a more detailed investigation, to find out about her ear openings, or whether she really had a swivelling toe and lacked a crop. On the whole, she resembled a tiny old lady in a grey smock who had fallen asleep over her knitting. She was perfectly nice and utterly old-fashioned. We would have taken her home and offered her a shelf in our bookcase to live in, but it probably wouldn't have been very easy to catch mice for her, so we left her, tiptoeing, followed by her unseeing, closed stare.

It is strange, you know, how some animals have an old-time sense about them, as if they no longer belonged to this world. Such an owl, for instance, gives an impression as timeless and antiquated as Puchmajer's verse,[1] or a bustle once owned by Granny. You are rather moved when you encounter something of the kind. So there we are, it's really true that in bygone days bustles were worn and there were still live owls around – who would have guessed? Suddenly you feel you are in a different and terribly old world – perhaps there is also a water-sprite in a green tail-coat under the weir, and a snake-maiden with a little golden crown on her head is basking in the sun, perhaps a post chaise with a little fellow in a red coat will come along this road bringing us a letter with a blue stamp from Mauritius. Everything is possible in this old-curiosity world – even barn owls and little owls do exist, and there are other mysterious signs too, only you must be careful not to overlook them like a small shabby stump in the grass.

Poor little owl, perhaps she has just got lost here, perhaps she has forgotten the way back to some older, undisturbed world. You know what, I'd put an advertisement in the paper: '*Bird*, with outdated opinions, seeks a bit of the old world. Flat roofs and houses with radio out of question. Offers marked "Ruins preferable" to Box No. . . .' Surely it should be possible to find a corner somewhere in this world, where there would be a place for owls, books and Athena's wisdom!

Vacations

The People's Paper, 13 June 1937

Dear me, no, grown-ups no longer have any idea what vacations are really like. No matter what he does, a grown-up can't give himself over to them as wholeheartedly as a child. Every spring he makes boisterous, futile noises about how much he's looking forward to having a break this year, where he'll go, and how he'll enjoy himself. But when he's in the middle of the much longed-for enjoying, he finds that it's too hot there, or that it's raining all the time, or that he's constantly being eaten by disgraceful midges, or that the food isn't all that good, or that there are masses of ants all over the place, or that the beer isn't worth a tinker's cuss, or that it's too far to walk to go swimming, or that there's a weird bunch of people and no one to have a decent talk with, or that he's bored, or that it was better last year, and about 3,740 suchlike thats. On the other hand, if I remember rightly, to a child, midges and ants are no bother, he doesn't worry about heat, foul weather or bad food, he doesn't care about the opinions of his fellow beings, and is in no need of the beauties of nature. To a child the great fact that it's a vacation is enough; his vacation is, I'd say, about itself. It is a Pure Vacation.

Pure, true, or childish, vacations are, taken etymologically, not vacations – there's no emptiness or vacancy in them, but quite the contrary, an astounding and undiffused fullness. The main thing is that you *don't have to go to school*. I'm not saying that school is torment and labour for a child; rather, to the child's eye it's a ferocious waste of time that could otherwise be used more fully and colourfully. So far as I can remember, school didn't strain me, it just bored me stiff (unlike, of course, the so-called school of life). The deepest pleasure you get from vacations is precisely the relish arising from no musts – it's the great bliss of freedom.

True, even during a pure vacation there are still umpteen regulations in force about what's allowed and what's not. For example, you mustn't eat unripe pears or pull cats' tails. On the other hand, commandments prescribing what has to be done markedly drop off. You don't have to go to school. You don't have to sit quietly. You don't have to do your homework. You don't have to do anything, almost; and you can do almost everything apart from what you mustn't do. Suddenly, there spreads around you a sort of free space for endless enterprises and idiosyncratic pursuits; there's more room, more breadth; there's engagement and infinite potential. The world is no longer cramped by dictates. And this free space isn't empty; it's packed with objects and happenings, it brims with abundance, it gapes wide with interests. It has no boundaries, even if it doesn't reach much further than the corner of our street or the fence of our garden.

And the second great pleasure of a true vacation is the savouring of Time. Vacation time isn't divided and crumbled by directives as to what has to be done in this particular minute; there's no time-table, just an endless, unbroken passage from morning to night. The vacation day isn't made of hours, but of pure extension and undisturbed flowing. It is without shore, yet full of mysterious bays, like an unexplored lake, which you can't sail around even in a whole day, and tomorrow, boys, there'll be a new sheet of time, you won't be able to see the end of it. It's a larger and more endless time than any other; never again in our lives shall we exist in such vast time, never again shall we experience time in itself, time in its greatness and glory, as we did during a day in the vacations.

But a grown-up no longer gets much from his holiday. In vain will he chase after the lost Pure Vacation at the seaside or on the

peaks of mountains. A grown-up no longer experiences that absolute pleasure from no musts and mustn'ts. Don't we see grown-ups,
here, there and everywhere, doing all they can to mould the world
out of dos and don'ts? For some reason grown-ups don't have much
feeling for the miraculousness of freedom any more. They can't
embrace it with genuine joy; and as for pleasure from the greatness
and glory of Time – they're even more useless in that department.
They can't have a vacation without feeling acutely and embarrass-
ingly: God, how time flies!

November

The People's Paper, 7 November 1937

You can't yet say that the year is ending. Take the fields and hedge-
rows – it's still far too lively out there. Goats and cows are hastily
stuffing themselves with grass before they are driven into the shed
for a re-enactment of the manger scene. Here and there the land
is bedewed with wild pinks still in bloom, the groundsel glitters
with gold, and the creeping cinquefoil has taken it into its head to
flower. As for the earth, it's working heart and soul – it has been
ploughed and harrowed and dug, and so it is now taking in moisture and air. It is fragrant, and aerates itself, it breathes and quietly
crumbles away into sifted topsoil. The boletus is still oozing liquid
in the forest, yellow chanterelles are turning numb and brittle, and
pale toadstools, which they call all the bad names under the sun,
are drawing magic circles. And there are ruddy oldsters everywhere
picking up and lopping off tangy brushwood and ferrying it on
wagons. Somehow, even animals seem to be more abundant than
in the summer. From each furrow a flock of partridges starts up,
a hare zigzags to the woods, grouse flap their heavy wings, and in
a clearing glisten roe deer with their little white behinds. As I've
said, there is enough liveliness; but all of a sudden, in two shakes of
a lamb's tail, there is a misty sunset, light leaps through in flashes,
and an immense forlornness lies on the whole world. Only a slow

wagon creaks towards the village and a lonely man, with hands in pockets, heads somewhere hastily and sullenly. The year is not yet ending, but the days are ending.

It can't be helped, autumn is dark, but even that's a kind of blessing. Otherwise the last autumnal colours couldn't glow with such pathos: the blush of rosehips and the rich red of barberries, the scarlet of sour-cherry crowns, the dark yellow of larches and the heavy gold of fallen chestnut leaves (look! – the russet-brown eye of a little chestnut among them, half-open, in a cracked shell). And if it weren't for the darkness, we wouldn't feel so strongly about the true, most glorious colour of autumn – the flickering light in the windows of our home.

It's said that in autumn nature is getting ready to go to sleep. It's roughly true, but she does it just as we do – she delays, undresses with slow indulgence, and still wants to talk about what happened today and what will happen tomorrow, and before she falls asleep, she mixes memories of past time with plans for future days. This year's leaves haven't yet fallen; even so the branches and twigs are already swollen with next spring's buds. OK then, now we can go to sleep, for even sleeping ought to be done for the future's sake.

Which brings me to what I've saved for the end – the real annual discovery of autumn. It's the discovery of our own little den. It's the annual return to bed. No other time does a man sleep more gratefully and sprawl in bed more blissfully than in this season when the days are drawing in. Poets have allegedly sung of everything, but I don't know of anyone who has sung the praises of an ordinary warm bed instead of bosoms or heavenly phenomena. Far too much has been written also about dreams, but who has described the smooth friendliness of a pillow and the familiar dimple worn by our lying down? So while extolling autumn, let's join voices in glorifying the little human den: may it be kind to the sleeping, tender to the sick and strengthening for the weary; may the hare, too, find a warm hollow, the roe deer a dry hole and the sparrow a shelter under the eaves, amen.

Trees

The People's Paper, 30 October 1938

Weeping willow

One night – it was during those massive rains – it suddenly cracked and rustled; there was a heavy thump, and then silence again. It wasn't until next morning that you could see what had happened. An old weeping willow had fallen. The most beautiful willow spreading over the brook, vaulted like a cathedral, fell in the night. God knows how it could have happened. It had withstood a gale before, one of the worst that had ever come this way – at that time the forests were blasted and uprooted, but the weeping willow didn't yield. Only now, on a still black night thrumming with infinite rain, did it collapse. Perhaps the soil beneath it got waterlogged and softened too much; that's what it must have been – it lost the firm ground, tilted and couldn't carry the weight of its heavy, branching crown. Its trunk, as strong as a cathedral pillar, split; only a huge white splinter remains, pointing woefully at the heavens, while the crown with its vault of boughs broke off and spread across the ground.

The old willow has fallen, and suddenly it looks like a quite different, more barren, fragmentary world; you wouldn't believe what a loss to a home such a fallen tree is. Oh well, what remedy? The only thing left to do is to lop off the branches, so that they won't crush the undergrowth, and leave the bare, shattered stump to God – let it go on complaining, though fallen.

So it is complaining, complaining to heaven, the sliver of bole as white as a bone and the lopped-off crown wearily resting its broken shoulders on the ground. God, what a misery! You walk round the fallen willow as if round a dead man. What can we do, old weeping willow, we too have been brought to our knees by fate; the world has changed so much that we can't believe our eyes. But wait, a bit of green leaf from somewhere has caught here on your knotty bark. No, it's not a bit of green leaf; a new green shoot is pushing its way out of you, and here's another one, and yet another . . .

I'm not a stump, human creature, I'm a living tree because I still have roots. And as long as your roots are in the ground, my friend, you can go on to grow in the spring. It's easy to say I'm a fallen tree, but just wait, wait till the bark closes over, wait till I take an even firmer grasp on the earth . . . Hush! Can't you hear the future crown humming?

November

One night frost fell strong and dumb. The sun rose in the morning and it turned festive and beautiful, and then, out of the blue, leaves started raining from the trees in the sunny calm. It was as if someone had whispered 'now', and the burnt leaves instantly separated from their twigs and quietly floated to the ground. Or as if the trees were silently weeping. Their faces did not twitch at all, they were only harder and more furrowed than usual, but those leaves are still showering in an unstoppable stream. Well, there, that's enough, that's enough, who do you think wants to look at this? Don't we have enough sorrow of our own?

See what you look like, you trees, what is left of you? Just gaunt little bare skeletons, so now you know; yesterday you were still rocking like loaded argosies in full sail. And your fame also is over, you ash trees, birches and limes, and so suddenly, so suddenly that one can't get used to it. It's a misery, isn't it? Now you can only creak your bare branches, put on a firm frown, and stand holding rigidly, stubbornly to your spot and wait . . . for cruel weather – is that right?

Why, no, you human fool. If you leaned carefully against the bark, perhaps you would feel something like a stream. We are building up our strength; we are withdrawing into ourselves, into the earth, into the roots. Can't you hear the crown of our roots and tendrils murmuring? The spring is all very well, but the growing time is now – it's now that we thrust deeper into the earth; we must keep fighting again and again for the ground we stand on. True, it's hard, black labour, but that's the right labour for hard, black times, my friend. You say cruel weather? Then it's the right time for roots.

V
LETTERS TO OLGA

From Letters to Olga

Karel Čapek met the actress and writer Olga Scheinpflugová (1902–68) sometime in 1920, possibly before the first night of his lyrical drama *The Robber* on 2 March. In her near-autobiographical *Czech Novel*, published in 1946, she describes how he waited for her after one of her performances and used his allegedly unfinished play as a pretext for arranging a private rehearsal with her. However, their earliest surviving correspondence dates from the summer of the same year. From Čapek's letters that autumn it is clear that Olga's initial response was reluctant or wavering, whether because of youthful carelessness, or a pretence at mature indifference, or a fear of fatal attraction. The relationship gained intensity at the end of 1920, and by the summer of 1921 Olga found herself pregnant. Karel's letters in the critical August of 1921 offer comfort, but no clear proposal of marriage, and even though he vehemently disagreed with the idea of an abortion, by the time she got his letter (Letter 11), it was obviously too late. It seems that Olga, aged eighteen, and afraid of her father and her future, took the advice of her elder colleagues.

Never in her reminiscences of Karel did she touch on this subject. Protectively, she always explained his subsequent reluctance to marry her by reference to his illness or the opposition of his family. It is true that his spinal disease was at its worst during the First World War and in the early 1920s. His father feared that if it continued to progress as it had done he would end up in a wheelchair. That he was often in severe pain, and could not then even think of physical love and marital life (see Letter 18), is beyond doubt. But his mother also had much to answer for. She is known to have said that he could marry anyone apart from a gypsy or an actress. That his mother, sister and brother disliked Olga is evident from the memoir *The Brothers Čapek through the Eyes of their Family* (Hamburg 1961–2, Prague 1994), which his niece Helena, his sister's younger daughter, wrote in reaction to Olga's novel. (His sister's book, *My Dear Brothers*, published posthumously in 1962, is mostly silent, or polite, about Olga.)

Karel was attracted by Olga's impulsive emotions, yet longed for peace for his writing (he compared himself to 'a sheet of water that mirrors everything but is static', characterising her as too 'glowingly, stirringly sensitive'). His letters describe vividly the fear and reclusiveness that sprang from his illness. They are understandably silent about another woman, Věra Hrůzová (1901–79), whom he met briefly at the end of 1920 and who renewed contact with him in the critical months of 1922–3 when Olga most pressed him for commitment. Though this relationship seems to have remained in the hinterland of his imagination, it may have contributed to his frequently voiced need for purification. He felt very guilty about Olga. Her trauma obviously did not help her oversensitive nerves, and she suffered from a congenital heart condition. Besides, as a result of the termination she could not have children. Her dramatic reactions must have made life difficult for him. Though they eventually seem to have agreed on very close friendship, and he, as an invalid nearly thirteen years older than her, did not expect her to confine herself to him, he could never give her up, and was possibly even jealous (see Letter 26).

She became a distinguished actress, performing in Čapek's plays among others, and an author in her own right, though she self-critically characterised herself as mediocre. Sometimes she used to say to him: 'Stand a bit further away from me so that I don't catch your greatness.' But their literary minds were in constant fruitful dialogue. She gave him, for example, the subject for his last play *The Mother*. Contrary to medical expectations, Karel's disease did not deteriorate but stabilised by the 1930s. In 1935, after fifteen years of an eventful relationship, and sadly only three years before his death, he decided to marry her.

We will never be able to unveil the full story, not least because we do not have Olga's side of it. She is said to have buried her letters in his coffin. For some reason Čapek, though he collected cacti, Persian carpets, African music and other artefacts, burnt most of his correspondence (see Letter 5), including letters from world-famous personalities – though he later gave some of these to his sister's second husband, the poet Josef Palivec, and to other collectors of such rarities. However, Olga recalls that when in the distressing months after Munich she wanted to burn his letters, he joked that they did not have anything to feel ashamed of, and that her brother, his literary agent, should keep them so that future literary critics could dissect them.

It has been suggested that his love letters to Olga read like a novel. They certainly have a unique place in his writings, and for both these reasons a small selection (twenty-eight out of 361 surviving letters) is included in this collection. However warm or passionate he sounds in his journalism and fiction, he remains a brainy writer, with a fondness for logic and the disentanglement of enigmas. Though his correspondence with friends shows his delight in nicknames and wordplay, nowhere else but in his letters to Olga does he reveal such spontaneous playfulness and intensity of feeling, or speak about his personal problems. What also gives them a special value is that he frequently discusses his art (e.g. Letters 9, 10 and 21). Olga used extracts, often unsystematically, in *A Czech Novel*, and writing it helped her to overcome bereavement and survive the war. When she was accused of faking the quoted passages, she pointed out that many publishers, including one based in England, had offered to publish her private correspondence, but that she had refused for emotional reasons. As long as she was alive she did not want to publicise what belonged only to her. It was not until 1963 that she gave way to pressure from Čapek's editor, as well as from scholars and friends of his generation, who feared that they would not live to see this part of his oeuvre. The letters, which, as Olga put it, bear the stamp of 'the poet's heart, co-feeling, and relation to life and man', finally came out in 1971, three years after her death.

I

[November 1920]

Forgive me, Olga, it's a weakness to be writing to you again; you owe me so many replies and all that, that I feel ashamed before both myself and you that I don't have enough patience to wait until you find a free moment or the good will to write me a few words or call me. But to write is my only means of talking to you today, even if it's without a response, I'm talking and so am able to bear at least one difficult hour. Once I've finished writing, I'll feel worse still.

So, I had the pleasure of seeing you on Friday, then, and the lesser pleasure of waiting for you on Saturday at Smíchov Station! Poor bunch of violets, which I laid on the tram rails so that nothing should be left of it! And then four more days; for four days my soul was freezing in an overheated room. And this night I dreamt of you; it was such a beautiful dream that I can't and mustn't tell you about it. And I saw you lunchtime; you offered me some tiny strange hand and were altogether like a stranger; I hardly recognised you, it seemed to me you got fat or something, and that perhaps you no longer existed and some other little girl, who didn't know about anything, had come instead of you. This afternoon I got back from Prof. Syllaba;[1] I wanted sleeping pills, he was fussing over me for half an hour and then said: There is no physical reason for insomnia, you've been tormenting yourself with something difficult; *I* can't help you with that. Yes, of course he can't help me with that. I can't help myself either; the proof of this is that against my better judgement I'm writing a futile letter and watching dusk fall. Another day has passed; when I was waiting for it yesterday I thought it would perhaps bring me something.

Little one, who treat me as you're used to treating others, do you know what I wish terribly? That you were just a typist or a shop-girl; a little girl who runs to her grey work the same time every day and back home at noon, and after lunch again, and again in the evening; that I could wait somewhere round the corner and catch you and have you a short while for myself, and please you and please myself. You'd have cold little hands that would move me; you wouldn't have anything else to think about than your workaday bloke and festive Sunday; you would need me as you do your little mirror, your thread gloves, your bed.

But you are an actress and think about art. Great art. Ah, if you want to be a great artist, you must undergo the torture of being a great human being. Little bird, little bird, that's not a merry thing. It doesn't mean to frown and be tragic. It means to sacrifice a lot for life; to give generously and give the best; to give your life without end and not crave anything so much as sacrifice. Little bird, your twitter is beautiful, why do you want to be a human being? It's not an easy thing; it binds you to give your blood and soul, not to be endlessly free, not to be beautifully irresponsible, but to drink humiliation zestfully, to yearn to feel your way into the weight and anguish and awfulness of life which hasn't yet caught you, little bird.

I have never been so lonely as I am now. I was far less lonely when I didn't know you. Only now am I getting to know what loneliness is. The one person who used to be closest to me sees my anguish and looks on it with impatience, almost with hostility, because he notices how it takes away and weakens the potential success of shared work.[2] My God, as if any success whatever mattered! All my books are dead; I write and don't care what I'm writing; it's enough when I manage to push it a smidge above mediocrity. Nothing in the world can make me concentrate; nothing can entice me. I used to like my work and it is a stranger to me; I used to like it that I had become somebody so early, and now I'd like to chuck everything, abandon everything and leave for somewhere where I'd be a nobody. I used to like my pictures on the walls, they were near to my soul; I'd like someone to take them down so that there would be only cobwebby traces left. I used to like people; ah, what a nuisance they are! They even used to like me; now their closeness suffocates me. I'd like to leave but not so as to travel, rather to erase myself, to stop somehow being. I'd like to make a sacrifice to something, but don't have anything to make it to, and that's the worst thing about loneliness.

And yet, I too could be happy, even the happiest. The very immensity of my loneliness shows me how much sociability and love have been wasted in me. So much love that it would be enough for a whole district. And now so much loneliness that I even have to give it an extension of my nights. Yes, Syllaba is right; the patient can't be helped.

For God's sake, enough about that! How could this theme entertain you? Forgive me, I'm writing out of weakness, and weakness is everything I'm writing. I have such a heavy feeling between my eyes, in my throat and on my chest; you don't know about that, but when you are thirty, you will also start to feel that anxiety when some hope will be slipping away from you. By then you will surely have become a great actress; then you will not think about success, or a wig, or togs, or this and that, or at least not in the first place; you will think more about the day or the hour that's vanishing and adding the whole of its weight to your forlornness. Besides, prophesying is a weakness too. I've actually wanted to write about something else. At times I'm overcome by anxiety and pity that I didn't want to accept the friendship you once offered me. Perhaps, perhaps, perhaps you would have enjoyed to call a friend and twitter with him. He would have sat next to you asking nothing; nothing would have been taken away from him. Ah, Olga, if only I knew what strange thing has fallen between us!

Well then, here is another letter, I suspect the eleventh; one of seventy or seven hundred that you will have counted by the end of the month. You are used to getting letters; it's not an unpleasant thing if it's not necessary to answer them, to answer not only the letters but also your own self. I want imploringly and inordinately that there should be something between us, anything, but not my weakness. I don't deserve to be driven into it; and yet, my God, what can I do? Where, how, by what means shall I get my way? Oh, if only the means were for once in *my* hands! You'd goggle at what a turn it would be.

2

[5 December 1920]

Olga, my great darling,

I must tell you something. I can't turn it into the most beautiful story in the world, but it is the most beautiful reality in the world. He found her for himself, a bud, a half-open flower, and reached out for it with his hand. The hand was timorous and weak and clumsy with love, pious with love, ruthless with love; the hand was love itself. Yet all of a sudden the undefiled flower breathed out a cry of tenderness and horror: 'You'll destroy me!'

And he felt as if he was tumbling down on his knees, and was weeping and praying and wringing his hands: 'Oh, sweet flower, how could I destroy you? I'd rather cut both my hands off, I'd rather perish, I'd torture myself to death with desire and love rather than destroy you! No, no, never, sweet flower. I would curse myself if I ever caused you the least pain. I'm not worthy of you. I am a burning, wretched man, and my breath will not bring you happiness.'

The undefiled flower is silent and fragrant; it is bending over and trembling. And its silence softly, with devotion, with immense shyness, breathes out: 'Pluck me!'

And now, something else, Ola. Today I realise very powerfully that something changed between us yesterday. At least in me. It was during the performance of *A Little Girl.*[1] There is more ahead of us than there has been so far. We *must* work together. Olga, I feel that that's the reason why we've met. I'd like to be able to say that I order it. Ola, starting with today you must give me your every role, even if it is a negligible one, so that I can think with you and work with you. You must understand me. I don't want to, and cannot, teach you anything, and you don't need that, but I want to be a mirror to you before which you grow into greatness, and an encouragement, and a comrade in work; I want to be a director to you; I want to co-create your career. Ola, you must become someone. You are such super-precious material that I now suffer terribly knowing that hands so unintelligent, and so without love, as those which are right now leading you through your acting career, interfere in it. Ola, you *must* let me work on you and with you. You are young, and I dread that you might be formed by those who don't love you and don't even understand you. You *must* grow, you must be something extraordinary. Ola, I love you too much. I'm not content with your present – I want to and must get deeply engraved in your future. From today on, Ola, I'm talking to you about nothing but this thirsty 'want'. I want to be a rung on which you will walk up. That's my task.

Ola, I miss you endlessly today. Be so good and write me at least one sweet word, will you, right now. Little girl, make my evening happy. I'll wait for you at a quarter to ten. Please don't slip away. I must see you – I must see you, love – I miss you with the whole of my body and soul.

I shall bring you that fairy tale of mine. It's poor, but the intention was good.[2]

3

24 December 1920

Bathed like a baby and alone for a while at last, I have nothing else and better to do but write to you: how I was glad when you came in the morning, what an event it was for me, and how I regretted that I couldn't have conjured Jizinka[1] into the left pocket of my grey waistcoat and kept her there locked in my wardrobe for half an hour. Or why didn't Jizinka die for half an hour? I'd have laid her on the sofa with piety, and above all, most of all, I'd have closed her eyes, and then, Ola, we'd have prayed together, and comforted each other because of that sudden loss, and when we'd comforted ourselves entirely, Jizinka would have suddenly sneezed, we'd have flown apart and she'd have said: Children, I talked to my Lord God; it was awfully beautiful. – And we, Ola, we wouldn't have said anything, not even agreed that it had been awfully beautiful. – But Jizinka's good for nothing – she was unable to die in time. May her Lord God punish her for that! May she get fat! May she attain ninety-seven kilos and ninety-seven years! – But I'm not grumbling, even as it was, it was a Christmas present for me, and you won't give me a better one, Ola.

Ola, I'm terribly ashamed that I haven't really given you anything. When I give you my books, it's as if a peasant had given you a basket of his own potatoes. When I walked from the office at one, I saw so many lovely, alluring things in shop windows, and my eyes, my hands, and money too, turned all itchy: no Ola, forbid me what you like, but you mustn't forbid me to bring you something occasionally.

About that room, you must decide quickly before the housing department gets involved; once again: a view over the Vltava, the Shooting Island, Žofín,² beautiful old Biedermeier furniture, a respectable aunt – a spinster, who once used to love Fibich.³ Decide by tomorrow.

My God, Ola, I didn't give you anything, me who'd like to shower you with gifts as Aladdin did his Badroulbadour! Tonight I'd like to bring you all this (in a military lorry):

(1) A sports suit made of English cloth, a little knee-length skirt, leather knee-high boots, a cap for the mop of sweet curls, and besides, a complete set of knitted underwear in khaki colour, endlessly long stockings and lamb's wool gloves – enough. (2) A batik 'tea-gown', as colourful as a parrot and as light as a morning love-thought; in addition, nice little slippers, fluorescent stockings *et le reste* – a dream, Olga, a pure dream! (3) A fur coat made of 'seacalf' (an English way of saying 'seal'), as shiny as fantasy, resembling dark grey silver. (4) A ball dress of your own choice (a chap mustn't meddle with that), and with it – for the neckline would presumably be rather low – a string of pearls. (4) A box of wigs – black, fiery and golden. (5) Fifty pairs of gloves. (6) Twelve pairs of shoes and high heels straight from England. (7) A box of sardines. (8) A jumper with a collar that can be rolled up to the forehead. (9) A packet of invitations for guest appearances from directors of theatres in America, Australia and even far-off Prague. (10) Furniture for a little blue room (designed by architect Janák⁴ – damn it, it's a bit cubistic). (11) A train ticket to Africa (Oran, the Continental Hotel). (12) The latest model of a hat from Paris (notice the gorgeous white

bird-of-paradise plume! A gem, isn't it?). (13) A ring that makes the person who wears it invisible. (14) The complete works of K.Č. in fifty-six volumes. (15) A beautifully dressed tree, all hung with candles, male scalps, rubies and diamonds, wigs, costumes of all eras and chocolates. (16) A drawer with charming love letters, sorted out in neat compartments and provided with dates, from 122 men head-over-heels in love and ready to lay down their lives for you. (17) A free first-class ticket for all rails of life. (18) (Because eighteen is your number) a longish chest, which two servants in perfect liveries (white breeches, white chamois leather gloves) would carry to your room, which you would (only after opening everything else) open, and in which you'd find the beneficent giver of all those treasures winking at you and saying: 'Ola, all of this is still too little; I must also give you a bit of myself, at least for this evening; pop me quickly into your room and don't tell anyone that I'm here. And if a smidgen of sadness comes over you at dinner, come and have a look at me; don't forget at dinner *that I am with you*, very, very near you, that I don't even breathe, and no one knows that I'm at your place.' – Ola, if all this is too little, forgive me; we must save something for next Christmas.

Strejda has just come with your present. Ola, it's so beautiful, thank you, I could have given her a kiss straight away; sweet girl, you've made me incredibly happy. And that fairy tale, my God – we must create and live through more of them. There will be fairy tales, Ola, you can be sure about that. It's beautiful, fabulous, your gift. I'm all the more ashamed for the nothing I've given you. Ola, I'm kissing your generous little hands that made me so happy. Good-bye tomorrow. And tonight, don't forget that I'm in your room.

Your devoted *K.Č.*

4

25 December [1920]

Ola, I wouldn't feel rested tonight if I didn't write you a few words. Good Lord, I made you cry! After an evening which we were allowed to spend so . . . so free of worries! Ola, I'm a brute and a fool; I shouldn't have talked about a thing which concerns only me, with which I have come to terms and which, after all, perhaps, probably, surely is not and will never be true. I don't know what your hot little tears were directed at; I only know that I brought them about, and I'm awfully ashamed, I feel like beating myself up. The moment I sat down to dinner, Jarmila told me:[1] Karel, something happened to you. No, nothing happened, but I did something terrible. For the second time already I've made my little one cry – I who want to set her peepers in the gold of an eternal smile! Ola, I talked utter nonsense. Sweet girl, you are my life, and if you love me, I have so much strength, both physical and mental, that I could give it away, that I'd like to pour half of it into you, who so often suffer more than I do, who are frequently more tired, who are a thousand times weaker. Ola, I say it's just the other way round: you need (at least sometimes) a little wheelchair, and I'm here to pull you; and you are right even in that – this is just the most beautiful thing. Ola, and forgive me one more thing – those eighteen years of yours. For a lot of the time you are older than me; so many times I'm a boy by your side; Ola, for God's sake, the years do not make any distance between us! Still, I want you to be eighteen permanently because it's just what I like so terribly! You are my life. I never want to make you cry again. If you only knew how much those little tears are smarting!

I'm writing to you with your sweet stockings on my lap. Forgive me, I've unwrapped them and keep kissing them after every sentence. My big-hearted, impulsive, crying little darling, I'm a brute, a savage donkey and an irksome raven, but I'm so much in love, you see! And besides, sometimes when I can't sleep, and still can't sleep, I think of so many things – mostly incredibly beautiful ones but sometimes horribly sad ones, and what happened yesterday was I involuntarily blabbed some of those sad ones. It was a thought from one of those bad nights – a phantom of insomnia, an illusion, nothing serious. Let's never talk about it again! – Ola, I *must* see you the moment you've finished singing the start of *The Flower*.[2] I must, infinitely must. I'm waiting in front of the theatre so that no one else can snatch you away. You are my life.

5

[The end of February 1921]

Dearest little one,[1] Karel[2] has just caught me tidying my room like a diligent Martha, that is, after three years I've once again been combing through my old papers, ties, and the general debris that a slightly untidy bloke manages to litter his pad with. This is the third day I've been doing it; three cartloads of the stuff have already been taken away, and I haven't even dared to look into the more tucked-away drawers. The result is dust, tiredness and very strong melancholy. Every trifling thing brings back the time when it was still alive for me. I'll have it all burnt in the afternoon, and I'll watch the fire with gusto.

My appetite for writing is growing almost incessantly. Little one, I'll soon plunge into work, but first we must write that summer film.[3]

This morning I had a brainwave, which would be nice if it were feasible; it's that the proceeds of the performance of *The Robber*[4] in which you'll be a guest actress should go to charity, I mean, I'd donate my royalty, say, to the building of a student colony. But only if it were announced 'For the benefit of' etc. The point would be that a lot of people would come then, especially if it were for some really popular purpose. So this is the morning idea; I haven't had another one yet.

Little one, sweetheart, think about the film, we'll talk about it this afternoon. I miss you, my voice is sad with catarrh; yesterday I looked forward to how much I'd be missing you all evening and thought that I'd write you a poem, and instead I got two new sheets of *Embarrassing Tales*[5] and had to be doing the proofs. Sweetheart, my O-darlin-ka, you made me very happy when you dropped me a few lines; you saved my morning. I'm looking forward to the afternoon – I'll come at four. A thousand kisses for each letter of the alphabet you wrote; when will you collect them? You are good and so, so sweet, darling Olinka, and I'm already completely and incorrigibly your

Káča[6]

6

[March 1921]

God, if I wanted to be anything,
I would want to be nothing but her hunger.
I'd never have to wait, she'd never linger,
I'd just happen to her three times a day
And she'd always, always without delay
Have to satisfy me.

And if I were her big and busy comb,
I'd pluck her hair for myself in the morning,
And hold it between my teeth all day long,
And softly hum a never-ending song.

And if I were, and if I were her heel
I'd be so cheeky and I'd be so proud
That I would grow very tall like a tree,
And she'd no longer be a little girl.

Lord, if you want me to bow to your might,
Make me a porter in Thunovská Street,
I'd open the door for her every night
Good God, I don't know what would happen then.

If I were a poet with a true gift,
I'd find a word to rhyme with the name Olga,
Mind you, that would be really something.

And if I were the moon, oh, I would dive
Straight into the house number twenty-five;
I'd sit on her bed quietly and listen
To her breathing, and I'd make her teeth glisten
With silvery light, on her half-parted lips.

If I weren't mad, I'd know what to do.
(To be repeated eight times, each time with a different expression.)

Who hasn't got a wench,
He has no thought to quench;
But I have got an actress,
Which is a sort of madness,
A smarting fever.

If I weren't writing nonsense to her,
I'd want to be walking under her windows;
If I were now walking under her windows
I'd want to be writing nonsense at home.

If I were the police president Bienert,
I would have all constables play guitars
And two French horns in Chotek's park at night.
Prague would then quiver and begin to heave,
Swing, toss and float, enchanted, it would weave
Through the dark waves of night weeping with love.

If I were this minute condemned to death,
I would die gladly;
I would say to myself: It's good to die
Being in love.

If I were Olga Scheinpflugová reading
All these crazy words, I couldn't help thinking
And saying to myself: I've found a man
Who has a screw loose, which means that he can
Count on his lucky stars in the first place.

What shall I do with this blithe silly fool?
It's hard to know. Blithe and silly and fool
Equal, when added up, one word – blissful,
Blissful thanks to my darling girl's grace.

7

[April 1921]

Ola, sweetheart, it's half past twelve and I've just got back from the Castle;[1] it's just the hour you're dancing, and perhaps, perhaps you are in a way happy. See, little one, I miss you: tonight people have flattered me so much, but I can't be proud now; amid that splendid society I kept drawing the picture of my sweet girl in a little skirt, with her mouth tucked into her collar and her glistering eyes; she threw me a look with those eyes, and I didn't know what I was saying or to whom. Little one, God knows, we don't belong among those people, oh God, tuck us away into a dark-black corner.

No, you're dancing now, little flame; I don't know who you're dazzling and who you're burning, but I'm looking at your pictures and am jealous, you see, I'm jealous of all actorkind, since as early as ten o'clock I've had a piece of ice in my heart.

But, no, you enjoy yourself; I want you to be madly happy and not to forget me at the same time. Sweetie, it's one o'clock and I'm thinking of you; I fear I won't sleep much, and that there's a lot of yearning ahead of me. I feel your mouth on my hand, and would like to shout how much I miss you. Ola, Ola, tomorrow at six, *come rain or shine*, we'll go somewhere; we owe it to each other, you know, Ola – tonight both of us belonged to too many people; next evening must be only ours. Ola, it's one; perhaps you're not thinking of me now, and I – a fool – had vowed to say Ola ten times when I was talking to Miss Alice,[2] and I did fulfil it, twice over; but you're not thinking of me; if you were thinking of me, I couldn't be so jealous.
Your *K*.

8

[The beginning of April 1921]

I'd feel restless if I didn't so much as greet my little one. So last night it wasn't filming, but a police raid across the worst slums in Košíře – I'll never forget what I saw.[1] Some time I'll tell you about it, my little one, so that you learn more about real poverty. There's no possibility you'd have been able to come along; it's good you'd gone to bed. We were walking for five hours; I didn't get back home until three. Yesterday I thought I'd go to see darling Olinka this afternoon, but I'll sleep instead, darling, because I'm as weak as a kitten and tired and utterly sad. But at six I'll look for you in the theatre, at six sharp; perhaps the little one could stand outside so that I don't have to call her, and then I'll wait for her at nine to take her home. My sweet, how horribly people live! I'm ashamed of how much luckier I am than them. Please me tonight.

Káča

9

[Trenčianské Teplice, 16 August 1921][1]

My dearest little one,

Yet again I'm opening today's letter with a nice thank-you: two letters have come at once. Sad little letters they are, like tattered butterflies. My sweet, I repeat once and for all: be cheerful and trustful; 'all's well that ends well'; there's nothing to fear. Calmness, calmness!

I'm writing very late at night; we played cards in the family circle till well after eleven. Even in cards I find a fate that fills me – my whole life – with tranquil resignation: neither to lose nor win, to remain in balance, to give life as much as it gives me.

And before that – a gorgeous autumnal walk. As if the sky itself wanted to show its stunts – the sun shone, it rained, two rainbows stood over the mountains, and the beloved moon at twilight; quaint vistas among the mountains, the mountains all around – light-green forests, indigo shades, brown pastures with big herds of white and black sheep, all in perfect tune with early autumn. It was so beautiful that I thought of you countless times with parching regret that you couldn't see it with me.

It's Tuesday, so you played in *Pussycat*² today as well; from this distance, from this rough, broad-chested nature it seems to me almost painful. Oh, little one, the greatness of life doesn't lie in a feverish swirling, ambition, a strenuous chase after success or whatever else. Anyone who looks at these big, strong, peaceful things almost ceases to understand the restlessness of us burned-out, hurt people. I, too, don't see a path to success or fame in my literature; in the most beautiful case all art is as matter-of-course as a mountain or a juniper tree; it grows, lives, simply *is*, and what people add to it is something as revolting as tourist signs in the countryside. To be an artist, yes, there is nothing better than that. But to be an artist in life, an artist in harmony and in the greatness of life itself, that's the most beautiful, most modest and purest thing.

Ola, my precious, I'm experiencing so much that a memory of your anguish is a thousand times more tormenting for me, because that anguish wouldn't weather the strict trial of this mature autumnal beauty and the chilly heavens. Everything seems to be telling me something, and I'm passing it on to you faithfully: 'Let what must happen, happen in peace. What is necessary is good. Bear what you are destined to bear. There is a deeper, useful sense in everything you can't escape.' Sweetheart, believe in the wisdom of those autumnal, heavenly powers; I, too, have come to believe them and have learnt two things: to accept what must be, and to fulfil bravely what is good and beautiful to do. I have inner strength for more than two; what good is it when I can't share it with you? Sweetheart, be strong; it counts more than 'be beautiful' or whatever else. If you can't be as strong as a silvery beech, be as strong as a juniper or hardy wild thyme, as everything that accepts, without grumbling and swirling, drought and cold, fertility and hurt. To be able to do it like nature! Be strong!

Enough, enough said, little one; I'm afraid that I won't be able to please you today either. You can see at least one thing – how *my* autumn has given me a lift. If you are afraid that it means a summer after a too short spring *for you*, OK then: be strong and content – your autumn awaits you too, and if you are wise, it will be beautiful, more beautiful than everything you've had before. Whatever is sad about it?

And so farewell for now, Olga; again I'm waiting for another letter. My health has much improved. Good night, darling Olinka, midnight is just striking.

A thousand times your *Čáča*

10

[Trenčianské Teplice] 17 [August], Wednesday [1921]

My sweet poppet,

I really don't have anything to write about today. Not only because I have toothache and have dulled myself through and through playing cards (and had annoying luck and won a lot of money), but because nothing happened all day, nothing, absolutely nothing that would have provided me with a single little farthing-worth of thought. I started writing chapter IX,¹ and frittered the rest of the day away on such small change that now in the evening I have nothing to hold on to. I dislike days like this. In the evening, when they are over, I don't feel the peace I long for. The only good day, or valuable day, is one that has made me feel or learn something good, and at least a bit great. I don't even say: a day that has allowed me to do a good piece of work. Work isn't what makes a man either. I can imagine years when I wouldn't take a pen in my hand and would only look and grow a little wiser day by day; perhaps such years would be less lost than those prolific and diligent years surround-ed by so-called success. I know, little one, it's all resignation in a way, but believe me I feel almost sick when I imagine that I'll start taking all those personal, as well as public, affairs, theatre, scandals, the talk of the town and heaven knows what, seriously. To be strong and wise in the first place, to be a master, to live one's life deeply and quietly – anything else is a useless fever, an intemperance and a distraction.

You can see I haven't got any letter from you today, so I'm writing only about myself, but during, or *precisely* during my writing I'm thinking so much about you. If it were possible, I'd like to divide you into atoms, and warm each atom with my own breath, make love to it and then reassemble them all. I've always said I'd like best to be your Pygmalion. Because I don't have you here, I'm working on myself, and that's why I keep finding old ridiculous qualities in me that I'd like to get rid of. The whole alleged importance (*Wichtigtuerei* is what the Germans call it) of the so-called artistic mission, the personal touchiness, the ferocious effort to find one's useful place, the ostentatiousness, and in fact the immodesty, of an artistic nature now seem to me to be the first undignified and comic thing I want to get rid of. And other and other things. About that another time. Today I am a poor man who has undignified, comic toothache.

Sweet girl, are you still tormenting yourself? Be quiet, stop it; I've thought up a lot of things for the future that are *completely* satisfactory, you will see. No fantastic plans; very realistic details. And again another day's over. I'm definitely expecting a letter tomorrow, a more cheerful and happier one.

And now good night. I'm kind of physically out of sorts. Poor pussycat, when will the *Pussycat* end? Farewell for now, and write, and if you can instruct me in something, or if you want to change me in some ways, start with it straight away while I'm experiencing my days of good resolutions.

Kissing you, *Čáča*

II

[Trenčianské Teplice, 18 August 1921]

Dearest little one,

Your two express letters of the 15th and 17th have just arrived. I don't consent to your doing anything, do you hear? I – if you care for me! – forbid you to do any such attempt, and you'll cause me horrible pain if you don't listen to me. I hoped you understood when I wrote: be calm and content. It meant that I myself took the whole thing on, and that you were to trust me absolutely. I didn't write more, I didn't want to write more, but I thought about everything, and am absolutely clear about what I am supposed to do and what you are supposed to do. I beg you urgently and supremely seriously: leave it to me, wait, be calm and don't be afraid. Live as if nothing at all has happened. All is well, I'll accept everything gladly, with hope, yes, with looking forward to it. I look forward to it, my sweet, and I beg you to look forward to it with me. I look forward to the responsibility and worry I'll take on. I look forward to the fact that only now I'll duly be your mum. I terribly look forward to what I don't name in my letters. I've thought through the enormous difficulties that are in the way, and I know how to triumph over them. Just rely on me. I'd travel to Prague right off to tell you everything, but it's dangerous to interrupt my treatment now; it could result in deterioration, and I'm afraid of that for both myself and you. That's why I beg you: wait patiently. I can see, and feel all but palpably, a completely smooth solution; I only ask you to trust me, wipe your darling eyes and look forward to it as I do. It's an awful nonsense that you're tormenting yourself; quite the contrary, quite the contrary, be happy. My present happiness, that turns bitter only by the terrible sympathy with you, is in great part based on the image I see before me. That's what it is, dearest Olga, and now be calm. Above all, don't do anything! Don't meddle with fate. Be happy about what is to be and must be! I'm only endlessly distressed lest you have done something I would regret terribly. God, how repugnant it is that I have to be so far away from you! I feel an itch to jump on the nearest train and not stop until Thunovská, but then I'd have to lie down and you'd be even more worried.[1] I want to be healthy, very healthy – you know why.

Child, child, now I'm asking you again – neither for heroism nor for self-restraint, but for one tiny thing: trust me absolutely. Everything will turn out as I wish: well for both of us. Promise that you'll leave it all to me. Promise that you won't lift a finger and will do only what I'll ask, but everything that I'll ask, you to do. Now farewell; I want to take the letter to the post office before noon so that you can get it tomorrow morning. Dearest Olga, I am by your side, I am fully with you; believe me, wait and be happy with me.

Love, *Karel*

12

[Trenčianské Teplice] 20 [August 1921]

My sweet poppet,

I meant courage and strength in a different sense – but what can be done, it happened. I don't want to reprimand you now, as you'd perhaps deserve. At present it's a big event in itself that you are at least a little bit happy. I feel tremendously weak – not physically, but morally and spiritually; weak for gladness, weak for blame, not entitled to either; both relief and pain are all one to me, somehow. Only wish you to be healthy now. That you start doing better. That you be happier than you've been so far. Better equipped. More capable of resignation. You've been through great pain. My sweet, it can be enormously useful. Perhaps you are richer now. Not from one experience – it wouldn't be worth living if all you bought were experiences of this kind. But richer from a few lives, other than those you have had. I'm seeking something good about all that happened, but somehow there is just emptiness around me. I'm afraid to think about it lest I have to blame myself too heavily. Oh God, if only I could atone for it! I, I, I, who keep gabbing about harmony and wisdom and happiness, have played a nasty trick on a nice young life! You don't know how bitter I feel. Because of that, yes, mainly because of that I wanted everything to be different, so that I alone could bear the weight of the thing and responsibility, and could force fate to turn a heavy mistake into some good. Now the good has eluded me. I have done nothing but a chunk of suffering. It's horrible, really. Now I'm standing over the debris of my good resolutions that were meant to make up for my guilt. And meantime only you were paying. Me nothing, nothing at all. I feel terribly bitter about myself. What have you done? What have I done? The latter question lies on me like a cloud. I will never make up for it. For me, too, some kind of childhood ends here. I've done evil – in fact I had never done anything evil until now. I'm still too stunned by it to be able to grasp it fully. It's been a few days since I wrote to you no less than unashamedly that I felt as if I had my life bang in my hands. And meanwhile, chance decides for me. Had I been in Prague, everything would have been different. I'm not saying better, and I don't believe worse, but completely different.

At the same time, an unbearable, anguished tenderness towards your suffering bursts out of me. There, you suffered, and I wasn't with you! I'd like to cause myself some severe pain to know what it is like. Last night, as a result of too much tiredness and exertion (I wanted to tire myself out to sleep like a log), I got a terribly painful bout of sciatica; I didn't sleep all night for the pain. I'll sacrifice that pain to you; it's little, but at least something. Even that pain came from love. I'd like to shower you with the most tender words, not because of what you did but because you suffered. Meanwhile I feel sad and bitter; I am ashamed of myself; I'd like not to be. Be at least healthy now. For God's sake, please do everything for your health – eat, live sensibly and carefully so that I am spared at least that worry. I don't know what I should be like, and what I could now gild your life with. I thought about so many things, but it all turned out differently. I now have different duties even towards you; even towards myself I now stand beyond excuse, somehow. Oh, little one, love remains even beneath shame and self-torment, and grows with compassion. I'm writing nothing but sad things, but at least this is clear to me – that I love you more than ever before. Please be healthy now.

Tonight little Helenka pressed me again for the picture of Eddy Pollo.[1] Please be so good as to send it to her – even that is a little bit of love.

Good night, my sweet girl; I am sad and in love, but perhaps I, too, will come out of this woeful bath better. Good night, good night, Olga!

All your letters have arrived.

13

Brno, 16 December [1921]

Dearest little one,

I just have a little free moment in the office, so am writing. I arrived after noon, half the journey I was freezing and half boiling, and since then I've been to the conservator to pick up my dear old pictures – they are beautifully cleaned-up, and I am very happy about them; I'll give them to myself for Christmas as I've been good for the whole year, except for some wickednesses for which may the earth consume me and one good girl tear off my ears and legs, but apart from that I've been diligent and will give myself these pictures as Christmas presents. Well, and then I went to Freda Stránský¹ and commissioned him to publish my *Factory to Manufacture the Absolute*; I thought he had been shamelessly robbed by my conditions (fifteen per cent of the retail price, that is a record fee for Czechoslovakia), but as he thanked me rather than anything else, presumably it wasn't so bad. I'm in the office now, where I have handed in the twenty-third to the thirtieth chapters of *The Absolute*, and am also waiting for chief editor Heinrich to put in a good word for Štorch-Marien.² He was given immediate notice, you see, and was hellish unhappy because he's unemployed after a doctorate, so I'm doing my best to save him here in some ways. Well, hopefully this will work out as well, while my inner voice is telling me a little scornfully: 'You want to help others and can't help yourself.' Yes, you are right, wretched voice, I can't help myself, but what's a hundred or a thousand times worse is that I can't shake any help out of my sleeve for the good, unhappy girl so that she will never be unhappy again, and so on. And that's as damned and bitter a helplessness as you please, and nothing perturbs me as much, but I don't want to write about it any more – as I'm done in and sleepy after such a taxing day; I dread that I'll still have to crunch my way through a mountain of pork (you see, I'm at a feast that has been specially prepared for me) before I can get to my den and close my tired eyes.

For the whole journey I watched how icy flowers formed on the windows of the carriage. It was terribly interesting, you know, when the train stood at the station, the flowers thawed every bit, and when we moved, they began to bloom and grow remarkably fast; one almost doesn't manage to follow the way the flowering fern expands, spreads and intertwines, the way it develops into palms and jungly brakes – well, something fantastic. In fact, it was the strongest impression of the entire day, and that's why my eyes are tired, and I'd like to close them to be able to see the icy flowers again. Compared to that, people are stupid and primitive.[3]

I shan't write tomorrow for sure, little one, because in the morning I'm looking for a box for my pictures and going to Štech's[4] and Mahen's,[5] and in the afternoon I'm seeing my sick friend Trýb,[6] and will have to keep an eye on the packing of the pictures and also go to the editorial office, and in the evening to the theatre for an opening night of some sort, and on Sunday morning I'll have to go to a concert, apparently a particularly big and beautiful one, and on Sunday I'll get back to Prague (or, Christ!, not until Monday afternoon, because it's just transpired they want to keep me here for a Sunday meeting of the whole editorial office, but I'd rather come on Sunday morning or afternoon), but I'll certainly come to the square on Monday at four and will wait for you, and now good night. Have a good time, and don't let anyone or anything torment you.

Čáča

14

[Tatranská Lomnica, after 20 June 1922][1]

My dear Olga!

For quite a few days now I've wanted to write to you, but there has been something between us that I couldn't let pass – and still can't let pass. It's your letter from Prague. My dear girl, there are things that shouldn't be written to a person who is alone from morning to evening, alone with himself, with his thoughts, and has nothing to divert himself with, and nothing to deafen him to them. Such a person gnaws his way, nastily and bitterly, down to the bottom of all that he has been told ...

Oh, you have never ever known how hurtable I am. – And now let's leave *this* sad chapter. Every day I wait for you to write me something about Your life, Your joys, if you have any. For my part,

I can't tell you much of anything that would interest you. Yes, I devote mornings to my Great Work you're so ironic about – with head bowed I trail my furrow behind, not caring if it's good for anything or not. In the afternoon I sometimes go for a short walk with Mrs Calma Veselá, who has also come here to write (poetry).[2] All the other things – longer walks and hikes, aimless roaming or rests – are solitude. More than solitude: forlornness. I see and meet inexpressible beauties; I often think if only Olga saw this, but I know all the while that these paths, these forests are nothing for her poor, clumsy, sprainable little feet; she wouldn't walk for longer than five minutes and would have to limp back home. The whole Giant Mountains[3] are a stroll in the park compared to these paths that are half bog, half stream or gorge, and the rest naked rock. It's a wilderness, but there are sublime places and moments; it's strange that great beauty always has something sad about it. A human feels he cannot appropriate it, that he is only a stranger in its presence. So in this great solitude I've made a discovery – that I am in fact a very sad person. All my feverish work, my activism, my enterprising spirit in life is just a way of deafening myself to it, of dispersing and diffusing myself. Oh, I'd be able not to work and 'live innerly', but then all my feeling would be such a sorrowful, horrible complaint that I'd be another Job. An infinite sea of bitterness has accumulated in me; I can disperse, but not overcome myself; I will never empty my bitterness, I can only not think about it.

My everyday life, that so much absorbs me in Prague, feels terribly far away. If the theatre burnt down, if Prague sank, if everything I have so much exhausted myself with disappeared, perhaps I wouldn't even think about it. It doesn't seem to me I should ever come back; perhaps I'd be able to leave for years and start a completely different life elsewhere; after all, everything one lives by, everything one does, is all one.

Right now the mountain peaks are being dimmed by cloud, and down there the entire Spišská plain is breathing with such subtle colours that one would like to dissolve. If only dying meant dissolving, simply evaporating! I'd finish writing this letter and the address, and would go to the balcony and evaporate for ever! I wouldn't even regret that my Great Work hadn't been brought to an end.

Well, farewell for today. My wish for us is that we were better.

Karel

15

[22 November 1922]

Dearest Olinka,

It's not for the first time, but surely and certainly not the last time that I'm thanking you not only for thousands of big reasons, but also as an author. I kiss your lovely hands for everything, but kissing hands is too little, I should kiss the whole path you daily walk along, but even that is not enough – for all you have done.

Thank you, thank you, my dear.

Your *Čáča* for always.

16

[24 December 1922]

Dearest little one,

My skin is crude and pays little attention to everyone's dreamy and better feelings, but as you can see, today I feel regretful about all sorts of things. Once again I've stroked the rascal wolf pelt that you will wear (and wear it gladly, for my joy), and thought that ultimately it would be better to come just empty-handed and give you nothing but joy. Even that is selfish, you know; I'd wish for myself that you walked by my side cheerful, jocund, clinking 'with glassy little voice', free of worries, healthy, nicely looking ahead – oh God, God, surely I'm an awful egoist: I wish you were happy!

And I'm also this old grey wolf that you wear and will wear on your young nape; sometimes I have red wolfish eyes, and sometimes I do lots of damage – I mean, I'm wicked, grumpy, biting and, in a word, a beast, even though I show an affable front to people. But if only, if only I felt light to wear! If only I kept you warm and stroked you and didn't weigh you down, and were always warm and gentle to you; and when I've finally grown shabby by moulting and am of no use, if only you could still cut me into pieces and make a muff out of me for your restless, light, pretty little hands! And perhaps also cuffs around your sleeves! And a little collar! What a wolf I am, I want to be useful to you for everything.

Today your clock will already be ticking for me. It will be talking quietly – fancy how much it will tell me, fancy what a prattler you'll become to me, you, who are sometimes so bitterly and painfully silent! I look forward to it; I'll have company even while working, you'll be so to speak tinkling over my shoulder when I – a diligent little craftsman – will be gluing, polishing and carving what I can do on my writing desk. That's why I wanted the clock so much. It's the most loyal gift.

Oh, but you won't give me the best thing, miserly you, you niggard, you won't give me your joy. Even though you don't have it yourself, you should seek it all over the world, in all earthly and heavenly shops, so that you can bring it to me. We don't usually have what we want to give; we must seek it. And so, I beg you, for God's sake, seek joy so that you can give a bit of it to me: just by being yours, it will be mine too. And if you love that black scoundrel a little, give it to him. As you can see, he is choosy – he wants the most beautiful in the world. But to want the most beautiful – a lot can be forgiven to the sinner just for that.

Dear little kissable mouth, I feel now as if I'm talking to you. Well, it's me talking, you are silent (because I don't yet have your clock here), and are hiding your chin and mouth in the fluffy old wolf, and you're just looking. If only I'm not mistaken! At this moment it seems to me that your eyes are somewhat brighter, starrier, and that somewhere behind them you are thinking about something nice. If only I were not mistaken! Something nice! Lord, in whom I'm beginning to believe in my stale heart, give to my poppet, my golden little one, something nice! You can try me (you know that, Lord) as much as you like, and inflict any cross on me; I'm a chap,

I can bear a lot, accommodate myself to many things and deny myself much. But to her, Lord, to her, give something nice. She is not made so fit for life, she is not so firm and hard, so coarse-grained and waterproof as others. She is woven out of sensitive and fragile fabrics, and terribly needs life to treat her if not with velvety hands, then at least with humanly decent ones. Lord, I'd enter into any contract with you if you promised me this!

But it can't be helped: the Lord God is playing the Baby Jesus today, and is giving out little sculptures, wolfies and other silly things so that he doesn't have to give people anything proper.

It's quite hard to turn from the Lord God to earthly things; I'm lacking in transition, so be, then, my footbridge from heaven to earth (or better from earth to heaven, or best both at once). So come on, lass, lassie, you tangle of a hirsute creature, you crazy moppet, my Christmas tree, my Baby Jesus, I beg you, for all the saints' sake, to think well of me when you read this letter, *only* well, and cheerfully. I want to write you words that will shine like a gazelle's pelt, and will be as silvery as a silver fox, as soft as a mole's fur coat, as warm as a beaver and as weightless as a chinchilla, as dear as a sable and as familiar as a goat under a little bed, and not grey, coarse-haired and matted like this particular wretched wolf skin; I'd like my words to warm you, stroke you, please you more than all the world's bristles, skins, furs and hides. What else? I shall see you in half an hour, and shall be again that irritating, clumsy Čáča, who sometimes wounds without meaning to, unintentionally hurts, and not knowing gives a chilling pang. But now, at this sacred moment, when I'm talking nineteen to the dozen, and your sparklers are so bright (if only I'm not mistaken), I feel immensely lovely: now I'm just very quietly stroking you with love, with infinite tenderness, and would like to – well, better not for now, even a letter, like the little wolf fur coat, has its end. So one more kiss on the cute nozzle (the wolf's, I mean), a kiss on your every finger (including the one that used to be chilblained), and a smile on your every sweet eyelash, and I can wish a happy Christmas.

Kissing you, dearest little one, a hundred thousand times,

Love, *Čáča*

17

[Palermo] 9 May [19]23

Dearest Olinka,

I wrote from Naples the day before yesterday,[1] but I know that this letter from where I am – as far away as Sicily – will take longer than a week to arrive, so I'm writing instead of going to bed.

I'm not in a good mood. It was in this region – the most beautiful of all I've seen so far, so beautiful that my head honestly swirled at the wondrous sight – that I experienced the most annoying afternoon. I made a mistake, as often happens, and got on the tram going in the opposite direction. Instead of arriving at the magical garden of Villa Giulia, I found myself in the factory outskirts of Arevella, and then for almost an hour I was trudging along the smelliest, dustiest street in the world to get to the sea. OK, I had a nice moment there, and returned to Arevella – then I get on the tram and something goes wrong with it; it won't start, so I have to walk among the stupid factories in staggering dust and heat for an hour and a half. Not a single cab, not a single car with free space, no loo, no decent pub. I got to Palermo splenetic, dead-beat, dusty and sweaty, at which point the problem was fixed and the trams started running. Imagine my rage!

Well, at least I had a nice moment at the seaside. It smelled of wild thyme there, and I looked towards the north where Bohemia lies, and said to myself: So you see, Karel, somewhere up there, there are your successes, your name, every reason why you've toiled away so hard, and here you are nothing and nobody, just a dusty little human creature sitting on a milestone, and it works – your heart isn't heavy, you could give up everything, and first of all everything that others find enviable. I recalled that once I wrote these lines: '. . . I sat on a rock, heavy with my own weight, And the sea was soughing at me, grim and graceful, And I said: Don't call me yet, leave me alone for now; One day I, too, will stop, not caring where, Strange, unknown and dumb to all people, Having neither an interest in, nor a word or reproach for anyone.' That's roughly how the lines were murmuring in my ears. I could see that my greatest bliss was peace, that's why I like sea and silence. I'm no longer young; perhaps the whole of my 'nervous illness' was just a transition from seeming, somewhat undermined youth to this state . . . I can't yet say of maturity, but definitely not youth. I'll probably never be exuberantly cheerful as I used to be, but I want to be calm, quiet and concentrated. I haven't enjoyed myself much, and I won't probably indulge in enjoying life, but I'm not sorry; I'm neither sad nor disappointed – it's good like this. If only I could find peace of mind so that I didn't have to torment myself. And if only I weren't wicked and glum! Didn't weigh anyone down and didn't suffocate anyone! You, Karel, must want a lot from yourself. You must make yourself better and purer, deeper and calmer. Oh, how much I still need to purify myself! My sweet, only I know and feel how much mire, badness and weakness there is in me. I know that I won't find peace until I find inner purity. Just because I've grown up somehow, I've started looking at myself more strictly. I must, I must reform a lot in me.

Other than that, I live intensely, strongly through my eyes, as you can imagine. I look and see, and that means a lot. I'd write you about everything I like, but there is so much that I'd rather tell you. And sometimes, as in Monreale, my senses weren't sufficient – it was as if I were drunk.

I'm still worried whether you're well. Please be careful, don't do anything so silly as running around with something as serious as lesions on the lungs. Perhaps now you've already played *The Romantics*.[2] I expect to have a letter from you in Naples or Rome to see how it turned out. Tomorrow I'm going to Agrigento where there are Greek ruins. My brother wrote to me in Naples to say that they had just had a healthy baby daughter.[3] I don't know about the Khols,[4] where they are going in the end; he wrote that he wanted to go to a seaside spa.

God, I almost forgot to tell you how much I liked the ferry. I was afraid of being seasick, but the sea was as calm as a pond. Now I regret that I won't be coming across again.

It's almost midnight and as warm as our summer. Strawberries and cherries, oranges, lemons and fruits yet unknown to me are ripening here already; in places, it's a paradise on earth, in other places, the dirtiest gutter, for the most part, it's a desert.

I mustn't forget to say that I am well, taking it easy, so all in all I'm fine – you mustn't worry about me at all.

Best wishes and kisses, *Čáča*

18

Naples 15 May [19]23

Dearest Olga,

I got your long beautiful letter this morning; I was particularly pleased that you were a bit better again and were thinking of me so much, but then my head started aching from it all, so terribly that I hadn't yet had it so badly before. It has eased a bit now, but you mustn't take any notice if this letter is a bit distorted.

Dearest Olina, there are a few painful and awfully agonising misunderstandings in your letter. The first, and the greatest, one is that you beg me, that you put me in the false, tormenting situation of someone who cares only about himself and who needs to be begged not to think only about himself. Now I'm begging you – for the sake of the merciful God who I bear in my heart – I beg you to believe me this one thing: in everything I have done and do I think more (and most in the world) of you, and not of myself; I have more regard (and most of all things) for you, and not me, as I love you more than you in a way understand. This must be clear in the first place. Don't beg any more, my girl, for it is such a pain and shame for me that it makes me want to cry; when you do, I feel base, selfish and brutal, and then have to defend myself before my own conscience until it gives me a headache.

But there is one thing about which I must ask you to have consideration for me. You've told me so many times that you would like to nurse me, make me gruel, give me compresses and nearly change nappies. Honestly, my girl, where did you get this from?

One isn't exactly the master of one's taste, but *this* image of life is precisely the desperate opposite of my own taste. I'm astonished how much you don't know me; forgive me – my notion of life is more manly, and perhaps harder too, and the moment I was confined to such humiliating care, I'd simply take my own life. My life – that's discipline, work, serious search for truth, love and other strong and strict relationships. I detest effeminacy and weakness. I even shrink from tender indulgence! May everything around me be hard, clear and calm; no moral cushions, no slipping into comfort, no pampering and nursing and growing infantile, for all that fills me with sheer horror. So never talk about these things in my presence. You really don't understand how intolerably repulsive I find it.

And now, to turn straight to the main point – without shilly-shallying and weakness – you write about our marriage and obviously expect a direct answer from me. Alas, three times alas: I don't have it. Not yet, I don't yet know what to do; there is no purity and clarity in my soul yet. God, help me! Above all I want to say that I don't doubt you the least bit; I don't doubt your love – I don't deserve it, but I don't doubt it – neither do I doubt your magnanimity and self-sacrifice, nor your fidelity. What I doubt is me, but I don't doubt my love for you either, but – God, how shall I put it? Imagine someone were to take on a job or create an artistic work, and before he got around to doing it, a terrible doubt as to whether he would be up to it, whether he had the required mental faculty and competence for it, stirred in him; he felt anxious that he would, in some irreversible, desperate way, spoil, destroy, devalue and splinter everything instead of making it. But these are just silly similes. The thing is simply that I am torn, feeling deep inner disquiet; you must have sensed that my journey was just a flight from this nasty state. It's called neurasthenia, but it's something terribly nasty. For example, there are days when one can't bear the voice and closeness of someone else, when he just wants to shout in aversion when someone comes near him. I've so far managed to overcome this, but you can't imagine with how much tension; you can't imagine how I sometimes suffered when you blamed me, for instance, that I didn't have anything to tell you, that I didn't love you any longer and this, that and the other, while it was just torment to me that I had to speak *at all*. I don't know if you can imagine these states of mind. Other times it's just the need for silence, just silence and solitude, and yet other times the need for love and quiet talk, and always, always the need for peace. My girl, it's not moods; it's suffering – it's a disease that must be cured, else ... else one is just unable to be in human company. And then, after such crises one has difficult moments of self-doubt – that he's simply unbearable, that he causes pain, that he hurts the dearest one and that he should disappear somewhere or whatever. There are moments when I feel condemnable, utterly heartless, without relation to other people. I don't know if you understand me; I'm seeking to write it more simply than it is, and am still afraid it's not clear at all. I didn't tell you this because you were so sore, and might at times interpret it that you were a nuisance to me. No, a thousand times no; it's me who is a nuisance, a disgruntled person who torments others. But then I hate allowances, attention and excuses; I feel embarrassed when I sense that people make allowances for me because of my condition. The only possibility is to remove myself, to withdraw into myself – that's the only way. The only possibility is to find balance again. That's what I keep writing about – peace, purity and the solidity of life. Oh child, if only you could understand me! That's why I've excommunicated myself so strictly, so that I can become stronger mentally and morally. Perhaps this whole state is just a transition to ageing, I don't know; I only know that *now*, in this crisis, I must live the life of a hermit. Just today, after having got your letter, I couldn't stand eating among people; I had the meal brought to my room and then I locked myself up, lay staring at the ceiling and defended myself before you, since my conscience has been tormenting me again. It's bound to torment me if you suffer, and my greatest dread is that I think that you'd suffer more by my closeness. Much more and much harder. God, if only these anxieties stopped distressing me! And don't think any longer that my worries concern the physical that is, or is not, or cannot be between us. God, that's the least I think about now, from far off. I think about it, and it distresses

me, when I am by your side and see you so young and richly beautiful. But here it's somewhat remote to me, I can't even imagine it;
here I'm only listening to the voices of my inner self and am waiting until I can breathe more calmly and more humanly, as it were.
Today everything is unpleasantly on edge; I detest Naples with its
sun, crowdedness, contented and noisy people; I dream of a frosty
reclusive place somewhere in the mountains where there is infinite
silence. Only the sea does me good; I'll get away from these mad-
ding cities, for I haven't found here what I was looking for. If there
were a monastery without religion I'd go there straight away. But
please don't treat me like a patient; you know that I hate it. Just
today I moaned and cried, surely next time I'll write you a calmer,
healthier letter. And if you want to have the greatest, most beautiful
consideration for me, then do just one thing – *never* torment yourself again; you really can't imagine how *desperately* it always stirs
my pain. I love you, that's my weakness; I am to blame if you suffer.
And I must, now I *must* lead a pure, unstirred life. If only I came
back with a clear soul! My sweet, be cheerful! Write to Florence.
I can't stand it here; it's beautiful, but too noisy. I feel lighter now;
the headache is better.

Best wishes and kisses, bad *Čáča*.

19

[Florence] 26 May [19]23

Dearest Olina,

I picked up your letter today (arrived in Florence last night), and
I'm replying straight away. First of all, my deepest sympathy with
your bereavement. I know how much you loved your Grandad, how
movingly lovely he was and how sad it feels at your home now. I
felt sorry about him. I became so strangely sad, and couldn't go to
see anything. I went to the nearest church and was sitting there
through the whole morning.

My girl, my sweet, how sorry I am about your pain! It wrung my
heart when you kept repeating that you bowed your head. I bowed

mine ages ago when no one yet knew about it, but you shouldn't. You are beautiful, you can joy in your success, you are right at the start of your career. And if you want to make me particularly happy, if I am to feel a great and unflagging happiness, be bright, trust yourself, grow, retain everything that's in you. You are the most precious and the most self-sacrificing person I have ever met, and perhaps you don't really know how much I love you even though I've caused you so much pain. Don't pity me. I am a weak person, but there is strength in my weakness. My sadness doesn't hurt; my fatigue is at once my thoughtfulness; my self-denial also my purity. I'm a bit different, a bit strange, not a bad chap, for I love, I love you, people and the whole world more than myself, and I still want to do lots of good. I want to do something good wherever I go, and you don't know how much it distresses me to see that I'm doing harm. I only lack inner peace – peace with myself and my conscience.

I want to be poor, simple and quiet, work as much and as best I can, and love as purely as I can. *It is* a sort of monasticism or something, people are either born with it or grow up to it. But don't pity me, there is no bitterness or envy in me. Oh, I shall be so happy when I see that I'm not hurting anyone! I adjure you, sweetie, my dearest soul, you must not suffer, or perhaps I shan't come back. My love – that's the most terribly sensitive spot in me. Believe me, believe me now, that many times I've felt like killing myself when I've seen you suffer so horribly. And I torture myself when you are ill, I despair when you cry, I want to sink into the ground for shame when you blame me. I'm happy when I see you calm and bright; it's music to me if you are pleased about anything; I revive when you revive. Do at last understand this delicate, faithful life-alliance; my God, it's all I can give you now with a clear conscience, without anxiety and disintegration, and I beg you, for God's sake, please don't say that it's little and worthless – that, as you can guess, would humiliate me horribly. I give you the whole of me in that alliance, but without my bad sides, without my reclusiveness, without my instability, which then imposes the humiliating task of a nurse on you, without my sensitive touchiness that drives me away from every human closeness. And I take from you endlessly more than I give, above all your dazzling self-sacrificing nature, and then your youth, an occasional flash of joy, and a lot of joy from your art, and even more from being with you, for you are wonderful and big-hearted, even though you're a madcap. Oh dear, I feel almost like crying, but out of pure tenderness. Don't think that I'm sentimental; I'm cruelly critical of myself, and even of you. Anyway, what I'm writing now is again, after a long time, a love letter and a declaration of love. There has been so much misunderstanding between us, my sweet. And now I'm humbly begging you, let there be peace between us! Don't be cruel to me any longer, don't cry, don't suffer, don't complain, don't blame – in *this* respect I'm coming back even more sensitive than I was before I left, for I have purified myself and kind of peeled. In many places I'm covered in a sort of new, tenuous and sensitive skin. And now I feel lighter again. Somehow I feel that you'll have a cry over this letter but with a kind of more moderate and less bitter tears, because at this moment you believe that I love you very much and that you can do a lot of good for me. Oh, you can! But you must be bright, darling Olinka, like that bright, splendid day that is now outside after a sultry storm – bright, erect, reviving so that I can, even at a distance, think of you with pride and delight. Sadness does not kill, only lowness kills, and between the two of us there must never be anything low. I shall then also revive, I shan't be young, but shall be happy. I think I'm babbling on in a muddled way. I beg you, for God's sake, I'm worried about your health again. Go to see Syllaba or someone, I have a feeling that today you're unwell again. I'm now on my way back, one more brief diversion through Genoa and Lombardy and I'll be finished. Please write me a letter to Verona *immediately, ferma in posta.* I'll then write to you again as soon as I stay somewhere a little bit longer.

Wishing all the best and kissing your hands,
Your faithful *Karel.*

20

Prague, 6 July [19]23

Dearest girl,

  I'm writing these lines with a heavy heart. I've just this moment
got your letter; there are words I should kiss with gratitude, but that
have touched the wound that has now been opened. You write with
all your simple and sincere love: 'When we get married, we shall
go, and so on.' Well, yesterday I wrote you that Mrs Tével¹ was here
and that I committed a certain foolishness; now I must confess it
all. She saw – apparently before I'd gone to Italy – some tension.
She talked to me like a mother, about you and me; I don't know
why, but I couldn't refrain from telling her the words I had written
to you before: 'Nature has drawn a circle around me that I can't step
over.' She got the point and was taken aback, then she was near
tears about you as well as me, for she likes you very much. What
she proceeded to tell me was the same as I keep telling myself in
my self-accusations: what I can do and mustn't do, what my duty
towards you and my conscience is. She was stricter with me than I
am; she said that I was spoiling your life, and would destroy it, and
other horrible things in which she was far too right. She wanted to
write to you straight away; I begged her not to, not to mention it
to you at all that I had said that. I was struck by her ability to guess
what torments me – that it's not the disease of my body, but the
disease of conscience, fear, distrust, escape into solitude, hermit-
like reclusiveness and all that; just like you (and perhaps like all
delicate women), she doesn't see a big hindrance in the weakness
of the body but in what grows from it – the illness of the will, the
sore and touchy love of seclusion, agonising doubts, the dread of
closeness, the thirst for silence and escape from the world – she
nodded and said she knew why I was suffering so much. I told her
that I hadn't told you, she said I must, else we would both go mad.
I won't repeat everything she told me; it was cruel wisdom; I came
out of that talk with sensitivities intensely heightened, but also a
bit comforted because she is the first person who understands me

entirely, and she talked to me like a mother. I like her very much for the few good words of comfort she gave me, and for speaking about you so well and with love. I think that she is the best friend you have in the world.

You must decide if I did a silly thing in confiding in a good, wise person at a weak moment. But I'm asking for just one thing: When you sometimes talk about our future, and I respond by drooping my head and by silence, and then you cry and pour bitter reproaches on me, and torment yourself and me with images of what everything could be like if I had more *good will*. Well, I beg you earnestly to ask that rare woman if my weakness deserves condemnation, and if my will is unmanly or irresponsible. I beg you earnestly, if you are tormented by doubts about my behaviour, to ask her if it isn't beyond my power and my conscience to act differently . . .

And now, please go to the seaside, let yourself be soothed by its singing and lulled by the waves, and then write to me that you aren't angry with me.

Your devoted *Karel*.

So far I haven't had any news about Mum; the last is: a considerable improvement in the lungs, a certain relapse in the bladder.[2]

21

Saturday morning [Jindřichův Hradec, Rudolfov, 4 August 1923][1]

My dear Olina,

Yesterday I didn't take my pen in my hand; I didn't feel up to anything, most probably I got light sunstroke when I went mushroom-picking the day before yesterday. One always pays dearly for what one likes. Today I feel all right, just the stomach is a bit funny. Yesterday I lived on pap all day.

I've already reached chapter 36.[2] About five more chapters and it will be all done; so in the end I'll bring it to you finished. It's becoming more and more romantic; it keeps me in suspense like mad; in the evening I can't wait to see what I'll be writing the following day. Writing is the most beautiful thing in the world. I don't think that what I write has any particular value, but I give – I give life and the world what I can, and as seriously and conscientiously as I can, and perhaps that's why other times I am a selfish wretch who doesn't think of human duties and thinks he's excluded from life's responsibility. I am happiest when I sit over my papers and feel it unfolding from me like a fabric, I don't know where it comes from. Where does it come from? It's so enigmatic that I sometimes marvel at it. Surely the person who writes is an instrument of something unknown.

And do you know that a whole shower of meteors is falling at the moment, during this month? I sit in front of the house late into the night and watch the sky; it's simply fabulous. Yesterday I saw a big green meteor flying; it drew a line crossing out the whole sky and was so wonderful that I forgot to make a wish. Anyway, I take a bit of a theoretical interest in astronomy as well; I can see how little I know, and how splendid it is to be getting to know more. From now on I'll study – piece by piece – everything, all the sciences and theories; I'd like to know the whole world. And then, as an Irish proverb says: 'The man who knows everything dies.' Amen. To die of knowledge would be a beautiful death!

Otherwise, I'm very much OK. I've put on weight, I sunbathe daily, I watch the stars every night; only everyone chivvies me about writing too much. You, too, would chivvy me, but I can't be helped. I keep writing, writing; it's my joy.

Best wishes and kisses, *Karel*.

22

[Jindřichův Hradec, Rudolfov] 17 [August 1923], Friday

My dear Olina,

I've just this moment got your letter – with great relief and joy. So you see how much futile bitterness there was on your part. I wish to God that your calm and joy, your trust without exaggeration, your love without storms and swirlings, your mutual consideration and the peace in your soul, have truly returned. I'd write more, but I'm already on my way to the post office with this crumb. No, I didn't run away from you, but I sought peace with my own self; I've found it a bit, but it's fragile and sensitive, please don't expose it to any trial. My Prokop is dying,[1] I must get him out of it; I'm moved as if it were a real living person, but since my sister is just coming, I won't have any chance of curing him today. But please be calm and cheerful.

You have written such a nice word – friendship. Any older love acquires this undertone – please value it and don't underestimate it. Friendship is such a calm, solid and self-denying feeling, one of the best given to man.

My pen is squeaky and I don't have another one at home. To write with a squeaky pen is like playing a piano that's out of tune; it simply doesn't work; one can't say what one wants to.

Friendship, the effort to be pleased by the other's joy; I don't know what joy ranks above that. I'm a bit sceptical about love; you hold it against me, but it's unquestionably natural. To use a geological analogy, an extensive drift of terrestrial strata is going on in me. It is maturing and coming to terms with things: you make a mistake if you can't see that I'm changing, or if you compare me just one-sidedly – love-wise, for instance – with the person I was in the past. There is a little more prudence, and hence more coolness in me; you make a mistake if you relate that coolness just to yourself, and don't realise that I'm a planet that shifts from a glowing state to a state of inhabitability by all living things. Imagine that you don't really know me, but will start getting to know me; then you'll definitely look at everything with quite different, clearer eyes.

It can't be helped, I've been wittering on while I should have gone to the post office. Come to that, I'm curious, you know, if your brightening-up will last till my return. If only it does! And forever!

Best wishes and kisses, your *KČ*

23

[London, Notting Hill] 9 June [19]24

Dearest Olina,

Today, on All Souls' Monday, I have a quiet morning, what I mean is that I can sit and write. However, in three quarters of an hour I'm going to lunch at Seton-Watson's,[1] then I'll pop on tails and am going to dinner at Nigel Playfair's,[2] and then to a theatre of some sort, I don't even know where. Tomorrow I'm lunching with some journalist or another, and am dining at Rebecca West's, a good writer. The day after tomorrow I'm going to the country to see the editor of the *Manchester Guardian*, coming back on Thursday morning, at which point I'm again invited to lunch and dinner. So you can see what my life here is like, and I can't get out of it. Everyone is so terribly good and polite to me. The day before yesterday I lunched at Bernard Shaw's; he was incredibly kind and so great when he talked. I still have Wells to meet. I've seen virtually nothing of London so far, on the other hand, I'm getting to know what hardly any Czech has done, that is posh English households, the best clubs and high society. But at the same time I feel somehow sad. I don't know, last year, in Italy, I was much happier. And at home – I'd love to be at home. I often close my eyes and imagine that, say, tomorrow I'll be going home. Instead, maybe on Friday or Saturday, I shall travel further into England – let me see her while I'm here. I think that I shall never come back over here. I'll travel without excitement, but still I'm glad to be leaving London behind. The whole of last week I was all over the papers here, there was something there every day. Hopefully I shall eventually start having a peaceful time now.

Physically I feel, by and large, all right as I did at home, but I'm depressed. I feel uneasy, I should tell you something, but it's hard to open my mouth. My sweet, before my departure Prof. Syllaba told me things that are a blow to me as well as to you.[3] I beg you, for God's sake, please don't ask me to repeat them to you, because it hurts dreadfully. It concerns certain very bad nervous (*just* nervous, I assure you) strains for which no one is responsible. It is, you see, such a strange type of neurasthenia, such nasty phobias – but I have determined that I shall never describe them to you, because you are such a sensitive person. I think that I must suffer something because of my mother – it's inherited. Syllaba comforted me that perhaps this mental frailty (please let's call it *just* that) gave me the gift for creating – maybe. I only ardently wish someone else didn't suffer because of my mental inadequacy. And now, my dear noble sweet girl, if you love me, don't touch on *these* sore points. Please tell your Dad to go to see Prof. Syllaba and ask him himself. I wouldn't like him to take me for a bad person. That you understand me and will be merciful to me, I know, and I kiss your hands for it as passionately and gratefully as you deserve.

And now away, away from these pains. I still joyfully think of the success your Dad enjoyed – tell him that I press his hand. Surely I shall still be able to see the piece after I have come back.[4] I wish you could see the theatre here. I saw Miss Evans and Miss Thorndike – they are wonderful, *very* simple in their expressive means, but, mind you, what a refinement of nuances! I think it's the kind of acting that you *in particular* would like – little stylisation, cultivated and refined realism. And it's purely the actor's doing in the first place, the director retreats into the background. You wouldn't, however, like London, little one, not a whit. It's without charm, only parks are spectacular here, so Rusalka-like. Heavens, I'd love to have a letter from you, but then I still can't give you a proper address. In Italy I had a plan of the journey, I could see at least a week ahead, but here, nothing, I know nothing of what I'll do, where I'll go and where not. Do you know what? Send me your next letter to the following address:

Dr K.Č. c/o Dr O. Vočadlo[5]
33 Adelaide Road
Surbiton (Surrey)
England

He's my good friend, and he'll immediately forward the letter to where I tell him on my card.

I don't have any news whatsoever from home; your letter has been the only one so far. How's Hilar doing?[6] I feel awfully sorry for him. Christ, I'd love to sit with you, say, in that garden in the Lesser Town, and talk, talk, talk about everything I've seen here. But I wouldn't like to have you *here*, not that, you'd be unhappy, and everyone speaks nothing but English here. When you write to me, remember that you're writing to a person who is full of anxiety, and distressed. Cheer me up, cheer me up, as you did so many times in Prague. Send me one of your good-hearted and non-weepy cards. Keep well, my girl – I'm trying to do so too. I implore you to send me a nice letter. Please apologise for me in the theatre, that I haven't yet had a single minute to be able to send so much as cards to my friends and the people I know.

With best wishes, movingly kissing your hands. *K.Č.*

24

[April 1927]

Dearest Olina,

Some things shouldn't be uttered at all or at least not too often. Even the bruised flesh grows calloused, you know, if it's touched too often. I won't react to your letter now; my nerves are more rattled than they've ever been before, and I'm so gripped by bouts of impatience that I have to stop myself from breaking something.

Now it's *The Killed Man*'s turn.[1] I'd like to know how it's going, and I'd like to help you a bit so that you don't have to bear it all alone. I know I don't offer you much, but let me blow on your hot porridge and be at least a little crutch for you when you've got too much to carry. Don't let anything upset you now, for God's sake. Tomorrow (Thursday) I'll come round to ask you again; you can turn me away from your doorstep, but you can't forbid my need to be near you and bear your worries. If you don't have time for me, at least give a more detailed description of how *The Killed Man* is going, and what worries you, to Božka.[2] So you see, Smolík won't be so bad – I hoped so.[3] I'll come fiveish again.

See you.

Kissing hands, *K.*

25

Topoľčanky[1] [the first half of September 1927]

Dearest Olina,

The only thing I can write at this moment, the only thing I'm allowed to write and to which I'm entitled before my own self is the longing wish for you to be happy. Not even death would force me to say 'farewell', but instead I am telling you and adjuring you to be happy. Unhappy creature, you have such a desperate gift for suffering that I can't think of anything else for me or you but this only prayer that you should be happy. I got your letter this morning, Olga, I can't even say that it hurt – I knew too many unuttered things beforehand, and it fell on me so, as if I had already experienced it some earlier time – I ran out into the rain to a park and was praying for you there. Only then could I torture myself and start settling my accounts with the past. By the time you read this letter a night and a day will have passed. Within that time I will have counted the tally of all I am guilty of, as well as of what is not wittingly my fault, I will have accepted all the pain that is still awaiting me, and will have taken as much human suffering as possible on me in order to pay my account. I no longer want to be happy, only reconciled. Darling, I don't have a bitter word to say to you. I'd like to beg you for forgiveness, but forgiveness is not as easy as you are willing to give it. I am afraid of you terribly. I am afraid that you will find even in these lines something that you will want to torment yourself with and that you will want to cry over. I beg you then, Olina, I beg you on my knees not to weigh me down by taking any of my words or deeds as the cause of your pain. I beseech you to believe me for once that I desperately want to write or do something that won't cause you a shred of pain. I cannot bear any of your pains any more. You have never seen that bearing them has been harder for me than bearing anything I have suffered myself. The only sweet thing I'm capable of telling myself now is what I'm saying to myself while running around the park: let you be happy, let you be happy, let you be happy. You can't imagine what comfort there is in those words.

Darling Olinka, I don't have a word for my apology. If I was harsh on you, I was also harsh on myself, and now I am ten times harsher – you no longer have to tell me by what and when I have hurt you. But to you, my girl, I want to say, I want to shout at you, be happy. I don't know what it is to be happy, indeed, I don't know how it is done, but I at least want to be able not to cause you any pain. Perhaps I've never been capable of love; the only thing I have been capable of has been a terrible pain from your every pain. Perhaps it's not love, what you call love, I can't clarify it for myself, but I know that it's been the strongest feeling that I have been capable of. Maybe you other people are capable of some other feelings, but my love of you, of people, of God, of everything that exists and that I know, is a passionate co-feeling. Christ, Olga, if you could see, if you knew how much my heart is overburdened by it all! And perhaps it's necessary for the salvation of my soul that I don't live my own life. I think that this talk with myself will have a great influence on the whole of my life, but that's not the point now – the point is not about me, but only, only about you. Darling, make an effort to be happy. It's your great duty. Please, Olga, make darling Olinka happy. For the sake of your love of me let her be happier. They say about me that I am selfish. Well then, at this decisive moment I'm asking for a relief for myself: let her be happy. If a day comes and you smile at me, I shall stop being haunted by the most difficult thing that clutches my heart. I know, I know, I know very well that by everything I can write today I'm only getting around what I should say, but there is a dread in me that I might press some of the sore spots of your heart, a terrible dread, darling. I don't want you to suffer. I can't bear it any longer. I beg you, please, for God's sake, do not torment yourself.

Kissing your hands. *Karel*

In the middle of the night: Darling Olinka, you have decided. I accept. I'm beginning to see the light, not in my heart, but in my head. Be happy. God, how much I'd like to make your decision easier for you! Oli, you deserve it, be happy.[2]

26

23 June [1928]

Dearest Olina,

I have a strong feeling that this letter isn't intended for me, but for some of the numerous other Karels, most probably for that obstetrician;[1] I'd have sent it straight to him, but I can't for the life of me think of his name – I have a bad memory for names. Simultaneously, I got another letter that is certainly meant for me; thank you for the remembrances from Kotlina.[2] But you are wrong to think that I'm somehow exasperated and that 'I'm weary of the world' just like the girl in that song. I'll fight a bit, and mostly because I haven't yet lost all sense of humour. And then again, we can't live prettily in this world if, helplessly and once and for all, we sell out to all those wheeler-dealers, windbags and slanderers. But I'll save it for the autumn – everyone is lazy now in the summer and public opinion has gone on holiday. Tomorrow I'm going to Brno, I'll be there for three days; it will probably be rather tiring because I'll have to write something about that exhibition. Other than that, I don't know anything new, not since yesterday; I'm just coming back to the admonition that this year you should really devote the entire vacation to that calcification. Go to the Tatras again and lie in ultraviolet radiation there; they won't cure your neglected catarrhs in two weeks, you need at least eight for that. You can go to Paris any time during the season, but use the long vacation like a sensible person. I'll be really angry if you don't listen; I'll write to your father and you'll get it in the neck. Tell me, would you let Boženka[3] go to Berlin or Vienna or somewhere instead of having treatment? You'd jaw and jaw at her and pontificate until poor Boženka obeyed. You won't have such a bad time in the Tatras, but if that doctor is also called Karel, woe unto him – you'll add him to your collection as well, then. What a pity Maxíček isn't called Karel too.[4] But wait, our chair Marek is also Karel,[5] then there is Dr Kramář,[6] Havlíček Borovský,[6] Toman,[8] composer Rudolf Karel,[9] our Poláček[10] and many other Karels.

No paper has reprimanded me for as long as three days – well, that's what they call the silly season.

But now I must write an article – I only wanted to return this precious little letter, that isn't intended for me, to you; and be careful, if you go on like this I'll learn all the secrets about A.S., Haas, Mary, Štěpánek and other Prague citizens.[11] Remember, one must never write an address on the sealed envelope, but put down the address first, then read the letter to remind yourself who it is written for, and then put it all together in a suitable manner.

Give my fond regards to Boženka, look after yourself and heal; health belongs to physical culture just like having a bath, clean underwear and a permanent wave.

Kissing both hands, *K.*

27

August 1935 (but even earlier)[1]

> In Lorenzago I was at an inn,
> To tell you where it is would be a sin,
> Best you don't know, else you would go there straight
> To see it, and you wouldn't think it great,
> And in your disappointment you would state:
> That K.Č. cannot but exaggerate.
>
> A buxom hostess with maternal breasts
> Brought frills to deck the windows for her guests,
> The curtains were like little starchy crimps,
> Or like an altar-cloth with lacy trims,
> And Mary's picture up above the bed
> Just like a little chapel overhead,

Why is it all so peaceful and so white?
All things in order, I must put things right,
Get into line, be good, and then at night
Won't look into the gaping pit of night,
With hands clasped I will lie in peace, unhurried.
Old fellow, why aren't you married? Married?

28

Monday [Osov, 24 October 1938][1]

Dearest Olinka,

I wanted to come back to Prague today, mainly because of you, so that I could be with you, but I now seriously fear that people might say that I disappeared from Prague just when bombs, to say the least, were hovering over her.[2] It makes me feel awkward. I think it will be better for me to stay in the country for a while and do my work from here. If you can't come to see me today or tomorrow, please give me your advice by letter.

I'd awfully like to go to Strž.[3] I'd feel a deeper relief there. Please ask Karel, as soon as he manages to get a couple of litres of petrol, or Dvořák or someone,[4] to give you a lift, and come to collect me and take me to Strž – we must finish all the works there so that we have somewhere to write in peace. Arrange it with Karel or Dvořák, and collect me please. Else I shall come to you to Prague tomorrow or the day after tomorrow– in short, write to me or telegraph.

Dearest little one, please don't get angry now and avoid angry people. Nothing can be done. To put up with the way things are is a sin because we have fallen victim to a great historic brutality, and to rail at those who led us into it is a sin too, because it could do us harm internally as well as abroad, and we cannot afford that now. We can't even curse the one with whom we were prepared to fight; there is no way out; we have no outlet for our frustration that might give us some relief. That's why I beseech you, I beg you with my hands clasped to clench your teeth, like many others, and leave all passions aside. If everyone does it, we shall come out of it at least in such a way that we pull together. Do it, little one, for my sake, and also for yours – you'd destroy yourself physically as well if you kept rending your heart by that anger. I'd love to have you here. I hate the theatre for separating you from me in such a distressing time.

Be calm, then, even if you are sad, my dear, forget all vain talk and shrink from it. Rely on me to still be seeking, as long as it depends on me, right words and right deeds, or little deeds, that might at least help at a particular moment. So don't be upset by anything any longer. Truly, we shall all need a great deal of strength and wisdom, and we must keep them for later. You and Boženka[5] hug each other tight, and as soon as you can, come to see me. For the time being don't puzzle your head over plans for the future. And write a poem again – everyone profoundly liked the Sunday one. To go among people is only a torment. I'm being reclusive here among most lovely people because I can't stand hearing the same talk and reactions all the time.

Dearest Olinka, the important thing is to see you again soon. Do everything to make it as soon as possible. I'm looking calmly into the future – it will be possible, it will not be so bad as one sees it coloured by emotional perturbation. And as for the two of us, I just thirst for us being able to snuggle up together and live more for ourselves than we've done so far.

Kissing you many times and as warmly as I can.

Love, *K.*

Let Růžena[6] stay at Strž! I *must* go there!

VI
COMMON THINGS

Save Yourself If You Can

(*The Path*, 18 August 1922)

Does man need salvation? It seems that he does. Despite all the reassurance the poets give us about the beauty and joy of life, we are by and large unhappy. And anyone who doesn't need salvation – may he go to hell in his pride and obduracy; don't stand in his way. But the rest of us want to be redeemed.

The idea of salvation (to start in a learned fashion) exists in two versions: subjective and objective. The subjective one asks: How and by what means shall I be saved? The objective one wants to know: Who will be saved? And since there are two questions, there are, with mathematical certainty, two potential wrong answers. And if it's possible to go wrong about a thing, it's likewise possible to philosophise about it.

1. How and by what means will I be saved? Presumably something will come to me through God's grace; some truth, an apostle, a revelation will knock on my door and enter so as to save me; I myself can only wait. At best I can watch for it out of the window to see if a great and redemptive something is already drawing near from somewhere. The emphasis is on the words 'from somewhere': from heaven, from the east, from the people, from a university, for I don't know where the one who is supposed to come will come from, and possess my soul, and make it into his soul, so that I'll be saved. A messiah must come somewhere from the outside to grant my soul eternal salvation, or at least a goodish hope of it. So I shall be redeemed by, say, the introduction of eugenic marriage, or lay morality, or the dictatorship of the proletariat, or prohibition, or universal education, or freethinking, or some new religion, or some old religion, or what not. But salvation is always something that I must needs be helped to obtain by someone or something else,

that I receive as a gift, that comes to me. It is not myself; it doesn't spring from me alone; I haven't done it of my own accord.

Now, I can understand quite well that man expects salvation from the outside, simply because salvation must be something other than he is himself. He can't believe in himself, so he believes in a 'something from somewhere'. If there is anything wrong about this concept, it is that man wants to be redeemed wholly and at once.

Suppose that 'to be saved' is the same as 'to ascend into the air'. Probably we all tried to lift ourselves when we were children. If I can lift Franta here, or Andula, the kid thinks, I bet I can lift myself. And he grabs his trousers and wants to go up in the air. To mankind's great disadvantage, it's impossible, I'm afraid. A man doesn't lift himself to any height. A man can't save himself. Some rope or other must be dropped to him from on high, or he must be given a lifting device of some sort. As likely as not it's the same with salvation. And yet, a man *can* lift himself. If it doesn't work vertically, it will work slantwise. If he can't grab his trousers and haul himself up, he can build a ladder and climb. With every step he lifts himself by his own power. So it's perhaps possible to save yourself even by your own power. Except that it doesn't go vertically, but slantwise, not all at once, but step by step, rung after rung, in small, everyday and partial salvations. Perhaps it's possible to replace absolute redemption with a thousandfold relative salvation. Maybe you can even save yourself a smidgen each day. And anywhere. In any ordinary mundanity. Perhaps the whole error of salvation lies in that we're used to saying 'to be saved' instead of 'to save ourselves'. And perhaps that ladder of personal, relative salvation can be Jacob's ladder, too, on which the angels will come down to him.

By all this I only want to say: surely salvation is possible, because we need it. So save yourself if you can. Save your own self.

2. Who is to be saved? A customary belief is this: if there is any salvation, it saves the whole of humankind, and everyone has to accept it. And if someone cursedly doesn't want to let it save him,

smite him! It's strange what a furious altruism there is in every salvationist faith. Everyone wants to redeem the whole world at all costs. He won't do it any cheaper. And if it doesn't fit his neighbour's purse, it's not salvation's fault but the neighbour's. For it becomes the definition of salvation, as it were, that it's universal and for everyone.

I belong among those short-sighted creatures who are unable to see the wood for the trees, or humankind for actual humans. I can't imagine an idea that would save both Professor Mareš and Professor Krejčí.[1] I can't imagine a great idea that wouldn't, besides having the miraculous power to unite people, also have the miraculous power to divide them. Given this state of affairs, there are only two possibilities: either to condemn all the unbelieving dogs whose heads don't fit under my hat of salvation, that's what usually happens; or to say to myself at last that there's enough room for all sorts of salvations in this protean world. Come to that, let's not speak about humankind and the whole world; these are words under which no one can picture anything at all. Let's speak about any person you care to choose and his salvation. Because he wants to be saved, the only thing that matters is for him to *be* saved. By what? From the perspective of the pure love of a fellow being, that is utterly indifferent. But it can't be a matter of indifference to us by what means all humankind is to be saved – it's such a terribly serious question that . . . that it should finally be left at rest. Communism – that, you might say, is a sin against humanity, but it's a fairly good thing for Jiří Wolker.[2] Eugenics is grievous nonsense for humankind, but it surely must have a lot of beauty for docent Brožek.[3] Religion will save Jakub Deml and prohibition Professor Foustka,[4] Professor Krejčí's soul will disintegrate into dust, whereas the soul of Professor Velenovský will be jiggling ouija boards for another thirty thousand years.[5] But it's horrendous to demand of humankind that all souls should disintegrate into dust or be harassed after death by spiritualistic hogwash.

The corollary of this is not resignation or indifference as regards the problem of salvation. On the contrary, you can seek salvation passionately, unremittingly and with all your fervent love and hope, but seek it for your own self in the first place. Save yourself if you can. Don't seek your salvation in saving others. Just give your example: even that is a lot.

If at this moment someone rang my doorbell and I went and answered the door, and if it were Christ on his pilgrimage through the world, and if he said to me: 'As you can see, I'm coming to save mankind once again,' – no doubt I'd cry, shattered by my unbelief and smallness, but no doubt I'd say (or at least think to myself): 'For Christ's sake, don't do it, it's good for nothing. Even if it were the quintessence of the beautiful and the wonderful ... Humankind cannot be saved, perhaps because there isn't really any humankind, but only people. Mankind can't be saved, but it is possible to help a man. Perhaps it is a low ideal, only helping instead of saving, helping only someone, on this spot, at this wretched moment, instead of saving the whole world at once for evermore. Perhaps it's a teeny ideal, just a farthing enterprise of salvation, but how can one deliver the world if everything is not all right here at hand?'

The Resurrection

The People's Paper, 1 April 1923

When I was a little boy playing marbles with beans and wiping my nose on the sleeve of my shirt, every year I experienced one moment of festive excitement, and that was the Resurrection. There was, you know, a deacon in our town, God rest his soul, and this deacon was supra-terrestrially fat, in a way that was somehow spiritual and dig-nified, nothing short of majestically fat; his fatness had no vulgarity about it as in secular people; rather it revealed a special divine grace – in short, it was a sinless diaconal fatness. And when in the moist vernal half-light of the Resurrection celebration our square lit up with lines of candles in the windows, and a stream of white servers with glowing tapers gushed out of the church, and behind them the big white Mister Catechist, and then Mister Deacon himself with a glistering monstrance, wearing a golden chasuble and walking under a silk canopy, and the canopy is carried by Mr Kuťák and Mr Blahouš plus two other aldermen, and all of them are downright black and all have their bald patches glistening, and Mr Těmín with a local band blow their trumpets, playing the famous, ultra-famous flourishes, and four servers ring little bells, and two boys emit smoke from their censers, and Churchman Nyklíček has swung the big bell, ding, dong, ding, dong, and hey, hallelujah! hosanna, hurray! Mister Deacon is now floating along like a bright stupendous cloud scented with incense . . . God, it's so beautiful, so immensely beautiful that I, a bad, impious boy, am throwing myself on my sinful knees and can't take my eyes off the lights, candles, brands, flags and banners, torches and monstrances and canopies and all that splendour slowly swimming by, and my innermost being is saturated with envious, wretched bitterness: why is it that my Daddy, my big, strong and dignified Dad isn't also carrying the canopy over Mister Deacon, or at least a banner or the smallest brand; and this was the yearly pain of the godless boy.

Since then I haven't seen the Resurrection, because I don't want to get that great and glorious impression spoilt, but on every Holy Saturday I'm swamped by a kind of Catholic nostalgia. And now tell me that it's an aesthete's pose! Oh yes, of course, I was then, at the age of eight, a remarkable aesthete, the same aesthete as the natives of the Congo or New Caledonia, who also marvel vastly at their own processions and dancing magicians and torches and other suchlike splendour, the same aesthete as a Prague or Madrid or Heaven-knows-where street gazing at famous funerals, parades, marches and celebrations. This form of aestheticism is as old as the world and as sophisticated as an American Indian; it's not really doing very well today, but . . .

'Yesterday at noon, on behalf of the broader administrative committee of Larger Prague and the inhabitants of the capital, Mayor Dr Baxa welcomed Spring in Kinsky's Garden. Accompanied by representatives of council clubs, heads of city councils, and also representatives of guilds, fire brigades, municipal officers, uniformed forces, etc., etc., he visited the First Flowering

Crocus, and in a longish speech he assured it of the joyous feelings with which the capital greeted the return of Spring within its olden legendary walls. Then the Police Band struck up and the Hlahol choir sang a moving chorale "So we have spring starting, lovey". At the same moment all the Prague bells began to chime, nine shots were fired from the cannon on the Marian Bastion and a squadron of aeroplanes circled over the River Vltava. Innumerable hosts of viewers are on their way to pay homage to the First Crocus, where a guard of honour is kept by members of the PT Association Sokol, the Police, civic societies and the Workers' PT Association . . .'

'The President welcomed Spring at an intimate celebration in the chateau garden. In the name of diplomatic staff the doyen of ambassadorial services Nuncio Micara conveyed the warm feeling of joy whereby governments and their representatives welcomed the arrival of Spring per se, not least on the territory of such a flourishing and wisely administered state as Czechoslovakia . . .'

'On the occasion of the arrival of Spring all political parties will organise meetings and rallies, whereupon they will form marches and proceed towards Stromovka Park, where they will join to make merry . . .'

'The Czechoslovak army welcomed Spring in a speech given by the general inspector at a festive parade held on the training ground near Invalidovna. Since early morning the sun had been suffusing the earth with its balmy beams . . .'

Why go on lying? Democracy is nice – great! – but it can't do a single celebration. Mayor Baxa may have welcomed the participants in the trade fair, but he did not, and will not, welcome the First Crocus, although the first crocus is something better and more blessed than all possible trade fairs. Mr Mayer will not carry out a ceremonial Crossing of the Frozen Vltava either, nor will he salute the spectacular and heartening Departure of Ice to the sounds of a military band. We still accept Christmas, Easter and All Souls' Day from the withering hand of the church; old Catholicism still upholds the sacred divisions of the year, but we infidels have found nothing, absolutely nothing, to take their place. I don't even know which our current democracy lacks more – a bit of poetry, or a bit of exuberance.

Kazi Ulaya

The People's Paper, 4 January 1924

In his reminiscences of East Africa Dr Hauer relates this: the natives are ever so curious. If they see anything they can't understand at all, like binoculars, or a compass, or a gramophone, or a tennis racket if you like, in the hands of a European, they squat on the ground and start up a most lively conference about what it is and how it is done, where the catch in it is and how come it's like that. And when they've racked their brains over it to the utmost, they say: '*Kazi ulaya.*' 'That's a European piece of work.' This settles everything, and any additional question is unnecessary; the Africans stand up in relief and don't think about the peculiar thing any longer. It is *kazi ulaya* – European work – that explains everything.

And we *bwani ulaya*, Misters Europeans, aren't any better. At the end of all our questions we have our *kazi ulaya*, some omnipotent cause that puts our minds at rest at once and rids us of the further strain of thinking. Whether it's called gravitation, electricity, energy or causality, it's again nothing else but *kazi ulaya*. We stand up feeling satisfied: everything is clear because it's been named. To explain anything means to substitute the nameless unknown with the named unknown.

The Africans from around Mount Kilimanjaro have quite the same scholarly method as the whitest sage. Because we don't know any more about magnetism than an African does about European work, we expound the principle of the compass no more accurately than a black man with his *kazi ulaya*, and are as satisfied with our explication as he is. Why does the compass turn northward? Well, it's European work, I want to say, it's the effect of the earth's magnetism. It's simply *kazi ulaya*, and now you know it all.

And another traveller, Detzner, describes how in West Africa, where Cameroon and the Congo are situated, the natives are afraid of such new things. An electric lamp, that's magic; it's juju – it's a demonic power. And a gramophone and a theodolite and other uncanny sleights of hand are also juju; no one must touch them, or something terrible will happen. Juju doesn't explain the thing with reference to its causes, but guesses at its hidden essence. *Kazi ulaya* is a causal explanation; juju is a metaphysical explanation. *Kazi ulaya* and juju are the two basic, universal categories of human thinking.

I think that the theory of human cognition would be a great deal simpler if these terms were introduced. All scientific cognition, as long as it's called empirical and positivist, belongs to the *kazi ulaya* class. All metaphysical cognition, all religion and mysticism fall within the juju sphere. Poetry and art, too, are mostly juju, whereas technical invention is *kazi ulaya*.

There are numerous, in large part very bizarre, combinations of the *kazi ulaya* with the juju type: for example, philosophy, justice, and not least politics. *Kazi ulaya* is a mark of progress; juju is on the conservative and prohibitive side. In the spirit of curiosity, *kazi ulaya* takes pleasure in new things that it can name and can play with; in mystical horror about things unknown, juju pronounces them demonic and bans all contact with them. The whole of life is permeated with nothing but *kazi ulaya* and juju. Everything we accept because we don't understand it is *kazi ulaya*; everything we reject because we don't understand it is juju. The circle of possible thinking is thus divided.

To *kazi ulaya*, juju is obscurantism, superstition and blind backwardness; for juju, *kazi ulaya* is godlessness, sin and blasphemy. But, when all's said and done, both *kazi ulaya* and juju are equally African, I mean equally panhuman.

From Murderess

The People's Paper, 16 March 1924

It's said that the deeper significance of the jury is to bring in a verdict in accord with the moral feeling of the people. But I'm incapable of believing that the moral feeling of the people would demand the death of Marie Töglová, a murderess. There's nothing to embellish her deed with; it's more than terrible – it's disconsolate, wretched, destitute and as helplessly sad as a ghastly autumnal day. What is there to excuse, to wash off; what is there to illuminate by throwing the light of deeper understanding on it? I only want to keep repeating: four crowns, two days of hunger, no shelter, no mercy, no helping hand; hunger, hunger again, a night somewhere in the forest or in a barn, harsh people, a hungry baby in her arms and nothing, nothing, nothing but the October cold. Is there still anyone who doesn't understand, isn't it clear enough yet? Then think about it, four crowns, and not even those any longer, two days without a morsel of food, all doors shut ... I could repeat these muddily grey, brutal facts without end; nothing more can be wrung out of them but greyness, poverty and some kind of unspeakable, cold-blooded hopelesness.

Pronounced guilty by eleven votes, since she committed desperation, let her be hanged then. God knows what these juries are up to: sometimes they're so lenient that you could beat them, but Marie Töglová is to be executed. Judges, Your Worships, Marie Töglová is not a mouse, but a human; if she is hanged, you won't rid the world of poverty, the helplessness of paupers, the stupefaction, the hunger and the despair of mothers who have no roof over their heads; the guilt for the death of her child will be neither punished nor atoned for. This time you have judged badly; you didn't ask whose fault it was that Marie Töglová had only four crowns in her pocket, that she had nothing to eat, nowhere to sleep, no milk in her breasts, nor even a human soul to advise her. You judged a victim; you sentenced her to death for not having enough strength to bear what none of us has ever experienced, for not having done – what, come to that? It's so horrible that there isn't a reply to that. Mothers, what should Marie Töglová, who hadn't eaten for two days and had been driven away from human thresholds, have done? Perhaps she should have died with her baby; so let her be sentenced to death for not having jumped into the river herself, then.

I'll never meet Marie Töglová; but if any of you can, tell her in her cell what I want to let her know on behalf of others: that people are not so vicious, and that there were very many who felt desperately sorry and ashamed when they were reading about her pitiful case.

The case of Marie Töglová is not a sensation, is no disclosure of the dark forces of the human soul. If it discloses anything, well, it's only that human justice is sometimes as ugly, brutal and grey as the facts, as the saddest histories of the poor.

About Scepticism[1]

The Present, 23 October 1924

Scepticism. Pessimism. Relativism. Nihilism. Individualism. And finally also *Ignoramus et ignorabimus* [We do not know and will not know]. All this Latin is liberally applied to the so-called pre-war generation, presumably out of the conviction that it amounts to a shattering disclosure of their covert vices. Since, out of pessimistic curiosity, I got myself born some twenty-five years before the war, these Latin words fall on my head too. I ought to defend myself against them, but surprisingly, now I've put them down, I must confess that I find them very appealing. So, for example, I like scepticism as inordinately as enthusiasm, and worse still, I'm capable of committing both nine times a day. Pessimism charms me, especially when it is, as is proper, in league with passionate optimism. Relativism provokes me to a hearty assurance that there are not only things in the world, but also relations and proportions between things. Nihilism somewhat throws me; perhaps it's nihilism when I believe that 'nothing is lost', for instance, or 'nothing is without value'. For in truth, I comfort myself with a great many negative sentences. Individualism is, in practical terms, a belief that the postman, who has just brought my mail, is a stunningly extraordinary personality; I was granted the privilege of noticing his sad moustache, and his wise, taciturn eyes – I tell you it's been a great discovery.

So what's left is the so-called ignorabism, or the belief that there are many things that we don't know and can never get to know due to the limitations of our brain, and so it's pointless to think about them. This is to an extent correct. I keenly own up to every limitation of my or other people's reason. I'm convinced that Prof. Krejčí will never get to know God's glory and I'll never understand Einstein's universe; it would be useless to think about it any further. But it's wrong if Prof. Krejčí thinks no one has ever known and will ever know God's glory because Prof. Krejčí can't understand it – that's simply a dogmatic statement, unsupported by any evidence. If our generation is sceptical, it can't exactly profess ignorabism, for the two are in opposition.

But in this contemporary use or misuse the words *ignoramus et ignorabimus* seem to mean something else – presumably they imply that our age-group, faced with various solutions to life's problems, can't opt definitively for one or the other party, thesis, truth or regulation; that it's inclined to see good and evil mixed here as well as there; that it sighs despondently – we don't and can't know which of all the possibilities is worse or more absurd or more catastrophic; and that this generation renounces any fundamental opinion, giving itself over to bleak fear, resignation and cowardly compromise.

Supposing that were true (though I don't think it is). Then I ask whether this position is in itself so tenuous or bleak. What's bleak is of course Buridan's ass who is dying of hunger between two bundles of hay because he can't decide which of the two he should tuck into. But an equally bleak ass is the normal, ideological ass who eats only from the bundle on the left, in the horrible belief that the bundle on the right is passé, bourgeois and putrid, or by contrast eats from the bundle on the right, full of contempt for the poisonous, unpatriotic and malign left bundle. As regards these alternatives, I believe that the healthiest view is that of an ass who may be limited but is practical, who sees just hay in both bundles and allows himself enough time to pick up the best mouthfuls from either side. This ass is, as they say, a compromise, but surely not an unprincipled one, for his principle is to search for the best, patiently and bit by bit.

But I should be speaking about people here, isn't that right? So, let's say you are symmetrical, and have two eyes and a brain in the middle, and you want to know too much, and you devour facts insatiably and can't shut your eyes to either good or evil. If you are like that you're nothing but indifferent, you indulge in fruitless scepticism, you're apathetic, half-hearted, dreary and pessimistic. Because an integrated, concerned, active, optimistic, and in a word, genuine person decides for one and only one truth; he follows and implements it, or to put it in another way, he bashes everyone else, shouting God's on my side.

A belief consists in accepting some other opinion as your own. A firm conviction is a decision that you already know enough, and no longer have to improve your mind with anything. Sticking to principle is an ability to act without taking into account the actual state of things. Positive action exhausts itself in fury at other opinions, and in a constant repetition of certain key words. A programme is a chance to do idiocies tenaciously. As you can see, all political advantages are on this side.

A worse, and more difficult, path is the 'indifferent' one. You never know in advance in which direction you will find good or evil. Where you might feel like condemning, a past or future value sparkles out, and where you might feel like jumping on the bandwagon, you find inhumanity or absurdity. You are never finished with weighing up; you are not spared a single disappointment; you are not blind to any hope. You don't see two bundles, but thousands of stalks; and that way your possibility of choice multiplies a thousandfold. Stalk by stalk you pick up what's good and useful in the human world; stalk by stalk you eliminate stubble and tares, and no king of ants comes to help you – you alone must accomplish the whole work by yourself. You don't cry out at the oppression of thousands, but at the oppression of every single individual. You have to abolish one truth to be able to keep finding thousands of them. Your inactivity means that you always have a lot to do; your indifference means that everything that exists concerns you; your pessimism means that you can't be dismissive. You can't be sublime because you want to stay close to things. You can't save the world because you want to help it. You can't fight for the truth because if you fight you stop seeing. For all your absorption in getting to know, you can't say that you know something. Your certainty doesn't rest on principles, but on facts; indecisive about principles, sceptical about words, you trust only what you see, but you are not like a doubting Thomas, for the wounds you find are not for sticking fingers into. Come to think of it, as there is nothing more perfect, you simply believe in people.

In sum, '*ignoramus et ignorabimus*' is a name for a free and endless path of cognition, testing and finding out; and I tell you what – seen in this light, it doesn't seem to me too bad. If I really have to choose between belief and criticism, I choose criticism, for belief robs me of criticism, while criticism enables me to save at least some little piece of belief – and even the beliefs of other people. And if I am to choose between ignorance and ignorabism, I go for the latter.

Tradition

Apollo: A Review of Cultural Life, 1 November 1924

I've inscribed this word at the head of my article so that I won't lose sight of it, but the more I look at it, the more perplexing it seems. Let's say that by definition a tradition is an upholding of old ways (all right, maybe this definition is wishy-washy, but just don't butt in for the moment). On the other hand, a hangover from the past is also an upholding of old ways. I don't know if the wigs of English judges are a tradition or a hangover from the past. I can't decide whether the university beadle is a hangover or a tradition. If the university beadle is a venerable piece of tradition, it is to his credit that he reminds us of the fifteenth century. If he's just a rotten hangover, however, the same thing is to his discredit. A tradition is an upholding of old ways *because* they are old. A hangover is an upholding of old ways *despite the fact* that they are old.

But the term 'old' is an even thornier problem. The beadle's fur coat is for us ordinary unhistorical folk very ancient, but for an archaeologist it is not old but recent. Lately I read in the work of one scholar that the statues on some portal or other were 'entirely modern', that is, from the fifteenth century. And for a palaeontologist a paltry two-thousand-year-old Roman or Egyptian amphora is nothing short of indecently recent. By contrast, it's possible that last week is like a golden age, a tradition, to a summer fly, while the bacteria in my tumbler may cherish the bygone tradition of the hour that has just passed. So, a tradition is an upholding of ways that we for more or less arbitrary and irrational reasons regard as old.

At times someone proclaims that we are to return to the traditions of the 1890s or the 1880s, or as far back as the tradition of our national revivalists. What's alarming about this tendency is not that it's reactionary, but that we count things that have been in the past for only twenty or forty or a hundred years as old. It may be that next year some new reactionaries will start calling for ye olde poetic tradition of Jiří Wolker.[1] Maybe someone is, from outrageously reactionary motives, going to dig up the tradition of Fráňa Šrámek from the silt of ages.[2] We no longer value the last century even as a source of classical traditions, whereas it could serve as a springboard for the present. Perhaps it's because of the lack of historical continuity that things and actions grow old so quickly in our land. Woefully, it's perhaps the reason why people here grow older more quickly than in the western, historically older, countries.

In any case, the word 'old' is a curious notion – it's impossible to work with it seriously. To a cherub of three years old, a kid of five seems past his prime; a young filly sniggers at the grey hairs of a grandpa of thirty; a teenybopper thinks a school-leaver a has-been. It's quite natural that young people should take the elderly for old buffers, it's worse when the elderly take themselves for old buffers. It's been suggested that the Czech Academy should be made younger. It's a splendid idea. I enthusiastically add my voice to the idea that the Czech Academy should be made younger. But not by taking in young members. Rather, its members should start thinking of themselves as whizzkids, with all their advantages and challenges.

With age a man tends not only towards the future but also towards the past. What looks like a far-off, outlived era to a twenty-year-old seems, when he is fifty, so near that he could touch it with his hand. I don't believe that Methuselahs would be so incontinently progressive as Bernard Shaw makes them. I think that they would approach closer and closer to what they had left behind, not through regression but simply through growth. They would grow deeper into the past than we short-lived people can.

As for me, I confess to a certain historical incompetence. I don't like old things, or more precisely, I like some old things enormously, not because they are old, but because they aren't old at all. Even the university beadle in his glory seems to me lovely not because he's ancient but because he's very colourful, and so closer to glorious youthfulness, as it were, than we in our little grey suits. Jaroslav Durych looks back to Erben not because Erben is old, but because he is absolutely not.[3] We take pleasure in the primitive and early arts not for their wonderful oldness, but for their wonderful youngness.

This is what I've wanted to say: what would do us good is greater love of the past and of old things, because plenty of truly fantastic youthfulness is buried in them. Only people who have never been wholly young can regard the past as a heap of old junk. There is something senile in speaking about old traditions. If even the oldest traditions aren't blazingly young, I can't honestly see what use they are. If they are really old, they are just hangovers from the past.

Why Am I Not a Communist?

The Present, 4 December 1924

This question has emerged, out of a clear blue sky, among several people who were inclined to pass their time with anything but politics. It's certain that none of them would have put the question 'Why am I not an agrarian?' or 'Why am I not a national democrat?'. Not being an agrarian doesn't need to mean you have a defined opinion or a life-belief, but not being a communist means being a non-communist; not being a communist isn't a bare negation, but a certain creed.

Personally, the question is a relief for me, as I was in woeful need, not of engaging in polemics against communism, but of defending myself before myself as to the reason why I am not a communist and why I cannot be one. I would feel lighter if I were one. Then I would live under the impression that I contributed to the rectification of the world as fiercely as possible; I would believe that I sided with the poor against the rich, the hungry against the money-bags; I would know what to think about what, what to hate, what to ignore. Instead, I'm like a naked man in the brambles, empty-handed, not covered by any doctrine, aware that I'm powerless to help the world, and often not knowing how to protect my conscience. If my heart is on the side of the poor, why on earth am I not a communist?

Because I am on the side of the poor.

I've seen indigence so poignant and unspeakable that everything I am turned bitter for me. Wherever I was, I ran from palaces and museums to look at the life of the poor in the humiliating role of a helpless onlooker. It's not enough to watch and it's not enough to empathise; I should live their life, but I'm afraid of death. This lousy, inhuman penury isn't carried on the banner of any party; and communism shouts from a glaring distance into those horrible dens, where there is neither a nail for a noose nor a dirty cloth for bedding: 'The social order is to blame. In two years, in twenty years, once the flag of revolution starts waving, then . . .'

How do you mean, in two years, in twenty years? How can you so indifferently permit that another two months of winter, another two weeks, another two days should be lived like that? The bourgeoisie, which is unable to or doesn't want to help, is alien to me, but equally alien is communism that, instead of help, brings the flag of revolution. The last word of communism is to wield the sceptre, not to save; its great slogan is power, not help. For it, poverty, hunger, unemployment are not an unbearable pain and shame, but a welcome reserve of dark forces, smouldering with rage and revulsion. 'The social order is to blame.' No, we are all to blame, whether we stand looking at human indigence with our hands in our pockets, or holding the flag of revolution.

Poor people are not a class; they are declassed, discarded and unorganised; they'll never be on the steps of the throne, no matter who sits on it. The hungry don't want to rule, but to eat; in the light of poverty it's irrelevant who governs, what matters is how we people feel. Poverty isn't an institution or a class, but a misery. When I look for some immediate human solution I find only the cold doctrine of class rule. I cannot be a communist because its morality is not a morality of help. Because it preaches the abolition of the social order, and not the abolition of social evil, which is poverty. Because if it wants to help the poor at all, it does it conditionally: first we must rule, and then (perhaps) it will be your turn. Woefully, even this conditional salvation isn't textually guaranteed.

Poor people are not a mass. A thousand workers can help one worker in his existential struggle, but a thousand paupers can't help one pauper even to get a piece of bread. A poor, hungry, helpless person is utterly lonely. His life is a history of its own, incompatible with others; it's an individual case even though it resembles other cases as one downtrodden piece of clay resembles another. Turn society upside down by whatever means, the poor will fall to the bottom again, and the maximal gain will be that some others will join them.

I'm not by a long chalk an aristocrat, but I don't believe in the value of the masses. Come to think of it, no one, I hope, seriously contends that the masses will rule: they are only the physical means of someone achieving certain goals; they're simply political material in a far harsher, more ruthless sense than partisans of other colours. It's necessary to compress a man into a certain mould so that he becomes mass material; it's necessary to give him a uniform made of a particular woollen cloth or particular ideas.

Alas, it's usually impossible to take off a uniform made of ideas after a year and a half. I'd begin truly to respect communism if it came up to a worker and told him honestly: 'I demand something from you and don't promise anything; I'm asking you to be a piece, a unit, material in my bailiwick, just as you are a piece and material in the factory. You'll listen and keep quiet, just as you listen and keep quiet in the factory. For that, one day, when everything has changed, you'll remain what you are; you'll be worse or better off, I can't guarantee which; the world order will be neither more generous nor sweeter to you, but it will be more just.' I think that most workers would hesitate over this offer, and yet it would be supremely honest. God knows it would be, for highly moral reasons, more above board than anything they have been offered.

Feeding promises to a poor person is robbery. Perhaps he finds it lighter to live when someone leads him up the garden path to show him fat geese on a weeping willow. But in practice, nowadays, just as a hundred years ago, a bird in hand is worth two in the bush, even in a government park, and a fire in the stove is better than a red weathercock on the roofs of palaces – and palaces, by the way, are considerably less numerous in this country than anyone who has been forced to think in terms of class consciousness rather than use his eyes might believe. For as regards our standard of living, we aren't, with few exceptions, exactly a wealthy folk, which communists as a rule forget to point out. It's usually said that a poor person has nothing to risk. Quite the reverse, whatever happens a poor person risks most because if he loses anything he loses his last crust – the poor man's crust isn't here to experiment with. No revolution is enacted on the backs of a small number of people, but on the backs of the largest number; whether it's a war or a currency crisis or whatever, it's the pauper who suffers first and gets the hardest deal, there are simply no bounds and no bottom to poverty. All the world over, the rottenest roof-beams aren't those belonging to the rich, but those over the heads of the poor. Shake the world up, and then go and have a look who has been buried under the debris.

What should be done then? I for my part don't comfort myself with the word 'evolution'. I think that poverty is the only thing in the world that doesn't evolve, but expands chaotically. And it's impossible to put off the problem of the poor till some future social order; if they are to be helped at all, it must start today. The question is, of course, if today's world has enough moral means for it. Communism states that it doesn't – well, this negation is exactly where we differ. I don't want to assert that there are enough perfectly just individuals in this social Sodom, but there's a bit of the just in each of us Sodomites, and I believe that we could after a longish effort and a good deal of hand-waving reach an understanding on thoroughly decent justice. However, communism says that we can't come to an understanding; presumably, it doubts the human value of the majority of people – but I'll come back to this later. Today's society didn't crumble when it enacted some kind of protection of the unemployed, the elderly and the ill, however unspectacular. I'm not saying it's enough, but it's important for the poor, and me too, that it's been possible to do at least that much now, on the spot, without the angry wait for the momentous time when the flag of revolution has started to wave.

To believe that the problem of the poor is today's problem, and not something reserved for a future order, that of course means not to be a communist. To believe that a chunk of bread and a hot stove now are more important than a revolution in twenty years, that indicates a very uncommunistic temperament.

The weirdest and most inhuman thing about communism is its peculiar grimness. The worse, the better. If a cyclist knocks down a deaf granny, it's a proof of the putrefaction of today's establishment; if a worker sticks his finger into the wheels of a machine, his poor finger isn't squashed by the wheels, but by the bourgeois, and to cap it all, with bloodthirsty gratification. The hearts of all the people who aren't, for one personal reason or another, communists are bovine and as repulsive as an ulcer. There isn't a good hair on the head of the entire current establishment – whatever is, is bad.

In one of his ballads Jiří Wolker says: 'Deepest in your heart, Pauper, I see hatred.' It's a horrid word, but the strange thing is that it's wrong. Deep down in the hearts of poor people is an extraordinary, most beautiful cheerfulness. A worker at a machine makes jokes with more gusto than the owner or the director of the factory; builders have more fun on a building site than the architect or landlord, and if anyone sings in the household, it's definitely the maid scrubbing the floor rather than her mistress. The so-called proletarian is by nature disposed towards a joyous and childish perception of life; communistic pessimism and sulky hatred are pumped into him artificially, and worse still, through unclean pipes. This import of desperate grimness is termed 'the education of the masses for revolution', or 'the strengthening of class awareness'. A poor person, who has so little, is deprived even of his primitive joy in life – that's the first instalment paid for a future better world.

Inhospitable and inhuman, these characterise the climate of communism; there is no moderate temperature between the frosty bourgeoisie and the revolutionary fire; there is nothing that a proletarian should give himself over to with delight and peace of mind. There isn't lunch or dinner in the world; it's either a pauper's mouldy crust, or a grandee's blowout. There isn't love any more, but either the perverted practices of the rich, or proletarian propagation of children. A bourgeois breathes in his own rottenness, and a worker tuberculosis; that way, air has somehow vanished. I don't know if journalists and writers have coaxed themselves into this nonsensical image of the world, or if they lie wittingly, I only know that a naïve and inexperienced reader, which a proletarian often is, lives in a horridly distorted world that isn't really worth anything but to be fundamentally uprooted. And since such a world is only fictive, it's high time to fundamentally uproot this gloomy fiction, by a revolutionary act – in this case I'm enthusiastically for it. No doubt there is too much unspeakable misery in our vale of tears, suffering beyond measure, little affluence and less joy. For my part, I don't think I have a tendency to depict the world through rose-coloured spectacles, but any time I trip over the inhuman negativeness and tragicalness of communism, I want to cry out in indignant protest that it's not true and that everything doesn't really look like this. I've got to know very few people who haven't earned a smattering of salvation with a mite given in alms, and very few upon whom a sober and prudent Lord God could possibly rain brimstone and fire. There is more ignorance than intrinsic badness in the world; at the same time there is enough sympathy and trust, affability and good will to make it impossible to write off the world of people as past hope. I don't believe in the perfection of today's or future man; the world won't become paradise through goodness or through revolution, not even by the extermination of the human race. But if we could somehow gather all the good that ultimately inheres in every single of us sinful human creatures, I believe that it would be possible to construct a far kinder world than the one we've so far had. Perhaps you'll say it's a feeble-minded philanthropy. Yes, I count myself among the idiots who like man because he is human.

It's easy to say that a forest is black, for instance, but no tree in the forest is black. It's red or green, because it's an ordinary pine or a spruce. It's easy to say that society is bad, but go and look for quintessentially bad people. Try to judge the world without brutal generalisations; after a while you'll be without even a sniff of your principles. The premise of communism is an artificial or intentional lack of knowledge of the world. If someone claims that he hates Germans, I'd like to tell him to go and live among them. In a month I'd ask him if he hates his German landlady, if he feels like cutting the throat of the Germanic vendor of radishes or strangling the Teutonic granny who sells matches to him. One of the most immoral gifts of the human spirit is the gift for generalisation – instead of gathering experiences, it simply replaces them. You read nothing about the world in the communist papers but that it's downright wretched. A person for whom ignorance isn't the apex of cognition finds that inadequate.

Hatred, lack of knowledge, fundamental distrust, these are the psychic world of communism. The medical diagnosis would say that it's pathological negativism. If a man becomes a mass, he may be more susceptible to this infection, but it's impossible to put up with it in private life. Stand next to a beggar on the corner for a while, and notice who of all the passers-by will turn out his pocket for sixpence. In seven out of ten cases it's people who themselves move on the margins of poverty, the other three cases are women. From this a communist would probably infer that a bourgeois has a hard heart. I, on the contrary, infer something more beautiful – I mean, that a proletarian mostly has a soft heart and essentially inclines towards kindness, love and self-sacrifice. Communism with its class hatred and rage wants to make this man into the *canaille*; such humiliation is not what the poor deserve.

Today's world doesn't need hatred, but good will, obligingness, concord and co-operation. It needs a kinder moral climate; I think that it would still be possible to work wonders with a bit of ordinary love and cordiality. I stand up for the current world not because it is a world of the rich, but because it's likewise a world of the poor, and of those in the middle too, those crushed between the millstones of capital and the proletariat, who nowadays uphold and save the greatest part of human values, at least tolerably. I don't really know those ten thousand rich, so can't judge them. Still, I have judged the class called the bourgeoisie, and in such a way that I've been accused of dirty pessimism. I say this only to acquire a greater right to stand up in some measure for those whose faults and guilt I'm by no means blind to. The proletariat cannot displace this class, but it can enter it. Despite all the flimflam of manifestos, there's no proletarian culture. By and large there isn't even ethnographic culture today, nor aristocratic or religious culture; what remains of cultural values rests on the middle, the so-called intelligentsia. If the proletariat claimed its own share in this tradition, if it said, 'OK, I'll take today's world over, and will husband it with all the values that there are in it,' we could perhaps shake on it and give it a try. But when communism pushes ahead first, while sweepingly brushing everything that it calls bourgeois culture aside as needless trash, then goodbye. At that point an even moderately responsible person begins to gauge how much would get wasted that way.

I've already said that real poverty is not an institution, but a misery. You can turn all the orders upside down, but you won't prevent a man from being struck by misfortune, from being ill, suffering hunger and cold, needing a helping hand. There's no escaping the fact that misery assigns a man a moral, not a social task. The speech of communism is harsh. It doesn't speak of the values of compassion, obligingness, help and human solidarity; it states confidently that it isn't sentimental. And it's precisely the worst thing for me, that it is not sentimental, because I am sentimental just like any housemaid, just like any fool, just like any decent man; only a rascal and a demagogue is not sentimental. Without sentimental reasons you don't offer a fellow being a glass of water. Sensible reasons don't lead you even as far as helping a man who has slipped over to get to his feet.

Then there's the problem of violence. I'm not such an old maid that I cross myself every time I hear the word 'violence'. I confess that sometimes I'd damn well like to beat up a man who delivers false reasons or tells lies. Woefully, it's impossible because either I am too weak for him, or he is too weak to defend himself. As you can see, I'm not exactly a brawler, but if the bourgeoisie started shouting that they'd go and hang proletarians, I'd be off right enough, and would run to help those being hanged. A decent man can't be in the same boat as the person who threatens. Anyone who calls for shooting and hanging overthrows human society not by a political coup, but by infringing natural and simple honesty.

I'm often called a 'relativist' for the special, and presumably pretty heavy, intellectual offence that I try to get a grip on everything. I keep dissecting all branches of knowledge and all literatures down to black folk tales, and find with mystical joy that if you have a little patience and common sense you can come to some kind of an understanding with all people of all colours or faiths. In all likelihood there's a common human logic here, and a wealth of common human values, such as love, humour, appetite for food, optimism and many other things which it is impossible to live without. And at times all of a sudden I'm seized by horror that I can't reach an understanding with communism. I can twig its ideals, but I can't twig its method. Sometimes it feels as if it were speaking a foreign language and its thinking were governed by different laws. If one nation believes that people should be consumed with the spirit of tolerance, and another that they should consume one another, it's admittedly a picturesque difference, but not an absolutely vital one. But if communism believes that to hang and shoot people in certain circumstances is no more serious than killing cockroaches, it's something I cannot understand, though I'm speaking Czech too; I have an awful impression of chaos, and am really anxious that like this we'll never agree on anything.

I've believed and still do that just as there are five senses, so there are moral and sensible nuts and bolts whereby a person gets to know what another person is like. The method of communism is a broadly-set-up attempt at international misunderstanding; it's an attempt to smash the world into pieces that don't match, and have nothing to talk to each other about. What's good on one side can't and mustn't be good on the other – as if people weren't physiologically and morally identical here as well as there. Let the most orthodox communist descend on me; if he doesn't floor me on the spot, I personally hope to agree with him on umpteen things, as long as they don't concern communism, of course. But communism fundamentally disagrees with others even about matters that have nothing to do with it: speak about the function of the spleen, and it will say that it's bourgeois science; similarly there are bourgeois poetry, bourgeois romanticism, bourgeois humanity, and what not. The power of conviction you find in communists is almost superhuman: not because the conviction is so elevating, but because they aren't fed up with it eventually. Or perhaps it's not the power of conviction, but a kind of ritual prescription, or ultimately a skill they acquire.

But those I'm particularly sorry for are precisely the proletarians, who are in this way cut off from the rest of the educated world without any other substitute but the beauteous prospect of the bliss of revolution. Communism places a cordon between them and the world, and it's you communist-intellectuals who stand with gaudily painted banners between them and everything that's prepared for them as a newcomer's share. But there is still room for the dove of peace, if not among you, then above your heads, or right from on high.

I feel lighter having said at least this, although it's not all; I feel as if I'd been to confession. I don't stand in any throng, and my contention with communism isn't a contention of principles, but conscience. And if I could contend with consciences, and not principles, it wouldn't, I believe, be impossible at least to understand one another – and that would already be a lot.

About Pessimism

The Spring, 10 December 1924

Like optimism, pessimism has two meanings, depending on whether we use it about ourselves or about others. If I say about myself that I'm an optimist, I mean I'm bursting with strength and hope, very buoyant, unfaltering and energetic, and in a word, a good chap. If I say about someone else that he's an optimist, I mean that he's a dreamer, impractical, naïve and foolishly trusting, and in a word, a softy. If I say about my fellow being that he's a pessimist, I mean that he's a spineless, cowardly neurasthenic, and a sourpuss, that he suffers from constipation or gallstones, exaggerates, and in short, is utterly wrong. If I call myself a pessimist, I imply that I'm more experienced than others, that, mind you, I never fall for any flimflam, that I see into everything, and am simply right – everything will turn out as I say, you mark my words.

For a person who parades neither the one nor the other, pessimism smacks of a skeleton in the cupboard or a dead rat.

As an example of pessimism, I could name Heraclitus, Schopenhauer or Eduard von Hartmann. However, I've chosen a more horrible test case, the quintessence of universal pessimism: it's the terrible and incontrovertible contention that 'a slice of bread always falls on the buttered side'.

You won't find an optimist in the whole world who would challenge this gloomy assertion with the crucial view that 'a slice of bread always falls on the unbuttered side', since – and herein lies the tragedy of optimism – *this* opinion is overturned, even if a slice of bread falls on the buttered side only once, whereas the pessimist's perspective isn't shaken, even if a slice of bread sometimes falls on the unbuttered side as well. On the face of it, it's because this case, having no serious consequences for the slice, or the trousers, or the carpet on which the buttered slice delights in falling, is irrelevant and doesn't carry the same weight as its opposite.

Unfortunately, it hasn't yet been mapped out statistically whether a slice of bread falls on the buttered side more frequently or not. But if it transpired that eighty times out of a hundred it falls on the buttered side, we'd conclude that it falls on it apparently because the buttered side is heavier. Well, this opinion would be as little pessimistic as Newton's idea that objects fall to the ground. Surely it's not a pessimistic claim that anyone who falls from a tree is likely to break a leg. What's pessimistic is the belief that people mustn't climb trees because the Ancient of Days punishes it. Pessimism is the attitude of the inhabitants of Melanesia who hold that anyone who falls from the top of a palm tree has killed himself, because a mythical forefather once killed himself in that way. From this you can see that pessimism doesn't consist in envisaging bad consequences, but in envisaging sinister and fatal causes. This means that real pessimism is purely metaphysical. It's pessimistic if I believe that the world is in a bad state because people are essentially and metaphysically bad. A more comforting and less pessimistic stance is that the world is in a bad state because people are oafs. OK, the result is virtually the same, but the cause is clearly less tragic.

To put it another way, true pessimism doesn't reside in the perspective that things look dim or will come off badly, but in the perspective that all round, and on principle, they can't come off any other way but badly. If they happen to turn out all right – well, you're not out of the wood yet, and don't count your chickens before they're hatched. If, however, they really turn out to be a disaster, they fulfil a higher necessity, to the pessimist's gloomy gratification,

for it's metaphysically correct that it has turned out a disaster. A
bad state of things fills a pessimist with a special kind of pessimistic
satisfaction that amounts to sheer excitement. Pessimism is a form
of self-indulgence; it's a way of getting joy from a bad situation.
Any accident, misfortune, scrape, mistake or suffering is something
that entirely fits in with the perpetual misery of the world; it's just
one more delectable detail, and a refreshing example of universal
bad luck. A pessimist has quite a good time over the bad progress
of the world – the worse, the better, for that's to him an inexhaustible source of contentment and diversion. Pessimism isn't a belief
that the world is wretched, but a belief that it's all right that it's
wretched.

However, if you take a mistake for a mistake, a silliness for a silliness, and a misfortune for a simple misfortune, you aren't and can't
be a pessimist. You are not a pessimist because you see the pain, the
idiocy, the cruelty and the absurdity of everything. If seeing this
hurts you, if you quiver with compassion or shudder with revulsion,
you are not a pessimist.

And as for that unfortunate slice, there's no refuting the dreary
opinion that it *always* falls on the buttered side except by holding
it in your hand more carefully.

Bethlehem

The People's Paper, 25 December 1924

Perhaps there was also a Bethlehem crib in the church of your
childhood at Christmas. And there were the Three Magi, and the
baby Jesus, and shepherds with little sheep and cows, and small
houses for the shepherds, and curly trees, and everything else that
can possibly be thought of, and you couldn't take your eyes off the
beauty of it. When I now recall what we liked about it so much, it
was, I think, mostly the charming circumstance that everything was
so minuscule. The mysterious poetry of the crib is that it is tiny; its
fairy-tale beauty lies in the diminution of all proportions. Imagine

a crib with seventeen-foot dummies – it would surely arouse horror rather than excitement.

We often claim that conditions in our part of the world are small. We are undoubtedly a small country with small means, but surprisingly enough, we don't find this charmingly beautiful and poetic. When we return home from abroad we quickly realise that the Creator didn't stretch out his arms all that far, and didn't roll up his sleeves. Rather, he worked in small measure, patiently fashioning pleasant plains and wooded hills, unturbulent rivers and closed horizons. We find that man, who came after him, didn't stretch out his arms very far either, and didn't make a big gesture and shout, 'This is all mine'; but he sliced the land into minute squares of fields and built small houses among nice little apple and plum trees instead of citadels, and when, coming back home, we see all this, we suddenly breathe out with excitement that it is like a 'Bethlehem' crib.

True, we are a small country, that's that. But somehow we are not enchanted by the fact that we are a small country. The conditions here are small, but we fail to see it as a poetic advantage, worthy of special praise and love. Our means are modest, but it doesn't seem to us a fairy-tale task to establish a neat, modest crib with them. We rather think that we must stretch out our arms, and establish, all at one go, seventeen-foot, multimillion-crown Central or Representative Offices, Institutes and other public edifices. Ever since the memorable day when we became an independent Bethlehem,[1] we have tried to imprint a sense of seventeen-footness or multimillion-crown enormousness on everything we have initiated or designed. What we have achieved is not greatness, but a kind of chaos. Suddenly we find that the crib is too small.

If a Czech wants to make love in words or thought, he uses a diminutive. He calls his beloved little one, or a silly little thing, or some such expression, not Giantess or Archwoman. If he likes his garden, he calls it 'a little garden'; if he likes his glass, he says 'a little glass'. If an Englishman wants to fondle something in words, he says that it's 'dear old' – that's because in England old things are valued. But we caress a thing by saying that it is small. If we wanted to caress a ministry, we would call it enthusiastically and tenderly 'our little ministry', and if we wanted to show it our love really intimately and as sincerely as possible, we would set up a small house with two windows and a little table for it, as if for a doll. But since our relation to institutions is gloomy and anti-pathetic, we design grim, fearfully huge buildings for them. Because we don't like Prague and its inhabitants sincerely enough, we keep speaking about a Great Prague. Because we don't like our country tenderly enough, we don't speak about a poor, dear little country, but about prestige, representation on the international scene and other seventeen-footers.

Bethlehem, too, presents itself on the international scene, but it presents itself as being small, though 'not the least among the princes of Judah'. It is not represented by some new town hall or other, but by an old cattle shed. It is not represented by a welcoming delegation of fifty members, paid for by the poor shepherds' money, but by fifty poor shepherds who show their joy at, and interest in, the happenings in the shed for free. It is aptly represented by having the baby breathed on by a bull and a donkey, modest and useful animals, instead of having him breathed on by two cere-monial speakers. It is, simply, a Bethlehem happy with being small, telling the world: Come and look how nice it is when we can be small and poor. And the world looks and cannot take its eyes off.

We arrange things badly on a large scale instead of arranging them well on a small one. When we arrange them on a large scale, we say that we are doing it for the future. But doing something just for the future is like preparing something for a rainy day. It is better and more far-sighted to prepare the future itself. Surely we shall never grow to be a great power, but we are very likely to become a small part of a great European or world order. No local and national megalomania, no powerful pretension, will be of any use to us then, but everything that we can do will be very useful. So the future is not to be organised in terms of monumental frame-works. For the future, there must be a preparation of people.

It is not hard to live as poor and small if we are honest with our-selves and admit that we are poor and small. All right then, if we are not a Babylon, let's be zestfully and proudly a Bethlehem. Some sort of saviour might be born, even today, in the manger of a shed rather than in the marble palace of a big insurance company. But woefully, because of all the palaces, we cannot get down to building Bethlehem sheds.

And let us not be vexed that Bethlehem is perhaps too small for three Magi or whoever from the east. It is worse when it is too small for Bethlehem shepherds, because it cannot provide a roof over their heads and food for them to eat. And that bright star up there can never be kindled by grandiose state expenditure.

About Women and Politics[1]

The Present, 12 November 1925

I don't mean to generalise in any way. I know that one Mrs Punkhurstová, or a Miss Zemínová for that matter, are worth a couple of us chaps, but as far as I can tell, women mostly don't like politics. They still consider it a male issue, in which view a certain admiration is mingled with a certain contempt. I think that this approach to politics is, besides other sexual impulses, determined by two female motives: the lack of a sense of abstraction and the lack of a fighting spirit.

Though being active in politics is usually a supremely practical activity, propagating politics and having a belief in politics presuppose a whole range of abstractions, starting with the word 'people'. A good half of political principles are what in German is called '*Prinzipienreiterei*', a kind of horsemanship that has from time out of mind been a male passion. You can inflame a man if you tell him that democracy is in danger. If you wanted to inflame a woman, you'd have to say that what's in danger is her husband or children. A man lets himself be beaten up for the sake of the autonomy of the Čáslav region. A woman lets herself get squashed so as to buy cheaper shoes for her kids. A clerical leader fights for Rome; a clerical granny fights, so she imagines, for her Lord

God. In lands like ours, where the primeval male predominance prevails, politics is played in the name of principles. In America, where the woman has the spiritual predominance, politics is played in the name of lowering the price of stockings or suppressing alcohol. Women are very little interested in politics because they are very little interested in abstract slogans. A woman lets herself be killed out of love, but she doesn't let herself be killed on principle. Many women have let themselves be killed for the love of Christ, but not one has let, or would let, herself be quartered for the theological question of the Holy Trinity. That is, so it seems, reserved for men. There have been female martyrs for revolution or liberty, but I don't know of a case where a woman has sacrificed her life, say, for the election victory of the Young Turks over the Old Turks. I have a somewhat chilling feeling whenever a lady delivers an oration against, for example, the *de jure* acknowledgement of Russia. It would seem more natural to me if she stood on a barricade with one of her breasts uncovered. Woman embraces politics quite as concretely as love, family or other matters of life. Man, if he doesn't use politics as just something to tear money out of, is capable of embracing it with a dogmatic fanaticism as if it were a theological controversy. If the promulgation of politics is reduced to such general ideas, it's natural for women to respond that we should give them a break or words to that effect. I'm convinced that the Parliamentary Review, or whatever, will never become a favourite read of the mesdames and girls of the Czech lands. I haven't even met a single married woman or girl who reads leading articles in the dailies with pleasure. For they have the blunt, and quite correct, feeling that the stuff isn't written for them. It is not adequate to say that they don't understand it; it is more relevant to recognise that they don't enjoy it in the least.

So far I have called the second motive that makes women dislike politics 'the lack of a fighting spirit'. Let's not deny that the male need to become a member of a political party answers the archaic male instinct to join a fighting force or a clan. Deep down in us is a certain military collectivism – we always own to some *our* flag or other, and we fling ourselves into *our* battle for *our* victory. In politics we talk about a battle, a banner, a shield, an enemy camp, a battleground, weapons, victories and defeats – the whole of this vocabulary is as obviously militaristic as Žižka's tract on the art of war.[2] Even if a man doesn't have an ulterior, usually economic, reason, he joins a political party out of the same simple bellicosity that made Diomedes, son of Tydeus, join the Achaeans. It gives him the epic delight of fighting in a male camp. A man leaves his family to fuse with a caravan, expedition, team, camp, party – his 'I' has an inclination to expand into larger wholes. The word 'our' is for the most part of a masculine nature: our village, our generation, our fire brigade, our party. Women are more likely to be happy with the word 'my', as in my husband, my family, my female neighbours. A genuine political partisan is born when he says 'our party', with a special emphasis falling on the image of 'we'. Man is a being of the crowd. A throng of women is always somewhat comical – woman loses much when she exists en masse. A political party is an organisation based on a mass instinct, an instinct which is ancient and male. That's why it is perfectly natural that women should enter political parties less often than men. A political party is a distinctly male formation. Political partisanship is male politics.

And now we are in the paradoxical situation that fully half, indeed probably the greater half, of the nation has political rights without having a real political interest. Half of the nation is forced to vote politically though they mostly don't know what it is about. It's not that good or bad political results wouldn't affect female lives and private interests in a good or bad way. It's because politics is carried out by methods that are fundamentally alien to them, in fact detestable. You might say that women don't have a feeling for politics. But likewise you might say that politics doesn't have a feeling for the female half of the nation. It's possible to maintain that women are short on brains, but perhaps an alternative formulation fits better – that male politics is short on brains. It is as if you offered women men's trousers and were surprised that they didn't appreciate this sartorial deal.

If a sensible person had a pub and found that a good half of his customers were vegetarians, presumably he'd begin to cook carrots and spinach and wouldn't force them to eat roast beef. If sensible politicians realised the surprising fact that a good half of political citizens are women, they wouldn't present them with a strictly male diet, such as abstract fanaticism and political partisanship, but would look out for something more palatable: not so much for a new programme as for a change of method. The politics of parties will never be the politics of women. You can't really win women over to the idea of a free market, but you can win them over to the idea of cheaper bread. You'll win them over to a range of specific things that are as important for men as for women, but you'll hardly get them excited about the ingenious achievement called the success of our party. Women never know who is the minister of this or that department – though they wouldn't mind someone being there who was an expert in what he's supposed to know about. It wouldn't necessarily be political progress if half the politicians were women, but it would be great progress if politics were done in such a way that the female half of the nation could be bothered with it. With a stroke of the pen we have added women to the political mass, but we have forgotten that this somewhat changes the mass. It is in no way apparent that political methods have changed to keep pace. Politics has remained as slogan-ridden, as belligerently party-minded, as loutishly power-driven as it was before. It has remained male politics.

About Relativism

The Present, 18 February 1926

All kinds of people write about it. Their habitual method is to touch on Einstein's relativity first, whereupon, rapidly abandoning this strict region of mathematical supra-sentience, they make a beeline for philosophical and literary relativism, and that's when, for some nebulous reason, I and some other people I know are publicly accused of relativistic vileness and get a wigging. Because they obviously mean something derogatory, I should perhaps defend myself by a blazing declaration that I have never committed relativism, or maybe I should defend relativism by claiming that it's not so bad as they say. Instead, I confess that I don't know precisely what their precious relativism is.

As for Einstein's relativity, I admit frankly that I don't understand it, just as I don't understand some religious mysteries, the logic of history, infinite space and suchlike. I tried to study it; I got to the point where it states that if I moved with the velocity of light, I'd, for some numerical reasons, get flattened like a biscuit; and then I gave up on the rest, very much reconciled to the fact that I don't move with the velocity of light. Because I move slowly and thoughtfully, I become round rather than anything else, and wouldn't like to be flat. Some people, who hurl themselves forward with enormous speed and who are ahead, as they say, of their time, really are remarkably flat. I find, then, that I have nothing in common with the principle of relativity.

Luckily, the relativism they often accuse us of has nothing mathematical about it; what's meant by it is simply . . . well, what, come to that? What's meant by it is, say, the relativistic view that new things are sometimes good, and old things are sometimes good as well. But this view (if you happen to hold it) is not relativism, but just ordinary, down-to-earth experience that is impossible to controvert. It may be true that a new radio is better than an old barrel-organ, but the barrel-organ had the advantage of feeding old paupers. Democracy is better than tyranny, but tyranny was by and large more straightforward. We don't need relativism to see that a stick has two ends – only a more homespun intellectual operation, viz. using your eyes. It's not necessary to labour under some relativistic system to come to the conclusion that in most human arguments the pot is calling the kettle black; it's enough to know people and their morals a bit. You don't need to be a relativist to find that Lenin may possess a fraction of the truth, but that Ford possesses a fraction as well; it's enough to take certain indubitable results into account. To explore experience as totally as possible is not relativism, but thoroughness. To find that big things aren't boundlessly big and small things aren't wretchedly and unforgivably small, that's not relativism, but empirical truth. I can't understand why these matter-of-course, commonsense assumptions are called relativism or scepticism. You hear people saying, 'The doctor sounded sceptical about the patient's state of health.' Well, if the doctor did that, we can't claim that he was an obstinate, dyed-in-the-wool sceptic; perhaps he just examined the patient thoroughly and objectively. When we say that one thing or another is relative, we aren't for that reason relativists. Supposing that it *really* is relative, then our assertion is as little relativistic as my claim that the blotter on which I'm writing is green and littered with blots. Let's not keep on asking what sort of badly understood Greco-Latin word we should employ to label and denounce some person or other. Rather, let's look to see what experience he calls on, and if he doesn't have a fraction of the truth.

Yes, a fraction of the truth: that's what is referred to as relativism. For some fundamental reason people demand that truth should be delivered to them complete and exclusive. They claim that this particular statement is the absolute and sole truth, whereas everything else is false, fraudulent and balderdash. Let's assume that it's possible to pronounce it absolutely true that digitalis is a medicine. Or that it's possible to pronounce it a truth worth dying for that digitalis is a poison. The reality is, I'm afraid, partial and a compromise: digitalis is sometimes in some doses a poison, other times and in other doses a medicine. But if I say that digitalis can be both a poison and a medicine, I don't do it, as God's my witness, out of some unconcern about its power, nor out of a comfortable indifference to human fates. I say it because I'm aware of certain limitations as to its usefulness and its relations to other things. Relations: that's the important word. If relativism makes any sense at all, then it contains the notion of *relation*. Socialism is good in relation to wages, but it doesn't say anything in relation to private and painful questions of life, to which I have to seek an answer elsewhere. If we are concerned about the true relations of real things and real people, nothing is left just to our arbitrary will. The only drawback is that life becomes incredibly difficult. No matter what you do, you can't disentangle yourself from it. You are not unrestricted in your pros and cons, you can't play with them at will, but your pros are restricted by real noes, and your cons are mitigated by hundreds of faint, imploring yeses. This relativism is not indifference; quite the contrary, you need a rabid indifference not to lend an ear to the voices of life that are at odds with your absolute verdicts. It's not a soft-soupy tolerance; if you want to give it a name, it's an anxious attentiveness to everything that exists.

But of course, when we fight for or against something, we can't do it with anxious attentiveness. Equally, when we create, we can't but concentrate on our work, and in a way not care about all the rest. Relativism is neither a method of fighting nor one of creation, both of which are straightforward and sometimes even ruthless; it's a method of cognition. But if there is to be fighting or creating, it's necessary these are preceded by knowledge that is as broad as possible. Knowledge isn't a belligerent activity; every fight is really a severing of relations. One of the worst confusions of this age is that it mixes up cognitive activity with ideological belligerence. Getting to know isn't the same as fighting, though a person who gets to know a lot will have a lot to fight for – so much that he'll be called a relativist even for that. The only alternative to not being a relativist is to be a monomaniac. Choose the better side: either the side of Mary, who listens to the sole truth, or the side of Martha, who is 'careful and troubled about many things'. On the side of 'many things', of course, there may be lots of petty-minded, bizarre, unknowable and waifish things – for on this side there is the whole of reality.

About Americanism

A letter to the publisher of the *New York Sunday Times*,[1]
The Present, 29 April 1926

Dear Sir,

I voiced my doubts about the ideals of Americanism to an excellent American. I don't know how this has reached your ear, but you are now asking me to repeat my objections to your American readers. Suppose I do, and having done so, decide to travel to America to see if what I think is the actual truth. Can you guarantee me that on stepping onto American soil I shan't get quartered by four Fords as a punishment? Or that within twenty-seven and a half minutes I shan't be hanged on a sixty-four-storey gallows, 230 metres high, built of iron and concrete? Let the responsibility fall upon you then, and here goes.

Admittedly, I haven't been to America; nevertheless, I have read, with scrupulous care, plenty of articles about America, written principally by Europeans, since no one else but a European, who has spent a couple of months there without having been run down by a car, can be so frantically enthused by the New World. Genuine Americans, whom I meet in Europe, usually talk about America with greater scepticism than these freshly made Yankees, who are more proud of having stopped being greenhorns than of having been born with a human soul. It seems to me that American ideals are more dangerous for us Europeans than for American-born citizens. I don't ask if American ideals are good for America, but if they are good for Europe. My question is whether Europe should get Americanised, as many people imagine. There are people who wish that one day America would civilise old Europe just as Europe once civilised the ancient empire of the Aztecs. I confess that I dread that image as much as the ancient Aztecs dreaded the cultural ideal of the European conquerors, and that, in my Aztec tongue, I'm raising a war cry against this endangered state of our European reservation.

I should perhaps start with cultural ideals, but let me start with something simpler – that is, bricks and mortar. I was building a house, a small, yellow-and-white one like a hard-boiled egg. You have no idea how complicated such a thing is in Europe. Before the house was finished, we had been through strikes by bricklayers, carpenters, joiners, parquet-layers and roof-tilers. The building of the house unfolded itself as a two-year social struggle. If work was done at all, people had, in between the laying of two bricks, enough time to have a little chat, enjoy some beer, spit and scratch their backs. For two years I went regularly to watch how my house was coming to light. It was a part of my personal history. My relation to the house grew into an endless intimacy. During those two years I got to know a host of details about the work and life of bricklayers, joiners, canteen-keepers and other hairy, serious and jocular men. All this got cemented into the bricks and joists of my house. You must see that after so many drawbacks I cling to it with a certain fierce patriotism, and that I wouldn't change it for anything.

Now, you in America would build such a house within perhaps three days. You would come in your Fords with a ready-made iron construction, tighten a few screws, pour in several sacks of cement, nip into your Fords again, and go and build somewhere else. It would be far cheaper and quicker; it would have all the technical and economic advantages. But I have the feeling that I would be less at home in my house if it had sprung into being at such an unnatural speed. Do you remember the way Homer describes Achilles' shield? One whole book of the *Iliad* is needed so that the blind poet can depict how the shield was done. You, in America, would cast and assemble it at the rate of ten thousand shields a day. I admit that it is possible to do shields more cheaply and successfully like that, but impossible to do the *Iliad* that way. For my small house, like Achilles' shield, is not only a chunk of work, but above all a chunk of life. A chunk of a hard and cheery life.

So far things in Europe have been developing slowly. It may be that an American tailor makes three coats while our tailor makes one. It is likewise possible that an American tailor earns three times more than ours. But I ask whether he also savours a three times bigger portion of life, whether he is three times as in love as our tailor's journeyman, whether he whistles three times as many songs while he works and whether he has three times more children. As far as I know, American *efficiency* concerns the multiplication of output, not the multiplication of life. It's true that man has to work in order to live, but he obviously lives all the time he is working. It is possible to say that a European man is a very bad working machine, but it's because he is not a machine at all. If he is a bricklayer, he is not one only to lay bricks but to talk the while about politics or yesterday, to drink beer and celebrate Blue Monday, and altogether live broadly in a bricklayer's manner. I take it that he would give a good telling-off to a person who wanted to prove to him that the highest aim of a bricklayer was haste.

Haste, speed! This is the new gospel that is constantly being shouted at us from the other side of the ocean. If you want to be rich, increase your speed and efficiency! Leave unnecessary talk and rest behind, and hurry up with your work! A human being is measured by nothing but the number defining his output! I don't know whether America really lives under this watchword's whip-crack, but it's a watchword offered to us by Americanised Europeans as a programme for the progress and reconstruction of Europe. Yet the question is whether haste and quantity are truly the only measurement of activity. There are things – and this old Europe in particular still abounds in them – that we couldn't really measure by units of work. We cannot measure the ideas of a philosopher in terms of how many of them he can do in an hour. Art is not measured by the time needed for making a sculpture or a poem. Indeed, it was necessary to be in very little of a hurry to start producing such things at all. Europe was in very little of a hurry when she accomplished her cathedrals and philosophical systems. A man who wants to conceive something doesn't rush about with a stopwatch in his hands, but seems like a person who idles and fritters away his time. I think that your William James must have seemed a bit of a lazybones to the people around him. I bet that in his lifetime your Walt Whitman enjoyed a reputation as a layabout and a good-for-nothing, knocking around Hoboken with his mane flying. If we wander around old Europe, we marvel at how little haste people who have left big footmarks everywhere made. Men who made revolutions didn't have their time measured out. Some of the greatest activities of the human spirit have developed only in the course of an unheard-of waste of time. Europe has been wasting time for many thousands of years – in this lies her inexhaustibility and fruitfulness. I have heard about a distinguished American who was very busy in Europe. On the train he dictated letters to his secretary; in the car he sorted out his conferences; at lunch he held his meetings. At lunch we primitive Europeans normally just eat, just as during music we normally listen. We may squander our time, but we definitely don't squander our life. One could speak of a magnanimous laziness that has endowed Europe with some of her highest values. Some laziness is necessary for the full appreciation of life. A man who hurries tremendously certainly arrives, but only at the expense of not looking at thousands of things he has missed on his way.

The second watchword that new America exports to poor Europe is the big word Success. Begin as a liftboy and become a steel or cotton king! Think every day about forging ahead! Success is the end and essence of life! It is truly alarming how this watchword begins to demoralise Europe. This old part of the world has a certain heroic tradition, you see. People have lived and died here for faith or truth or for other rather irrational things, not for success. Saints and heroes are not people who want to forge ahead. There are certain deeds and tasks for which it is necessary to sacrifice success beforehand. It's to Europe's credit that Shakespeare didn't prove a success and didn't become, for example, a great ship-owner, or that Beethoven didn't prove a success and didn't become the greatest manufacturer of bad cotton textiles. Balzac attempted in vain to become a rich man; luckily for the world, he wasn't successful and never got out of debt. This foolish Europe has been able to care about thousands of other things rather than successes – those things, then, have remained, while the successes, for all that history has seen, have gone to hell. What a lot of things would have remained unaccomplished if those who accomplished them had had success in mind! If we judged people by their success, it would transpire that ninety people in a hundred have bad luck in life rather than success, and scarcely one in a thousand would dare say that he had really met with success. European morality, which has known this since the age of King Croesus, has always assured us of values of life different from success. If I'm not mistaken, quite a few times it speaks of the vanity of all successes and encourages us to seek higher values – loftier and more lasting. Very well, so far we haven't lost the eagerness to seek them.

The third watchword that threatens us is Quantity. People from America bring over the uncanny and fantastical belief that only the biggest is sufficiently great. If a hotel is to be built, it will have to be the Largest Hotel in the World. If something is to be worth seeing, it must be the biggest in its sphere. The Creator of the world was not, as it seems, touched by this magnitude mania, since he did not create this world as the biggest of all the celestial bodies. The Creator of Europe made her small, and further divided her into small parts so that our heart could delight not in magnitude but in diversity. America corrupts us by its fondness for magnitudes. Europe will lose herself as soon as she adopts the fanaticism of dimensions. Her measure is not quantity, but perfection. She is a beautiful Venus, not a Statue of Liberty.

Enough said. I could introduce a dozen other ideals that we European natives term American – the twelfth one would be called the Dollar. That would, however, be another story, and the space you have promised me has been used up, so I'm ending with what more prudent, more political people than I am would probably have started with.

From New Year's Eve to Epiphany

The People's Paper, 9 January 1927

If my memory doesn't fail me, people always say after every New Year's Eve that last year it was more fun – this time it was nothing, but last year it was really hilarious! They said this last year about the year before, and the year before about the year before that, and so on. Heavens alive, if this decline of New Year's Eve's gaiety has lasted since the beginning of the world, how paganly jovial must New Year's Eve have been in the youth of the late lamented historian Wáclaw Wladiwoj Tomek! Or during the reign of Maria Theresa! Or in the time of Boleslav the Cruel! But I think that even then those who remembered olden days used to say in a flush of New Year melancholy: 'This is nothing like last year, like in the time of Duke Wenceslas – that was a completely different New Year's Eve; needless to say, that was a real hoot.'

Everyone with whom I've talked – and they were not just skiers and chestnut-vendors – says that it should freeze and snow properly. Call this a real winter? If it really decides to be winter, it should crunch under your feet, chill your ears and there should be some good icy slides on the ground; and, furthermore we'd like to have red noses, icicles on the roof, frosty flowers on the windows and a nice high drift of snow by the path so that you can squeeze it into a lump and whack someone with it in the back or in the neck (especially in the neck). From this it's manifest that the need for order, and the inclination to think that everything in the world should be the way it has been from time immemorial, haven't yet died out in people. At least in the case of the natural order, people have a firm grasp of what is only right and proper. In matters of life and death, such as snow in winter, we remain tenacious traditionalists, and don't wish any climactic somersaults to take place. If we started building this world, insofar as this was in our hands, on premises as firm as the one that there should be snow in winter, we would find no end of other things that ought to be, just because they're proper. There is a 'should be' in any proper and healthy thing. In the republic, and in parliament, and in the army and in people as well. We like to chase after a tradition. But a real tradition isn't what used to be, but what ought to be. A tradition isn't last-year's or the year-before-last's snow, but this year's pretty, completely fresh snow, that should be here. I'm telling you, it should be here. Everyone says so.

* * *

It's an old experience of all occasional poets and columnists that the moment they sing of snow, it starts thawing, and when they assure readers that it's black and bleak out there on the muddy ground, it starts snowing. It's just happened to me: while I've been snowed under with writing, a sprinkling of snow has settled on the earth. I think that we scribblers, although we're pure as the driven snow, have no personal impact on snow itself. Rather, the gods want to prove that the papers are never right. The minute the typesetter typesets that there's no snow, lo and behold, snow arrives. The moment he typesets that there is snow, lo and behold, there's none. Perhaps there's a sign of some sort in it. Perhaps when the leader-writer announces in the paper that the situation is tense, it's not in fact tense but kind of shrunk and crinkled. Perhaps at the very moment when the papers insist that the time is highly critical, it is utterly non-critical. It may not be true that the speech of MP Dr Kramář made a profound impression. It may not be true either that Prime Minister Švehla is negotiating with the Slovak nationalists, but quite the contrary. But if this is the case, it's not the journalists' fault. There's a special intention and providence of the gods in it, who presumably don't wish anyone else apart from themselves to be omniscient.

The other day I stumbled on the Three Kings again after a long time. They were, however, just two, and the taller one was as thin as a flick knife. All the same, they kept singing unwaveringly at every door: 'We three Kings are coming to you.' If they had struck up with, 'We two Kings are coming to you,' they would have been factually correct, but would have ceased to be the genuine Kings of the Epiphany, and no one would have believed that they were bringing us 'happiness and health', or would have given them a single farthing. But listen, my good sirs, we grown-ups do exactly the same. We sing in our political carols, 'We the majority of the nation', or 'We agricultural workers', or 'We the working classes'. If we sang truthfully, 'We the party-secretariat', or 'We the inner circle of the executive committee', or something like that, our carol would lose all mysterious power and no one would give us a farthing of credit.

If . . .

The People's Paper, 1 January 1928

If on New Year's Day I woke up to find myself the Lord God – or rather not, that wouldn't work, for God never sleeps – so if on New Year's Day I woke up as St Peter, I'd say to myself: 'What should I do for those misbegotten Czechoslovaks? They're heretics, right, and often an ungrateful shower, a plague on them!; even so, something could become of them. I think that the air they breathe is a bit harsh. Perhaps that's why they're so splenetic and sulky. It's sweltering and stormy in summer, so they're tetchy and growl at one another; in winter it freezes so hard that everyone thinks just of himself and is like an icicle to others. The climate is to blame, that's what it is. That's why they aren't happy with anything. Winter is too cold for them, summer too hot; if something's black, it seems too black to them; if something's white, it seems too white. Nothing can ever be quite right. Their weather's got into their bones. But wait, you scallywags, I'll make you first-rate weather, it'll be just like at the seaside. I'll give you gentle winters – with snow, of course, a crisp covering of snow is scrumptious – and delicious summers full of sunshine and dewy spray. And I'll be damned if I don't change you! If you yourselves were kinder to one another, your weather would be milder, and if you don't want to start, I'll start. God help you in the New Year!'

If on New Year's Day I woke up as Prime Minister, I'd greatly wonder at it and, feeling at a loss, I'd start stroking my chin. ('Aha,' I'd say to myself, 'I must have a shave.') If, after a while, I got accustomed to the miraculous transformation of my existence, I'd stay in bed for another couple of minutes, as I used to do when I was still an ordinary citizen. However, I wouldn't go back to sleep, but would think something like this: 'Heavens, so it's this year we are to celebrate the jubilee of the Republic. I know what, I'll summon the Cabinet and say: "Boys, last year we were still remembering Austria when we governed; this year we must govern remembering the Republic. Look, we must make it up somehow, the right camp with the left one; it's going to the dogs, the way things are, I mean. A republic, that's like . . . like a circle – could there be a right wing and a left wing in a circle?"' Now a lot of other arguments would enter my head, but I'd keep them for the Cabinet meeting. At which point I'd get up, being careful, so as not to ward off good luck, to rise on my right foot first.

If on New Year's Day I woke up as the Mayor of Prague, I'd stare out into a better future for a while, and then I'd say to myself: 'That Čapek's right, I suppose. It should really get started, the work on the green belt around Prague. I like to imagine pretty avenues of trees . . . and meadows for children . . . and groves here and there . . . OK then, let's have a go.'

If on New Year's Day I woke up as a millionaire, a man of disposable means, I'd say to myself: 'Is it the year 1928 already? Good Lord, how time flies! It can't be helped. Something must be done with my money this year, something commemorating the anniversary must be built or founded, but I mean something really worthwhile. Must be well thought out, though. But the money won't be a problem, we'll see to that.'

If on New Year's Day I woke up as a twenty-year-old lad, I'd turn on the other side and go back to sleep. Quite so! Why should I be thinking anything after New Year's Eve, so there!

If on New Year's Day I woke up as my little bitch Minda, I'd keep scratching myself with my hind leg for a while (for I'd have a beastly flea on my nape), and then I'd say to myself: 'This year I won't be naughty, I'll be good to my master, I'll go out nicely, I won't scatter bones all over the staircase, I won't make messes, I won't sleep on the couch, I won't run across the plots in the garden . . .' At which point I'd get a sugar cube and would vastly rejoice in life.

The Rescued and the Rescuers[1]

The People's Paper, 14 July 1928

Just at a time when the so-called public was so passionately interested in the trial of Margita Vöresmartyová's murderers, I noticed
with surprise that the man in the street, that is the man on a tram
platform, the man on a cab stand, the man talking to a constable,
was far more interested in the fate of the airship *Italia* than in
the sensational crime. I've been observing this demotic interest for
weeks. The man in the street has criticised the unfortunate General
Nobile, censuring the poor leader for allowing himself to be
rescued before the wounded steersman Ceccioni.[2] He's got his
tongue around the names of Amundsen, Viglieri, Malmgren
and the others;[3] he's woven plans about how to get to the men
marooned on an ice floe. There's been a lot of healthy romanticism, both boyish and manly, in that demotic interest, but there's
been a no less marvellous human nobleness in it, a nobleness that
marvels at heroes, is excited by danger and sympathises with
knightly adventures. Amundsen has become the darling of the
anonymous man from the Prague quarters of Košíře or Vysočany.
Another name has now been engraved in his fantasy – the icebreaker *Krasin*. It looked almost helplessly cumbersome as we read
day after day that the icebreaker *Krasin* was making its way at an
elephant's pace of a few dozen miles a day, that it was stuck in
mist or drift-ice, that it was still forty minutes as the crow flies
from the survivors, and that they were practically already lost. We
looked for a light aircraft that would somehow descend from the
heavens to help the lost expedition. It was so desperately slow, as the
iron ship crunched yard after yard through the polar ice towards a
bunch of people half-mad with hunger, cold and hopelessness. But
the icebreaker *Krasin* eventually crunched all the ice away and got
to them, while the light aircraft with Amundsen had disappeared,
and the plane with the brave Chuckhnovsky had crashed.[4] See, it's
impossible for help to plummet from heaven like the lightning of
grace; it's more likely that it will crawl on earth or water at the cost

of endless patience and strain. Our ways still run, if laboriously and crawlingly, on earth.

In this century of mine accidents, train crashes and shipwrecks, on this crust of the earth tossed about by earthquakes, cyclones and floods, amidst this civilisation hurling millions of soldiers against cannon and gas clouds, in this world of enormous, yet quickly forgotten human hecatombs, there are such beautiful moments when it seems that the whole planet joins hands to save a few lost people. Governments send one expedition after another, individuals plunge into the ultimate risk, and the rest of us – we'd all like to be where a few people are still waiting for help from the human world. These are festive moments of human solidarity, festive because in everyday moments we would invoke it in vain. Nobile and his companions were to discover the Pole, but they had to fly as far as to the Arctic waste to discover the man of this world once again.

Yes, this is about being human. Amundsen, who parted company with Nobile in bitter indignation, sacrifices his life for Nobile. With the utmost difficulty, with overheated boilers, the Soviet ice-breaker inches forward to rescue an expedition sent out by Italy in its fascist pride. A government which has no particular scruple about judicial murders and massacres – if we can at all trust the current history written by press agencies and papers – sends its best pilots and ships to save a handful of foreigners from a nation that is in fact its enemy. The real triumph from the proud voyage to the north is carried off by the icebreaker *Krasin*. With a slight uneasiness we feel that we should like to shake the Soviet government by the hand and say: 'Congratulations and thanks.'

At which point the Soviet government would grumble in visible embarrassment: 'Stop it. Goes without saying. Naturally, we do what we can.' And true, it's ultimately matter-of-course because all great spontaneous symbols are matter-of-course. It's natural that the Soviet government should help the Italian survivors, just as it's natural that a man from whatever quarter of Prague gets wildly emotional over the fate of the Soviet icebreaker and the shipwrecked Italians. Here we suddenly appear in a purely human order that does not bear the flimsiest resemblance to the political one. The good thing is that this human, it-goes-without-saying naturalness exists. It would be rather inhuman if someone started shouting: 'Lo and behold the high standing and beautiful conduct of the USSR.' For this enterprise was carried out not by the government of the USSR, but by the government of human impulses. We couldn't take our hats off to a government's political gesture, but we do take our hats off to the people who ordered and performed this deed just because they felt like proper men. It's not a Soviet success; it's a success of all those who watched this fight for the lives of a few men with suspense and passionate sympathy.

It wasn't a political gesture, only a human one, but it speaks volumes and so tellingly that we, looking towards the motherland of the icebreaker *Krasin*, would like to say: 'Wouldn't it be possible now to talk with one another as people with people?'

The Hero of Our Days

The People's Paper, 9 October 1929

What do you want, Mary? – I'm writing, as you can see. – What am I writing? Well, an editorial about the election. No one's interested in anything else now, you know ... So tell me quickly, what do you want? – What, the neighbours next door have had a dust-up again? Forgive me, Mary, but it's none of our business. I'd rather . . . It doesn't matter that you heard it, but ... OK then, so he's cheating on her, but really it's none of our ... Let him booze, it's his problem, isn't it? – Far above their tight budget! What's it to us, how they live? Remember I never stick my nose into other people's kitchens. It's just you women ... Sorry but it's a matter of principle: never to care about what others ... I don't like gossip, you know. – It doesn't matter if it's true or not. On principle I don't believe in what's whispered. – I beg you, Mary, get that awful womanly habit out of your head and don't bother yourself with other people's intimate affairs.

You know I hate it. – I'm a preacher? You needn't have come up with all this tittle-tattle, so there! – Yes, I have my principles. And perhaps you could let me write now, don't you think? – Goodbye. – Bloody women! Where did I get to? Aha:

'As we learn from a confidential source, gentlemen from the executive committee of the opposition party are at one another's throats; according to hearsay it didn't stop at words. Rumour has it that the funds of this party have been exhausted; the opposition severely censures the executive committee for allegedly over-burdening the party co-operatives with debt. In a word: rank disintegration. Besides, the old personal tensions between the trade unionists and the party's political leadership have resurfaced, it's said. We have received reliable news that the party leader has been accused of perfidy . . .'

What do you want, boy? Can't you see I'm working? – You've lost your ball? You should be more careful. – What? Young Ivan Vahalík has pinched it? Did you see him? You didn't? – Aha, you only think so. Listen, Johnny, and remember: you must never blame anyone if you don't know it for sure. You mustn't do that, do you understand? A decent man doesn't do that. Just imagine if you did him wrong! It's a horrible thing to wound someone's honour. – It's your fault that the ball's gone: if you hadn't left it lying in the corridor . . . Look, Johnny, in a couple of days you'll be playing with Ivan again. Would you be able to look him in the eye if you accused him now of theft? – You mustn't, Johnny, I know you're stronger, and that's just why you mustn't beat him. – Faugh! Suspicion is bad. – What did you tell him? That he's a scoundrel? You'd deserve a slap for that, Johnny. If it happens again, I won't let you play football for a week. Go away, I'm cross with you! An honest man doesn't slander anyone, is that clear? Go away! – Flaming kids! Where did I get to?

'. . . of perfidy and peculiar underhand dealings. We ourselves could ask the gentleman in question where the two million earmarked to revitalise a certain co-operative have disappeared. We could ask why the case of Mr V., against whom a charge of embezzlement has been brought, has been hushed up. Enough is enough!

We'll be on our guard to ensure that our republic doesn't get dismembered by political rogues and notorious liars. Our party will look into the practices of these abusive hooligans ...'

What is it, Fanny? – A horse has fallen over down in the street and the coachman is kicking it? Well, what am I supposed to do? – That's a policeman's job. – And why should it be you who runs to look for a constable? Mind your own business. That's enough. – All right, you can't bear to look at it, but I only say that everyone should sweep their own doorstep. – Don't even think – it could get you into an awful scrape. – Oh please – you want to make people better! Don't meddle in it, and that's that. – If you say anything, he'll just get angrier. Let it be, Fanny; let everyone take care of their own affairs, and that's it. And don't disturb me any more; I have urgent work to do.

'. . . of these abusive hooligans, because it is inherently in the interest of public morality. In speaking out ruthlessly against them, we are doing our national and moral duty. Where would it all end if we kept silent about the embarrassing embroilment, corruption and indecency of our opponents? That's why we are calling all honest, unafraid and idealistic citizens to arms ...'

Confession

The People's Paper, 14 February 1931

So this is how it was in its true, authentic reality: I feared for my vegetation. I feared for the Japanese anemones and the chrysanthemums, for the roses and the freshly planted *Abies concolor*, and for the brooms and the new phlox, as much as for everything else that grows and flowers in the part of the cosmos that I call my property. A dry winter like this without a blanket of snow, a winter with black frost, a bleak, barren winter isn't worth a brass farthing. The soil doesn't get any rest, and doesn't warm up under the snow, and doesn't soak up moisture; the naked shoots of plants freeze, and the little roots break up, and the buds are burnt by frost, and all round what happens is that nature is turned into a horrible wilderness. So that's how it is, and that's why every gardener maintains that there should be a snowfall, and worries from November right through to March, and goes and knocks on the barometer to bring on an abundance of precipitation. And when winter is bare and like a wasteland, black and dry as a bone, good for nothing and desolate, then man in the office of gardener . . .

Well, that's it: a gardener doesn't turn to heaven reproachfully and say: Oh Lord, if only it would snow, at least on my garden! At least on my anemones and roses, and when it's about it, it might just snow on the shoots of my tulips, come on, they're right next to them, and why not, on the other beds as well! I insist he doesn't do any of this to settle his personal account with the climatic predicament, but goes among the people and incites them against the governing weather, saying:

'No wonder there's a flu epidemic! There's always flu when the winter's dry. If it snowed, it'd be the end of flu straight off, you'd be surprised, old chap. The germs get buried in the snow and just snuff it, you see, and the air clears when it's snowing, and that, mark you, is the end of illnesses. That's what it is, it should start snowing.

'Unemployment! No wonder there's unemployment! If there were snowdrifts the roads would have to be cleared, and there'd be tons of work straight off. But when it's such a beastly winter . . .

'And what about the kids? They'll have no sledging to enjoy this year, they won't even be able to build a snowman – is this hygienic? But if there was snow, the kids would look different there and then – fit as a fiddle, sound as a bell, in the pink.

'Anyway, I'll tell you what, when *I* was little, it was quite different: snow up to your knees every year, icicles reaching down to the ground – oh well, those were beautiful winters! Everything just sparkled with cleanliness and beauty. Is it any wonder people are sad and fed up when winters are so black, foggy and dirty! As I say, it's all jiggery-pokery . . .

'They keep on about "the age of sport". But will it snow? So that people can have a good time skiing here under the crematorium in Strašnice? Will it heck! Not everyone can pack up their boards and go to the Swiss mountains or Jilemnice, after all! If I had my way, there'd be lots of snow so that everyone could have their bit of sport, and all would be in order.'

I too carried on like this when I was ranting against the black, dry winter, perhaps because I couldn't have moved people to pity my anemones, or because it's in man's nature to enrobe his own interests and needs in public concern.

And come to that, tell me, hand on heart (I have an elevated vision of the hands of fifty thousand readers touching their hearts this minute): isn't it the same with legions of public and panhuman issues? Don't we smuggle the precious little goods of our private interest or intimate pain or personal dream in under some public, democratic declaration? Aren't our general ideals and protests and programmes only a mask to hide from ourselves the desire for a private and selfish gratification?

Perhaps so. And lo, snow has fallen, and I'm confessing my self-ishness, casting off my hypocrisy and revealing my true colours. And while I'm admitting to my egoism, out there it's squeaking and squealing with kids on sledges, the shovels of the unemployed are clattering, the world is more beautiful and people have a more cheerful outlook making footprints in the snow. So once again (while we're at it) tell me, hand on heart: aren't a lot of our egoisms ultimately and in fact good for the world? It's not snow any longer, but politics and other big things. We may feel them just in that selfish way, but perhaps our – maybe unconscious – point is that the world should be more beautiful and its hubbub happier, and that the shoots of future things shouldn't wither away.

About Tax Returns

The People's Paper, 31 January 1932

Ash Wednesday is drawing near, slowly and inexorably, and what it portends is: 'Remember, son of man, that you are a tax-payer; where-fore get yourself the preordained tax forms and confess your sins.'

A normal citizen doesn't like to pay taxes, indeed, he groans, as he says, under their yoke. He may want everything he can possibly get from the state or city council, and he may swear, with lively gusto, at the fact that there isn't enough money for it all, but nothing makes him more elated than when he manages to conceal a crown or so from the Treasury – in that endeavour he invests a massive amount of ingenuity. I'm not exactly a normal citizen, I think. I don't groan under the yoke of taxation so much as I do under all the paperwork. I hate it like toothache. My whole year is darkened by the glum vision that February, that ill-fated month, will arrive, and I shall have to fill in forms relating to income tax, and housing tax, and capital gains tax, and pension tax, and a tax for running a freelance writer's business. Perhaps there are even more forms than these, I don't know. I just fill them in, 'to the best of my knowledge and conscience', but don't understand a single section. Year after year I keep asking practical, experienced people how to fill them in. They always go on something like this: 'Oh, it's quite easy: just put this here and that there, deduct this from whatever, and then you do something with the whatchamacallit, and Bob's your uncle.' And I normally reply 'Aha', or 'now I know', because I worry that they might otherwise feel offended. But then I sit down and bend over my forms feeling doubly confused, anxious not to muddle up anything whereby I might burden the best of my knowledge and conscience.

If I were the Inland Revenue, I rather think I'd occasionally get stricken by grief. I'd say to myself: Oh God, no one likes me. Well, it's true that wanting money from people is a rather unsympathetic activity. But that's not my fault. Others are responsible – the Exchequer, the government, parliament – I, the Inland Revenue, just have to do what I'm told. Don't blame me, I'm only a cog in the machine, I'd say to myself if I were the Inland Revenue. And suddenly I'd have a brainwave: I know what, I'd say to myself (if I were the Inland Revenue), I could at least make that yearly nuisance easier for people. Why should they have to do so much scribbling and head-scratching? I'll sit down and think up a new form – just one for all the taxes. Put your income in here, my dear chap, your property has earned you this, this comes from your craft or business, this is your salary and this is from your shares if you happen to have any. And you just put all the allowances you're entitled to there, and it's over with. I'll check it over, add up and subtract, and work out what's due to whatever individual tax myself. Besides, I (the Inland Revenue) have to do all the calculations again anyway, after you've done them. Imagine how much work and paper you'll save, not having to do it all bit by bit! And you'll say to yourself: That Inland Revenue, well, it really screws us up, but at least it does it smoothly and comprehensibly – quite a pleasure, really. All right, we can't avoid paying, but we're relieved it's not such a hassle and bother as it used to be when we lived under all that cumbersome and voluminous bureaucracy.

From Fragments

The People's Paper, 12 February 1933

Caiaphas's idea: I'd really like to know who paid this fellow from Nazareth, and how much.

The critic: To criticise means to inform the author that he doesn't do it as I would if I were able to.

One of the greatest catastrophes of civilisation is a learned fool.

Better obey a bailiff than a cliché.

During a debate: What do I care about the truth if I'm not right?

Only little people fight for prestige; great people have it.

Imagine the silence if people said only what they know!

Fighting was created by nature; hatred by man.

Infection

The People's Paper, 25 May 1933

As is well known, yawning is infectious; to an extent laughter and weeping are infectious too. Anger, on the other hand, is not infectious. If you are a passive onlooker when someone loses his temper, and really throws a tantrum, you won't start shouting like him. On the contrary, you'll remain critical and detached. It's true that grumpiness is catching. If someone is just in a bad mood, everyone else is seized with a kind of irritability. A grin is usually untransferable; thinking is not catching either.

It's a bit different in a crowd. There anger is highly infectious. Nothing is easier than projecting your rage into a crowd, and arousing so-called elemental feelings of aversion, opposition and resentment. Such a collective arraignment as we are witnessing now, a political movement that is, as we watch, sweeping through a whole neighbouring nation on our very borders, clearly shows an unusual infection of passions that are more complicated than boredom or laughter. When we are part of a crowd, we are often open to influences that we would not dream of supporting in private. Private life is more critical than public. When the time comes that people start weighing and measuring in private what they have succumbed to in a crowd, there will be a bitter disenchantment – and a return from infection to normality.

Europe

Life xii, 1933–4, January 1934

Look at the state of Europe today. All in all, you could say:

1. that nationalism, whether economic or political, is growing; states and nations are becoming separated from one another by the ever sharper, sensitive boundaries of political suspicion and economic isolation; and despite all expectations and

human progress, we witness that the gulfs between nations and states are widening, thus enhancing the motives for distrust and hatred;

2. that by contrast, from the perspective of civilisation and culture, Europe is levelling out, though here and there we can see an endeavour to use even culture for political and nationalistic ends. One might say that differences in national life are gradually getting blurred – people live ever so similarly but in ever deeper trenches. This is the paradox of today's Europe.

It is obvious that every state feels economically and politically suffocated within its own frontiers because they cut it off from the rest of the world. From this, however, arises an effort to move them, spread them further, and expand the country's living space by revising its borders, through aggression or alliance on the one hand, and a dire need to defend its own palisades tooth and nail on the other. Several possible paths diverge from this. Europe will either get involved in another war, that is, in a series of catastrophes, for war does not solve border problems. Every form of political and economic nationalism will always clash with the national emblems of other states.

Or – and this possibility has not so far been eradicated – Europe will decide on the other path. If it is the frontiers that stand in the way of peace in Europe, well then, let's make them less of a frontier. If what divides us is economic and political nationalism, let's try to administer the world by means of international economics and world politics. We have no right to think that in a thousand or ten thousand years humankind will still be so stupid and primitive as to settle their conflicts like dogs in the street. One day they will arrive at less animal methods: why should not Europe start using them now? Not to believe in such a possibility is to be convinced that the human spirit is terminally impotent – a spirit that prides itself on having gained control over natural forces, but is unable to manage and regulate human society either socially or politically.

To overcome economic and political nationalism: these days the idea is almost utopian – or, to use a different formulation, a revolutionary programme. Either way, it is the only path of reason and hoping. It is possible to free the world from the nationalism of profit and prestige, but nations will remain after you have got rid of that. Even if it is no longer necessary for countries to dig themselves in within their borders, which then become redundant, nations will still be here, and will want to persist and retain their speech, their awareness, their great I, shaped by history, land and language. If Europe follows the only path that is not catastrophic, national conscience will no longer find expression in the threatening national egoisms of politics and economics. But it will not disappear from the world – that baby cannot be thrown out with the bath water. As a natural phenomenon the nation will keep its vitality and will want to express it – well, this is and will be the mission of creative culture. Once politics and economics do not have to fight for the nation's being, the nation will gratify its need for identity in what distinguishes it on a spiritual scale. Politically and economically it will be a part of Europe. In its national culture it will perceive its singularity.

Let's make a mental effort to reverse the course of that strange process happening to Europe. Let's think of politics and economics from an international viewpoint, and of culture as the enactment of specific, living and natural values of each nation. For the time being, it is utopian, yes, but think how already today this could change and deepen our relation to art enormously, and how much it would inspire us to seek for in it.

The gifts of civilisation are international, but culture returns to national sources. Photography is international, but wherever it turns into art it becomes the individual, essentially inimitable expression of a nation. Russian film is as Russian as Russian theatre or Russian literature; it has not become Russian because it has wanted to be folklore, but because it has wanted to be art. Fashion is international, but the taste with which a Parisian girl stitches a dress and wears it is national. Good working-class houses are an achievement of civilisation, but Oud's estates, for instance, are a manifestation of Dutch culture. And so on and so forth. Anywhere where things are accompanied by the special values of love and perfection, belonging and intimacy, they transcend their general usefulness and become a portion of national culture. I would put it simply – beauty can be neither imitated nor appropriated; it is necessary to beget it on the spot. It is precisely culture that has about it that special grace, carrying with it the kiss of the genius loci. Truths are general and valid for the entire world, but love is specific – to love means to give preference to someone. Art is a big preference-giving: it grants beauty to a nation, to a native land or a continent, above others. Europe will never stop being a continent of individual nations as long as it is a continent of creative, that is national, cultures.

Beneš 1915[1]

Saturday, 26 May 1934

Forgive me that I must start about myself. Already in the first weeks of the Great War, a lot of us felt that something should be done – it was in the air, somehow. At that time I was on corresponding terms with the Italian futurists, especially their leading figure Marinetti. I knew that Marinetti passionately hated Austria – in one poem he expressed the desire to hover over Vienna in an aeroplane and drop the last pope on it *comme une crotte noire* [like a black turd]. It wasn't yet certain then whether Italy would enter the war and on which side. To cut a long story short, I took it into my head to go to Italy and win over the futurists for a campaign against Austria.

I submitted an application for a passport to travel to Spain, pretending that I was studying art history and wanted to collect material for a dissertation on Mudéjar architecture. Professor Chytil[2] signed it for me. I enclosed an application for a special

medical examination, and was waiting for it to be processed. I
didn't talk about the business to anyone and had no idea if anything
was going on on our side.

Some time in the March of 1915 Docent Beneš stopped me in
front of Kaulich's house; until then I had spoken to him only once,
something about sociological sources. 'Mr colleague,' he blurted
out, 'you're going to Spain, aren't you?'

I had no time to wonder. 'I hope so,' I admitted.

'You'll go via Switzerland,' Dr Beneš said. 'And you'll
smuggle some papers for us. Think about how you can best hide
them. You'd get the rope for it, you know, if they found them on
you.' Apparently it didn't even occur to him to wait for any possible
objections. 'Agreed?'

'Agreed.'

And he was gone that very minute. The next time I saw
him was five years later when he was Minister of Foreign Affairs.
I had waited for the passport for another half year, while it
had gone, in succession, from the police headquarters to the
governor's office, to the Ministry of Defence and the Ministry
of War, and from there got back to me in the form of a bunch
of papers with a rejection and a warning that I should be careful – but all that is another story. At the time, in front of Kaulich's
house, however, I stood for a while until I had my fill of indignant
marvelling:

where Mr Docent had got it from that I was trying to get
abroad,

how bloody careless of him to turn to a person virtually unknown
to him,

how he could take it as read and beyond any possibility of refusal
that I would risk my life for such a precarious task,

who were those 'we' whose papers I should smuggle through,

but what I most marvelled at was that everything was really so
matter-of-course, and that I didn't hesitate for a minute before
deciding that I must do it and that Dr Beneš had the right to ask
me.

I Don't Know What It Means

The People's Paper, 4 August 1934, in the section 'The week's "Little Broadcast"'

I don't know what it means,
What import one should find
In that old rigmarole
I can't get off my mind.

When God created Adam,
Or so the myth implies,
He added Eve to him
To seal their paradise.

The serpent was there too.
He envied them their bliss,
And dropped a hint to Eve,
Whispering in a hiss.

So when they were in bed,
'Tell me, Adam, my dear,'
Eve started, with a sigh,
'Where shall we go this year?

'There are no mountains here,
No seaside in this place,
Summer in Eden is
Too horrible to face.

'Really it's such a bore
Sitting here all year long,
We must go somewhere else,
Please, darling, come along.'

The Lord, of course, heard this,
And thundered, looking peeved:
'Joy's over, Adam, now
You're hearkening to Eve.

'Right! Go where she commands
To spas or swimming pools,
But hear my judgement first,
You hereditary fools.

'In the sweat of thy face
Shalt thou eat bread each day,
And leaving rest and peace
Shalt go on holiday.'

March 1935

The People's Paper, 15 March 1935

Prague, 14 March. (Special correspondent)

Among the issues that were under negotiation at today's Cabinet meeting was the date when the spring was to commence. The prevailing opinion is that it will not be possible to postpone its launch until the day allocated to it by the calendar, that is, 21 March, or an even later time. No definitive consensus has been reached; some of the parties are in favour of maintaining the status quo as long as possible. It seems that the signs that spring is unstoppably on our doorstep have proliferated in the countryside too. The Prime Minister insists that the decision will have to be made by 21 March at the latest. The issue will be further discussed throughout the whole of next week.

Sezimovo Ústí, 14 March. (Spec. corr.)

Minister Beneš told a distinguished foreign journalist that the issue of when the spring would actually commence must be addressed from a European perspective.[1] The spring either happens everywhere, or unfavourable weather will continue to dominate, albeit it is of course necessary to allow for specific conditions in individual countries. 'We are prepared for the spring,' Dr Beneš asserted, 'and I can make the same claim about the allied states – for the countries of the Little Entente, the coming of the spring will arrive in a matter of a very few days.' In any case, there is reason to hope that the whole of Europe will adopt a policy of solidarity on this matter.

Prague, 14 March. (Spec. corr.)

With reference to the rumours that the spring is to be shortened, the Governor of the National Bank told us that the ongoing high level of barometer readings corresponded to conditions abroad, and could not be challenged by any measures that our Bank might take. This high pressure naturally precludes any accumulation of airflow coming into circulation especially from western countries: what we are facing is a temporary predicament that usually happens at the end of winter, and is then shortly succeeded by a sharp fall on the barometer. But these barometric deviations do not undermine the strength of our currency, and least of all the financial policies of the National Bank.

Prague, 14 March. (Spec. corr.)

At a big meeting of the National Unification held in the Lucerna, the Reich leader Hodáč railed against the dependency of our weather on foreign countries.[2] It is undignified for a sovereign nation that decisions about its climate should be determined by continental or overseas meteorological conditions. We want to have a spring of our own. (A storm of applause.) Whereat the speaker, amid ecstatic cheers, announced that the momentous beginning of spring would be brought about only by the next election, which would ensure the victory of our cause.

Geneva, 14 March. (Spec. corr.)

Rumour has it that the commencement of the spring will not fall on an earlier date than that of Sir John Simon's visit to Berlin. Hence a strong sense of exasperation has been apparent in Italian circles; the possibility of Mussolini's ordering the beginning of the spring much earlier, so that Italy retains an independent strategy even with respect to this international affair, cannot be ruled out.

Athens, 14 March. (Spec. corr.)

During a reconnaissance flight over the positions of rebels in Macedonia the government pilots discovered the first signs of spring. (These are probably primroses.)

Erfurt, 14 March. (Spec. corr.)

At a mass meeting of the National Socialist Party, Minister Dr Goebbels denied that a change of the governing weather in Germany had ever been under consideration. 'This weather is the result of our work,' he said, among other things, 'and we will persevere in it forever. Any rumours about signs of spring in Germany are', he insisted, 'a sheer fabrication, spewed out by the usual mendacious propagandists.'

About Easter Magicking

The People's Paper, 21 April 1935

It's really true, you know: Easter used to be as richly embroidered with folk traditions and superstitions as Christmas. It used to be

a festive season as potently magical and pagan as the winter solstice. But with one big difference: the mystery of Christmas is to
a large extent prophetic, whereas the mystery of Easter revolves
solely around magic. At Easter there is no dripping molten lead
into water, apples are not cut in halves, nuts are not cracked, candles are not set in their shells, and there is no staring into the
water's depth so that the future can be revealed. At Easter no
dog barks to betoken which side a bridegroom will be coming
from. All these prophecies belong to Christmas. At Easter we do
magic in order to be healthy, so that there's a good harvest, or whatever. At Easter you don't ask mysterious fate what will happen,
but you try to exercise a magic influence over the future. Wash
yourself in a stream at dawn, my girl, and you'll be healthy all the
year long. Do this and that, fulfil this one or that other magic formula and everything will be all right – your future's in your hands.
It's not in your power what will come out of the molten lead at
Christmas; you can't control whether the seeds of a halved apple
will arrange themselves to form a cross or a star; you can't stop
your little candle in its nutshell boat from being the first to be
put out. But at Easter you are more or less master of your destiny
again. If you do this and that, you'll stay alive and be as fit as a flea.
So go and do it.

Night wields the sceptre over Christmas, but God's daylight
over Easter – that's what it probably is. At Christmas nature sleeps,
there's no work to do. A man bound up in nature sits with his arms
folded, waiting until the winter is over. He can't interfere with the
course of things in any way; it's just a matter of surviving the winter.
And so a man, who is dreaming and waiting, is seized with a sooth-
saying mood. If there's nothing else to do, he at least feels like fore-
telling the future. A man with a plough in his hands doesn't enquire
helplessly what the harvest will be like because he's to a certain
degree already making it. Come hail or drought, at least a man will
do his level best so that his field will yield crops. He does magic so
that evil powers won't harm his work or health. That's why he lights
consecrated candles during thunderstorms, and keeps catkins at
home to ward off pernicious illnesses. He doesn't foretell the future,

but helps to shape a good destiny. During the winter solstice he sits in half-darkness and longs for prophecies and portents: reveal what will become of me and us because it's beyond my power to bring it about of my own accord. In the time of the vernal equinox he has work to do – thank God, he is again a bit of a constructor and workman of his own fate. And everything around him stirs. Nature sets out on its titanic move – there's no longer the wintry clinging and numbness. And that's why the spring magicking is entirely different from the winter one. No more metaphysical impotence or feeling at a loss or asking fate what will befall us. Here is some action at last, at least we can spend a little effort and affect our happiness.

And I think we could all have enough of that wintry sooth-saying. The whole of Europe has had a go at it – you hear nothing but that anxious question, what will happen, and how will it turn out. Perhaps it's time we started with spring magick-ing everywhere, and did something so that it will work out well for us. If we do this or that, if we fulfil these or those other con-ditions, we'll stay alive and healthy. And with this magicking everyone can help. Anyone who does something doesn't have time to ask destiny helplessly what awaits us. I say, do not think that we can't have an impact, however infinitesimal, on the future. Even the minutest influence is better than mere prophesying. In this lies the whole mystery of spring magicking – that it's at least in our power what will happen.

On Mother's Day

The People's Paper, 12 May 1935

It's common experience that at election time women become the focus of public attention and political flattery distinctly more than at other times. What's more, they are talked about and even talked to in leading articles that otherwise minister only to the male pas-time of political knockabout all year long. They'd be crazy if they felt grateful for this sort of electoral attention. By sheer coincidence this year *their* festive day, which comes round just once a year, falls on the Sunday preceding the one when they go to the polls. On Mothering Sunday *they* have the right to demand publicly that those seeking their political support should devote their precious male attention to things that are closest to, and most important for, women – motherhood and family, childcare, education, children's hygiene, social security for women, and a range of other things that could be summed up as respect for the life mission of womankind. Let's admit our debt to women; it can't be rectified by pre-election kowtowing, but only by taking the protection of mothers and children more seriously. The subject of discussion on this Mother's Day should be what the politically enthroned could do, and what they have the will to do, for women. In my view they should concentrate specifically on the things that are most sacred to women and mothers: peace-making, both external and internal, humanness and equality – for women have learnt far too well what inequality and injustice are like.

Relief

The People's Paper, 10 April 1938

What are you doing here, my friend?

Oh, can't you see? Raking. Raking out stones and dead leaves and all sorts of muck from this patch of earth, to be precise. Here at least I can do it. Look, it's been like a rubbish-tip, and I'd like to put it straight.

Why?

Just because. Just to make it more beautiful. I can't be putting the whole universe straight, can I? You know what it's like in the world these days.

And that's why you're raking out stones and weeds?

Why, yes, that's part of the reason. Now you know. You just have to do something. You can't sit waiting all the time to see what comes up . . . At least you've got something in your hands. I know it's just a rake; it doesn't look like a flagpole or a gun. But if you spend a couple of hours raking out stones, you do have a feeling you've done something, my friend, no matter what. The whole of your body has that feeling, and your head joins in too; it knows that you've done what you can. Look – it does show – all that work, I mean. If someone came over tomorrow, he wouldn't be able to tell that there'd been such a rubbish-tip here. No one will appreciate what a hell of a lot of work needed to be done. If you knew how devilishly sore the palms of my hands are . . .

And are you content?

Yes. With that, I'm content.

I see. So it's as if you didn't know, as if you didn't even want to know how serious the times are. You're raking away here as if nothing were at stake. Didn't you at least think about the fate of the world when you were fiddling with this?

No, to be honest, I didn't. I only wanted to rake out that muck, my dear chap; you have to go at it hammer and tongs – you don't really have time to think about anything, except finishing the job by the evening.

There are more serious tasks before us today, my friend, for example . . .

I know. But to be waiting for tasks isn't a task at all. I tell you that nothing cheers you up more than putting something in order, whatever it is.

Like a bit of the garden, eh?

Yes. Like a bit of the garden, just that. It's a fragment of the world too, and it takes quite an effort, don't think otherwise. Just try it yourself – to sort something out, and you'll have that feeling too . . .

What feeling?

Well, a special kind of feeling that things in the world could ultimately be made better. I for one never believed that I'd get rid of those stones and muck; I even thought that it wasn't in human power to make this place into anything. And see, I knuckled down – out of anger, if you like.

What kind of anger?

Oh, perhaps at the fact that you're so helpless. Something bad is happening to the world, and what can you do? Nothing, just frown and think to yourself, damn it, it'll be a massacre again! I frowned as well, my friend, and bit my lip and all that. And then I said to myself, OK . . .

What?

I'll have a go at that rubbish-tip. I'd never have knuckled down to a sweat of that kind if it hadn't been for such hard times. First I was raking out of sheer rage to get it all out of me, but then I found I was really obsessed with those stones, and that I just had to clean this spot out thoroughly. And I was raking, my friend, I was raking, as if that were the only thing that the world's fate depended on.

So what? What's it good for?

Perhaps just a little. Perhaps just that a piece of good work has been done somewhere.

About Dowsing

The People's Paper, 11 September 1938

So once a stout, russet man came along – there was absolutely nothing mystical or extraordinary about him; he looked more like a publican or a cattle-dealer. At once he took what looked like a metal hose out of his bag and trod with it slowly, somewhat woodenly across the meadow. Suddenly the hose started twisting in his hand and the man said: 'So there is a spring here, seven metres down.' Further off he stopped again. 'Here's another one, but this one is ten metres deep.'

Of course, you know, folk like us don't believe just like that. They look on with polite scepticism, thinking that anyone would be able to do that, to move a twig around in his fingers and claim that there's water there; you're not going to hoodwink me, old chap. 'So now *you* must try,' the russet man decreed. 'I'll cut a willow twig, it'll be easier for you with that.' The sceptical man takes the thin willow fork in his hands and treads with it slowly, somewhat woodenly across the meadow, and suddenly the twig bends towards the ground with all its might, bang on the spot where the water-diviner's hose was twisting. On principle, the sceptical person tries to exert resistance on the twig, but it seems it would be able to wrench his fingers round, such force is inclining it towards the ground. So the unbelieving man tries it again and again; ten times he treads somewhat woodenly across that particular meadow, and each time the twig dips precisely on the same spot. Whereupon the doubting creature draws two conclusions at one go from his experience: (1) that there's really something to dowsing, and (2) that he himself has a talent for dowsing, and he feels something like pride in this exceptional gift of nature. It's perhaps because I'm so sensitive, or it's some special force, he thinks with satisfaction.

From that moment on the new convert swoops on everyone who appears within reach. 'Come and try how the twig works with you!' Usually the people in question try to get out of it, but eventually they're forced to tread somewhat woodenly across the meadow with a twig in their hands. 'You don't get it doing anything much,' admonishes the brand-new diviner. 'See how it bends with me!' Some eight people dawdle about the meadow with twigs in their hands; they look like loonies or sleepwalkers. 'There's a spring here too,' a voice echoes every so often. Quite simply, it transpires that there are at least twenty underground springs on that patch of earth, and that every other person with a twig responds to it. Some have the twig turn right over, others, presumably less talented, hardly make it tilt ('but I can feel a kind of jerk in my hands,' they assure you eagerly), while, for yet other people, it doesn't move a bit. This last sort put their twigs aside, making it clear to the others that they consider the whole thing is humbug and superstition or an undignified toy. 'I'm too strong a character for that,' is written on their faces, 'it seems to react only with feeble, oversensitive natures and neurasthenics.' On the other hand, those for whom the twig wriggles as if alive look down on these strong types with slight disdain. Oh well, they think, he's a bit thick for this, poor chap; he obviously doesn't have a flair for nature and its forces. From this you can see that even the diviner's twig divides people into two camps and makes mutual understanding between them difficult.

But there we are. May an honourable testimony be rendered. There really is something to the dowsing rod, and it is possible to find underground springs, and perhaps even quite a few other things, with it. God, if I had such a twig that would lead me to a place where there are springs of peace among people, albeit fragile, I'd walk with that twig (slowly and somewhat woodenly) across the whole world and would say: 'Careful, careful, here it is, and it's not too deep for it to be released.' My God, the world is full of such hidden little springs . . .

But there would certainly be strong characters who would consider it humbug or feebleness: in their hands such a twig wouldn't even quiver.

A Prayer for This Evening[1]

The People's Paper, 22 September 1938

God, you who created this beautiful country, you see our pain and disappointment – we don't have to tell you how we feel and how we are bowing our heads. Not in shame, for we have nothing to be ashamed of even though fate is smiting us with an iron rod. No, not us – we haven't been defeated, we haven't failed to show enough courage. Our nation has not lost a shred of its honour; it has only lost a part of its body. We are like a man who has been caught between cogwheels – at once, with the first and most horrible pain, he feels that he is alive. Our nation is alive, and it is precisely this intense pain that makes us feel how intensely, how deeply alive it is.

God, you who created this nation, we don't have to tell you anything, but our lips and hearts are trying to formulate, at least for our sake, what we must never lose, that is, faith. Faith in ourselves and in your history. We believe that we have not been and will not be on the wrong side of history. We believe that there is more future, more of what will grow and bear fruit, on our side and in our effort than on the side of violence and temporary power. Truth is more than power because it is everlasting. But even at this difficult moment we must realise that our obligation is not to wait for the future with folded arms. We shall work for our nation, for its inner strength and unity, more than we have done so far. The better we make our people and our nation, the more we'll do for the better side of history.

Even in our fate world history is being enacted, and it will continue with great and glorious necessity. There is no reason why we should fear the world's evolution – quite the contrary; violence pales before the universal human need for freedom, peace and equality among people and nations. We must do a great deal for ourselves, we must love our nation even more than we have done, we must love one another more. We believe that even in that, especially in that, is our great mission to the world: to make ourselves into a nation that will be capable in every respect of a better future than the current and transitory dark episode of European history.

God, we are not asking you to avenge us, but we implore you to breathe the spirit of trust into each of us, not let anyone despair fruitlessly, but make them already seek the ways in which they can be useful for the future undertakings of an everlasting nation. We don't need despondent people now. We need faith. We need inner strength. We need effective love that will fortify us tenfold. A nation will never be small so long as it does not allow itself to waver from its belief in the future and work for a better time to come.

Studánka[1]

The People's Paper, 14 October 1938

I'm reading and I can't believe my eyes. Malé Svatoňovice has been taken over by the occupying German forces. Malé Svatoňovice, my birthplace, Malé Svatoňovice that the local folks call Studánka, after the miraculous spring of Our Lady of Svatoňovice. Listen, not a single German has ever settled there, except for the surveyor and the foreman of the local coal mine, who were once appointed by the Duke of Náchod. It's the most Czech of the Czech nooks; right next to it lies Rtyně, where there used to be rebellious peasants; further away from it is Granny's Valley,[2] and over there round the corner is Jirásek's Hronov;[3] it's a region of miners and weavers, old Protestant sectarians and spiritualists. Only further off beyond Žaltman, beyond the Hawks' Mountains, beyond Brendy, as they used to say, towards Markousovice and Sedloňov do you find Germans. There it's all purely German just as it's purely Czech here, right down to the marrow. The two nations have never mixed there, nor have they squabbled; they've lived good-naturedly side by side: here a Czech, there a German – both as true as steel. And good Germans they were. They went to Czech churches to listen to the German Word of God and spoke the German dialect of Hauptmann's weavers;[4] even a German didn't understand them. The problem of minorities arose further away, in Trutnov, but never in this place; so matter-of-course were neighbourly relations here, so clear the linguistic boundary. It's either one of the minor errors, or one of the major injustices; either way, it's absurdly and grotesquely distorted. Studánka occupied by the German army! Nothing in the world is clear and certain, then.

That spiritualist from *The Robber* is a miner from Svatoňovice.[5] Today he can't go to the colliery. It stands there shut, and before it stretches a delimitation line.

From One Human Being to Another

The People's Paper, 4 December 1938

There isn't much that the human eye can rest on with relish, or with certainty, without it suddenly starting to twist and distort and wink at you differently, somehow, and uncannily. Everything has changed, everything has changed – worse still, not just states, but also people; and you used to think that you knew them! – Oh well, I did think so, but it's not their fault that everything has changed, is it? Look, there was so much pain and panic in what has happened, no wonder that a face you used to know has contorted! Even nations have their faces, and there are moments when we should look somewhere far off rather than straight into people's faces. You must come to grips with this and look far off – see, it is still our old horizon even now.

So you go around, fixing your eyes on the far distance (for that is also a way of seeking your own path). A person you used to know visits, or a letter arrives from a small, remote place, whose name you haven't uttered for a long time, and whose taste you at that moment feel sweetening on your tongue. Or a new acquaintance, who you're meeting for the first time, shakes hands with you. No need to talk much in the meanwhile. No need to say anything at all, and suddenly you know with certitude: continuity hasn't been broken here. Everything has changed, but here is someone who has remained the same, equally decent and believing, equally even-tempered, of the same spiritual fabric as before. No matter what has happened, something faithful and steadfast has remained here, something firm as the ground beneath your feet. And suddenly you realise that while fixing your eyes on the distance, you keep discovering what's nearest: that you discover people, that you find a nearer nearness and a deeper concord among them than you had ever done before. Hark! A lot must have changed for you to find what is constant; an awful lot must have been broken for us to feel palpably with our hands what holds together. So you see, it's not so bad, for did you get such joy from people when we weren't being tested so harshly?

Yes, a lot has changed, but people have remained the same, except that we now know better who is who. Anyone who is decent has always been decent; who was loyal, is loyal now too. Anyone who turns with the wind turned with the wind before. Anyone who thinks that his moment has come has always cared only about himself. No one becomes a defector unless he has been one always; anyone who changes his faith never had any. You can't transform a person, he'll just come out in his true colour. You can't transform a nation, unless you have centuries to do it; only a rabble can be led here today and there tomorrow. Anyone who hates has had hatred in him always – where else could it spring from so suddenly?! Anyone who served will carry on serving; anyone who desired the good will desire the good still. The will does not change. Don't look into a face that has changed – no one becomes more beautiful by being two-faced.

A harsh test is also a harsh recognition. The future folio of our history of this time will bear a single subtitle: Who was who. A retentive memory will also be part of that steadfastness that is and will be needed.

A lot has changed, and even more has shifted to a state of restless swarming; and so your eyes must seek something that lasts and is steadfast. Praise and give thanks to God that you are not watching out for it in vain any more. You will find it in people, you will find it matter-of-course, unbroken and patient. You will find it in people, reading the Word of God in Czech and believing, as they did after the Battle of the White Mountain.[1] You will find it in people, as a quiet summoning of strength. You will feel the quiet and steadfast beside the most deafening; the quiet and the quietest are the true history, for there is no history without steadfastness – swarming and uprooting are not history. Nothing true is without steadfastness. If someone tells you to believe, what he means is be steadfast to the utmost!

Greetings[1]

The People's Paper, 25 December 1938

One thinks all sorts of things about other nations, and they wouldn't always make that particular nation walk tall. It is a kind of habit to identify the country or the people with its politics, regime, government, public opinion or whatever it's called. But what's different is to be able to imagine the nation in some illustrative way – you can't just invent it or do it by will power. A memory enters your mind of its own accord, a memory of what you have seen, of something quite random and mundane. God knows why just this small experience, and no other one, has so strongly imprinted itself on your memory. Suffice it to say that you recall, say, England, and the very moment you see . . .

Well, I don't know what *you* see, or if you have any picture at all, but with me it's simply a little red house in Kent. There was nothing special about it. I caught a glimpse of it hardly for a second as the train was speedily puffing its way from Folkestone to London. Actually, it was hard to see the house because of all those trees. There was an old man in the garden trimming the hedge with a pair of shears, and on the other side of the green thicket, along a straight path a girl was cycling. Nothing more. I don't even know if the girl was much to look at. The old gentleman in black was perhaps a local parish priest or a retired businessman, it doesn't matter. The house had high chimneys and white windows, as all the little red houses in England do, and I can't tell you any more about it. Still, the moment I say to myself England, I can clearly see that ordinary house in Kent, the old man with garden shears in his hands and the girl pedalling solemnly and straight on her bike, and I begin to feel I miss it a bit. I've seen all sorts of other things there, like castles and parks and ports, I've seen the Bank of England and Westminster Abbey and whatever historic and monumental sights you like to mention, but that's not the whole England to me. The whole England – that's that naïve little house in a green garden, with an old man and a girl on a bike. Why, I don't know. I'm telling you only what I see.

Or if I want to imagine Germany, what arises in my mind is an old inn in Schwaben. It's not my fault that it isn't the Potsdam Gate or a military parade. I have never ever been in that inn, I only caught a glimpse of it from the train somewhere past Nuremberg. It was early in the evening, and there was not a single soul to be seen, and the inn was high and spread out like a cathedral, in the centre of an old toy town squeezed together as if it were in the palm of your hand. In front of it bloomed elders, and there were stone steps leading up to the taproom. It was almost laughable how dignified and broad that inn was – somehow it was reminiscent of a mother hen slumbering in a small warm pit. True, I've seen finer and more notable and more German things in Germany than that antique Schwaben Gasthaus. I've seen umpteen towns and houses and monuments there, you know, but that venerable, sturdy inn has defeated them all. I don't know why, but to me that's Germany.

Or consider all one can imagine if one recalls France. My relentless image is this one: a Parisian street, virtually on the outskirts of the city, on the border line; there are still a few pubs and petrol stations among vegetable gardens. In front of a pub, on the awning of which is written Au Rendez-vous des Chauffeurs, is standing a heavy two-wheeled cart pulled by a fair Norman gelding. In front of the pub a peasant in a loose blue shirt and a broad-brimmed straw hat is slowly drinking white wine from a thick glass. That's all, nothing else is going on there. Only the sun is blazing with white-chalky hardiness and the ruddy peasant in a blue shirt is finishing up his glass. I can't help it: that's France.

Or Spain: that's, by contrast, a cafe on the Puerta del Sol. A black-haired mother in a black dress is sitting at the next table, and she is holding a black-eyed baby with a sweet little round head and festively grave black eyes in her arms, and a father with a black sombrero on his nape is excitedly and jovially grinning at his black-eyed niño. There's nothing about it, a wanderer could see it anywhere in the world, yet down there mothers look more like Madonnas, you see, and fathers more like fighters and babes more like mysterious toys, compared to anywhere else in the world. When I read about Spain, I don't see any Alhambras or Alcázars, that's for sure, but a festive niño in the arms of a black-haired Madonna.

Or Italy: one could imagine the Colosseum, pines, Vesuvius, or whatever, but not that! It's a train, a jerky passenger train, from Orvieto to Rome, I suppose. Night has already fallen, and there is a workman asleep sitting opposite you, except that his fluffy nut is heavily and limply dangling. Then the Italian woke up, snorted, rubbed his eyes with one of his paws, and told you something, do you remember? But you didn't understand him and didn't trust him, and suddenly he put his hand in his pocket, took out a chunk of cheese, wrapped up in paper, and with a casual, matter-of-course gesture offered it to you to cut a piece for yourself. It's a sort of custom there. That rough hand with a scrap of sheep cheese, that's to you the whole of Italy in a nutshell.

I know, today it is so terribly far from one nation to another, and one thinks all sorts of things. Indeed, one is cross with many, and keeps saying to oneself, what has happened can never ever be forgotten: how can we possibly communicate with one another in the midst of this unprecedented distance and alienation? And then you think of, say, England, and suddenly you see the little red house in Kent before you. The old gentleman still keeps trimming the bushes and the girl is pedalling away swiftly and straight. And see, you'd like to greet them. *How do you do? How do you do?* Nice weather, isn't it? *Yes, very fine.*

So you see, that's it, and you feel lighter. Now you could go up the stone steps into that Schwaben inn, hang your hat on a stand and greet everyone: *Grüß Gott, meine Herren.* But they would recognise that you were a foreigner, and so would start talking a bit quieter, at times eyeing you searchingly. But when they saw you wiping the bottom of your jug on the red tablecloth just as they do, they would be less distrustful and would ask: *Woher, woher, mein Herr? Aus Prag. – So, so, aus Prag,* they would wonder, and one of them would say that he had once been to Prague. Thirty years ago. *Eine Schöne Stadt,* he would say, and you would for all that feel a little bit happier.

Or you would stop at Au Rendez-vous des Chauffeurs. The peasant in a blue shirt is just finishing up his glass of pale wine and is wiping his moustache with his palm. *Fait chaud,* you would say, *à votre santé! – À la votre,* says the peasant. There is really nothing more to say, except you would tell him: No, *mon vieux,* honestly I'm not cross, not with you – how about having another glass together?

And you could also grin at that Spanish baby. It would fix its grave, festive eyes on you, the black-haired mum would suddenly look even a little more like a Madonna, and the caballero dad with a hat on his nape would start jabbering on in Spanish, but you wouldn't understand him. It doesn't matter, it doesn't matter, so long as you haven't frightened the child!

And now, also, you must cut a morsel of that sheep cheese for yourself. *Grazie, grazie,* you're mumbling with your mouth full, offering a cigarette in return. And nothing more. Well, there's no need to talk loads of God-knows-what to make all well among people!

What can we do? It is so far from one nation to another; all of us are more and more lonely. You'd better never stick your nose out of your house again; better to lock the gate and close the shutters, and now others can wish us well as much as they like! I have finished with everyone. And now you can close your eyes and softly, quite softly keep saying: *How do you do*, old sir in Kent? *Grüß Gott, meine Herren! Grazie, signor! À votre santé!*

Notes

INTRODUCTION

1   'From our Region', *The People's Paper*, 9 May 1926.
2   From a letter to Otakar Vočadlo (1895–1974), a scholar of Czech and English literatures, 16 December 1924.
3   'An Unknown Artist', *Musaion*, spring 1921.
4   *From the Life of Insects*. In English *And so ad infinitum* (1923), new trans. *The Insect Play* (1999).
5   In English 1923.
6   In English 2008.
7   In English *The Makropoulos Secret* (1925), *The Macropulos Secret* (1927), new trans. *The Makropulos Case* (1999).
8   In English 1929.
9   In English *Power and Glory* (1938), new trans. *The White Plague* (1999).
10 In English 1939.
11 'An Interview about Theatre', *The People's Paper*, 26 February 1933.
12 In English *The Absolute at Large* (1927).
13 In English 1925.
14 In English *Three Novels* (1948, 1990). *Hordubal* (1934), *Meteor* (1935), *An Ordinary Life* (1936).
15 In English 1937.
16 In English 1939.
17 In English *The Cheat* (1941).
18 '70° 40' 11" N', in *A Journey to the North* (1936).
19 'English Theatre', *The People's Paper*, 17 July 1924.
20 From a letter to Olga (from London, 30 June 1924).
21 'Let's Be Revolutionary', *The People's Paper*, 24 November 1925.
22 'To Forestall Any Confusion' (II), *The Present*, 9 April 1925.
23 Karel Steinbach, *A Nearly Hundred-Year-Old Witness* (1988).
24 From a letter to the English dramatist Hermon Ould (1885–1951), after 30 September 1938.
25 Died in 1944 at Auschwitz or, according to new testimonies from the 1990s, in January/February 1945 in the concentration camp at Dora.
26 From the novel *Meteor* (1934).
27 Olga Scheinpflugová, *A Czech Novel* (1946).

28 'A Colonnade', *The People's Paper*, 30 May 1926.

29 Meanwhile the editorial team founded a literary weekly, *The Path*.

30 *The People's Paper*: founded by Adolf Stránský in Brno in 1893; between the wars it developed into a highly respected newspaper, presenting itself as a broadsheet for the independent-minded.

31 'About the Social Status of a Czechoslovak Writer', *U-Bloc*, 10 March 1937.

32 'Talks with Karel Čapek' (interviewed by the poet Vilém Závada (1905–82)), *Aventinum Discussions*, 22 October 1931.

33 'A Dispute about Foreign Influences', *The People's Paper*, 23 November 1924.

34 'A Colonnade', *The People's Paper*, 30 May 1926.

35 From a letter to Otakar Vočadlo (about 23 March 1924).

36 In English *Intimate Things* (1935).

37 In English in 1931; new trans. 2004.

38 In English *How They Do It* (1945).

39 Čapek did not keep his much-corrected manuscripts. Readers and scholars are indebted to the courageous enterprise of Čapek's editor, Dr Miroslav Halík (1901–75), who secretly retrieved his journalism from various periodicals during the Second World War.

40 In English *Apocryphal Stories* (1949) and *Apocryphal Tales: With a Selection of Fables and Would-Be Tales* (1997).

41 See 'I Don't Know What It Means' in Part VI.

42 'Room for Jonathan!' (Walt Whitman's name for a typical American), *The Present*, 21 March 1934.

43 Ibid.

44 Marsyas – a symbol of condemned art – was a satyr who taught himself to play the flute and challenged the god Apollo to a contest, but was flayed alive by him when he lost. In English *In Praise of Newspapers, and Other Essays on the Margin of Literature* (1951).

45 'An Interview about Criticism', recorded by the journalist and director Josef Kodíček (1892–1952), *The Present*, 15 February 1933.

46 From a letter to Otakar Vočadlo (16 December 1924).

47 From Ferrara, 20 April 1923. His travel books include *Letters from Italy* (1923; in English 1929), *Letters from England* (1924; in English 1925, new trans. 2001), *A Trip to Spain* (1930; in English *Letters from Spain*, 1931), *Pictures from Holland* (1932; in English *Letters from Holland*, 1933) and *A Journey to the North* (1936; in English *Travels in the North*, 1939).

48 From the end of the novel *Krakatit* (1924).

49 Even his brother and sister sometimes thought he wasted his talent, especially on his popular detective *Tales from One Pocket* (1929) and *Tales from the Other Pocket* (1929). In English *Tales from Two Pockets* (1932; new trans. 1994).

50   From a letter to Otakar Vočadlo (about 23 March 1924).
51   'A Bit Personal', a reaction to a reviewer's criticism of Nigel Playfair's English production of *The Insect Play*, *The Present*, 3 November 1927.
52   'Do Ghosts Exist?', *The People's Paper*, 31 January 1926.

I CULTURE

Two Kinds of Joy
    1   An allusion to Goethe's Faust: 'I am on a par with the spirit I understand.'

Where is Heaven?
    1   Eduard Bass (1888–1946), writer, journalist, author of literary cabaret acts. In 1933 he became *The People's Paper*'s editor-in-chief.
    2   Karel Zdeněk Klíma (1883–1942), nicknamed Kazetka, journalist. In the late 1920s and 1930s he became *The People's Paper*'s editor-in-chief, and was executed by the Nazis.
    3   Jaroslav Kvapil (1868–1950), lyric poet, playwright (author of the libretto for Dvořák's opera *Rusalka*) and director, head of the National Theatre, and subsequently of the Vinohrady Theatre where Čapek worked as dramaturge.
    4   Bohuš Zakopal (1874–1936), actor in Čapek's plays.

The Age of the Eyes
    1   Vítězslav Nezval (1900–58), avant-garde poet.

Karel Čapek about Himself
    1   Addressed to Otakar Štorch-Marien (1897–1974), founder of the Aventinum publishing house (the Čapek brothers' chief publisher until 1932), and publisher and editor of the journal in which this piece appeared.

Culture and Nation
    1   Brno: the capital of Moravia, regularly hosting Trade Fairs.

About the Čapek Generation
    1   Charles-Louis Philippe (1874–1909), French writer, influenced by Dostoevsky and Nietzsche.
    2   Pergamum: an ancient city in western Asia Minor, famous for its library and as a major centre of Hellenistic culture.
    3   Logicism: a theory emphasising logic in philosophy and mathematics, introduced by Gottlob Frege and developed by Bertrand Russell. The *Oxford English Dictionary*'s first reference to the logicists is from the American philosopher William James, to whom Čapek, himself a doctor of philosophy, devoted a chapter in

his book *Pragmatism, or a Philosophy of Practical Life* (1918, revised edn 1925).

4   Georg Simmel (1858–1918), German philosopher and sociologist. Heinrich John Rickert (1863–1936), German philosopher, one of the leading neo-Kantians.

5   Alphonse Daudet (1840–97), French novelist and dramatist.

6   Tomáš Garrigue Masaryk (1850–1937), Czechoslovak philosopher and statesman defending minorities within the Austrian monarchy, taking a stand against anti-Semitism, clericalism and the genuineness of the allegedly Old Czech epics known as *The Manuscripts*. During the First World War, as exiled leader of the resistance, he facilitated Czechoslovakia's independence and international recognition, and became the first Czechoslovak president (1918–35).

7   F. X. Šalda (1867–1937) criticised Čapek for reasons that were partly personal, partly generational and political, and appreciated his literary qualities only with the publication of his 1930s trilogy.

8   Paul Zech (1881–1946), German writer and expressionist poet.

About the Čapek Generation during and after the War

1   Jasina: a town furthest to the east of pre-Second World War Czechoslovakia, in the region known as sub-Carpathian Ruthenia, now in Ukraine. Cheb: a Czech town on the western border with Germany.

A Personal Letter to President Masaryk

1   Anna Maria Tilschová (1873–1957), novelist.

2   *Talks with T.G.M.* (1928–35) – a three-volume book of Masaryk's memoirs, opinions and philosophy that Čapek recorded faithfully and poetically, and published with his epilogue in 1936. In English *Masaryk on Thought and Life. Conversation with Karel Čapek* (1938), new trans. *Talks with T. G. Masaryk* (1995).

About a Pussycat, a Puppy and Little Flowers

1   A reaction to an article by the Czech expressionist and cubist artist Emil Filla (1882–1935) published in *Free Directions* 30 (1933), a critical periodical on the modern visual arts, which Josef Čapek had edited (1912–14) before he parted company with the Association of Fine Artists (Mánes), and for which Karel had written. Josef's reply to Filla appeared in the cultural weekly *The Act* vol. v, No. 21, 1933.

2   *Dashenka (Dášeňka), or The Life of a Puppy* was first published in book form, with the subtitle 'For children – written, drawn, photographed and endured by Karel Čapek', in 1932 (in English, 1933). Josef Čapek wrote and illustrated the well-known children's *Stories about Pup and Pussycat* (1929), in English *All About Doggie and Pussycat* (1996).

The Nation Doesn't Need Us

1   Rudolf Medek (1890–1940), 'legion' writer drawing on his experience of fighting in a Czech legion in Russia in the First World War. The so-called Czechoslovak legions, made up of prisoners of war, were formed in 1917–18 in Russia, France and Italy to help the Allied Powers (in Russia they also helped to fight the Bolsheviks), and contributed to the recognition of Czechoslovakia by the Allies.

2   See Čapek's essay 'Why Am I Not a Communist?' (1924), which earned him a bad press from communist writers.

3   Stanislav Kostka Neumann (1857–1947), anarchist and communist poet, critic and journalist.

4   František Ladislav Rieger (1818–1903), patriotic politician active under Austrian rule.

5   Vítězslav Nezval (1900–58), chief representative of the Czech 1920s avant-garde movement 'poetism'.

6   Karel Toman (1877–1946), lyric poet frequently evoking the motif of home.

7   Vladislav Vančura (1891–1942), one of the leading novelists, known for his highly poetic style and experiment with language.

8   Fráňa Šrámek (1877–1952), author of poetry, prose and drama characterised by lyricism and sensuality. Josef Hora (1891–1945), highly metaphorical, reflective poet. Jaroslav Seifert (1901–86), lyric poet of intense eroticism and melancholy, who started off as a proletarian and avant-garde (poetist) poet; the first Czech Nobel Prize-winner (1984).

9   F. X. Šalda (1867–1937), the most important of all Czech literary critics, who considered criticism equal to creative writing. Čapek's polemics against this leftist critic were well known.

10   Karel Havlíček Borovský (1821–56), satirical poet, critic and journalist, persecuted by the Habsburgs; symbol of the anti-Austrian resistance.

11   Jan Neruda (1834–91), poet and journalist, author of realistic, atmospheric stories; Čapek followed his journalistic example.

12   Svatopluk Čech (1846–1908), popular author of social and political poetry and humoristic, dystopian prose.

13   František X. Hodáč (1883–1943) and Jiří Stříbrný (1880–1955), nationalistic politicians.

A Flu-sufferer

1   *Michelup and the Motorbike*: a new novel by Karel Poláček serialised in the paper.

The Protection of Authors

1   *The Turbine* (1916) and *Antonín Vondrejc* (1917–18), novels by the writer Karel Matěj Čapek Chod (1860–1927), who adopted the

differentiating name 'Chod' after Čapek joined *The National Newspaper* in 1917.

2   Karel Poláček (1892–1945), humoristic and satirical writer and journalist of Czech-Jewish origin, Čapek's close friend and colleague.

3   František Langer (1888–1965), writer, playwright and journalist of Czech-Jewish origin, and Čapek's close friend. He associated with Jaroslav Hašek and Franz Kafka. In the First World War he served as a doctor in the Czechoslovak legions; during the Second World War he joined the exiled Czechoslovak armoured brigade that fought at Dunkirk, contributed to BBC broadcasting, and published essays on England and the Čapek brothers. He was disapproved of by the Communists. *A Wonder in the Family* (1929) – his humoristic novel.

4   Vítězslav Novák (1870–1949), composer, Dvořák's pupil.

5   Vítězslav Nezval (1900–58), avant-garde poet.

6   Josef Maleček (1903–82), ice-hockey champion.

7   Max Švabinský (1873-1962), artist.

8   Jarmila Novotná (1907–94), world-famous soprano.

9   Jan Antonín Baťa (1898–1965), entrepreneur and economist, owner of the Baťa shoe company.

10 Comenius: Jan Amos Komenský (1592–1670), educational reformer and pansophist.

11 Between the wars Ruthenia was part of Czechoslovakia; after the Second World War it was ceded to the USSR; now part of Ukraine.

II WORDS

From Criticism of Words (1920)

1   A Preface to the 1918 column 'We versus I' which initiated a series of reflections on language. The first nineteen appeared in *The National Newspaper* in 1918, another five in the 1919–20 issue of *The Stem*, and the remaining twenty-eight were written and published, together with the earlier pieces and a new introduction (see below), in book form as *Criticism of Words* in 1920.

2   'Dog's weather': a Czech idiom meaning 'awful weather'. 'It's fit for a cat': an idiom implying that something is vile.

3   Antonín Slavíček (1870–1910), distinguished Czech landscape painter and leading representative of Czech Impressionism. The word *slavíček* means 'a little nightingale'.

4   Václav Beneš Třebízský (1849–84), popular writer of historical prose.

5   Jean Henri Fabre (1823–1915), French entomologist.

6   Eduard Vojan (1853–1920), notable actor.
7   Vlastimil Tusar (1880–1924) resigned as prime minister on 15 September 1920.

Against Little Goose Legs
1   Jan Žižka (1370–1424), Hussite war leader.
2   An allusion to the ancient Czech legends variously rendered by nineteenth-century poets and writers, most notably by Alois Jirásek (in prose, 1894), and immortalised in Smetana's symphonic poems *My Country* (Part IV is called 'From the Czech Leas and Groves'; in Part VI, 'Blaník', the legendary knights fulfil an old prophecy by coming to the devastated country's rescue).

About the Word Robot
1   František Chudoba (1878–1941), scholar of English literature.
2   From the Czech word *robota* meaning 'forced labour'.

IV NOTICING PEOPLE AND THINGS

Decadence
1   Jules Payot (1859–1940), French educationalist and philosopher.

The First Step on the Path of Vices
1   See 'Beneš 1915', about Čapek's attempt to travel abroad during the First World War and smuggle some papers.

An Invention
1   Jaroslav Veselý, scientist-writer.

From Philemon, or About Gardening
1   František Langer, writer and Čapek's close friend.

How I Have Come to Be What I Am
1   Karel Havlíček Borovský and Jan Neruda – classic nineteenth-century Czech writers.
2   Granny's Valley (Babiččino údolí): a region in northeast Bohemia, the setting of the classic of Czech literature *The Granny* (1855) by the radical female writer Božena Němcová (1820–62).

A Legend about the Horticultural Species
1   Krč Forest: a park in south Prague; Spořilov and Záběhlice: quarters in southeast Prague.

Owl
1   Antonín Puchmajer (1769–1820), writer, one of the earliest national revivalists.

V LETTERS TO OLGA

I.

  1 Čapek's doctor Ladislav Syllaba (1868–1930).

  2 His brother and co-author, Josef.

2.

  1 *A Little Girl* (1905), a play by the feminist writer and playwright Božena Viková-Kunětická (1862–1934), in which Olga acted.

  2 Karel edited the Sunday supplement for children and wrote a fairy tale for it, and so did Olga at his request.

3.

  1 Jiřina Schubertová-Tůmová (1890–1968), Olga's fellow actress, later translator and secretary of PEN.

  2 Shooting Island, on the river Vltava, so named for its fifteenth-century shooting range. Žofín, a building on the Vltava's Slavonic Island used for balls and cultural gatherings.

  3 Zdeněk Fibich (1850–1900), composer.

  4 Pavel Janák (1882–1956), cubist architect.

4.

  1 Jarmila Čapková (1889–1962), his brother's wife. At the time she, her husband and Karel shared a flat.

  2 *The Little Flower of the Prairie*, a play by Antonín Fencl.

5.

  1 The use of diminutives is frequent and richly varied in Czech; diminutives are the most natural way of expressing affection. Karel's choice of 'little one' (literally 'little girl') partly reflects the title of the now forgotten play in which Olga acted (see Letter 2, note 1).

  2 Karel Scheinpflug (1899–1987), Olga's brother, lawyer and author of the memoir *My Brother-In-Law Karel Čapek* (1991).

  3 Čapek planned a film of *Rusalka* (the naiad in Dvořák's opera) with Olga in the leading role, but it was never made. His manuscript got lost.

  4 *The Robber* (1920), Čapek's poetic play.

  5 *Embarrassing Tales* (1921), Čapek's second book of short stories; in English *Money and Other Stories* (1929) and *Painful Tales*, in *Cross Roads* (2002).

  6 *Káča* (or *Čáča*): Olga's nickname for Karel.

7.

  1 Prague Castle, the official seat of the republic's president.

  2 Alice Masaryková (1879–1966), President of the Czechoslovak Red Cross and social worker, President Masaryk's daughter.

8.

  1   Košíře: a quarter in south Prague. Čapek reported on what he saw in three articles, published in *The People's Paper* in April 1921, urging the government to take action to rescue children from poverty, which he called worse than any disease.

9.

  1   Trenčianské Teplice, a spa in Slovakia, where Čapek's father worked. Čapek spent summers with his parents, undergoing treatment for his spinal disease.
  2   *Pussycat*, a farce by Walter D. Ellis.

10.

  1   Čapek's dystopian novel *A Factory to Manufacture the Absolute* (1922).

11.

  1   Čapek's family's dislike of Olga complicated his situation. In his next letter to her (19 August 1921) he writes: 'Mum clings to me more than ever, or at least she shows it more than she's ever done. It's near tormenting and horrible; I know that if I left, she'd hate you for a long time. I feel terrible because of her love, her kisses, her serving me; I don't belong to her, that love doesn't pertain to me, my mind is elsewhere. And then there's the duty to pretend, not to show my anxiety; the moment I think about my own business and you for a second, there're four women around me: that I'm sad, that something must have happened to me, perhaps that letter, and so on.'

12.

  1   Little Helenka – Helena Koželuhová (1907–67) – Čapek's niece, the younger daughter of his sister Helena. Eddy Pollo: popular film actor.

13.

  1   Alfréd Stránský, brother of the founder and owner of *The People's Paper*, and publisher.
  2   Otakar Štorch-Marien, Čapek's first publisher, wrote film reviews for *The People's Paper*.
  3   Čapek's column called 'Icy Flowers' appeared in *The People's Paper* on 13 December 1925.
  4   Václav Štech (1859–1947), head of the Brno National Theatre.
  5   Jiří Mahen (1882–1939), playwright, director and dramaturge at the Brno National Theatre.
  6   Antonín Trýb (1884–1960), poet and novelist.

14.

1   Tatranská Lomnica, a tourist centre in the High Tatras mountains in Slovakia.
2   Marie Calma (Veselá) (1883–1966), opera singer and writer.
3   The Giant Mountains (the highest in the Czech lands) in north Bohemia, where in July 1921 Karel and Olga, chaperoned by his sister and a woman friend, were on holiday together.

17.

1   Čapek's trip to Italy was primarily an escape from the emotional crisis. Still, he sent reportage to the paper and subsequently combined his feuilletons into a book (*Letters from Italy*, 1923).
2   *The Romantics*, a play by the French playwright Edmond Rostand (1868–1918).
3   Josef Čapek's daughter: Alena Čapková.
4   František Khol (1887–1930), dramaturge and owner of a drama agency (which promoted Čapek's plays abroad), and his wife Bohumila.

20.

1   Anna Lauermannová (1852–1932), pseudonym Felix Téver, writer and hostess of Prague literary society. Both Karel and Olga attended her salons and at one he met Věra Hrůzová.
2   Čapek's mother fell ill and, after a period in a sanatorium, died the following spring. His father came to live with him in Prague until his death in 1929.

21.

1   Rudolfov: a small country hotel near Jindřichův Hradec (Henry's Castle) in south Bohemia, where Čapek spent the summer with his brother's family.
2   Of the dystopian novel *Krakatit* (1924), with its two interweaving romances, which seem to reflect Čapek's complicated relationships with Olga and Věra Hrůzová. He met Věra in December 1920, and, possibly frustrated by Olga's unstable response, arranged a couple of meetings with her and invited her to the first night of *RUR* in January 1921. After that she disappeared from his life until she wrote to him in the summer of 1922. Her reappearance certainly did not facilitate his crisis with Olga. After a year of occasional letters and meetings, during which his family made it clear they preferred her to Olga, she married a mine-owner, by whom she had three children. Čapek kept up a witty correspondence with her until 1931.

22.

1   The main character of a scientist in Čapek's novel *Krakatit* (1924).

342

23.

1   Professor R. W. Seton-Watson (1879–1951) was a historian of Central Europe who influenced Allied policy towards the region at the end of the First World War.

2   Nigel Playfair (1874–1934), actor and director, introduced the Čapeks' plays on the English stage.

3   Prompted by Čapek's sister Helena, Prof. Syllaba wrote to Olga about Čapek's neurasthenic tendencies in July 1924, and advised her that she could do more for him as his girlfriend, offering inspiration and comfort, than as his wife and nurse.

4   Olga's father, Karel Scheinpflug (1869–1948), writer, poet, playwright and journalist, worked for the same two papers as Čapek. The reference here is to his play *The Second Youth*.

5   Otakar Vočadlo, senior lecturer in Czech literature at the Institute of Slavic Studies, University of London (1922–8), arranged Čapek's visit to England.

6   Karel Hugo Hilar (1885–1935), playwright, director and head of drama at the National Theatre. In 1924 he had a stroke.

24.

1   *The Killed Man*, a play (comedy) by Olga; the first night was on 26 April 1927.

2   Božka: Olga lived with her sister Božena Scheinpflugová (1901–84).

3   František Smolík (1891–1972), distinguished actor.

25.

1   In September and October 1927 Čapek spent six weeks in Topoľčanky, a small town in southwest Slovakia where Czechoslovak presidents had their summer residence, working with President Masaryk on his memoirs *Talks with T.G.M.* The first volume was published in 1928.

2   It seems to have been this letter that prompted Olga to attempt suicide, which almost proved fatal. From one of his letters to Mrs Tévér in July 1923 we know that Karel dreaded Olga's threatening him 'with a white pill'.

26.

1   Dr Karel Steinbach (1894–1991), Olga's close friend and admirer. He proposed marriage to her in the spring of 1935, and this seems to have spurred Čapek to marry her in August 1935. He became Čapek's close friend and one of the doctors who attended him in his last illness. He emigrated to the USA and wrote the memoir *A Nearly Hundred-Year-Old Witness* (1988). In the early 1930s Olga was also close to the President's son, Jan Masaryk (1886–1948).

2   Kotlina: in the Slovakian High Tatras mountains.

3 Boženka: Olga's sister.
4 Maxmilian Schwarz, farmer in Slovakia, Čapek's friend and host.
5 Karel Marek, chairman of the co-operative of the National Theatre.
6 Karel Kramář (1860–1937), chief representative of the home resistance movement during the First World War and politician.
7 Karel Havlíček Borovský (1821–56), classic poet and journalist.
8 Karel Toman (1877–1946), lyric poet.
9 Rudolf Karel (1880–1945), composer, the last pupil of Antonín Dvořák; tortured to death in the concentration camp at Terezín.
10 Karel Poláček, distinguished writer, Čapek's close friend and colleague.
11 Anna Sedláčková (1887–1967), actress, the first Czech film star. Hugo Haas (1901–68), actor, director and celebrated comic film star. Zdeněk Štěpánek (1896–1968), acclaimed actor.

27.

1 Alarmed by the prospect of losing Olga to Karel Steinbach, Čapek offered to join her on holiday in the Austrian Alps and the Dolomites in the summer of 1935. Apparently he slipped this poem into her hand at breakfast one morning, and woke her up at 5 a.m. the following morning to propose. They married on their return to Prague on 26 August 1935.

28.

1 Seeking peace from the political persecution, Karel stayed at the little Osov chateau in central Bohemia, which belonged to his sister's brother-in-law, Václav Palivec. He could not have used his and Olga's country house, because the telephone line was requisitioned by the army.
2 As part of its libellous campaign, the fascist and clerical press denigrated Čapek's autumnal visits to the country as cowardice precipitated by the late September general mobilisation. He defended himself in an article called 'What Truly Happened', published in *The People's Paper* on 26 November 1938.
3 Strž: a solitary old country house in central Bohemia, south of Prague. In 1935 Karel and Olga were given the right to use it as a wedding present from Václav Palivec. Karel planned the reconstruction of the house and cultivated the garden. In the Communist era Olga saved the house by helping to turn it into the Karel Čapek Museum, opened in 1963.
4 Karel Scheinpflug, Olga's brother; Karel Dvořák (1893–1950), sculptor, who had a house near Strž.
5 Boženka: Olga's sister.
6 Růžena: Olga's housekeeper.

VI COMMON THINGS

Save Yourself If You Can
1   František Mareš (1857–1942), doctor of medicine and philosopher. František Krejčí (1858–1934), psychologist and positivist philosopher.
2   Jiří Wolker (1900–24), proletarian poet.
3   Artur Brožek (1882–1934), the first Professor of Genetics in Czechoslovakia.
4   Jakub Deml (1878–1961), Catholic poet and writer. Břetislav Foustka (1862–1947), sociologist.
5   Josef Velenovský (1858–1949), botanist.

About Scepticism
1   This title adopted for the collection *About Common Things, or Zoon Politikon* (1932); first appeared as 'Ignoramus and Ignorabimus'.

Tradition
1   Jiří Wolker, gifted poet of proletarian leanings, who died aged twenty-four earlier in the year.
2   Fráňa Šrámek (1877–1952), lyric poet, Čapek's contemporary.
3   Jaroslav Durych (1886–1962), Catholic writer. Karel Jaromír Erben (1811–70), classic poet.

Bethlehem
1   The reference is to 28 October 1918, when Czechoslovakia was formed, gaining independence from the Austrian Empire.

About Women and Politics
1   First appeared under the title 'Woman and Politics'. This title in *About Common Things, or Zoon Politikon* (1932).
2   Jan Žižka (1370–1424), Hussite war leader, author of Hussite military regulations.

About Americanism
1   Written in Czech for *The Present* under the title 'Americanism'; this title in *About Common Things, or Zoon Politikon* (1932). An English version was published in the *New York Times Magazine*; an answer to 'the Criticisms of Karel Capek' called 'In Defense of Our American Ideals' was written by Glann Frank, President of the University of Wisconsin, and published in the same periodical on 6 June 1926.

The Rescued and the Rescuers
1   This is about the fifty-day international effort to rescue the survivors of the Italian polar expedition led by Umberto Nobile (1885–1978). His airship *Italia* crashed on 25 May 1928 during the second series of flights around the North Pole. Nine survivors were thrown onto a drifting ice floe; the six members of the crew trapped aboard vanished.

2   The chief technician Natale Ceccioni was among the seriously wounded whom Nobile wanted to be evacuated first, but the Swedish pilot Einar Lundborg, whose plane could take only one survivor, forcibly removed Nobile.

3   Alfredo Viglieri, Italian navigator and hydrographer. Finn Malmgren, Swedish meteorologist and physicist, died of exposure trekking for help. Roald Amundsen (1872–1928), Norwegian explorer and Nobile's rival, died in the rescue operation when his seaplane disappeared.

4   The Russian pilot Boris Chuckhnovsky was also rescued by the *Krasin*.

Beneš 1915

1   Edvard Beneš (1884–1948), Czech statesman. During the First World War he worked with T. G. Masaryk for Czechoslovak independence and in 1935 became president after Masaryk. During the Second World War he was head of the exiled government in London, and resigned from his presidency after the 1948 Communist coup.

2   Karel Chytil (1857–1934), art historian.

March 1935

1   As Minister of Foreign Affairs, Beneš championed the League of Nations and was its chairman, and created the Little Entente (alliance of Czechoslovakia, Romania and Yugoslavia).

2   František Hodáč (1883–1943), Czech economist with fascist leanings.

A Prayer for This Evening

1   On 19 September 1938, after Chamberlain's negotiations with Hitler in Berchtesgaden, the British and French representatives pressed the Czechoslovak government to cede the German-and-Czech-speaking border areas to Germany. When the Czechoslovak government refused, on 21 September at 2 a.m.(!) they presented President Beneš with an ultimatum: Czechoslovakia could either fight Germany alone, and be held responsible for another war in Europe, or submit to the proposal. The ultimatum was accepted on the afternoon of the day for which Čapek wrote his 'Prayer' (21 September), and then he was given the 'sad task' of helping to put together a broadcast announcing the news to the nation (in 'What Truly Happened', *The People's Paper*, 26 November 1938). However, by 22 September, when Čapek's 'Prayer' was published, Hitler had extended his territorial demands, calling for the immediate annexation of the Sudetenland. Czechoslovakia ordered a general mobilisation, but the Munich Pact was signed by Britain, France, Germany and Italy, without Czechoslovak participation, on 29 September.

Studánka
1 Studánka (Little Well), a popular name for Malé Svatoňovice, a small town in northeast Bohemia: Čapek's birthplace.
2 Granny's Valley , the setting of the classic work *The Granny* (1855) by Božena Němcová.
3 Alois Jirásek (1851–1930), realist, classic author of historical novels. The town Hronov, his birthplace.
4 Gerhart Hauptmann (1862–1946), German writer. *The Weavers* (1892), his social drama.
5 *The Robber* (1920), Čapek's lyrical comedy.

From One Human Being to Another
1 A battle fought near Prague on 8 November 1620. It marked the first major victory of the Roman Catholics over the Protestants in the Thirty Years War, and enabled the Austrian Habsburgs to establish an authoritarian government in Bohemia that lasted until 1918.

Greetings
1 Čapek's last journalistic piece, published on Christmas Day 1938. He died on the evening of the same day.

Index

recognition of states 110–11
and trust 146
and use of language 106
and women 284–7, 319–20
Pollo, Eddy 224
poor, the
cheerfulness of 274
and communism 270–3
generosity of 156–7, 275–6
popular taste
and culture 276
and epics 5–6
relative to cultural production
24
positivism 90
pragmatism 33, 37
Prague
green belt 299
People's Paper office 14–15
spring in 167, 259–60
primitivism 76
principles 74–5, 266, 267, 275, 279
Procházka, Dr 12
prophesy 87
proposals
charitable plans 214
coughing in theatres 10–11
humour in theatres 10
at New Year 298–9
welcoming spring 259–60
world politics 310–11
psychology 33
Ptáková, Mrs 13
Puchmajer, Antonín 193
Pussycat (Ellis) 219, 221
Pythagoras 91

radio
advantages of 27–30
as anaesthesia 43
narration on 20
railways
in England 118
ice on windows 225–6
landscapes seen from 147–8
reading
misreading words 54
of old texts 55

and old people 19–20, 54
by word, not letter 53–4
reason
characteristics of 78–80
dismissal of form 89
Rejzek, Mr 13
relativism
and absolute truth 90–1
appeal of 264
Einstein's 287–8
exceptions to 91
as intellectual offence 277
as method of cognition 290
and notion of relation 289
Simmel's 33
religion
Bible-reading 54
cathedral building, speed of 293
celebratory and ritual forms 88–9,
258–9
female martyrs 285
God as judge 81, 134–5, 137
God and seeing 81
as juju 262
lacks inverted commas 98
monasticism 236, 237
prayer 140–2
problematisation of 89
and relativism 90
and response to dictatorship 51
role of Holy Ghost 25–6
salvation 255–8
source of 23
see also Christmas; Easter; God
Rembrandt 3
resolutions, good 152–4, 298–9
Rickert, Heinrich 33
Rieger, František Ladislav 57
Robinson Crusoe (Defoe) 6
'robot', origin of word 103
Rodin, Auguste 3
The Romantics (Rostand) 232
RUR (Rossum's Universal Robots)
(Čapek) 103
rural life
and the radio 29
seen from trains 147–8
Russia 37